D1454535

YOUN

RACIA

Young Children and Racial Justice

Taking action for racial equality in the early years – understanding the past, thinking about the present, planning for the future

Jane Lane

national
children's
bureau

NCB promotes the voices, interests and well-being of all children and young people across every aspect of their lives.

As an umbrella body for the children's sector in England and Northern Ireland, we provide essential information on policy, research and best practice for our members and other partners.

NCB aims to:

- challenge disadvantage in childhood
- work with children and young people to ensure they are involved in all matters that affect their lives
- promote multidisciplinary cross-agency partnerships and good practice
- influence government policy through policy development and advocacy
- undertake high quality research and work from an evidence-based perspective
- disseminate information to all those working with children and young people, and to children and young people themselves.

NCB has adopted and works within the UN Convention on the Rights of the Child.

Published by the National Children's Bureau

National Children's Bureau, 8 Wakley Street, London EC1V 7QE
Tel: 020 7843 6000
Website: www.ncb.org.uk
Registered charity number: 258825

NCB works in partnership with Children in Scotland www.childreninscotland.org.uk) and Children in Wales (www.childreninwales.org.uk).

© Jane Lane 2008

ISBN: 978–1–905818–25–9

British Library Cataloguing in Publication Data
A catalogue record for this book is available from the British Library

The paper used for the text pages of this book is FSC certified. FSC (The Forest Stewardship Council) is an international network to promote responsible management of the world's forests.

Printed on totally chlorine-free paper

FSC
Mixed Sources
Product group from well-managed forests and other controlled sources
Cert no. BGS-COC-2482
www.fsc.org
© 1996 Forest Stewardship Council

Contents

Foreword

If only we could create the environments for all children to develop positive attitudes about themselves and other people unlike themselves, as well as to have the opportunity to learn with, from and about each other in multicultural settings, the world would in future be a much better place for human relationships. Yet it is patently obvious that virtually all people who have an interest in young children are striving to do their best to help them achieve successful outcomes in their early years as a sound basis for their future growth and development. But, in spite of our care, love and concerns, we are still not getting it right for many children.

Some time ago, my number two grandson (HG aged 3 then) was most upset with me for sternly challenging his behaviour. His angry response was a loud 'I hate you Grandad.' My immediate shocked reaction was to tell him that we do not do HATE in our home and that hate was much too strong an emotion to have as a child, or even an adult. My reaction at the time did not perhaps sufficiently acknowledge how important it was for him to express his feelings. I am sure, even though he hated me at that moment, that he did not really hate me in the long term, but his passionate scream indicated a deep dislike for his treatment. A year later HG observed me watching a live football match on the television. So disgusted was I with the unpleasant antics of one of the players that I expressed a loud hatred for such behaviour. HG was quick to point out that 'we do not do hate in this home, Grandad', his younger brother (CJ aged 3 then) repeated the same words but even louder and their older brother (number one grandson, TJ, aged 8 then) chipped in with his own rebuke. Not to be outdone, their grandmother capped it all by accusing me of hypocrisy.

Children are as sharp as a blade in the way they pick things up so quickly. They are so vulnerable to the influences of those people closest to them; and our own negative attitudes, views and behaviour become theirs. They are born free of prejudice and bias but they soon pick up those in the home, from parents, families and friends. We, the adults, are ourselves influenced by the attitudes and behaviour of our colleagues, peers, politicians, friends, families, media personalities, newspapers and day-to-day anecdotes. We then reflect such influences in our own attitudes, views and behaviour.

Each of us has a personal responsibility to help all children to grow free of prejudice, bias, ignorance, hatred, intolerance; to challenge unacceptable behaviour; to be exemplary in how we conduct ourselves; and to help them to become open and broadminded through guidance, care, education, teaching and learning. Jane Lane, in producing this comprehensive guide on early years experiences and practices, has dedicated her life in the service of others in securing equality, justice and fair treatment for people of all backgrounds. This book is a reflection of her passion for early years settings and getting it right for the children, their parents, the carers, educators, the institutions and ultimately our future society. She has invested her life in this project and there is something in here for all of us, especially those who are the professionals in the early years learning, caring and developing environments, which are most important to every child's future. It is in parts most challenging, sometimes arguably contestable, always interesting and, above all, thoroughly informative. There is a lot of learning (and unlearning) to do.

Herman Ouseley

Cherishing all the children of the nation equally

(extract from the 1916 proclamation of the provisional government of the Irish republic to the people of Ireland)[1]

In memory of Kathleen Wsama, who talked about her life of challenging racism in the East End of London between the world wars in a BBC *Opinions* programme during the 1980s, moving many of us to tears. And of my father, who always stood up against injustice and encouraged me to think critically about it from an early age. He is my mentor.

> *How society rids itself of such attitudes is not something which we can prescribe, except to stress the need for education and example at the youngest age, and an overall attitude of 'zero tolerance' of racism within our society.*
>
> (Report of the Stephen Lawrence Inquiry (Macpherson 1999) para. 7.42)

> *To shift something as ingrained as racism is in British society requires commitment, passion, a visceral hatred of injustice.*
>
> (Home Secretary, Jack Straw, in an interview with Gary Younge in *Connections* (Commission for Racial Equality), Autumn 2000)

---

[1] 'The [Irish] Republic guarantees religious and civil liberty, equal rights and equal opportunities to all its citizens, and declares its resolve to pursue the happiness and prosperity of the whole nation and all of its parts, cherishing all the children of the nation equally…' (extract from the 1916 proclamation of the provisional government of the Irish Republic to the people of Ireland).

My vision for the early years

As individuals we cannot make the world free of racism and a safe place to be, but we can do our very best to ensure that our early years settings are small models of what we would like the world to be.

Jane Lane

About the author
Jane Lane is an advocate worker for racial equality in the early years. She was formerly the policy director for Early Years Equality (EYE) and an education officer at the Commission for Racial Equality and was largely responsible for writing their publication *From Cradle to School: A practical guide to racial equality in early childhood education and care*.

Acknowledgements

I wish to thank those people who gave their time to read the original text of this book, or specific parts of it, during preparation, all of whom made constructive and helpful comments. They are Margaret Andrews, Rashida Baig, Babette Brown, Cressida Evans, Sue Griffin, Pat Joseph, Sue Owen, Cath Sinclair and Norma Wildman. Others who gave their time to discuss particular issues or contribute their ideas and experiences are Bill Bolloten, Bebb Burchell, Sarah Cemlyn, Julie Cigman, Lucy Davies, Andy Dorn, Mary Jane Drummond, Rose Drury, Samidha Garg, Ramani Gopinath, Jan Hardy, Ginny Harrison-White, Alison Hatt, Tina Hyder, Julie Jennings, Haki Kapasi, Fazlehussein Kapasi, Jennifer Larché, Jennie Lindon, Paul Luper, Joshua, Heloise and Michael MacAndrew, Sandra Mohamed, Herman Ouseley, Charlie Owen, Jools Page, Diane Rich, Robin Richardson, Ann Robinson, Gerri Ross, Sumen Shah and Syed Shah. Their comments are very much appreciated.

A very particular appreciation to Maud Blair for coining the term 'getting it' in a speech to the DfES entitled 'Getting it – the challenge of raising black pupils' achievement in schools and local authorities' (paper presented to the DfES in November 2006). And to Peter Wanless, Inderjit Dehal and Richard Eyre for getting the term into the public domain (2006) and for clarifying its meaning – clearly denoting a concept that is becoming daily more relevant and pertinent.

A very special thanks to Brenda Parkes from the Legal Department at the Equality and Human Rights Commission for providing legal advice and so willingly checking the accuracy of the chapter on the amended Race Relations Act 1976.

And to Ann Marie McAuliffe for her unerring faith in me and the causes for which we both strive.

And thanks to everyone at Reading Council for Racial Equality for always being so incredibly obliging and helpful.

And to all my family and friends who have put up with and supported me while I wrote and agonised over this book, especially Marjory Barnes, Babette Brown, Mary Dickins, Pat and Doug Green, Bhajan Hunjan, Haki Kapasi, Jennifer Larché, Greta Sandler, Christine Wilkinson and the Train Gang (Rebecca Adnitt, Gillie Francis and Andrea Hood) who have always been there for me when things were bad (and they often were). And to my soulmate: you know who you are.

And to Shirley Whitehouse who edited the text with unbelievable patience and ability to get to the crux of an issue.

Finally, my thanks go to four special people.

Sue Owen (Director of the Early Childhood Unit at the National Children's Bureau) who encouraged me to update the original version of this book. She provided the mechanisms and determination to ensure it was published and put up with all the vicissitudes in this process. I am very grateful to her for her continual support and commitment to getting racial equality issues on to the early years agenda.

Berenice Miles, who read and made comments on the book, my unfailing admiration for her authority, sensitivity, knowledge, awareness and understanding of the issues involved in addressing racism in the early years. This made her the most appropriate person to undertake this onerous and time-consuming task. We laughed together endlessly at our struggles to get every nuance of every word to be the best available in the context, both sharing and knowing the importance of getting it right. She understood completely why I initially put so many words in inverted commas to address this but persuaded me that this really was too much and that we must begin to accept them in their own unadorned right. She was absolutely magnificent in her care, commitment and thoroughness and made many very helpful, succinct, pertinent and practical suggestions from her wide experience. I am indebted to her for her wisdom.

Patrice Lawrence, who was a constant ally and support throughout the writing and editing process. Her understanding of how racism operates, allied with her literary skills and passion about what we were trying to do made me feel that I was never alone in the struggles we faced. It is at this level that one realises who one's true friends are.

Dorothy Y. Selleck, who was unfailingly constructive in discussing issues concerning very young children, always encouraging and supportive and raised pertinent issues and discerning questions to challenge any comfort zone into which I might have inadvertently slipped.

None of them, however, is in any way responsible for this text; the responsibility lies solely with me.

Jane Lane

The British

By Benjamin Zephaniah

Serves 60 million
(from *Wicked World,* Puffin Books)

Take some Picts, Celts and Silures
And let them settle,
Then overrun them with Roman conquerors.

Remove the Romans after approximately four hundred years
Add lots of Norman French to some
Angles, Saxons, Jutes and Vikings, then stir vigorously.

Mix some hot Chileans, cool Jamaicans, Dominicans,
Trinidadians and Bajans with some Ethiopians, Chinese,
Vietnamese and Sudanese.

Then take a blend of Somalians, Sri Lankans, Nigerians
And Pakistanis,
Combine with some Guyanese
And turn up the heat.

Sprinkle some fresh Indians, Malaysians, Bosnians,
Iraqis and Bangladeshis together with some
Afghans, Spanish, Turkish, Kurdish, Japanese
And Palestinians
Then add to the melting pot.

Leave the ingredients to simmer.

As they mix and blend allow their languages to flourish
Binding them together with English.

Allow time to be cool.

Add some unity, understanding, and respect for the future,
Serve with justice
And enjoy.

Note: All the ingredients are equally important. Treating one ingredient better than another will leave a bitter unpleasant taste.

Warning: An unequal spread of justice will damage the people and cause pain.

Give justice and equality to all.

List of abbreviations

BAME – black (or Black), Asian and minority ethnic groups [only explained, not used in book]

BME – black (or Black) and minority ethnic groups' [only explained, not used in book]

CACHE – Council for the Awards in Children's Care and Education

CLG – [Department for] Communities and Local Government

CRE – Commission for Racial Equality (now part of the EHRC)

CWDC – Children's Workforce Development Council

DCSF – Department for Children, Schools and Families

DfEE – Department for Education and Employment (no longer in existence)

DfES – Department for Education and Skills (now DCSF and Department for Innovation, Universities and Skills)

DH – Department of Health

DWP – Department for Work and Pensions

EAL – English as an Additional Language

ECF – Early Childhood Forum

ECO – Equalities Coordinator (same as ENCO and EOCO)

EHRC – Equality and Human Rights Commission

EMA/EMAG – ethnic minority achievement grant

ENCO or EOCO – Equalities Named Coordinator

EOC – Equal Opportunities Commission

EYDCP – Early Years Development and Childcare Partnerships

EYFS – Early Years Foundation Stage

GOR – Genuine occupational requirement

GOQ – Genuine occupational qualification

GTCE – General Teaching Council for England

IRR – Institute of Race Relations

JAR – Joint Area Review

LEA – local education authority

NAA – National Assessment Agency

NALDIC – National Association for Language Development in the Curriculum

NESS – National Evaluation of Sure Start

NIPPA – Northern Ireland Pre-school Playgroups Association

NOSCCLD – National Occupational Standards in Children's Care, Learning and
        Development

NNEB –National Nursery Examination Board

NUT – National Union of Teachers

NVQ – National Vocational Qualification

NCMA – National Childminding Association

OECD – Organisation for Economic Cooperation and Development

Ofsted – Office for Standards in Education, Children's Services and Skills

PC – politically correct

Pii – Peace Initiatives Institute

PLA – Pre-school Learning Alliance (formerly the Pre-School Playgroups Association)

PLASC – Pupil Level Annual School Census

QCA – Qualifications and Curriculum Authority

REIA – Race equality impact assessment

RES – Race Equality Scheme

RRA – Race Relations Act, i.e. the 1976 Race Relations Act

SENCO – Special Educational Needs Coordinators

SSLP – Sure Start Local Programmes

TESS – Traveller education support services

TDA – Training and Development Agency for Schools (formerly the TTA)

TTA – Teacher Training Agency (now the TDA)

VIP – voluntary, independent and private sector

WGARCR – Working Group Against Racism in Children's Resources

Introduction

What kind of school do we want to learn in? We want a school where ALL pupils LOOK OUT FOR EACH OTHER.

('Listening: Pupils' voices, experiences and advice', from *Preventing and Addressing Racism in Schools*, Ealing Council 2003)

Young children are like sponges. They absorb the attitudes and values of the world that surrounds them and usually reveal this in the way they behave. Until they grow older and their experiences are wider, it is unlikely that they will be able to discern whether prejudice plays a part in such attitudes and values and even then they may not do so. Their world has a powerful potential to influence their futures. Their world, our world, should treat children tenderly so they may learn tenderness, to themselves and others, at an early age. In so doing, a climate of equal respect and acceptance of difference is being fostered. We all know that a loved child is more likely to become caring and tender than one who is not loved.

The notion of 'tenderness' is developed in the Plowden Report (Plowden 1967), a seminal report in its time:

> *to care tenderly for individuals and yet retain sufficient detachment to assess what they are achieving and how they are developing.*

(para 873)

To feel secure, confident, comfortable, content and able to pursue our ambitions as members of society, we need to be valued for ourselves, to feel included, to be respected and treated with dignity and fairness and have a sense of belonging to that society. Most of us think that we should have equal access to services. For example, we think we should have equal access to health treatment, whatever our financial situation. And we want teachers, carers and other practitioners to give each of our children an equal chance to thrive in early years settings and to succeed to their best ability at school.

Do we expect everyone else to be treated in the same way as we expect to be treated? Looking around, we can see that some people do not have the same chances as others – they are not treated as fairly as they would like to be. In fact *we,* ourselves, may not be treated as we would like to be. How much are we prepared and able to get equal chances for ourselves? How far are we prepared to consider others who may have fewer chances than we have?

Whatever our individual wishes, they are likely to be influenced by the beliefs, values and attitudes of our society. Thinking about equality usually means continually examining the world around us, continually rethinking what we do, what we say and how the influences on our lives have determined our attitudes and behaviour.

Britain is largely a tolerant and accepting society. For example, few people would deny every citizen's right to have a vote or access society's welfare benefits equally. But while we may all value Britain's precious qualities, be glad that we live here and rejoice in its diversity, it remains an unequal society – inequalities remain embedded in it. While workers in the early years cannot alone remove these inequalities they can contribute to their removal, by ensuring that settings are places of belonging for all children and their families and where the principles of equality are integral to all their policies, practices and procedures.

Practitioners and others working in the early years are busy people usually with continuing responsibilities occupying every moment of the day. Requiring them to rethink their practice in order to implement racial equality may appear onerous, but the best practitioners constantly review the way that they work anyway. Hopefully, reading this book may make the task less daunting, rather than increasing the burden. However, there is no point in pretending that the task of getting rid of racism is easy or that a few quick adaptations will suffice. Although the statutory requirements of the amended Race Relations Act may perhaps initially feel overwhelming, they comprise a powerful and effective engine to drive through the principles of racial equality, an objective that is long overdue. It is hoped that the voluntary, independent and private sectors will be committed to this objective and, with the support of local authorities, will take it as seriously as the statutory sector is required to do. The principles of racial equality apply equally whether children and their families belong to an early years setting in the statutory or non-statutory sector.

Getting rid of racism means addressing a wide range of things. It means fundamentally:

- acknowledging that racism is deeply embedded in society
- recognising that this has serious implications for everyone involved in the early years of children's lives, that every one of us has a role to play
- acknowledging that children are beginning the process of learning their racial attitudes and behaviour long before they go to school – no child is born racially prejudiced
- accepting that active work needs to be done with children if they are to learn positive attitudes and behaviour to racial differences between people, and to unlearn any negative racist ones that they may already have learnt
- ensuring compliance with anti-discriminatory legislation
- understanding the power of stereotypes and the making of assumptions and judgements on all work done in the early years
- opening our eyes and minds to what is going on around us and in society generally
- being willing to give time to consider and reflect on issues of racial equality
- being committed to implement racial equality

- wanting personally to get rid of racism – like Blackpool rock, committed all the way through – because, whatever our ethnicity, culture or religion, racial justice is important in the lives of every one of us. Only then can we be at peace with ourselves.

It means 'getting it'. It means 'owning it'.

This book reflects the scale of the task.

The purpose of this book

It is well known, at least among those working with young children, that the early years of children's lives are critical for learning the basic skills that enable them to benefit from schooling and in life generally. Anything which interferes with this learning process, or which distorts reality, may have long-term consequences. Both prejudice and discrimination may damage children's life chances, chances that may be determined by the adults around them. None of us involved with young children can allow any differences between them to influence the principle of their entitlement to equality and justice. This principle also entitles them to be provided with opportunities to learn that *differences* are just that – they are not about superiority or inferiority, more or less value or more or less worthiness. They are all part of our common humanity.

Adults are in a position to exert a strong influence on children's learning, including learning their attitudes to differences. Therefore, if prejudice and discrimination are to be fully addressed, it is important to develop strategies to counter any prejudicial attitudes and behaviour, however unintentional, among adults as well as children. And it is important to acknowledge the early age that children learn their attitudes to differences between people.

Children have a right not to be subjected to prejudiced attitudes and behaviour. But, while they also have a right *not* to learn such negative attitudes, they have a right to *know* about them and to reject them in order to make that distinction – to learn *how* to reject them and how to support others subjected to them. Being prejudiced denies children access to many of life's experiences and opportunities, but learning *not* to be prejudiced opens up possibilities for the child – and has benefits for everyone else too.

All children learn to categorise things. They learn to make judgements. Evidence shows that children as young as three are able to use racial cues as a basis for identification and categorisation, and even babies recognise difference. As they grow older they are likely to be learning whose physical appearances and backgrounds are most valued by society and, unless this learning is countered, some may grow to discriminate against the people who are wrongly seen as less valuable.

Learning to respect the opinions, differences, similarities and needs of others is an important aspect of children's overall social development, and valuing racial and other differences is just one aspect of this. Whatever their racial attitudes, children are capable of considering another point of view. They can build up a balanced interpretation of what they have already learned when provided with accurate information in a non-threatening and sensitive atmosphere where everyone has equal value. In this kind of environment, children can learn to consider a variety of different opinions, analyse them and make up their own minds about what is fair and just.

All children should have opportunities to learn to be open- and broad-minded, to appreciate each other equally, to understand one another better and to share their happy or not so happy experiences together. They should have opportunities to develop their enquiring minds, to learn to be intellectually curious, stimulated and stimulating so that they enjoy learning and embark upon their educational experiences with enthusiasm, excitement, commitment and positive anticipation. Their families should also have opportunities to share and be involved in this learning process and to support their enthusiasm for it. This is a vision for all children and one to which they are all entitled. Anything that interferes with this diminishes us all. Childhood is a one-off chance, one that can seldom be repeated because some aspect has failed. As workers with young children we cannot allow anything within our control to block this process.

But the world of the early years and, in particular, an early years setting (for a description of this term see page 9), does not exist in isolation. It is part of a local community or neighbourhood which, in turn, is part of our wider society. This society is, at present, experiencing many symptoms of not being at ease with itself – a fear of crime (real or imagined), especially violence; an increase in racist attacks, including antisemitism; a rise in hostility to refugees, asylum seekers and other migrants and antagonism to some religious groups – particularly Muslims (Islamophobia); and dissension and sometimes violence between communities. There have been the terrible bombings on London's transport system. All these factors have implications for children and the world they will grow up to live in (see page 156 for further discussion). They are not conducive to the creation of a harmonious[2] society but all have implications for children and the world they will grow up to live in. While government tries to address these issues nationally in various ways it is clear that a local community, where people live and where early years settings are sited, is potentially the locus for action to be taken at a more fundamental and possibly more long-lasting level. It is a level where friendships are built up and where there is the opportunity for developing those friendships across ethnic and cultural boundaries and breaking down barriers between them – the process of inclusion.

---

[2] Harmonious – over recent years, in the field of race relations, this word has become associated somewhat negatively and perhaps sentimentally with concepts of people living side by side but not really fully communicating with, understanding or accepting one another. This is because the inequalities structured into our society caused by racism are not addressed. I believe this should be reclaimed as a positive word whose origins are in music – the various instruments or voices playing together in their differing role, as notes to create a harmony of sound each contributing equally to the whole. In such harmony there is no hierarchy between the instruments or voices, each complementing the other(s) and uniting together to make a totality more profound than the individual parts.

The impersonal hand of government can never replace the helping hand of a neighbour.

(Hubert Humphrey, Vice President of the United States 1965–69)

Early years services and settings, as part of these local communities, are in a critical position to be advocates for them and to be pioneers for racial and other aspects of equality. Where settings value everyone equally, where families all feel welcome, where both children and workers reflect the ethnic composition of the local community and where everyone feels that they belong, there is the foundation for extending these principles of good practice into the community outside the setting. In multicultural areas there are more readily accessible opportunities for building up friendship patterns between cultures than in largely white or monocultural areas. But the principles based in practice in the settings – of acknowledging, understanding and belonging to a wider society, wherever they are sited – are the same.

If change doesn't start in the early years where will it start? Where else can there be a grass-roots movement to establish links, a solid foundation, where people know one another, respect each other and care about each other because they have learnt in settings that this works for children. Thinking about what this might mean in reality is important.

The five outcomes for children is the mantra of *Every Child Matters,* the basis of the national childcare strategy. If we can implement racial equality for all children in settings in terms of these five outcomes, together with the sixth outcome identified in Chapter 10 ('being equal – feeling that you belong'), there is also likely to be a positive spin-off in the outcomes for their families, for their local communities and, in turn, for our wider society. We have to start somewhere.

A postscript

Action for racial equality in the early years was originally published in 1999.

Although this book addresses many of the same issues as the first publication it has been completely revised to take account of recent government commitment to the early years, race equality legislation and nearly a decade of changes in thinking and practice. It is consequently virtually a new book.

There are five million children under the age of six in England. Since the publication of *Action for racial equality in the early years,* the effects of the government's acknowledgement of the importance of the early years as determinants of children's life chances have been demonstrated in many ways.

Funding for early years services has been hugely increased; the United Kingdom now invests more per child in the pre-primary years than any other European country (OECD 2005 – 2007).

The pot of money available to help parents with childcare costs has similarly been greatly increased. The process of addressing the legacy of historical neglect has begun. Furthermore, books and many articles have been written about equality and its implications for practice in early years settings. Training, conferences and seminars have been organised and supportive audio/visual resources made. And, compared with the past, government has made considerable inroads into addressing inequalities. Issues of equality are at last on the early years national agenda, although there is still a long way to go to break down the barriers of institutional and structural inequalities. Sexism, racism, homophobia, classism and disableism remain entrenched.

In the specific context of racism (see Chapter 2 for discussion of this term), until the government takes a lead towards its identification and the development of a comprehensive strategy to eliminate it, the likelihood of a significant reduction of it in the lives of children and their families from black and other minority ethnic backgrounds is diminished. Similarly, the damaging effects on many children of learning to be racially prejudiced will continue. Existing government strategies on improving opportunities, integration and community cohesion, while addressing education in the mainstream and placing a statutory duty on schools (including children's centres run by schools) to promote community cohesion, do not acknowledge the importance of this work with very young children in helping them to unlearn any racial prejudice they may have already learnt (see, for example, Home Office 2005, CLG 2006 and Commission on Integration and Cohesion (CIC) 2007a and 2007b and comments on the consultation, Ouseley and Lane 2007). Children grow up to be adults, as members of their local communities and of the wider society. We ignore racism at our peril.

Who is this book for?

Young Children and Racial Justice: Taking action for racial equality in the early years has been written for people who plan for, work with, care for and educate young children; those who train, advise and support them; and those who plan services and develop policies and guidance for them. It aims to inform and offer practical material for discussion and considered reflection. But it has implications for everyone in the whole early years sector (including in national government) who wishes to ensure that racial equality is an integral part of all that is done. It is hoped that the issues raised will be taken seriously by everyone working with children up to the age of eight.

In considering our present society, it is not suggested that racial equality will be achieved overnight. National government plays one role but working from the top down cannot be as good as building genuine relationships from the bottom up. Racial equality cannot be contrived, although legislation plays a part in making discrimination unlawful. It is about people and the way they relate to and care about each other. But it is a task worth striving for in every early years setting and, within its local community, to establish long-lasting changes and understanding with families and their children – the ones that really matter.

This book looks at general issues of fairness and equality, and how they should be an integral part of early years services and settings. It discusses specific issues of racial prejudice and the attitudes and behaviour that may result from them as a consequence of our history, and focuses on the practices that may help or hinder racial equality in early years services and settings in Britain. It discusses the omissions that contribute to continuing inequality. It suggests how services and settings might actively engage in advocating racial equality in their local communities. In summary, it considers the need to examine all those policies, practices and procedures across the early years field in order to ensure that all forms of racism are removed.

The wide range of issues covered should not daunt those who are in the early stages of considering racial equality. Dipping into the book for specific issues may happen initially. But it is hoped that such issues will be considered within a wider context at a later time.

The order of the book has been planned with the needs of a reader working through the issues as part of a process. This has unavoidably resulted in some issues not being addressed in the order that a particular reader might wish. For example, the legislation for racial equality may initially seem complex and is therefore in one of the later chapters. But some readers may nevertheless wish to understand these legislative complexities at an earlier stage and so will change the reading order.

Except for those who are truly passionate about wishing to engage in discussions about racial equality, it is not expected that anyone will read this book from cover to cover. Most will probably read bits according to their interests and needs. But it is hoped that it will be of general interest and stimulate a commitment to making our world a better place for all our children, their families and their future lives. At the present time there is a daily deluge of documentation, including consultations and reports, emanating from the early years field. It is impossible to take account of everything that is published, however important it is. This book does not claim to raise all the issues involved in implementing racial equality nor that every issue raised is addressed in sufficient depth. It certainly does not have all the answers to the many questions that consideration of the issues raises. But it is hoped that in considering the *process* of working for racial equality, it will be a stimulus for everyone to identify for themselves what need to be done to achieve it.

In a sense the premise of this book is a plea for all of us to question everything we do and to examine, reflect on and re-evaluate the basis of the attitudes on which we live in relation to others – the assumptions, judgements and stereotypes that play such a critical role in the way we live our lives and our attitudes and our behaviour towards those who we may perceive as different from us. This may influence all our practice with them and is the prerequisite for our work with and care for children and their families.

Terms used in this book

For a brief definition of the words used when talking about racial equality and racism, see Appendix 1 and the latter part of Chapter 2.

The meaning of 'black' and 'white'

The term black is used here in a political sense to include all people who share a common experience of colonialism and are likely to be discriminated against, although perhaps in different ways, because of their skin colour. It includes most African, African-Caribbean and South Asian people, and those people from other minority ethnic communities where skin colour is a determining factor. Using the term black is not an ideal alternative to listing every minority ethnic group throughout the book and some people do not wish to use it, but it removes the need for clumsy repetition. When a specific group of people is being referred to, this is made clear.

In recent years the phrase 'black (or Black) and minority ethnic groups' (BME) has come to be used to incorporate all groups who experience racial discrimination. Even more recently the phrase 'black (or Black), Asian and minority ethnic groups' (BAME) is sometimes used to incorporate specifically Asian people who do not define themselves as black or Black. Both phrases, however, somehow imply that black people are not a minority ethnic group. This is clearly wrong. While recognising that the term 'black' is not an ethnicity, the phrase 'black and *other* minority ethnic groups' will be used here to ensure that black people are included as a minority group, despite its apparent contradictions, and to take account of the terminology in common use. The abbreviations BME or BAME will not be used here – the relevant full terms are spelt out where appropriate.

To a certain extent, the term black is being used here for simplicity. No term should ever be imposed on a child unless the child's family or carer has indicated that that is the way they wish to be described. For more discussion about the term black see page 76.

The term white is also used here in its political sense. It includes all those people who are not usually discriminated against because of their skin colour. However, Travellers, Gypsies, Roma, Irish and Jewish people and some refugees, asylum seekers and other migrants who are white are exceptions to this as they often experience discrimination based on their appearances, histories and nationalities – sometimes called xenoracism (see Appendix 1, for a definition of this term). The word white also covers those people of European origin and those who migrated from Europe to places like New Zealand, Australia, Canada, some South American countries, South Africa and the United States of America. Of course, there are also black people living in these countries, in some cases for centuries prior to white people. Interestingly the obvious corollary of BME, the phrase 'white majority ethnic' groups (WME), is rarely if ever used.

Using the terms black and white can be problematic because they have tended to become tainted as being descriptions of people who are inevitably subjected to racism (black) and people who are racist (white). They are clearly unacceptable as such because not all black people experience racism and many white people oppose racism or do not see themselves in any way as racist. Furthermore many people prefer to be described by their ethnic or national origins and sometimes religious affiliations. And many white and black people experience discrimination themselves on the grounds of their sex, gender, disability, socioeconomic status (class) and on other grounds in our society. So the issue remains complex if only because the terminology and understandings are so varied. However, until there is a greater consensus and clarification the terms black and white, despite all the associated misgivings, will be used. Thinking about equality always means continually re-evaluating what we say and do, in the same way as most people change aspects of their lives to take account of the times in which they live.

Describing the early years environment

In the early years field, children are cared for and educated in a variety of settings, including: nurseries, day nurseries, nursery schools, nursery classes, children's centres, neighbourhood nurseries, early excellence centres, Sure Start local programmes, crèches, playgroups, pre-schools, extended schools, kindergartens, family centres, drop-in centres, parent and toddler clubs, after-school clubs that cater for young children, and childminders. In this book, the phrase early years setting (often abbreviated to simply 'setting') is used to cover all the above, except where otherwise stated. However, childcare is often the preferred term in government documents. Young children are also cared for in their homes, although 'an early years setting' does not perhaps seem an appropriate term to use for this because a child's home is much more than a formal setting for care and education.

The phrases 'people who work with children' or 'workers' are used to refer to the wide variety of people working in the early years field. It includes: childminders, practitioners, carers, pedagogues, teachers, lecturers, educators, leaders, researchers, early years professionals, nursery nurses, nursery assistants, support staff, visiting staff, supervisors, caterers, cleaners, administrators, directors, chief executives, policy-makers, trainers, development workers, officers, helpers, volunteers, managers, leaders, Ofsted inspectors and school improvement partners, clerical staff and receptionists. There are also people who work for children but not necessarily with them. They are also workers in the early years field and this book has implications for them too. Sometimes, however, the term 'staff' is used where it more appropriately refers to a team of workers working together.

Notes

(1) The inevitable time lag between the writing and publication of this book means some recent events or government documentation may not be included. For example, in mid-2007 the Department for Education and Skills (DfES) was replaced by two new departments – the Department for Children, Schools and Families (DCSF) and the Department for Innovation, Universities and Skills (DIUS). And, since October 2007, the Commission for Racial Equality (CRE) is now incorporated into the Equality and Human Rights Commission (EHRC). It has not always been appropriate to change these terms in the text.

(2) Because it is anticipated that people may dip into this book, reading particular bits that are of interest to them, some issues appear in different sections giving a different perspective as relevant.

(3) It should not be assumed that instances cited here that took place several years ago have no relevance in today's society or in early years practice. Some legacies remain entrenched for many years. And although some books and articles were written a while ago many aspects, or all, may still have relevance today.

(4) In this text 'Race Relations Act' means the amended Race Relations Act 1976, that is, the Race Relations Act 1976 as amended by the Race Relations (Amendment) Act 2000. Where the Race Relations (Amendment) Act 2000 is mentioned specifically this is because it is the particular provisions and perspectives of that Act that apply.

(5) This text does not claim to have identified and made reference to all the many examples of good practical and written work that have been produced.

(6) Every example or issue discussed in this book has been experienced by me or raised by early years workers or others.

(7) There are a large number of references in this book. They are intended to be helpful, rather than overwhelming, in enabling readers, trainers, educators and others to access resources and support for their work wherever they are available.

(8) The use of inverted commas is intended to indicate the sometimes nuanced meaning of words. For example, the use of the term 'foreign' indicates the fact that some people may use it in a pejorative way. Where such words in inverted commas are used, any subsequent use does not have these commas. However, there remain some words that are nuanced or loaded because of the ways that they have often been used, even though they have no inverted commas – words such as 'other', 'different', 'normal' or sometimes 'diverse'. Care should be taken not to interpret them negatively, sometimes apparently reinforcing 'them and us' or somehow implying hierarchies of ethnicity.

(9) At the time of publication there was not yet sufficient clarification as to the actual status of children's centres – whether they were run by schools or other agencies – with regard to whether they were defined *as* public authorities (and therefore required to have a race equality scheme) or *as run by* public authorities (and therefore required to have a race equality policy).

(10) At the time of writing, a few local authorities still had early years development and childcare partnerships (EYDCPs). After the first reference to EYDCPs in the text it is assumed, where appropriate, that the term 'local authority' includes EYDCPs where they still exist.

(11) The Contents page flags up the main areas covered. The index lists more specific issues.

(12) There are sometimes no agreed terms or words used to describe something or someone. This is just how it is.

1 What do we mean by prejudice and discrimination?

The problem is that these f— people are rubbish in their own country and they come over here; they bring nothing except problems; they have no interest in learning about us and our ways; they just live among their own.

(An angry Spaniard telling a reporter from *The Times* what he thinks about the 300,000 Britons living in the Costa del Sol, quoted by Herman Ouseley in the *Guardian*, 10 April 2004)

There are many forms of inequality in our society. They include unequal treatment on the grounds of being a woman, a black person, a person from a minority ethnic group, a particular socioeconomic group or class; being a Gypsy, Roma or Traveller, a Jewish person, an Irish person; being disabled, lesbian, gay or bisexual, poor, homeless; being a refugee, asylum-seeker or other migrant, living in a particular place; having a particular faith, religion or belief; speaking a particular language; being of a particular age; having a particular accent or dialect; having a particular job, dressing in a particular way or attending a particular kind of school.

Most people would like the world to be a place where issues of equality are irrelevant, a place where everyone already has an equal place in society. But in the real world everyone is not equal. Many people, for all sorts of reasons, have to struggle for the necessities of life that others take for granted. They do not have the same life chances as others. For instance, some deaf people get left out of events because it is assumed that they cannot take part and, despite disability legislation, some wheelchair users may be unable to use the facilities that non-wheelchair users can.

There are laws in Britain that make discrimination on grounds of sex and gender, race, disability, sexual orientation, religion or belief, and age unlawful. Under the Race Relations (Amendment) Act 2000 public authorities are required by statute to have race equality schemes, which apply to all their services, functions, policies and practices. Maintained schools, most children's centres and any other early years settings run by the local authority are required to have race equality policies. Both the schemes and the policies have to be linked to an action plan. An equivalent statutory duty with regard to disability took effect from December 2006 and with regard to gender from April 2007. These three duties should be addressed within a single equality duty. A Single Equality Act, incorporating all six equality strands, is in process.

People who work with children nearly always aim to do the best for all the children in their care. They wish to treat every child as an individual though perhaps not realising that some children are also members of groups that as a whole do not experience equality. Treating every child as an individual appears to be a laudable aim but may not take account of the reality of a child being of a particular ethnic or gender group as well as being an individual. Children have family members who are of the same gender or ethnic group as themselves so the implications of any prejudiced behaviour against them as individuals includes other people in their families too, as well as their whole ethnic or gender group.

Our concern here is with young children. They are among the most vulnerable members of our society, and everyone working with them needs to strive for them all to be given an equal chance to succeed and fulfil their dreams. But equality does not yet exist and it is therefore important that all of us involved with young children consider how to achieve it.

Prejudice and discrimination

Prejudice is forming an opinion about a person with little or no information or evidence on which to base that opinion. It means that a person is pre-judged by others, maybe even before they have met.

Anyone can be prejudiced. Men and women can be prejudiced. Black and white people can be prejudiced. Disabled and non-disabled people can be prejudiced. Lesbian and gay people can be prejudiced. People from all social classes can be prejudiced. Rich and poor, homeless and housed, employed and unemployed, old and young, British and 'foreign', religious and non-religious; all people can be prejudiced against any other group of people, not because of who they are but simply because they are perceived to be a member of a certain group. People who are themselves discriminated against as a group may also discriminate against others as a group. Furthermore, some people who are discriminated against may be prejudiced against a particular group of others who also belong to the same wider group that is discriminated against. For example, some African and Caribbean people may be prejudiced against each other though both experience discrimination as black people. Some people from asylum-seeking communities may be prejudiced against others coming from areas of war and conflict. It is a reflection on our society that such behaviour continues to occur.

But this does not make it any better and does not make it right.

How is it that we may sometimes be prejudiced against others? Is it because:

- we do not understand them?
- we think they are less deserving, and getting the benefit of something that they shouldn't?
- we think they have not earned privileges we think they might have?
- we blame them for something in our histories or in our present society?

- we are afraid of something – of losing our own identity, culture or way of life?
- we think we do not like them?
- we really think we are superior to some others?
- we may have been misled or misinformed by media reporting?

Do we know that we are prejudiced?

Do we mind if someone says that we are prejudiced?

The reasons for people being prejudiced are complex and varied, but they include our different histories and the legacies they leave, different economic and social situations, different power relationships between people and groups, and ignorance and misinformation. As a result of all these factors, inequality has become embedded in the fabric of our society and 'accepted' as part of the way that it is organised. Inequality is part of the 'system'.

Prejudice and discrimination exist because they are allowed to exist. Prejudiced attitudes and behaviour, reinforcing and perpetuating inequalities, are passed from generation to generation in subtle (and sometimes not so subtle) ways. This process may be unacknowledged and its consequences largely unrecognised. It is only when attitudes are expressed in behaviour that discrimination occurs and recognition is possible.

Whatever the reasons, if any action resulting from prejudice disadvantages or discriminates against another person (a negative attitude or action), that action is morally wrong. If it is covered by legislation, it may also be unlawful.

Forms of discrimination

Some aspects of inequality are obvious, such as overtly prejudiced comments and discriminatory behaviour. For example, some people believe that women cannot make good Members of Parliament and they believe this because they are prejudiced against women doing that sort of work. Perhaps they think women have duties elsewhere.

Other forms of inequality are not so obvious. They are hidden in complex practices and procedures or built into the way society has been organised over long periods of time. For example, some meetings or social events are held without access to a loop system to support deaf people or access to alternative forms of print information for blind people, so that people with hearing or visual impairments cannot participate fully. Or public consultation meetings are planned during periods of particular religious festivals or at times of family responsibilities. No single person deliberately arranged for these to happen but the effect is that some disabled people, people of particular faiths and family members / carers are being discriminated against, if unintentionally. This is sometimes called institutional discrimination (see page 18).

Although circumstances are changing, women are still more often responsible for running a home and looking after children than men. The provision of affordable childcare, although increasing, is still insufficient so that, overall, women with children have fewer opportunities and greater difficulties in pursuing a career. They are discriminated against because of the traditional structures in our society and, despite well-established legislation (the 1970 Equal Pay Act and the 1975 and 1986 Sex Discrimination Acts), earn significantly less than men overall. This is sometimes called structural discrimination (see Appendix 1 (b)).

Stereotypes and assumptions

Prejudice is sometimes associated with stereotyping. Most of us make assumptions about others from their outward appearances. On seeing someone for the first time, we move into an almost unconscious mode of assessing what they are like, what they do, what their specific 'identifying' characteristics are and what is being felt about them. For example, people who see a white man, with tattoos, pierced ears and a shaved head might assume that he is a racist, but he may have no association whatever with racist people or racist views. Many young black men say that they notice white women clutching their handbags more tightly in their presence. The stereotype is that black men are muggers and the consequence is to make them feel as if they are a threat to 'civilised' society. Such feelings do not contribute to a society based on equal respect.

Discussion 1

Imagine when sitting in a train that you are the person sitting opposite you, behind their eyes and face looking out, with their body and skin colour and wearing their clothes. What do you feel like? Do you feel comfortable about your appearance or feel that people are hostile to you or embarrassed about being near to you? How might you (if you are a non-disabled person) feel if you were visibly disabled in some way, had a skin colour different from your own or were the opposite gender? How do other people around you react to you? Might you learn something from this exercise?

Our assumptions may mean that we treat people unfairly. For example, if we assume that Muslim fathers always speak and act on behalf of their families, we may not even try to find out what Muslim mothers think. This may lead us to believe that 'Muslims think so and so' when it is only some Muslim men's views that we have listened to.

A key concern is the damaging way that stereotyping, and the making of assumptions, may influence workers' attitudes to children's behaviour (for evidence of this see Gilliam 2005).

A simple example demonstrates how deeply assumptions may influence our behaviour and reactions to others.

The stick waver

While walking along the pavement Elizabeth sees a youngish woman behaving in a slightly odd fashion, waving a stick aggressively and shouting at a man on the other side of the street. Her immediate assumption from what she sees is that the woman is drunk or deranged in some way. Her reaction is to plan a way of avoiding her as she passes.

As she gets closer she sees the woman is wearing dark glasses. Instead of crossing the street she begins to realise that the stick the woman is holding is white – she is blind and the stick is her guide. She asks if she needs help and the woman then says gratefully that she is looking for a particular street and had been trying to attract someone's attention. Elizabeth guides her to where she wishes to go.

What appeared to be a potentially unpleasant scenario is transformed to a situation where someone with a disability is just trying to attract the attention of someone else to help her find her destination.

Point for thought and discussion

- How can we prepare ourselves to avoid making such negative assumptions?

Looking at situations from a different perspective may make them more positive. Instead of seeing something as a problem, seeing it as a window of opportunity – for example, seeing illiteracy as possibly revealing the story-telling skills that less literate people often have.

However with regard to racist assumptions, no truly effective work can be done unless there is a real understanding of racism: what it is, what it is not, and how it affects the lives of us all. It is more than being friends and content to live in a multicultural and multiethnic society, important though these are – it is about being observant of, sensitive to, aware of and countering the 'system', the way society works in practice to disadvantage and discriminate against people from black and other minority ethnic groups. Such understanding, and its inevitable commitment, facilitates the process of analysing the role of individuals, groups and organisations (including government) in countering racism. Without this understanding, practice can only be a palliative, and procedures only hit or miss in the continuous struggle for equality. It is not about berating ourselves for past actions but about consolidating actions for the future. It is about 'getting it'. For this reason the book takes considerable space to examine what racism means for everyone with the intention of helping progress towards this understanding.

Speedy Joe

Joe, a four-year-old black boy of African-Caribbean heritage, joins a local nursery. He doesn't know any of the other children. He feels a bit shy and so plays alone on a bicycle for a few minutes. No one interrupts him and he moves on to play on the slide. He then returns to the bicycle. He gets braver and starts going quite fast, riding it all over the place.

One of the workers, Rita, has a particular responsibility for Joe and is pleased to see him occupying himself. Although she would not actually say it, or perhaps does not even know she thinks it, she has an idea that black boys have difficulty in concentrating and that they like physical activity.

Several days later, Joe is still mainly occupied on the wheeled toys. Despite the requirements of the Early Years Foundation Stage (EYFS), no one really ensures that he plays elsewhere, with jigsaws or painting, working with a group or looking at books. No other child is unsupervised in this way. Because Rita's assumption, based on a stereotype, is that Joe is doing what he is best at doing and what he likes doing, she is happy for him and happy that he appears to be content. But Joe has had no opportunity to develop a range of learning skills or to cooperate with other children. Rita's assumptions have helped to create the behaviour that Joe is displaying – and he is being denied access to vital parts of his all-round development. Rita's discrimination is unintentional, but it is based on stereotyped attitudes and assumptions that can remain hidden and may have serious and long-term implications.

Points for thought and discussion

- What are the long-term implications for Joe if this practice continues?
- What should Rita be considering?
- What should Rita be doing?
- Who has overall responsibility for this situation, and what actions should they be taking?

Stereotyping is about believing that the characteristics of one person are found in all members of the group to which that person belongs, based on some notion that may or may not have an element of truth in it. Stereotyping may be about 'good', 'neutral' or 'bad' characteristics. The point is that all stereotypes are untrue:

- South Asian girls are *not all* passive
- African-Caribbean boys are *not all* good at sport
- *not all* blind people love dogs or are pitch perfect
- parents with little education themselves are *not all* indifferent to education
- *not all* Irish men drink a lot and neither do they *all* have the gift of the gab
- *not all* Jewish people are rich
- girls are *not all* incapable of playing football.

Prejudice can allow groups of children to be stereotyped. For example, whole cultural groups of children may be labelled as being 'not properly brought up'. Their families may be criticised for 'not taking them to the park', 'not teaching them to eat properly', 'forcing their religion on their children', 'keeping them up late' or 'bringing them up differently'.

Stereotyping and conditioning may also affect people who are usually the victims of stereotyping themselves, thus demonstrating its ingrained nature, as Archbishop Desmond Tutu describes.

> In 1972 I was Associate Director of the Theological Education Fund of the World Council of Churches based not in Geneva but in London. I had to travel extensively mainly in sub-Saharan Africa. On my first visit to Nigeria I had to fly from Lagos to Jos in the north. I boarded the plane and the entire crew was black. Both the Captain and the First Officer were Nigerian and my heart leapt. I grew inches with pride at this realisation that they contradicted all that apartheid South Africa asserted about blacks. We took off smoothly but some time later hit turbulence. Wow! It was scary. You know one time you are up there and then bump, the aeroplane descends and leaves your stomach on the ceiling. To this day I am shocked at what happened next. I really did not know the power of conditioning. I got quite scared because I said 'Hey, there's no white man in the cockpit. Will these blacks be able to land us safely?' Can you believe it?

> (Archbishop Emeritus Desmond Tutu giving the 'Steve Bantu Biko Memorial Lecture' at the University of Cape Town, 26 September 2006)

Prejudice into practice

> 'You know what your trouble is, man?' he said. 'Your white skin. You think it makes you better than me. You think it give you the right to lord it over a black man. But you know what it make you? You wan' know what your white skin make you, man? It make you white. That is all, man. White. No better, no worse than me – just white.'

> (Gilbert, in *Small Island* by Andrea Levy)

Some actions can be seen to be the direct result of prejudice. For example, if the governing body of a nursery school refuses to consider a man's application for a job simply because he is a man – because they think that women work better than men with young children or they are suspicious of his motives – that is discrimination due to sex and gender-based prejudice. It is sex discrimination and would be unlawful.

Other discriminatory actions may not result directly from individual prejudicial attitudes. They may be so embedded in the system that few people really think about or notice them. Even so, they have a clear effect on particular groups of people. Looking around our society it is clear that certain groups of people, usually white men, predominate in positions of power and authority – for example, the judiciary, political parties and 'captains of industry'. These forms of discrimination are institutional and structural. They are part of the way society operates.

Institutional discrimination

This is not usually a result of deliberate, individual action. It occurs when long-established practices and procedures, which may be official or unofficial, either fail to acknowledge the implications of our diverse society or combine with thoughtless (often unconscious) prejudice, stereotyping and cultural assumptions to produce discrimination. While many members of the institution may believe they are not personally prejudiced or that they do not hold stereotyped attitudes, their failure to recognise or challenge forms of discrimination within the institution means that they are part of the institutional discrimination. Only those people who recognise and challenge discrimination can genuinely claim to be exceptions.

In some early years services, white men lead some staff teams disproportionately though they are a minority in the workforce. Whatever their beliefs about equality this imbalance often goes largely unchallenged because it is historical and there are nearly always apparent explanations to justify it. And, in a sense, it is welcomed because it is clearly important to have men in the workforce. But the ethnicity and gender differences have important implications.

Case study 3

Thinking of equality; practising inequality

In one local authority ethnicity and gender differences resulted in a style of management and personal behaviour that did not address equality, despite an apparent commitment to it. This was in no way hostile or macho but ultimately led to a defensiveness and a lack of receptivity and understanding of the issues facing women and, in particular, black women. The women felt their expertise and skills were not being valued or recognised – in particular that their concerns were usually not taken with the seriousness that they deserved and were all too readily dismissed as unnecessary and unimportant whingeing. They felt marginalised and disempowered in challenging the situation and feared subtle hostility and repercussions if they did so.

Points for thought and discussion

What underlying stereotypes and assumptions do you think you might identify?

- Are white men better at managing early years services?
- Do black people have the same opportunities to apply for jobs, but just don't do so?
- Are black men interested in working with young children?
- Are women more accepting of the inevitability of inequality than men?
- Is it assumed that working with children is 'women's work'?
- Does a discussion about these questions, based on the kinds of statements that are often made, lead to a better understanding about how inequality works in practice?

It is important to be open in discussing equality issues on every occasion and to provide regular space for doing so, whether or not the opportunity is taken up. It is also important to create specific opportunities for discussions and to monitor all workers' recruitment processes and procedures to ensure they are free of discrimination on sex and gender, disability and ethnicity grounds (see page 33 for details of the specific form of institutional discrimination – institutional racism).

Monitoring information reveals practice

Some people are initially reluctant to collect and evaluate data, particularly ethnically monitored data. There are many explanations given for this – for example, that 'it labels people', 'everyone is a human being', 'it is in itself racist'. It is important that the reasons for monitoring are clear and lucid, explaining that monitoring is about identifying any possible discrimination and patterns of discrimination, and that without it much discrimination would remain hidden.

Collecting, analysing and evaluating information to monitor the implementation of practices and procedures helps to reveal any apparent discrepancies, inequalities or discrimination. It is also part of the race equality impact assessment, and identifies gaps in services and enables providers to design and target provision appropriately. For example, details about sex and gender, ethnicity and disability can be gathered from people who apply for and are offered a job, or from children (and their families) who apply for and are offered a place in early years settings. In this way, it is possible to check whether all communities are accessing the service equally. And it is through ethnic monitoring of attainment (for example by the Foundation Stage Profile) that schools and the education authorities are able to monitor whether all pupils are achieving equally, or if there is any cause for concern that needs to be addressed. It is therefore vital that everyone involved in monitoring truly understands and owns the reasons for doing it.

Any discrepancies in the analysis may be due to discrimination. But discrepancies themselves do not prove discrimination – there may be reasonable explanations for such discrepancies. And, equally, differing success rates within a group may be disguised by an apparent overall equitable result for the group as a whole. For example, using the category 'Asian' may not reveal different success rates for Indian, Pakistani, Bangladeshi and Sri Lankan groups. Monitoring provides the information by which to examine and analyse discrepancies and, where discrimination is proved, demonstrate the need to remove it. For example, train drivers may be found to be disproportionately men. Examination of the reasons for this may reveal that the work does not appeal to women for various reasons, perhaps that they do not want to be the first to break the mould or that the culture of train drivers themselves alienates women or they just don't fancy trains. These reasons can then be examined further to focus on the issues revealed and remove any discrimination or stereotypical assumptions about train drivers, for example by advertising pictures of black and white women train drivers.

Name-calling is particularly hurtful to any child and has sometimes been under-acknowledged for the damage it can cause. While all forms of name-calling are totally unacceptable some inflict particular pain because of their associations with actual incidents of physical violence and hatred in society. For example, racist name-calling may accelerate into racist incidents as children grow older. Both racism and homophobia seek out victims for attack and they are sometimes literally 'hunted'. It is important to recognise this reality and, while in no way belittling name-calling such as 'Fatty' in the hurt it inflicts, it is unlikely that anyone is murdered for being fat. This is in contrast to attacks on black and gay people because of who they are. Monitoring racist name-calling is therefore a key element in identifying its particular implications and the need, as with all forms of name-calling, for action to be taken against it.

Other areas of practice and procedure should be monitored for potential forms of discrimination. Audit checklist 1 can be used for this.

Audit checklist 1: Monitoring practice and procedures for potential discrimination		
Issue for consideration	Yes/No	Action required
Does everyone have equal chances of promotion and access to training and relevant information?		
Do the resources used – toys, books, jigsaws, dolls, videos and posters – have any hidden negative messages or omissions?		
Do any assessment arrangements give all children an equal chance to succeed, including when they are learning English as an additional language?		
Are the cultures, dialects, accents and languages of all children and adults given equal value?		
Are all children and adults given equal value, whatever their gender, ability or disability?		
Are all forms of name-calling taken seriously, and are staff aware that racist name-calling is particularly damaging?		
Are some children seen as more 'naughty' than others or do the names of certain children appear to be 'called out' more than others and possibly be on records of behaviour? Could this be due to stereotyping?		

For more details of monitoring considerations, see page 252.

Prejudice, discrimination and young children

Being treated unfairly is hurtful, but do young children always know when they are being treated unfairly? They certainly know when another child has a bigger portion of their favourite ice cream than they do, but do they react to unfairness in the same way as adults, and do they know when they are treating someone else unfairly? In fact, even young children soon cotton on to which children are favoured, and which are not.

Case studies 4, 5 and 6 give three examples of situations that might arise in an early years setting. Discriminatory behaviour of the sort shown in each example may happen in early years practice. Recognising it doesn't mean that an individual adult or child has to be singled out for blame. Blame is seldom appropriate when addressing discrimination with children (or adults), especially as it is crucial to help them to understand its effects rather than make them feel guilty about it. However, the complexities of the situations and the need to take both an immediate and a long-term approach illustrate that dealing with prejudice and the behaviour resulting from it take time, effort and commitment.

After each case study, there is a list of questions focusing on how the children involved might feel and the responses that might be needed from adults and other children. They are questions that people working with young children might stop and ask themselves every day.

All three examples have similarities and differences, but the main principles that should be used to address them are the same.

1   *Differences* between people should not be linked with ideas of superiority or inferiority.
2   No child or adult should ever be made to feel unhappy because they are different.
3   Being sorry for or pitying someone for being different does not address inequality or remove any notions of superiority.
4   No child or adult should be treated less equally than others because of differences.
5   All children should be enabled to grow up with positive attitudes to those who are different from themselves as well as those who are similar to themselves.
6   Being sensitive to another's position and learning to empathise are among the first steps to being committed to doing something about prejudice and discrimination.
7   Not being directly involved in, or being an observer to, such situations does not remove any responsibility to take action.
8   Combining and sharing information from a variety of sources – observations, listening, experience, knowledge, skills and reading – often empowers everyone to deal with the situations they face, whether daily or rarely.
9   By discussing issues in advance of potential negative situations, they can often be avoided – prevention is preferable to having to deal with them on the spot or later.

It is important to recognise that an apparently minor situation may add to and compound similar negative episodes regularly experienced by the child and members of his or her family because of who they are.

Asking the right questions

As well as the more obvious expressions of prejudice given in the three examples, there may be occasions where prejudice is hidden from adults unless they watch very carefully. For example, children may whisper remarks or play only with white, non-disabled dolls. But if adults are observant, listen and themselves play with all dolls, prejudice – as opposed to lack of familiarity with the dolls – becomes a more likely explanation for the behaviour.

Young children seldom express prejudice openly. Unless people working with children, parents and other family members or carers raise the issue, they will not necessarily know what children are thinking, especially when they do not really want to believe that such young children may be learning to be prejudiced. But it cannot be assumed, just because no obvious incidents occur, that young children are not already prejudiced or learning to be so. (See Case study 30 on page 101 for an example of this and Case study 54 on page 223 for children's hidden attitudes.) And young children, who have been exposed to prejudiced attitudes in their environment, may naively repeat them or let them affect their relationships with other children.

Case study 4

Playing doctors and nurses

Roger goes to a childminder. His left leg is shorter than his right, so he cannot move very quickly. Josie wants to play hospitals. She asks Altaf to join her and Roger indicates that he would like to play too. Josie says she will be the nurse, Altaf can be the doctor and Roger can be the patient. Roger says he wants to be the doctor but Josie waves him away, not unkindly, saying he can't be the doctor 'because of his leg'.

Points for thought and discussion

- What might Roger be feeling?
- Why did Josie assume that Roger cannot play being a doctor?
- What might the childminder or another child say to help Roger not to feel hurt?
- How could Josie be helped to understand the effect of what she has said? And Altaf helped to understand too?
- What could the childminder do to ensure that this doesn't happen again?
- What strategy could be developed so that the childminder, children and their families take responsibility to prevent this sort of incident occurring?

Kitchen sink drama

Alice is at her playgroup playing at making tea in the home corner. Brenda is doing some ironing. Ben comes in and wants to help serve the tea, but both Alice and Brenda shoo him out saying that 'boys aren't allowed' because the mummies are in the kitchen.

Points for thought and discussion

- What might Ben be feeling?
- What might a worker or another child have said or done to help him not feel hurt or rebuffed?
- If he was not feeling hurt, what else might he be feeling? Might any stereotypes he has of girls be reinforced?
- How could Alice and Brenda be helped to understand the effect of what they did?
- What could workers do to ensure that this doesn't happen again and to help the children have a different understanding of roles?
- What strategy could be developed so that workers, children and their families take responsibility to prevent this sort of incident occurring?

Ring-a-ring-of-roses

The children in the nursery class are playing ring-a-ring-a-roses with their teacher. Felicity, who is four years old and white, refuses to hold Paul's hand. Paul is black. The teacher tries to encourage Felicity to hold Paul's hand but she won't. The teacher holds Paul's hand and afterwards she asks Felicity why she wouldn't hold his hand. Felicity says she doesn't want to because his hand is dirty.

Points for thought and discussion

- What might Paul be feeling?
- If he appeared not to notice or feel hurt what might be a reason for this?
- What might the teacher or another child say or do to make Paul feel less hurt?
- How could Felicity be helped to understand the effect of what she did?
- How could all the children be made aware that this behaviour is inappropriate and hurtful?
- How might other children, who might have heard what was said, support Paul?
- What could staff do to ensure this does not happen again?
- What strategy could be developed so that the staff, children and their families take responsibility to prevent this sort of incident occurring?

Prejudice, discrimination and adults

The attitudes of people working with and caring for young children can have a significant effect on them, either in the early years setting or in the home. Whether conscious or not, a hidden attitude may influence practice in favour of some children and away from others. Below are some examples of prejudicial beliefs that people might bring to work, followed by questions that look into their possible consequences.

1   *If you go to live in another country you should adopt the way of life of that country*
   - What effect would this belief have on work with children and families who have migrated to Britain?
   - Would people working with children expect parents to speak only English?
   - Would they expect Muslim children to eat tomato sandwiches from the same serving plate as ham sandwiches are being served to other children?
   - Would they expect everyone to wear the same sort of clothes?
   - Would they expect all children to join in Christian Christmas prayers?
   - Would they feel the same about all families? For instance, would they feel that French, Japanese, Russian, Bangladeshi and South African families should all adopt the 'British' way of life equally?
   - Would they expect to adopt the German way of life if they went to live in Germany, the Argentinean way of life in Argentina or the Kuwaiti way of life in Kuwait?
   - Would they expect asylum-seeking parents of children in the setting to take a relaxed part in its activities?

2   *Men are more capable of grasping scientific and mathematical concepts than women*
   - What effect might this belief have on science and numeracy work with girls?
   - Would people working with young children encourage numeracy skills to be learnt more by boys than by girls?
   - Would they praise boys more than girls for completing project work?
   - Would they encourage boys to use computers more than girls?
   - Would they think that reading stories is more for girls than for boys?
   - Would they think that construction play is more for boys than girls?

3   *The families of 'working class'[3] children are not as interested in learning as those of 'middle class' children*
   - What effect might this have on the time and effort put into helping working-class children develop literacy and numeracy skills?
   - Might workers encourage working-class children less than middle-class children?
   - Would workers make every effort to involve and include working-class parents in all parental activities, including finding out their wishes from them themselves?

---

3 See Appendix 1 (a) for a discussion of both this term and middle class

- Might workers really expect only middle-class parents to attend parental sessions on supporting children in their learning and just accept it if it happened?

4 *Some groups of children, such as deaf children or children learning English as an additional language, are not as intelligent or capable of success as other children* (this may be an unconscious belief)
   - What result would this have on the way adults relate to any of these children?
   - Would they talk to them slowly, loudly or with unnatural emphasis?
   - Could their actions make the children feel awkward and stupid, and perhaps reluctant to speak at all?
   - Might they refer to children learning English as an additional language as 'having no language'?

It is good if parents and people working with children are provided with opportunities to think carefully about their own attitudes to differences in a non-threatening environment, free of the need to be defensive. It could be likened to listening to contemporary music or looking at a work of modern art that is so unfamiliar, even alien, that one cannot begin to understand it or even necessarily want to do so. Is it possible that, instead of rejecting it, one could in a sense force oneself to listen or look with no pre-conceived ideas and with an open mind? By taking time in this way and talking about it, might one learn to appreciate something previously dismissed?

A few issues about equality

All children should be provided with accurate information and opportunities to learn about the world outside their immediate environment – to counter both overt and covert misinformation, to extend their horizons and to learn to be open-minded. Otherwise such inaccuracies may pass unchallenged and form the basis of myths about people and cultures which are different from themselves.

> Overheard in a restaurant. A family was sharing photographs of animals in a zoo that they had visited. A young boy, aged about six, said he would like to see where the animals usually lived – in Africa. A young woman at the table with him screwed up her face with disgust and said 'Oh, we don't want to go to Africa – it smells.'

On hearing such an incident, it would be easy to jump to entirely negative conclusions about it. While not denying its likely intention, the woman did not actually say that African *people* smell and many countries have smells that others may find offensive. By addressing an incident such as this in an open way, both adults and children will be enabled to develop their analytical, investigative and discerning skills and consider other possible explanations for it – skills that are useful when learning not to make negative assumptions and judgements about others. They are also vital for their future learning successes and for their ability to operate in the 21st century. From this perspective it can be seen that the principles of equality apply in all areas – whether rural (often largely white), suburban or urban. In terms of racism they apply whether people from black and other minority ethnic communities live there or not.

Why is equality seen as different?

There is plenty of anecdotal evidence and reports from local authorities, trainers, the Office for Standards in Education, Children's Services and Skills (Ofsted) and elsewhere that there is a general reluctance and resistance to participate in discussions, training, seminars and conferences when the subject is equality, particularly racial equality. Might potential participants be worried that they will be made to feel guilty about their own attitudes? Or that someone may call them racist? Or that it is irrelevant to their work situation? For more discussion about the possible reasons for any reluctance see the section on Training and education on page 152.

Such feelings, often defensive ones, reveal possible past experiences, guilt, anxiety and the hope of avoiding any unpleasantness. They may even spill over into discussions and training on issues, other than equality, where the relevance of racial equality becomes part of the agenda. This barrier leaves many workers, often even those professionally thoughtful and questioning and working in multicultural areas, ill-informed about important aspects in the lives of many black and other minority ethnic people compared with their knowledge and understanding about most other important early years issues. But, significantly, it leaves many black workers and families feeling marginalised and that few others appear to want to know about them, include them or involve them. The resultant situation may then reinforce distance between communities. This all makes the task of addressing inequalities, particularly racism and promoting racial equality, often more complex than many other issues. How can these fears and feelings be addressed?

Are there positive ways of addressing them? Are there triggers or experiences that touch people's hearts (but are not about taking pity on someone) and which make them more receptive to listening to a variety of viewpoints? Many people report that something they experienced as children or young adults provided an insight for them into the reality of aspects of racism – a film, a book, an incident or hearing the real-life experiences of someone different from themselves. There are plenty of examples of antiracist films and books available on websites – everyone can devise their own examples according to the situation. The following are a few suggestions that may provide a stimulus, a trigger, to this process.

- **Reading pertinent books**, for example *To Kill a Mocking Bird* by Harper Lee; *A Fine Balance* by Rohinton Mistry; and *Bury my Heart at Wounded Knee* by Dee Brown).
- **Seeing a film**, for example *Crash, Guess Who's Coming To Dinner? Bowling for Columbine, The Colour Purple, Rabbit-proof Fence, To Sir with Love, Hotel Rwanda, Cry Freedom*.

- **Portraying reality using film**, particularly *The Eye of the Storm* by Jane Elliott about differentiating children with blue or brown eyes. Although this was made in the 1970s it still has relevance today in demonstrating the effect on children of feeling distress and being powerless in the face of unfairness, even though they knew this was only an experiment.
- **Starting gently to engage people's emotions**, for example, by focusing on differences, moving to disability and when principles have been established moving to racial equality.
- **Working in small groups** so everyone has to listen and contribute.
- **Listening to real life experiences** as told by someone who has observed racism from a white perspective and can share their feelings, the process of their learning and their present commitment to antiracism. In a context where they can trust everybody, black people may be able to describe their own, different experiences of racism, which may be very effective in helping people to understand what it is like. But the personal price each may pay for exposing such feelings to others should never be underestimated or accepted without a serious understanding of what it involves.

It is often unfamiliarity with the issue that leads to the reactions and the reluctance to address equality described above. Meeting, talking and making friends with people who are not normally met in everyday routines is perhaps the most positive way of reducing apprehensions and building up the confidence to begin the process of addressing racial equality.

Actions can change individual attitudes

Sometimes an unlikely or quite-by-chance experience given to a child or an adult may redirect his or her thinking as the following examples show.

And I also remember being in Gloucester, and performing in a school, and talking about martial arts. And there was a young boy who did the same martial art as me, in the front seat. And after the performance we did a little bit of sparring. I went home, and that was it. A couple of, well months later, the teacher sent me a poem which this boy had written. This boy's father and parents basically were just racist, and they were involved in this organisation 'Combat 18', and they were teaching him to be a racist. And he wrote this poem to his father, saying, 'Dad, I met a black man. I talked to him, y'know, he was so nice. He read some poetry, and I was very inspired by him. And Daddy, I'm not going to be a racist any more'. Y'know and so I know – I don't think or believe – I know that my poetry changes individuals, and I just hope that those individuals just go on to be good people.

(Benjamin Zephaniah, *Belief*, Radio 3, 4 January 2007)

Black man, white boy

In the early part of the last century a six-year-old boy was walking into town with his mother. He saw a black man coming towards him. He asked his mother why he was dirty, why didn't he wash? Embarrassed by his questions his mother retreated. The boy approached the man and asked him why he was dirty. The man sat down with the boy, their feet in the gutter. He asked the boy how often he had a bath. The boy replied 'Three times a week'. The man said that he had a bath every day and that he was not dirty. They then talked together for some considerable time – about the country he came from in Africa, about his skin colour and why it was not the same colour as the boy's. He told him that his name was Haile Selassie, later to become the Emperor of Ethiopia, and that he was visiting his sister. The boy never forgot this incident and later became a priest in South Africa, helping people escape the apartheid regime and was forever pursued by BOSS (the South African security organisation).

Points for discussion

- Are such honest conversations helpful in contributing to understanding?
- What might the mother have done to assist in such understanding?

Moved by a movie

A tutor teaching humanities in a further education college in the 1980s decided to get a group of students (with overt racist attitudes), on a motor vehicle mechanics course, to consider racism in Britain by initially discussing the apartheid system in South Africa. While they were shocked at apartheid they couldn't make the links with racism in Britain. Their expressed racist attitudes continued as before. Finally she showed them a film *Last Grave at Dimbaza* about life and death in the Ciskei – one of the South African bantustans set up by the government. Mick, one of the students, was so overcome with emotion at the shocking conditions in which black Africans were forced to live that afterwards he said to the tutor 'Miss, I have to admit it, I was wrong about the wogs!' His heart had been touched by what he had seen – he changed his attitude (if not yet his use of language) and was willing to say so.

Points for discussion

- What is it about this story that enabled Mick to reflect on his previously held ideas?
- Without engaging in pity, what might you do with young children to develop their concepts of empathy with others?

The marginalisation of equality issues

Issues of equality sometimes fall by the wayside. Despite having been raised in the same way as other issues they somehow get ignored. For example, when someone raises an equality issue of concern to them or to others, it is as if the person raising it is the problem rather than others who marginalise it.

Case study 9

A lone voice

In a small informal workshop discussion group with no leader, all the participants were white and only one man was present. Mary offered to take notes of issues raised. Stuart started the discussion and was followed by two women. Stuart then spoke again, again followed by two other women. After Stuart's third contribution Sue raised the issue of equality issues that she felt needed to be part of the agenda under discussion. Immediately Stuart spoke again on another topic, thus cutting out the possibility of further comment on that topic. One other woman then spoke and then Stuart before the end of the session. Stuart spoke five times, no woman spoke more than once and some not at all. Mary did not record Sue's issue about equality; neither did she report it in the subsequent feedback. No one questioned this omission. Sue felt too disempowered and afraid of appearing difficult to question it herself.

Point for thought and discussion

- What might Sue have said or done that might have alerted Stuart and the others to the situation, without causing discomfort?

Sue could have asked for her point to be recorded and fed back. She could have explained to Stuart afterwards what being marginalised felt like.

There are similar instances occurring in some conference reports, summing up of seminars and meetings, and follow-up actions. It is important to question omissions and provide clear guidelines for equally recording all points, all feedback and all follow-up actions.

The process of change

Process is care and thoroughness; it is consultation, involvement and co-ownership; it is legitimacy and acceptance; it is also record and clear accountability. It is often a significant component of outcome itself; and the more awkward and demanding the issue – especially amid the special gravity of peace and war – the more it may come to matter.

(Michael Quinlan, former permanent secretary at the Ministry of Defence, *Guardian*, 22 October 2004)

The need for change often represents a difficult balance. There is a conflict between wanting to change things quickly and the knowledge that sudden changes may work temporarily but may not last. But the process of change nearly always takes time, time that is well spent in making sure of a secure basis and its acceptance by everyone involved. And changes *are* possible. People *can* change their negative attitudes. Institutions *can* change their practices and take action to monitor what happens. Inequalities *can* be identified and procedures set in place to get rid of them. Changes may take place for many reasons.

Case study 10

The consultant and the director

The director of a voluntary organisation, very committed to addressing racial discrimination, told a consultant on implementing the Race Relations Act that he had no intention of asking his staff to collect and monitor the ethnic data of employees and clients. He believed it was intrusive, counter-productive, and irrelevant and he didn't like 'labelling' people. Years later, in another forum, he advocated the need for ethnic monitoring. He did not go back to the consultant to provide an explanation. But he had had time to think about his original views and had changed his practice.

However, where discrimination is found it must be removed as soon as it is identified. People who experience discrimination and prejudice should never be expected to wait until the people who are not experiencing discrimination feel the time is right. Change in such a situation is urgent.

2 Talking about racism – 'Getting it'

*In terms of race equality, individuals and organisations can broadly be categorised as either **those that 'get it'**, or **those that 'don't get it'**. A risk inherent in any policy to tackle racial inequalities is that those that 'get it' will act on the policy (if they are not doing so already), whilst those who 'don't get it' will view the policy as an unfair/pointless/bureaucratic burden…*

(Wanless, Dehal and Eyre 2006)

Understanding the true nature of racism is fundamental to understanding how it influences early years practices and procedures. Without such an understanding and, hopefully, a resultant commitment, any work done to counter racism will be unlikely to be successful. It is not about blaming anyone but just about 'getting it'. And 'getting it' does not mean feeling smug about it, 'holier than thou', getting an antiracism award or achieving a state of nirvana. It's not about being perfect but knowing that it is all right to acknowledge the power of racism (see Archbishop Desmond Tutu's quote on page 17) and, at the same time, not feeling guilty when mistakes are made. Everyone makes mistakes. Understanding means being fully alert to how racism operates, considering and being aware of its many manifestations and seeing it for the 'system' that it is. And understanding may remove many of the apprehensions that at present often prevent people from even giving themselves time and space to really consider it. This chapter attempts to address some common misunderstandings and remove some misapprehensions in order to 'get it' – to try to remove the elephant in the room that unless identified remains hidden and lurking with its threatening presence.

Racism is a word that is often misunderstood. So, before we can talk about it we need to know what it is and what it is not. It is nearly always difficult to define it exactly. Definitions often refer to racial prejudice and perhaps discrimination as well. But racism is more than these – it is more complex. Racism can be defined as:

All those practices and procedures that, both historically and in the present, disadvantage and discriminate against people because of their skin colour, ethnicity, culture, religion, nationality or language.

Taking this basic definition, it may be helpful to think of those 'practices and procedures' as being a package of different things that, all together, comprise racism. It can then be seen more clearly as complex but with distinct components, some of which are obvious and others less so. One or more components may be relevant in any situation. In Britain, as in most other countries where racism is rife, some components arise from the history of the society and socioeconomic circumstances and others are more recent. The package might include:

- racial prejudice
- racial discrimination
- racial harassment
- racial hatred
- racial violence
- racial assumptions
- racial stereotyping
- cultural racism
- sectarianism and anti-religious racism
- xenoracism
- institutional racism
- structural racism
- state racism.

The various component parts of this package of racism are defined in Appendix 1(b).

Considering racism in this way helps to explain its complexity and clarifies the struggles, misunderstandings and misinformation that many people have when trying to define and understand it. It helps to explain that any racist incident is fundamentally part and parcel of the whole and not just a one-off event without a context. It points to how history has fashioned and still does fashion the notion of racism. Some of the components are more pertinent to the early years than others, but all may impinge in some way.

Talking about racism and even using the word may appear to be daunting to some early years workers and perhaps induces emotional feelings of apprehension and guilt, often resulting in impotence to discuss it and, therefore, to address it. But because its origins are in world history, and Britain's role in that history, it is something for which none of us was personally responsible. However, we *are* responsible for recognising it today, and for playing our part in eliminating it, at least in our own contexts. Understanding it enables us to better know what to do about its consequent present day manifestations in the early years and, in so doing, helps us to take responsibility to counter it. This is important because to do nothing about it or to pretend that it does not exist, especially in largely white areas, is to collude in its perpetuation. It flies in the face of the evidence, of over fifty years, that shows that young children recognise different skin colours by the age of three – indeed how would they *not* do so when they can recognise other colours – for example, the difference between blue and red bricks, and when babies recognise the people who care for them? And unless action is taken to enable them to learn positive attitudes to such differences the evidence also shows that they may be learning to be racially prejudiced, racial prejudice that may lead to racist behaviour in adulthood. The power of racism to affect young minds cannot be ignored.

In talking about any aspect of racism it is always important to be specific about exactly what is being talked about – is it racial prejudice, racial discrimination or what? Or is it the whole package of racism, of which prejudice and discrimination are a part? If it is racial prejudice then to talk about racism may give a wholly different impression and imply it is something that it is not. While clearly racial prejudice is unacceptable, it is mostly when such prejudice is put into practice by omission or an act of discrimination that it affects others. Being clear about what is meant avoids misinterpretations. However, when a person is racially prejudiced against any other ethnic group, whether they realise it or not, this will inevitably affect the way they relate to and deal with people from that ethnic group, both personally and in the context of any situation.

Institutional racism

Because institutional racism and its implications for early years services is so important, it is described in detail below. Institutional racism could be basically defined as:

> Organisational structures, policies, processes and practices that result in some people being treated unfairly and less equally than others, often without intention or knowledge because of their ethnicity, skin colour, culture, religion, nationality or language.

Although, in principle, institutional racism can occur anywhere, in Britain it is the organisational power of, usually, white people, combined with prejudice, that results in detrimental, unfair and differential treatment and biased decision-making. The effects would be the same (that is, institutionally racist) if the power lay in the hands of black people. There is nothing specific about white people and racism – it is just the different historical and socioeconomic implications that determine who is powerful. It is critical that, whoever has the power, gives consideration to the potential for negative outcomes and takes appropriate action to avert those that are the result of discrimination.

The report of the Inquiry into the murder of the black student, Stephen Lawrence (the Stephen Lawrence Inquiry), defined institutional racism as:

The collective failure of an organisation to provide an appropriate and professional service to people because of their colour, culture or ethnic origin. It can be seen or detected in processes, attitudes and behaviour which amount to discrimination through unwitting prejudice, ignorance, thoughtlessness and racist stereotyping which disadvantage minority ethnic people.

(Macpherson 1999)

Although this was not the first time that institutional racism had been defined, it was the first time that it became widely known, through the publicity that the report of the Inquiry raised. It is a very important definition because it takes away the concept that racism is always intentional, deliberate and personal. It also identifies some aspects that are almost certainly outside the control of each of us as individuals within an institution, whether we are black or white – although, as black or white individuals or groups, we can challenge them. The definition partly focuses on those policies, practices and procedures that may have been in place for many years and were never deliberately intended to discriminate but have the effect of discriminating. But it also identifies a lack of attention by institutions to its consequences for those people affected by it and a lack of evaluation of the policies, processes, procedures and structures which have led to adverse outcomes. The term 'institution' here covers most national organisations and all local authorities and early years settings. Institutional racism has some similarities with the concept of indirect racial discrimination referred to in the Race Relations Act 1976 but has a wider application not limited by the Act's strict legal aspects. (Indirect racial discrimination is described in Chapter 8.)

Case study 11

Putting your foot in it…

One rather bizarre but clear example of institutional racism is of a hospital in a multiethnic town that offered a white foot, or the option of paying a considerable sum specially for a black foot, to a black woman requiring a prosthetic foot. The offer was not intentionally discriminatory or deliberately offensive on the part of the person offering it but reflected a lack of thought, sensitivity and preparation for the potential needs of a multiethnic community by the hospital, the institution. There is another dimension to consider – if the situation had been reversed and the woman seeking a prosthetic foot had been white would she, ever, have even been offered a black foot or given the option of paying for a white one?

Another particularly personal and intimate example cites a black woman requesting a prosthetic breast after a mastectomy and being offered a white one, an experience which was very emotionally upsetting.

Points for thought and discussion

- In what way could this be seen as institutional racism or, perhaps, as indirect racial discrimination?
- How could it have been avoided?
- What might be the barriers to addressing it?
- What similar issues might arise in early years settings?

While the use of limited funding might have meant that only white prosthetic feet were bought, the thoughtlessness that allowed a white foot to be offered reveals the lack of attention given to the issue. An alternative buying practice would have ensured that people from black and white communities were offered an appropriate service.

As a result of the Stephen Lawrence Inquiry, the Race Relations Act 1976 was amended by the Race Relations (Amendment) Act 2000 to place a statutory duty on all public authorities to ensure that racial equality issues were placed firmly in all their policies, practices and procedures. (See Chapter 8 for details; for an excellent discussion on institutional racism see Bourne (2001); and for a discussion of racism, and training and education to remove it, see Bhavnani (2001).)

Institutional racism in the early years

Significant and pertinent terms used in the Stephen Lawrence Inquiry report (Macpherson 1999) include 'unwitting' and 'thoughtlessness'. Very few people working with young children would deliberately discriminate against children because they are from a black or other minority ethnic group. Most would probably accept the reality and advantages of a multiethnic workforce, especially in urban areas. But institutional racism may occur because people have not had the opportunity or the concern to think about the issues involved. They may not have given themselves the time to do this. Perhaps they carry on doing what has always been done in the same way without considering its implications for living in a multiethnic society, in which racism is embedded, and the consequent changes that might be needed. Being alert to the possibility of institutional racism occurring is especially important if the research, policy or any other project has national implications. It is also important if the particular area is largely white and is not seen as a part of the wider society.

For example, an early years setting that operates a waiting list and offers places on a first-come-first-served basis, with those at the top of the list having priority, may well be operating institutional racism.

At first sight the waiting list seems as fair a method as any, but in practice families who are unfamiliar with the concept of waiting lists or the way early years services are organised, or do not yet live in the area, do not put their children's names down as early as others. This means that their children will be lower on the list and so less likely to gain a place than children from families who are familiar with the system and are already resident. People who are unfamiliar with the system are likely to include families:

- for whom English is not the first language
- that have recently arrived in Britain or do not yet know about early years organisations – are not part of the 'system'
- that move about a lot
- that have been placed in the area under the dispersal arrangements
- have not yet arrived in the area.

The waiting list will disproportionately affect Travellers, Roma and Gypsies; refugees, asylum seekers and other migrants; South Asian and some other minority ethnic families; as well as majority or minority ethnic families moving to the area. Looked after children (that is, those for whom the local authority shares or has exclusive parental responsibility) and children in emergency accommodation, such as a refuge or hostel, can also be disadvantaged by the waiting list system. There may be no specific intention to give them less of a chance but that will be the effect. This does not mean that waiting lists should be dispensed with altogether, as they are useful sources of information about the people who wish to use the early years setting. However, fair, clear and open ways of organising admissions should be implemented alongside waiting lists (of those children wishing to attend), and attempts should be made to contact families of all groups living in the community. Such admission arrangements should be part of the setting's policy for equality as required by legislation and/or government. A setting could consider holding back a small number of places to cater for transient families or late arrivals, especially where it is known that some communities may settle temporarily but regularly, for example where there is emergency accommodation used by the local authority nearby or a women's refuge.

The early years service or setting (the institution) needs to be aware of the pitfalls – factors, actions or lack of actions – that could bring about a collective failure to address potential institutional racism and could, thereby, contribute to discriminatory outcomes. These actions or inactions include the following.

Not examining all aspects of the local authority early years service, for example having an effective non-discriminatory selection procedure for potential employees but not considering whether the ethnic composition of those applying at all levels reflects that of the local community, and how this may be affected by the advertising strategy.

Not considering post-employment practices, that is, whether other aspects may be discriminatory once people are employed, including access to training, attendance at conferences and promotion.

Not being given, or having sufficient, time to reflect on these issues and to understand them (for example, in management or staff meetings, in training and in talking with families).

Not enabling people to raise issues of concern about racial equality, that is, not ensuring that regular opportunities are provided for people, including those with less authority than others, to raise such issues (within an ethos of trust and no-blame – see page 56). Often the result of not facilitating this is that people fear reprisals if they do raise their concerns and this allows frustration and feelings of powerlessness to fester. Such situations may cause workers from black and other minority ethnic backgrounds to feel that they are not valued and that there is deliberate discrimination against them.

Not examining all aspects of the workings of a setting, for example, not considering how the admissions procedures or recruitment of employees or volunteers might discriminate on racial grounds, even though there has been very careful thought given to the need for positive and anti-discriminatory curricular practice.

Wondering, in passing, why no black people appear to apply for jobs, or not particular jobs, but doing nothing to find out the reasons for this – or, worse still, not even noticing.

Thinking that collecting and monitoring ethnic data is irrelevant, either because it is seen as too bureaucratic, too difficult to implement or because the workforce is already multiethnic, without considering whether all ethnic groups are treated equally; or, more commonly, collecting data but not using it to monitor outcomes.

Not spotting whether racial discrimination applies, that is, when the general facts of racial discrimination are known, doing nothing about finding out if they are relevant within an institution, even when in a position to do so.

Not noticing that it is mostly white people who make important decisions

Not realising that one does not know what one does not know and, instead, assuming that you already know 'enough' about issues of racial equality.

Not offering a platform, that is, not understanding that it is crucial to encourage black communities to contribute to discussions from their own experiences and to listen to them and take them and their stories seriously.

Applying 'fault' where none is due, that is, where research or other findings indicate inequality of outcome for different groups, assuming some apparent 'inadequacy' or 'failing' on the part of the particular minority ethnic groups or families; and not questioning whether there might be alternative explanations before coming to final conclusions. The explanations might concern the methodology of analysis; negative stereotyping; inappropriately trained people carrying out all aspects of the research, including interviewers; or inappropriate procedures.

Being proud of black people being appointed to jobs, but... not really noticing that they are at low grades and not doing anything about the fact; or noticing that they are not appointed at higher grades but thinking that racism is not possible because the director or leader is black.

Not questioning a disproportionate impact of decisions and policies on particular racial groups of people.

Not thinking about the ethnic composition of participants when setting up an advisory or planning group, speakers at or invitees to a conference, or making a list of delegates; or just asking black people to speak (only) about diversity issues.

Using ethnocentric resources, that is, not considering whether a display, resource or journal presents an ethnocentric view of Britain.

Not using positive images to reflect a multiethnic society in the resources used; and not discarding resources which give a negative or stereotypical image of people from black and other minority ethnic communities.

Thinking it doesn't matter because everyone 'here' is white, that is, thinking there is not an issue about racism because everyone in the setting, or living locally, is white.

Thinking that there is only one way to bring up children – 'our' way, the 'best' way.

Audit checklist 2: Monitoring practice and procedures for potential institutional racism		
Issue for consideration	Issue for consideration	Issue for consideration
Do we examine all aspects of our early years service for inequality between different ethnic groups? – Do our resources and curriculum reflect a diversity of cultures, ethnicities, religions or beliefs, languages and communities? – Are our practices, processes and procedures appropriate for all of the communities we serve?		
Do we have an effective non-discriminatory selection procedure for potential employees? – Does the ethnicity of applicants at all levels reflect the local community? – If the area is largely white, does the practice take positive account of the wider society? – Does our advertising strategy ensure that it is widely known? – How do we know that all ethnic groups are aware of what we offer? – If people from some ethnic groups are not applying, have we identified the reasons for this and taken action if necessary?		
Do our employees from all ethnic groups have equal access to and take-up of training, attendance at conferences, and promotion?		
Is there enough time and regular opportunity in our meetings and training to raise and discuss race equality issues? Does everyone feel confident to raise and discuss race equality issues in a no-blame environment?		
Do we look at all aspects of our provision to ensure they do not discriminate against any ethnic groups?		
Do we collect data monitored by ethnicity? Does everyone understand the reason for ethnic monitoring? Do we use the data to monitor outcomes?		
When new findings about inequality or racial discrimination are publicised, do we check whether they might apply to our provision?		
Is it mostly white people who make important decisions in our provision?		

Audit checklist 2: continued		
Issue for consideration	Issue for consideration	Issue for consideration
Do we keep ourselves open to learning more about issues of racial equality, even if we feel we already have a good understanding?		
Do we encourage black communities to contribute to discussions from their own experiences? Do we listen to people from black communities and take what they tell us seriously?		
When we learn of research or other findings indicating inequality of outcome for different groups, do we look for reasons within our own provision rather than automatically assume that the reasons lie within the groups themselves?		
Are black people being appointed to jobs at all levels in our provision?		
Do we understand that racism can exist in an institution even where the director or leader is black?		
Do we question whether our decisions and policies have a disproportionate impact on particular ethnic or racial groups?		
When we organise training or conferences, do our advisory or planning groups, speakers and participants include people from black and other minority ethnic backgrounds? Do we only invite black people to speak about diversity issues?		
Do we ensure that our displays and resources do not present an ethnocentric view of Britain?		
Do we pay attention to our resources to ensure that they reflect a multiethnic society with positive images? Do we discard resources which give a negative or stereotypical image of people from black and other minority ethnic communities?		
Do we ignore racism because everyone in the setting, or living locally, is white and we think it does not apply to us?		
Do we accept that childrearing practice varies in different cultures, and there is no one right way to bring up children?		

Institutional racism needs to be very carefully thought about. Leaders in the early years field, in government departments, in services and settings need to be willing to acknowledge publicly that institutional racism is a fact and that the long-term challenges that it represents need to be addressed.

As well as the situations cited above it is often the way people behave in ordinary situations that builds up resentment on the part of people subjected to it. For example, not including everyone in everyday activities (going out for a drink – it doesn't have to be alcoholic), consulting only some people about putting up displays and decorations or just not talking with some people for whatever reason. Fear of offending or upsetting someone because you don't know for sure how they might react may be used to explain some situations. But it may result in not communicating, a reluctance to use words to describe people, not understanding some forms of body language or fear of saying or doing (or not saying or not doing) something that would normally be said or done in other circumstances, for fear of causing offence. Avoidance of the everyday mechanisms of friendliness, befriending others and concern by some people for people who are less powerful (not necessarily in terms of job status) is a denial of our common humanity and creates barriers by default. The consequence may be, however unintended, a form of racism, a form of exclusion.

Some issues in talking about racism

> *It is an irony that although racism is a reality, and a harsh one, race itself is a complete fiction. It has no genetic or biological basis.*
>
> (AC Grayling, 'The last word on Racism', *Guardian*, 4 May 2000)

Because racism is so deeply embedded in our society it is often misunderstood and becomes an enigma, causing unnecessary fear, anxiety and reluctance to embark on discussions about it. Trying to defuse these apprehensions is important. De-mystifying it helps everyone to feel able to talk about it as a fact rather than as a topic to be avoided.

Misunderstandings about what racism is, and is not

Many people think of racism and about 'being racist' as being about violence, national organisations demonstrating against people from black and other minority ethnic groups, hostile racist marches in areas where such people live, racist and cultural abuse and racist murders and attacks. And, because such behaviour is anathema to people who work with young children, they may not think that anything that takes place in early years services ever constitutes racism. Racism does indeed include such behaviour – it is all a part of racism. But this is not the whole picture. Racism also includes those often unconscious or subconscious practices that disadvantage and discriminate against people from black and other minority ethnic groups.

Discussion 2

Example 1: Requiring a worker to have a particular nursery nurse qualification in order to work in a setting may mean that a potential worker, who has an equivalent qualification from another country and who otherwise fulfils the requirements, cannot apply to do that work. Whereas this is unlikely to have been the intention, the effect is discriminatory and possibly unlawful. A requirement to have a particular qualification *or its equivalent* would have prevented any such discrimination. Additionally, particularly in a multiethnic setting, there could be benefit in employing a worker from the local community, possibly someone who has worked with young children in a voluntary community organisation. That may be as important a qualification as a professional qualification in those circumstances; someone from the local community can help to bring parents and workers closer together, and better understand the children and how to support them. However, there should be a back-up of appropriate training and opportunities for access to relevant qualifications.

Example 2: A setting might advertise a vacant post by word of mouth among existing families and staff – without realising that other potential employees might not know the present families and staff and are therefore, in effect, excluded from the opportunity to apply. If all the families and staff are white and do not know anyone who is black to tell about the vacancy, the effect could discriminate against black people albeit unintentionally (see page 87 for evidence of the low percentage of white people with black friends).

Points for thought and discussion

- Are there circumstances in which it would be of more benefit to an early years provision and the children in it to have a member of staff with knowledge of that community, but who is not yet qualified, than a white nursery nurse-qualified staff member?
- How could an early years setting go about informing people from black and other minority ethnic communities about vacancies, and attracting them to apply?

Because discriminatory practices are seldom intentional or people do not recognise the implications, they may not be perceived as a part of racism or, indeed, be seen at all. But their effect, in discriminating and disadvantaging, means that they also play a part in the whole gamut of racism. Word-of-mouth recruitment is likely to constitute indirect racial discrimination; and the report of the Stephen Lawrence Inquiry describes it more widely as institutional racism.

Surveys of the racial attitudes of people may appear to indicate that attitudes have become more positive over recent years. This may or may not be true. But, as Jenny Bourne from the Institute of Race Relations, wrote:

'testing' attitudes, i.e. an individual's prejudices, is not the same thing as measuring racism. Racism involves the power to act in a discriminatory way. Prejudice is about ideas and stereotypes.

(in a letter to the *Guardian*, 7 February 1997)

It is therefore important to distinguish between overt racism and the more 'subtle' or institutional forms of racism that seldom involve hostile negative attitudes, behaviour or intention.

It is also important to make links between various forms of racism – antisemitism, Islamophobia, and racism based on skin colour and other factors – and to recognise it as the seamless web that it is.

The power of racism

Everyone looks so comfortable, so relaxed, walking about as if they owned the place. So this is what black people look like when they are not having constantly to look over their shoulder, or justify their presence.

(from *My Fathers' Daughter*, by Hannah Pool (2005) a black woman born in Eritrea and returning there for the first time, aged 29)

Extreme forms of racism can occur anywhere in the world, for example in Uganda in 1972 when Idi Amin expelled Asians; in the United States of America before civil rights were built into the law; or in South Africa under the system of apartheid. In 1967, when the United States Supreme Court ruled that anti-miscegenation laws were unconstitutional, 16 states still had laws prohibiting marriage between different races. Alabama did not repeal its law until 2000.

Also, as can be seen from the example of South Africa, it does not always mean that the group with the greatest number of people are the most powerful – there were, and still are, far fewer white people than black people in South Africa.

The histories of exploitation and subjugation of peoples through slavery, colonialism and imperialism vary. It is well known that South Asian people have a history in terms of, for example, music, dress, religion, art, architecture and literature. In contrast, black African people are often wrongly described historically and portrayed in the popular imagery with such terms as 'primitive' (a term seldom associated with South Asian or white people) and as having relatively little history. The human race is of sub-Saharan African origin. Clearly African societies are complex and have a long history with great civilisations – for example, in Timbuktu some of the earliest known manuscripts in Arabic were written from as early as AD 1198 – but it has been marginalised.

But those who subjected African people to slavery had first to dehumanise them in order to make it acceptable for this cruel and barbaric trade to continue. This is serious and likely to have implications for how people of South Asian and African heritages and African Caribbeans, both adults and children, are perceived in Britain, including in the educational system. It is important to unpack these historical and negative characteristics, as they may lead to dangerous stereotyping, assumptions and low expectations of the abilities of African and African-Caribbean children.

If you want to know more

See Walker 2006 for a detailed history of Africa.

The facts of slavery, its history, its abolition and its legacy today are only recently becoming accurately known and even then only by a minority. However, the publicity given to the bicentenary of the abolition of the slave trade has made the facts about black African societies more widely known. For example, the writings of former slaves such as Olaudah Equiano describe the varied social and cultural activities of a rural community and demonstrate, along with other more recent writings about Africa, the existence of organised societies prior to the arrival of slave traders and counter the misrepresentations about Africa described above and elsewhere (Equiano 1789). But the way history has distorted the facts, by implying that black Africa has no heritage, that slaves did not oppose their circumstances and that only white people were actively involved in the abolition of the slave trade, reinforces negative stereotypes of African-Caribbean families and their children. Although indentured labour, a form of slavery mainly from India and China, replaced the freed slaves in the Caribbean after the abolition of the slave trade it was not so systematic and ultimately cruel as the enslavement of Africans. The legacy of slavery cannot be underestimated including the myth that black people did not take action against it, thus victimising them. Although there are also many current factors contributing to the situation faced by black people today, it fostered an acceptance of them by many white people as less than human in order to justify their mistreatment in this appalling trade – a legacy whose influences are still around.

In Britain the whole edifice of racism, its many parts and its insidious nature mean that it is nearly always white people who hold financial advantage and such influential authority positions that they are able to discriminate racially against others. Many may be unaware that they are in positions of such apparent power and influence. But whether they wish for it or not, white people, whether they are in positions of power in society or not, nearly always benefit from racism and need to understand the often invisible power they hold. Being white therefore means understanding the advantages this almost inevitably brings in most aspects of life in Britain compared with the everyday experiences of most black people. Most of these advantages are unspoken, unrecognised, invisible and largely seen as 'normal'. It is particularly when comparing such situations with the experiences of black people that the advantages of being white are demonstrated – in life's general opportunities and in advantages such that they do not even have to think about the possibility of being racially abused on the street, of not being included in some work activities, being stared at, being avoided on the bus or in the group of parents collecting their children from a setting, being told there are no vacancies when there are or wondering whether a negative reaction could be due to racial discrimination. These automatic and hidden assumptions may prevent them recognising the often different circumstances of black people, not least the subtle and everyday humiliating, unwelcoming and distrustful experiences to which they are often subjected.

Case study 12 illustrates this point.

Case study 12

Someone will 'say something'

Loretta, a black woman whose daughter, Rose, looks white, describes her experiences and her feelings

'I wish I could explain to them how vulnerable I feel as a black person, especially when I'm with Rose out of London – that additional vigilance and nagging fear that most white people would never understand. There is always that fear that someone will "say something", or I find myself explaining something to Rose that she has read or heard. I took her to a photography exhibition and she wanted to know why one woman, who looked like me, was standing by a wall with "Keep Britain White" graffiti. How do you explain that to a 5 year old?'

Points for thought and discussion

- Try to put yourself in Loretta's and Rose's position and imagine the day-to-day effect on her of her experience of racism.
- How are young children in families from black and other minority ethnic backgrounds affected by living in a racist community?
- Do providers understand and take account of this?
- What should providers do?

There is one aspect of being white that gives differential power, and that is social class. In general middle- and upper-class people are more affluent and have greater power in Britain than working-class people, however that is defined. But class and race interact. Ironically the commonalities between black people and white working-class people are many, especially when they live in relatively disadvantaged areas. But, where black and white people live in the same area, they may be forced to compete with one another for the often-limited resources allocated to communities in such areas, thus feeding racist attitudes; rather than working together to challenge that limitation. This may partly explain why working-class white people are sometimes perceived as being more overtly racist than middle-class white people living in more affluent areas; though many trade unions with membership across all social classes have been at the forefront of challenging racism both locally and nationally. In a similar way, local race equality councils have brought people from all social groups and ethnicities to work together against racism. Ironically, it is often the case that those communities with the fewest economic and educational resources are those expected to deal with the most profound changes in society, for example in dealing with new migration patterns and the dispersal of asylum seekers. In general white middle-class people do not live in or experience such disadvantaged areas or meet black people on a day-to-day basis, so any racist attitudes they may hold remain more hidden, even to themselves.

Both black and white people even with little societal power can, and sometimes do, express their prejudice in racial hatred and racist violence against others.

And both black and white people can potentially be racially prejudiced. But racially prejudiced white people (even if they lack societal power) have more power than black people and cannot help acting in a discriminatory manner towards black people in some situations. Their communication, their body language, their likely lack of friends among black communities inevitably distorts their behaviour, their actions and the way they relate to black people. Even where they have relatively little effective power as individuals they may express their racial prejudice in hostility to black people in senior positions in the workplace and elsewhere by undermining their positions in a variety of ways. In effect they are discriminating – they are conforming to a norm of racism. Furthermore, they can join overt racist organisations and express their power in their voting behaviour by electing racist people to positions of authority and influence.

Sometimes white people suggest that everything done seems to favour black people. All the evidence confounds this. What may not be recognised is that the power that white people hold is just taken for granted and goes largely unchallenged, so that any action taken to counter this is seen as favouritism. It is important to explain this in some detail rather than just dismissing the assertion out of hand, or denying what has been misinterpreted without an explanation.

While it would be possible for individual organisations run by black people to discriminate against white people, they can at present rarely do this in the powerful, national, prestigious institutions and structures that now dominate and control our society. White people do not experience institutional forms of racism in Britain although some – Jewish and Irish people, Travellers, Roma, Gypsies and some refugees or asylum seekers and other migrants – may be subjected to racism on grounds of their nationality, ethnicity, religion or asylum status (xenoracism). They are, whether they like it or not, in powerful positions compared to black people. Sharing this power may mean giving up some previously held, but perhaps unrecognised, privileges. This is the reality of what getting rid of racism means in practice.

Sex and gender, class and racism

While racism is the subject of this book, both gender and class issues impinge on it. In considering the impact of racism on children from black or other minority ethnic communities, it is always important to consider whether gender or class, or both, are factors in any situation. In monitoring by ethnicity on achievement levels, for example, the overall results may disguise the fact that boys and girls may achieve differently. Gender and ethnicity both need to be monitored. There may be different achievement outcomes for boys and girls; and aspects of the lives of boys and girls, who are from the same ethnic group, that are different.

The issue of whether social class is a factor in monitoring should also always be considered. Assuming for example that different results, collected by ethnic monitoring, are due to racism may be incorrect, they may in fact be the result of possible discrimination on the grounds of class. Furthermore in considering racism issues, the situation facing children from white working-class backgrounds must always be taken into account. To deny their experiences may deny the reality of poverty and powerlessness and how this affects their self-identity. It may also only collude with feelings that black children are favoured at the expense of white working-class children. Some of these attitudes were experienced and identified in Manchester when Ahmed Iqbal Ullah, a Bangladeshi boy, was murdered by a white boy in the school playground, allegedly because he believed that the school's antiracist policies favoured black boys at the expense of white boys (Macdonald and others 1989). Acknowledging the situation of such white children and their families, and recognising their possible experiences of discrimination by class and disadvantage due to poverty, may help alleviate potential hostility between black and white members of disadvantaged communities.

Racism and the media

Over the last fifteen years or so the media in general have made great strides in showing a more representative view of our multiethnic, multicultural society. Most young children can at least see some visual representations of people like themselves. However, many newspapers lag behind this progress in terms of addressing racism in the early years in positive ways.

During the 1980s, the tabloid newspapers and some of the broadsheets were at the forefront of attacking the so-called 'loony left'. Everyone, of any political persuasion, who tried to address racism in education seriously, was lumped together and accused of causing trouble where none existed before. A positive education programme in the London Borough of Brent led to the media accusing teachers of being 'race spies'. The media largely failed to support those who were trying to raise issues of racism in terms of the needs of both black and white children.

Emotive words like 'toddler', 'innocence', 'indoctrination' and 'censorship' were used to draw attention to the work that people were trying to do with young children. They implied that 'these people' were causing trouble where none existed before and that if they would leave things alone everything would be all right. For example, a widely circulated myth alleged that a London council had decreed that the nursery rhyme 'Baa baa black sheep' must no longer be used unless it was changed to 'Baa baa green sheep'. This was not true. Nevertheless the story turned up in many parts of the country and still resurfaces today. A media group in the Department of Communications at Goldsmiths, University of London, monitored the bizarre progress of this story over a period of several years (see page 79, Nursery rhymes and political correctness).

Another example concerned a tabloid newspaper which, on hearing that a home counties education authority had introduced a policy on racial harassment as a result of wide consultation, questioned an education officer of the council. He said that even children as young as four could be racially prejudiced and the next day there appeared in large bold letters, on the front page of the paper – 'Racist check on toddlers' (Doughty 1988). It was followed up the day afterwards by a feature article and an article in a London evening paper.

More recently, an ill-informed feature may appear. For example in 1996, the *Daily Telegraph* ran a full-page article ridiculing the 'multi-ethnic muddle in our nurseries' and implying that British children are being denied their Britishness. The reporter failed to acknowledge the existence of racist attitudes and behaviour in our society. She also belittled genuine attempts by nursery staff to counter racism by providing positive resources (Hardyment 1996). And in 2006, the issue of racial prejudice in young children again created negative headlines in the media (see Lane 2006c).

Although there has been an encouraging trend over recent years for most early years journals to publish features on young children and racial issues, articles and news elsewhere are rare. There is still some considerable way to go before the mainstream media acknowledge the importance of the early years in addressing racial equality issues, as well as recognising the links to this critical developmental stage as the foundation of future harmonious local communities.

The media play a very critical role in forming racial attitudes. Although evidence shows that, in general, people do not trust what they read and hear in the media – for example in 2004 only 7 per cent of people trusted most tabloid journalists to tell the truth – nevertheless their main source of information comes from that very same media (Mori 2004/2006). Although some white people living in multiethnic and multicultural areas of the country may hold strong racist attitudes, most have them ameliorated (or at least controlled in public) by the reality of their environment. Some, however, find the presence of black people intolerable and so vent their venom on them in a variety of ways – ranging from verbal abuse to physical attacks. Where disadvantage, poverty and poor housing collectively provide a forum for overt group racist activity, some particular local areas may become no-go areas for black people. The local media often stoke up the fires around such activities.

There are also largely white areas where hostility to such people as asylum seekers (and sometimes Travellers) may be widespread, despite the fact that they do not live there and are not seen in the locality. The media often play a disturbing role in portraying them as problems. People living in these areas may have no countervailing information about such communities to present a different and more positive view. Consequently negative attitudes flourish, unchallenged. Somehow attitudes towards asylum seekers and Travellers are not seen as racist or equivalent to racist attitudes towards African, African-Caribbean and South Asian people. They do not arise from personal experience or involvement but derive mainly from certain sections of the media which consistently and relentlessly whip up hostility towards them. The non-tabloid press cannot totally be exonerated from sustaining stereotypes, both by commission and by omitting to take a lead in countering them by positive reporting. Research shows that a negative portrayal in the press has a direct and immediate adverse impact on readers' assumptions about asylum seekers in general and the effect is often unconscious and automatic even among people with relatively low levels of prejudice. Furthermore any neutral or positive coverage in the press has no similar positive impact on readers (Brown and Lido 2006). Similarly, attitudes about 'our culture' being taken over by 'theirs' often abound – mainly in the absence of any particularly different cultures. Such attitudes are constantly fed by the media. Workers in early years settings need to take account of any negative local attitudes and their possible origins and provide children and their families, wherever possible, with accurate and positive information about people who they may have heard about but of whom they have had no personal experience.

Some of the media are responsible for a continual misrepresentation and distortion of the reality of the lives of black and other minority ethnic people in general – even though we are living in an increasingly diverse community, the media (especially the printed press) do not yet consistently reflect or report their lives in positive and sensitive ways.

If you want to know more

see the 1971 report of an important contribution to the discourse on racism in the media by Stuart Hall (1971) that is still relevant today.

Being called a racist

I can think of only one thing worse than being accused of being a racist and that is being accused of being a paedophile.

(white principal of a college on being cleared of allegations of racist, bullying, aggressive and discriminatory behaviours and attitudes)
(*Times Educational Supplement*, 30 September 2005)

There are probably very few white people who calmly accept being called racist. Only those who actively flaunt their racism are proud of the title but, even then, they may try to justify it by using pseudo-economic or social arguments to try to make their attitudes appear more generally acceptable. This is especially true since laws against incitement to racial hatred were enacted. These racists tend to promote their views in groups, perhaps for the camaraderie it provides, and it is less certain they would be willing to admit to being racists when challenged as individuals. But the existence of violent and offensive racist ideology in our society, though limited, needs to be acknowledged. Not only does it create a continuous potential tension in and between communities for those subjected to it but members of racist organisations will have children who attend early year settings – this potential cannot be ignored and workers need to be prepared to address any implications of this. (Evidence of racist activity is reported regularly in *Searchlight* – www.searchlightmagazine.com and in the Institute of Race Relations weekly bulletin – http://www.irr.org.uk/subscribe and on the 1990 Trust Blink website).

Nearly everyone else, whether they ever behave in a racist way or not, probably resists the idea of being called a racist. This may be particularly so where people feel they are professionals and so cannot be racist. They may become defensive and deny that anyone could consider their actions or language to be racist. Their mortification then prevents them from reflecting on the issue. Why does this particular word cause such a reaction? Is it a trigger word? Cecil Gutzmore, a former lecturer in Caribbean studies at the University of North London (now London Metropolitan University) suggested at a seminar in London that there is a long list of words that describe aspects of racism, ranging from milder words such as being patronising, through tokenism to the serious issues of discrimination, racial attacks, slavery and genocide (Gutzmore 1995). He suggested that when it is indicated that a white person is being racist in some perhaps 'minor' way, they may react as if they are being accused of running the gas chambers. A trigger mechanism going up the list is set into action and the reaction is out of all proportion to the initial incident. Whatever the circumstances, this reaction may have long-term consequences in terms of their withdrawal from any further discussions about racism or being racist.

Most white people don't want to be called racist. They know that black and white people share a common humanity. Is it because they know, whatever they may think themselves, that it is unacceptable to be racist in our society? Even so, some people really do not feel ashamed of holding racist attitudes. However, there is a certain generally agreed code of values that demands 'tolerance' towards all who live in Britain, whatever individuals may do. Even though some white people may make racist 'jokes', be unpleasant about black people or make 'unwittingly' negative comments, somehow they may not see this as part of racism. If challenged they may deny that they are being racist. Some may say that their best friend is black and he doesn't mind the jokes. They don't seem to make the connection. They don't 'get it'. (See page 70 for a discussion of 'jokes'.)

The only explanation for this appears to be that even though some people may say or do racist things, they are ashamed to be *caught* at it.

Because for most white people to be called racist is painful, it is important to be careful about using the word correctly. A more accurate term might sometimes be 'racially prejudiced', involving attitudes, not behaviour. When prejudice is put into practice in behaviour it is correct to call this racist. The trouble is that using this word evokes concepts of violent behaviour and overt racist groups on the streets. Early years workers are not to be seen in such situations so that may be why it is painful. Perhaps one tentative solution might be to make a point of referring to what has been *done* as discriminatory or possibly racist thus de-personalising it instead of calling someone a racist. By doing this the person may feel less under attack and may be more willing to reflect on the issues later. And, at the end of the day, many people (black and white) have been part of an organisation that is institutionally racist.

The subject of racism or being racist, when raised among white people, can kill conversation. There may be several reasons for this inhibition. Perhaps the people in the group are afraid to talk about it in case someone implies they are racist. Perhaps they don't like black people, but can't explain, reasonably, *why* they don't like them, so they clam up. Perhaps in the past someone had implied that they were racist when they had innocently referred to 'coloured' people or had said they loved their golly when they were young. Because they did not feel this was true and had been unable to defend themselves effectively, they had been made to feel guilty – an experience they did not wish to be reminded of. These examples demonstrate people's vulnerability and how important it is to be sensitive with people who genuinely think that they hold no racially prejudiced views, would never dream of going to a racist rally or who do not see themselves as having anything to do with racism. Being sensitive and understanding in such circumstances is essential if early years workers are to be enabled to consider their own attitudes in constructive ways. Such consideration is more likely to lead to them being confident and effective in working with young children on these issues – rather than to backing off from anything to do with racial equality if they can possibly avoid it.

Moreover where people feel guilty about racism they may become inhibited in their communication with black people for fear of offending them or scared of doing the wrong thing. Guilt, real or imagined, often paralyses people into inaction. Where such situations arise on training courses there is a need for great sensitivity to be used, if understanding and an acceptance of the work needed to be done are to emerge. (See Training and education page 150.)

Can black people in Britain be racist too?

Sometimes white people say that black people are racist too. Of course black people can be racist. Racism is a worldwide phenomenon. Individual black people can on occasions be in positions where they are able to demonstrate their prejudice, for example where they are in positions of influence with children. But the reality is that in Britain, while clearly some may be racially prejudiced, they are seldom in positions of authority to put their prejudice into practice. So, if white people mean that black people may be racially prejudiced, this is true. People from black and any other minority ethnic groups may be prejudiced against white people or against people from any minority ethnic groups other than their own – African Caribbean against African (and vice versa); Indian against Pakistani (and vice versa); Eastern European non-Roma against Roma (and vice versa); and Turkish against Greek (and vice versa), for example. There is no reason (apart from, as with all groups, their history) why, just because they are from a black or other minority ethnic group, that they cannot be racially prejudiced. And many are. Similarly people may be prejudiced against others on religious grounds – Jews, Muslims, Christians, Hindus and others. However this does not justify it.

And black people may be racially prejudiced against other black groups for a variety of reasons, including their histories. For example, some South Asian people who left African countries under threat of their lives, are prejudiced against some black African people and, in turn, some people from these African countries resented the economic position of South Asian communities living there and so supported their evictions. A similar situation existed in Trinidad where, after emancipation, cheap indentured labour was transported in from India thus undermining the bargaining power of freed slaves and casting many into poverty. The legacy of the most appalling racism still exists between Indian and African-Trinidadians.

But the fact that anyone can be racially prejudiced does not make it acceptable. Perhaps what is meant is that because some black people are sometimes racially prejudiced it justifies, or at least explains, the universality of racial prejudice and why white people may be prejudiced. In a sense they are perhaps saying: 'So what's so wrong with it, then? It is natural, we can't do anything about it!' This is not true – no one is born racially prejudiced, they learn it.

In some situations racial prejudice may manifest itself in personal racial discrimination. Hypothetically, just as a white woman might refuse to employ a black woman in her business because she is black so, too, a black man might refuse to employ a white man in his, because he is white. Both situations are possible and both could be unlawful under the Race Relations Act, according to the circumstances.

Where racial prejudice develops into hostility or hatred the principles are the same. Where there are inter-ethnic conflicts, any racial or religious prejudice and hatred, from whatever source, is equally unacceptable. The fact that white people are more able to use their power to manifest and institutionalise their racial prejudice more effectively against people they are hostile to than black people are able to do, for whatever reason, does not detract from this basic premise.

Reports of disturbances in Birmingham, and earlier ones in some northern towns and cities in the early years of this century, demonstrate the reality of social disadvantage and pinpoint underlying factors contributing to it. These factors include perceived preferential treatment and relative success, economic issues, misinformation and social exclusion. Where racial or religious prejudice and hatred fuel such perceptions, resentments may build up – aggravated by rumours, ignorance and jealousy – leading to the reinforcement of divisions between different communities. While such communities usually share aspects of poverty and disadvantage, these factors – sometimes fomented by a few perhaps opportunistic individuals – perpetuate and reinforce such divisions. This may turn some people against each other rather than uniting them in opposition to the basic causes of their common circumstances and conditions. In such situations, even where basic causes of disturbances are really economic, sometimes accentuated by individual greed, they may get labelled as racist. Whether inter-ethnic conflicts are between white and black, white and white, or black and black, the principle of racial prejudice and hatred being contrary to our common humanity is the same.

Racism and phobias about religion

Issues of hostility to or prejudice against particular religions sometimes gets mixed up with racism because racial prejudice combines with religious prejudice to target a particular group of people. In general people do not actively and independently chose their religion if they have one – a person's ethnicity and place of birth largely influence or determine it. But if you are born into a western European family, for instance, and have a religion, you are most likely to be a Christian and, depending on who your parents are, either Protestant or Catholic. Similarly, if you are born into a family in Saudi Arabia or Pakistan it is most likely that you will be a Muslim, even though they may adhere to different strands of Islam. And if you are born in northern Nigeria, it is likely you will be Muslim and in southern Nigeria, you will be Christian. And if you are born in India, it is likely that you will be Hindu, Sikh or Muslim – interestingly it is seldom acknowledged that there are more Muslims in India than in Pakistan and Bangladesh together. So any antagonism to Hinduism and Sikhism becomes associated with Indians; and antagonism to Islam with Pakistanis, Bangladeshis and Arabs (often called Islamophobia). Racism against black people combines with phobias about their religions, with Muslims currently being the specific recipients of hostility. White people are seldom the focus of anti-Christianity phobia.

In 2005 some black British people (who subsequently identified themselves as Muslims) perpetrated acts of criminal terrorism in London against whoever happened to be around them. It is crucial that, at such times, negative assumptions and hostility against *all* Muslims are not made – if the terrorists had been fanatical Christians would *all* Christians have been blamed? All Catholics were not blamed for the terrorist activities of the Irish Republican Army (IRA). Active work needs to be done in settings with all children and their families to counter such negative attitudes and behaviour. Victims of the attacks also need support, as do Muslim families who may feel threatened by Islamophobic attitudes and believe they may be perceived as potential terrorists. Since the events of 9/11 and 7/7 there has, indeed, been an increase in Islamophobia and Islamophobic incidents in Britain. Specific and very sensitive work is needed in settings to discuss these issues with young children.

Case study 13

The butcher's and the mosque

A large new mosque was being constructed in a multicultural town. Opposite the mosque was a butcher's shop that sold pork and had a life-size model of a fat butcher and a cut-out picture of a pig outside the premises – a well-known landmark in the town. A man having his hair cut at the other end of the town reported that the barber had told him about the mosque and that the Muslims there were demanding that the butcher's shop be shut down in deference to the wishes of those attending the mosque.

A woman concerned about such a rumour asked her Muslim pharmacist if this was true. He turned out to be the person responsible for the building of the mosque. He said it was absolute rubbish, that the butcher was there first and had every right to be there and that Muslims had no reason or intention to make such a demand. Indeed, on the contrary, he said the butchers had been very helpful in reporting an incident of vandalism to him.

Points for thought and discussion

- Why and how are such rumours allowed to circulate?
- What might workers and family members do to counter such rumours, both in the long and short term?
- What might they do with the children to provide them with accurate information about this sort of thing?

On such myths and rumours negative attitudes towards Muslims fester and are fostered and spread, possibly unbeknown to the people concerned. Islamophobia is nurtured.

If you want to know more

about specific work in settings, see Baig with Lane (2003), and Lane (2005g and 2005h); and for a discussion of the implications of violence, war and terror in settings, see Adams and Moyles (2005) and Hyder (2005).

Xenoracism against white people

Some people who are white experience hostility, prejudice and discrimination in some of the same ways that black people do, although their visibility on grounds of skin colour is not the same. This includes Irish people, Jewish people, Travellers, some refugees and asylum seekers and, more recently, people who have migrated here from countries newly joined to the European Union. This form of racism may be described as 'xenoracism', based on factors such as nationality and asylum-seeking status. While the historical reasons for such hostility to the different groups are varied, their experiences share similarities. The basic premise of unjustifiable differential treatment on grounds of who you are is the same for all forms of racism. They must all be taken seriously.

Solidarity

Surviving with integrity

(a phrase used by Beverley Prevatt-Goldstein in a talk, 'Racism and its denial in the Victoria Climbié Inquiry 2002: Suggestions for responses by black and antiracist workers at a London conference', NCB 2007)

It is important that everyone and every organisation working for equality – whatever aspect of equality – sees themselves as a part of the wider approach to countering inequalities overall. This is because the commonalities are greater than any particular differences; and to support one another in principle ensures that divisions are avoided. Solidarity between those working for equality should override destructive criticisms of one another, undermining what should be a common sense of purpose. Working for racial equality is seldom easy. So solidarity among people is important – not only for support but often as a critical aspect of being able to continue when things are difficult.

Disunity often results in all being marginalised. Unity is strength.

Inequalities should not be ranked in a hierarchy of oppression where some are considered more or less awful than others. All inequalities are unacceptable and attempts to prioritise one at the expense of another should always be resisted. Competition is more likely to limit the effectiveness of identifying and working towards common goals overall and of supporting work to address any specific differences. To people subjected to a particular inequality (and sometimes to more than one), it is *that* issue that is important to them. Who can judge the reality except the person or people concerned and affected? This common recognition and acceptance and building of alliances between groups working on particular equality issues fosters a shared understanding of the similarities and differences. It provides strength for all and offers a united and informed front against all inequalities.

This principle applies both in macro or micro situations – in national and local organisational terms as well as in any group or team discussions. Time spent in advocating one cause at the expense of another is nearly always time wasted. And it usually leads to ventures into irrelevant concerns and diversionary tactics, where the real issues can be dismissed or ignored by those not wishing to understand them. However unconscious and unintentional, such tactics should be recognised and countered. To allow such diversions means that the seriousness of the principles of equality can be treated as just the in-fighting of others and apparently justify any marginalisation of the issues raised.

Even when there are no obvious disagreements it is always important to demonstrate, in practice, that sense of solidarity that embraces all people and organisations struggling for equality. To be explicit about this solidarity removes the opportunities for anyone to play off one equality issue against another even if it is unintentional.

Case study 14

Speakers not in harmony

A speaker on racial equality at a conference in a rural area was followed by a speaker on Travellers. Even though the first speaker had included Gypsies, Roma, New Travellers and other Travellers (including Irish Travellers) specifically in the talk, the second speaker criticised aspects of what the first speaker had said, thus undermining his credibility. There was no opportunity to address this apparent contradiction, nor would it have been appropriate in the circumstances to do so. The audience was thus allowed to dismiss the arguments given as well as the possible credibility of either speaker.

Points for thought and discussion

- What is the role of the chair of a conference, and what should have been done to address this situation?
- How might the conference planners have prevented such a situation happening?

Any disagreements or misunderstandings would have been better addressed at the time in a friendly manner or dealt with after the talks and between the two speakers in private together, where differences were accepted as just a part of what happens. A sense of solidarity would have avoided any apparent lack of credibility.

But this principle of solidarity needs to be planned for. Ranging from conferences, local authority services to early years settings, there is a need to be explicit that all equality issues are important. For example with conferences, plan to explain this to speakers in advance; introduce them to one another beforehand where possible, perhaps with a written rationale seeking an endorsement for mutual support and respectful disagreements where necessary. In this way, the situation described above could likely have been prevented. It would also have obliged each speaker to consider the other more sensitively.

Groups in local authority services and settings, because they are more likely to work together regularly, usually have more opportunity than conference planners to clarify objectives and practise the actual processes of solidarity and the inclusion of everyone equally. Considering the way existing groups of early years workers operate in practice should be a part of this process. Groups sometimes, perhaps unconsciously, develop specific styles of operating among themselves that may reinforce conformity rather than valuing innovative ways that extend their experiences. A culture of behaviour becomes one where raising an issue that might possibly offend any member of the group, or even a particular member, is taboo. This then becomes such common practice that to even disagree respectfully is felt to be contrary to what is acceptable.

Newcomers to such groups or people who are in their own developmental process may consequently feel inhibited, powerless and pressurised to conform and to try to adapt to the expected behaviour – it becomes incumbent upon them to learn the particular style of the group. They are, in effect, prevented from an equal participation in the group unless they conform – they are excluded. Should they break the taboo barrier they may get a reaction of shock, visible upset and apparent personal hurt or injured innocence at daring to rock the boat – and then dismissed as 'having a chip on your shoulder' instead of everyone accepting the validity of the point being made.

People must be able to disagree with one another and yet still maintain respect and their commitment to countering all forms of inequality. If people feel unable to offer an opinion or dissenting voice because of the way the group operates, not only are they being excluded but, also, everyone else in the group is denied the opportunity to listen to that voice and possibly learn something of benefit from the experience or have a disagreement without rancour.

Because equality issues often involve strong emotions – some of which may have been repressed due to politeness or used as a mechanism for survival – there should be an explicit acceptance that disagreements are viewed as part of the process of coming to an understanding.

Operating within a no-blame culture (see page 56) and having respectful disagreements, opens up possibilities for being honest with one another and avoiding situations where everyone is trying to keep the lid on any potential discomfort by being nice to one another. In such situations there is little opportunity to listen to and learn from sometimes strongly worded and uncomfortable discussions; to suddenly realise the logic of another viewpoint, or the depth of hurt and extent of damage; to cope with dissension in constructive ways; or to have possibly unrecognised but entrenched attitudes questioned within a safe environment. Patterns of defensive behaviour (often stemming from understandable earlier experiences) usually block the realisation that disagreements can be positive and not damaging, that reflection can lead to changes and that everyone benefits from this acceptance of the differences between them. Disagreements, managed courteously, can lead to real exchanges of ideas where learning takes place and where everyone feels free to express their concerns without others feeling 'got at' or under attack. The writer Suzette Haden Elgin, describes this succinctly as 'How to disagree without being disagreeable'. Such an ethos of trust frees people up to ask potentially difficult questions, raise tentative concerns and genuinely listen to each other. From such discussions a greater understanding can emerge and the fear of the consequences of disagreements can be lessened.

Similar instances sometimes occur in training about equality – a subject which often means that participants bring fraught and apprehensive attitudes and behaviour with them to the situation. One of two trainers may fail to support or back up the other trainer when difficulties arise between participants and the trainer, even where both agree about where the difficulty lies. Such solidarity is vital. Failure to be supportive means that participants are left wondering what is going on and querying the value of what one or other trainer is saying. This is untenable. It points to the importance of trainers being very careful to work out how any potential difficulties will be dealt with, should they arise, in advance of the training taking place. Preparation for this is essential.

However, it is not always possible to anticipate what might happen. No one should be made to feel hurt or defensive because they have got it 'wrong'. No one can be sufficiently prepared for every eventuality. Recognising the difficulties facing trainers on equality issues, and having the confidence to persist and learn from these experiences, are things on which all such trainers can share and demonstrate their solidarity.

Solidarity, joining together and supporting one another in response to whatever inequality is being addressed or whatever disagreement is raised, is immensely affirming and important and confounds those who try to divide the issues and set one group against another.

Working within a no-blame culture

For all the reasons given above, talking about racial prejudice, discrimination or the wider issue of racism may create barriers when workers discuss how to develop a policy or scheme for racial equality (where required by the Race Relations (Amendment) Act) or how to deal with a particular set of circumstances. In these situations people are often overcome by being charged with the responsibility of addressing racism, feeling that this is automatically a basic part of their professionalism and is therefore unnecessary to be spelt out. White people may have already reacted in the way described above about 'trigger' words and feel compelled to deny the possibility of institutional racism or their part in any aspect of it.

Everyone comes to talking about racism and racial equality with a unique personal background, set of experiences, knowledge base and understanding of the subject. Everyone brings these different understandings to discussions. Past experiences may have made them feel reluctant to take part in future discussions. Even the rumours they have heard about such things may make them anxious.

It is easier to raise issues and ask questions if an atmosphere of mutual trust and respect between people has been built up. In this situation it becomes more comfortable to correct or discuss particular terminology without giving offence or being offended. It is easier to discuss potentially sensitive issues when workers feel confident and secure together. This is sometimes called working within a no-blame culture, where issues of concern can be raised, confident that no one will be belittled or made to feel stupid or inadequate. It is *not* about doing nothing. But it *is* about really listening to what is being said. Because everyone reflects their own backgrounds no one should be blamed for what that may mean for them. Everyone, however, within a common shared humanity and a commitment to countering racism, needs to listen, to share and to talk things through in an atmosphere of learning together. This can be difficult – but constant, open discussion generally makes it easier. For example, asking people how they wish to be described and which words they prefer to use when talking about race. It also makes discussion of difficult issues possible, some of which are seldom articulated. It is often a real relief to realise that something imagined as a uniquely personal and embarrassing question to ask is, in fact, something that many others share. For example, talking in detail about different skin colours, nose and mouth shapes; why some languages don't use the words 'thank you' as much as others; why languages other than one's own appear to be spoken very loudly or in front of us when we don't understand them; why some people (of all ethnic backgrounds) are unaware that the smell of the food they have cooked and eaten may linger on their clothes; why people who are oppressed are not apparently more grateful for what they have; and why different communities have different customs for greeting each other and different customs for permissible body contact (especially between men and women). It is nearly always preferable to talk things through respectfully and acquire a better knowledge and understanding than to build up a repertoire of impossible questions, irritation at apparent rudeness and lack of consideration for others or resentment at perceived ingratitude, imagined rejection or hostility.

> *Any intervention to combat racism has to be inclusive. The strategy to combat racism has to question, be critical and say the unsayable. The relevance of racism to people's lives and work has to be made clear to all. Racism must not be sidelined from other initiatives to make changes in the organisational culture. It is imperative that all groups are involved in these processes, not just black minorities or white middle managers.*

(Bhavnani 2001, p. 121)

Even where there is a serious difference of attitudes, as opposed to a lack of information, approaching the situation within a no-blame culture is more likely to result in some sort of resolution than would a direct confrontation or a bottling up of attitudes. At least the reality is now out in the open. This means that discussion has an opportunity to continue rather than being locked up in half understood (or misunderstood) behaviour. The temptation to be defensive is lessened and mutual acceptance more likely. This allows time for people sometimes to acknowledge having got it wrong without losing face. It provides a more productive forum for 'getting it'.

While by no means an exact parallel the following words may be relevant:

> *The fundamental commitment entailed by rights is not to respect, but to deliberation. The minimum condition for deliberation with another human being is not necessarily respect, merely negative toleration, a willingness to remain in the same room, listening to claims one doesn't like to hear, for the purposes of finding compromises that will keep conflicting claims from ending in irreparable harm to either side. That is what a shared commitment to human rights entails.*

(Ignatieff 2005)

It is, however, important to be sensitive, non-threatening and empathetic in dealing with vulnerable feelings. What is the best way to address an issue without making someone feel hurt, or affronted, or another person feel guilty? Occasionally it may be best to deal with an incident privately after the event. But it is important to remember that any witness may interpret it differently so it may be propitious to deal with it there and then. The question to ask is 'What might be the most effective way of enabling that particular person to consider what has happened and change without feeling bad about themselves and, at the same time, not allowing any circumstances involving racism to continue?' But the most difficult part of working within a no-blame culture is learning to receive comments, however mildly critical and well intentioned, in a positive and accepting way. Asking ourselves 'How would I wish to be told about something critical?' and prefacing any comments with positive ones may alleviate negative and uncomfortable feelings. It is the responsibility of everyone taking part to be supportive, kind and aware of how hurtful and humiliating such experiences may be.

If you want to know more

about addressing racism in a non-threatening manner, see Lane (2002a) and Responding to emotions, on page 216.

Case study 15

No, no, no…

One of the workers at Leaside nursery raised at a meeting the issue of what words they used with children which might be seen as negative, how children were affected by them and if they involved particular children. They agreed to monitor the use of the word 'No' with children by being aware themselves, listening out for each other and recording it wherever possible. This meant being honest about whatever they themselves did. They agreed to discuss how and why it was used, at the time if possible, or later if it was not appropriate.

At the next meeting they tried to unpick the reasons for using the word. It led to intense discussions and self-reflections. They found that once they started to think about it they used the word less frequently. They also began to question which child or children were most likely to be said 'No' to. They explored together whether it was useful to use the word and if there were other words or actions that might better replace its use. They realised that it would be important to use it in a dangerous situation and that if it was used too often the danger signal might become less meaningful.

They decided to continue the monitoring and collect information on the gender and ethnicity of each incident. This proved an eye-opener for them and made them much more aware about how and to whom they used it in the future.

Points for thought and discussion

- Are there other issues that might be pursued in a similar way?
- How and when might it be possible to raise and discuss them?

A no-blame culture can only be ultimately effective if it is backed up by a strong policy for equality, one that provides a framework for anyone or everyone to challenge what is perceived as racist. It can never be a protected area where such things are ignored or colluded with. The point about no-blame is that things are accepted for what they are, that personal blame is not appropriate and that everyone agrees that blame hinders reflection on what is said or done – that no-blame allows such reflection, opening up the way for change to be possible without recriminations.

Children can also work in a no-blame culture or in a 'be kind to one another' way. It could perhaps start on one day every two weeks when everyone knows that they must not make fun of someone, criticise anyone unfairly or belittle someone who doesn't understand something and that everyone will be watching out for this. After seeing how it works in terms of encouraging listening, thinking before you speak, realising how hurtful unfairness can be and that if you do anything unfair others will know about it, children may become more aware of hurting others and of their power to inflict hurt on others – a factor that bodes well for dealing with any racial incident later on. It may also reduce the development of notions of superiority in some children rather than fostering concepts of inferiority in others, which often lead to fears of getting things wrong instead of a motivation towards resolving a situation or problem. If the idea is successful in raising awareness it could be extended until it is the same for every day.

For an example of how a no-blame policy might work, see page 216.

Side by side, living in the same area

A racially integrated community is a chronological term, timed from the entrance of the first black family to the exit of the last white family.

(accredited to Saul Alinsky)

It is important to understand and acknowledge the experiences and feelings of people from different cultural backgrounds who find themselves in unfamiliar situations living in the same area. In all such situations where people meet, who were previously unfamiliar to each other, there is a need for mutual tolerance and understanding. There is a need for discussions wherever possible about how people are welcomed and what makes them feel comfortable or uncomfortable.

A black person newly arrived in a largely white area may experience racial hostility both from people already living there as well as from the wider society. This can feel particularly isolating. On the other hand there may arise situations where white majority ethnic people, who have been living in an area for a long time, feel disempowered when communities who are unfamiliar to them come to live in their area, even though they still remain the majority ethnic group in society overall. They may perceive, rightly or wrongly, that their traditional way of life, their culture, has been taken over by people with very different ways of living from themselves. These feelings are not unique to white people but would probably be felt in any similar situation anywhere in the world. There is then a potential for alienation, resentment and latent racial hostility to be expressed.

The reasons for communities arriving to live in particular areas are many and varied. They include any community's natural wish to live with others who are familiar to them and the availability of work. But it is often also the result of earlier discriminatory housing allocation policies and practices, manipulation by estate agents funnelling people into certain areas and recruitment practices into areas where there are employment vacancies.

When such situations arise, a mutual recognition and acknowledgement of each other's circumstances should be the basis of behaviour if the community is not to break down into separate enclaves that do not communicate with one another. It is often the case that both communities are subjected to the same disadvantages, specifically poverty. Recognising these shared circumstances should be the basis of action rather than focussing on their differences, leading to dissension instead of a combining together to challenge the adversity. Failure to do this may lead to 'white flight' away from the area thus leaving it as territory for a particular minority ethnic community, with no opportunity for communities to learn from each other. This is not a basis for arriving at community understanding and the reduction of racism. It is not even an effective basis for challenging poverty.

Whatever the explanations for 'white flight', if it results in an apparently segregated community this is not usually due to minority ethnic communities determining to dominate or not wishing to integrate (popular myths of explanation) but because of the exodus of white people – a concept that is widely misunderstood. Interestingly, largely white areas are only rarely described as segregated. Research from the 2001 census however shows that there is an increasing amount of racial mixing rather than segregation in the UK, both within households and in neighbourhoods (Simpson 2006).

Of course many people may adjust to both these situations and come to welcome the newcomers. But others may not. Both black and white people respectively may experience isolation and feel bereft of traditional landmarks of comfort. Extending welcoming signs and friendly body language and talking together about how people can be made to feel comfortable should be important ways of breaking down barriers between people and build up support networks between them. Members of all communities will benefit from communicating with each other, even if it is only by body language. Early years settings can be models for this.

Talking about racism in multiethnic settings

Working in multiethnic groups can be challenging. Some black and white people may never have sat down and talked with each other before. Both may come with fears and apprehensions, with anger and resentment. Everyone has to try to understand this. It can be painful and hurtful. Insensitive things may be said and once they are said it is difficult to unsay them. But when things are out in the open, it is easier to deal with them than when they are hidden. So in order to feel free to express what is felt, there must be an agreed confidentiality about what is said and an ethos of not blaming anyone. At the same time, not blaming does not mean accepting or ignoring comments that offend or misinform.

Talking about racism among people may be uncomfortable and add an extra dimension to an already challenging situation. There may be no shared experience or understanding based on trust from which to work. Even in all-white groups, people may need to learn to talk and listen to others before raising emotion-laden issues such as racism.

Valuing values

A multicultural infant school with a nursery class developed a policy for equality. It took many months to devise and include guidelines, issues for examination, objectives with time scales and 'who would do what'. When asked what they would do differently if they could do it again, they said they would have learned to talk with one another first about their values. When it had come to talking about racism it had become very difficult because they had not already sorted out their basic values together.

Point for thought and discussion

- What strategies might have helped to start this process?

Accepting that this may be the very first time that a white person has appeared to want to listen to what a black person has to say, and vice versa, is important. Because of this – and because this may finally be an opportunity to release the feelings of a lifetime – what is said may be difficult to hear, may be distressing and may appear to be out of all proportion. White and black people are equally able or unable to express themselves endearingly and black people as well as white people do not always get everything right. But taking time to listen to what people really feel is important. People who have been through these experiences have sometimes come together years later and shared their mutual feelings of stress – a recognition of the process of change.

It may be helpful to forestall potential difficulties and differences of opinion by devising a way of communicating with each other beforehand – setting up some ground rules and a structure for discussion. And it may be more appropriate to meet somewhere that is neutral to everyone or to consider having an independent outside facilitator who is experienced in working in such situations. Sometimes early years groups may decide to split into white and black groups to work on particular issues or for particular reasons. Each may have something specific to raise. This may be one of the results of coming to terms with the legacy of racism.

There has to be a shared objective – the removal of racism in the early years and a concern for all children. But it may be necessary to aim to achieve other objectives first. For example, to be able to talk with each other, then to decide what to do next – working with a series of objectives together before embarking on racism. Ultimately, the welfare and well-being of all children comes first, over and above any personal differences between adults. There is no miracle button to press. And if everything appears to be going smoothly it may be necessary to question whether people are suppressing their true feelings.

The power of culture and its implications for racism

Religions are usually tied up with a community's culture, and are often interpreted in varying ways by different adherents. Cultural influences to conform can be immensely strong: for example the pressure to marry within the faith or not admit to wishing for a same-sex partner. Fear of not conforming and being seen as outside accepted norms and consequently ostracised, create situations where individuals and families put pressure on their members to conform.

Furthermore, when this pressure combines with a genuine wish not to upset other family members, some individuals may feel an overwhelming need to be 'loyal' to their family. This form of pressure can be seen in most cultures and societies at various times, for example the shame that having a child born to an unmarried mother would bring on a white English middle-class family until the changes brought about by more open personal relationships in the latter part of the last century.

Where apparent religious requirements are added to such cultural influences the situation is compounded, creating an often almost insuperable pressure to conform. It is well known that, when some communities migrate to another country, the pressure to keep their traditions is greater than in the community left in the country of origin. Where such cultural pressure becomes associated with the religion practised by that community, and is seen as unreasonable and unjustifiable by those outside the community, the religion itself may be held responsible for what is, in fact, cultural pressure alone. It often becomes a form of racist attitudes within some of the majority community – a newly arriving community becomes the target of forms of hostility, ridicule and discrimination. The tenets of the religion may wrongly be assumed to equate with the culture.

This set of circumstances can apply to all religions but at the time of writing this book, many Muslims and their religion, Islam, are being targeted. It is of critical importance that workers and families in settings recognise and accept that Islam is a religion of peace and equality even when some of its apparent adherents appear to believe otherwise.

Blaming Islam or the 'culture(s)' of Muslims for the recent terrorist attacks is wrong and inappropriate – these attacks were criminal and antithetic to the tenets of Islam. The victims were attacked indiscriminately – the motives of the perpetrators were in some way political and were condemned by nearly all Muslims from whatever particular cultural background they belonged.

But blaming Islam for other particular aspects that are considered by some non-Muslims to be unacceptable may also be incorrect – they may result from particular cultural norms, behaviours and traditions that differ between the variety of cultural backgrounds to which Muslims belong. They act independently of religion. While, for example, some may believe that it is contrary to Islam for Muslim children to read nursery rhymes about pigs, others will know that Islam and the Qur'an do not require this. The perceived interpretations are cultural. Similarly wearing particular forms of dress, for example the hijab or *salwar kameez*, are cultural or personal.

Both Islam and Christianity are world religions and their practices will, inevitably, be influenced by local traditions and cultures. The languages, lifestyles, and cultural and historical traditions will temper the way each is understood and practised by each individual culture. And, like all other traditions and cultures, the expression of Islam by Muslims is undergoing continual changes because of access to information and ideas through media and other communication technology. As with particular Christian faiths, where women and gay priests are now being ordained in some countries, Islam is now as open as it was in its early years to the influence of both local and global cultures. Furthermore, society's attitudes may exert a more powerful influence than independent religions. For example, Indian Christians may have similar cultural patterns of behaviour and requirements to those of Indian Hindus or Indian Muslims.

For practitioners, this means, understanding the pulse of their communities and the influences that are shaping children's lives, both in their religions and cultures and the wider society which shapes their attitudes and behaviours.

Early years services and settings as part of the wider society

Subtle and sometimes not so subtle forms of non-communication, exclusion or racism are part of a wider issue in our society, a society that is not at ease with itself. Starting in the late 1950s, there have been episodes of community uprisings, hostilities or riots, and an ever-increasing number of racist attacks. There has also been an increase in hostility towards Jewish people, Muslims and their religion, Islam, and asylum seekers, partly explained by external events in Afghanistan, Iraq, the Middle East and elsewhere and fuelled by their vilification in the media and by some politicians and others. Although there was already an awareness of some disaffected young Muslims, the 2005 bombings in London highlighted concerns about individual alienation and the consequent implications for early years settings. These all contribute to what is sometimes called a lack of community or social cohesion, a lack of harmony.

Because people in the early years are members of communities, and services and settings are a part of their local communities, they all have a role to play in considering how they can contribute – in perhaps small but positive and active ways – towards breaking down barriers between people and communities. Government can contribute nationally by promoting community cohesion, and schools (including children's centres run by schools) now have a statutory duty to promote it, but the reality is that barriers between communities usually include barriers between individuals. Individuals live in their own local communities.

If they continue to live 'parallel lives' with no meaningful contact at any point, the ignorance will grow into suspicion and fear (see Cantle in Bunting (ed) 2005).

One of the ways that people (adult family members and children) meet one another is in the early years settings that their children attend – taking them and collecting them and perhaps participating in the setting's activities in some way. It is an almost unique opportunity to begin the process of breaking down barriers between people and between communities – where day-to-day contact is possible and where friendships can be made and communication established. Starting somewhere can begin by talking to one another. (For more detailed discussion, see section on Communities and neighbourhoods, page 156, and other references to community cohesion.)

The shy communicators

Mrs Shah and Mrs Taylor often passed one another when they collected their children from Penguin Nursery. They smiled at each other while their children put their coats on. Mrs Taylor felt a bit shy about talking to Mrs Shah – perhaps she would not understand her, perhaps she didn't speak English and she, Mrs Taylor, certainly knew no Panjabi, if that was the language that Mrs Shah spoke. She also pondered to herself if Mrs Shah might not wish to talk with her anyway. Mrs Shah, at the same time, felt a bit apprehensive about Mrs Taylor's fluent English and how she communicated so freely with the workers at the nursery. She felt shy in her presence. She had no idea if Mrs Taylor was prejudiced against Muslims – she had experienced some 'bad looks' when she waited in the waiting room at the doctor's surgery and she was aware of the prejudice that she had seen on the television. She did not wish to appear intrusive. So there was no real communication between them.

One day Mrs Taylor touched Mrs Shah's *salwar kameez* and said 'Nice'. Mrs Shah nodded with appreciation, although touching the clothes of someone you don't know (and the possibility that it indicated prejudice) was not something that would be generally appreciated within her cultural background. But so began a friendship, despite these initial feelings, that extended over many years, with their children sharing tea together, learning about each other's food, joining together in celebrating Eid and Christmas, talking about their holidays and laughing together. Mrs Shah's English improved quickly. They both learnt a lot about each other's cultures and enjoyed the experience of being together. Some things about each other they did not understand – but that didn't seem to matter.

The nursery workers took a cue from this budding friendship and organised little get-togethers for family members. They organised an English class for nursery family members. Mrs Shah, three other South Asian women, two Portuguese women and a Somali woman attended. This all led to local visits together with the children, which led to many other activities in the local community – joining in the local carnival, organising a campaign for a local playground to be refurbished, being explicit about their opposition to local racist graffiti and just waving at one another across the street.

Case study 17

Points for thought and discussion

- What might have been the country of origin of Mrs Shah?
- What might have been the languages spoken in Mrs Shah's country?
- How might Mrs Taylor guess that Mrs Shah was a Muslim?
- What in particular would Mrs Taylor have to think about if she was inviting Mrs Shah's children to eat at her house?
- What would Mrs Shah have to think about if she was inviting Mrs Taylor's children to eat at her house?
- The case study tells us that Mrs Shah and Mrs Taylor's children joined together in celebrating Eid and Christmas. Would all families from these religious backgrounds be happy to do this?
- What can we learn from the case study and the points for thought and discussion above, about making friendships across cultures?

Early years settings can and should be advocates for their local community. This issue is discussed in more detail elsewhere (see page 156; Ouseley and Lane 2006; and Lane 2006b).

So, what are the implications of racism for all people working in the early years?

The range of equality issues around us is daunting for nearly everyone. Most of us know that we are not doing everything that we should be doing to remove inequalities in society – the task is so enormous. Most people feel unsure about how to deal with the various aspects and have a sense of not knowing the answers or feeling apprehensive about possibly giving the incorrect answers. It is easier not to talk about things where we feel we do not have a strong knowledge. It is therefore understandable that many blanch at the very thought of having to address equalities, let alone racism, which may appear to many people to be one of the most scary of all aspects of equalities/inequalities. Nevertheless it is critical that they are faced because inequalities undermine the equilibrium of society, are contrary to laws and flout concepts of justice. As James Baldwin said:

> *Not everything that is faced can be changed, but nothing can be changed until it is faced.*
>
> (James Baldwin, *Reader's Digest* 1971)

At the beginning of the 21st century there are people, nationally, locally and in early years settings who, while clearly caring about and committed to equality issues, do not see what more needs to be done, or that they could do, to counter the wider implications of racism, both professionally and in their own lives. Others, perhaps less committed to equality issues, may allow such possibly difficult concerns to be put aside. Yet they are all mostly caring people truly committed to making the lives of all children worthwhile. So what exactly is it that in some way prevents them being involved and taking action? This is a serious question that requires equally serious consideration. But despite this there are no easy and obvious answers. Furthermore it is difficult to address without appearing to be patronising or 'holier than thou'. But not addressing it means the present situation continues, an unacceptable choice.

What might be going on?

Undoubtedly there is, with rare exceptions, no longer an overt hostile resistance – among local and national government and its agencies in the early years or among most national voluntary organisations – to recognising the existence of racial prejudice or, indeed, the need to address discrimination. There is not really a resistance to doing something in principle to ensure racial equality. But many of those with the responsibility and power to devise documents and promote policies, both within and outside government, do not seem to understand what needs, fundamentally, to change – many of those in positions of influence do not see it as important at present. Worthy terms like 'respecting or reflecting diversity', 'valuing different cultures', 'addressing needs' and vague references to 'equal opportunities' are often threaded through the various texts. But unless what they mean is known or spelt out in detail, the practical implications may not be understood. For example, 'assuming a commitment to equal opportunities' is just pie in the sky for many people and relatively meaningless in any particular situation. 'Equal opportunities' may be seen as treating children all the same, rather than ensuring they are treated equally according to their needs; or having an 'equal opportunities policy' but not monitoring whether it is being put into practice. Such documents and policies singularly fail to deal with the basic underlying racial inequality and discrimination in society, an inequality which is already required to be addressed in some measure by stringent statutory obligations. These obligations include making race equality impact assessments and monitoring policies and practice by ethnicity (see Chapter 8 for details of these).

These obligations tend to be ignored and it is largely because the law is not enforced, together with the lack of understanding, that the situation continues – in effect it is *allowed* to continue. The will to understand and the determination to enforce the law are not present. A race equality policy or scheme, unless followed through with training, implemented and effectively monitored and evaluated, does little to ensure racial equality. Similarly, government requirements and targets about racial equality are not followed up. For example the requirement in government guidance for early years development and childcare partnerships to ensure the identification and training of an equality coordinator, in every early years setting, to implement the setting's equal opportunity strategy by 2004 has, so far as is known, not been monitored (DfES 2001). Certainly very few local authorities have implemented this requirement.

With all the good will that there certainly is in the early years sector to make children's and their families' lives better and with all the evidence available to demonstrate what is going on in terms of racism, it is salutary to realise that so much that *needs* to be done, and *could* be done, is *not* being done. This is serious because it means that there is no overall strategy to prepare leaders, trainers, advisors, support and development workers and practitioners to effectively deal with the racism in our society, which affects early years services, settings and, ultimately, children and their families. It is relatively rarely that a few committed individuals are determined, despite the barriers, to ensure that what they are providing addresses it. If those in positions of responsibility to make the changes required don't make them, how can such trainers, leaders, advisors, support and development workers and practitioners, despite any commitment and determination that they might have and often in isolated situations, be expected to address racism and promote race equality by themselves?

Understanding what needs to be done does not mean passing a test or being somehow more 'right on' than others. It is not about being better or superior to others or dividing people into worthy and less worthy groups. It is about justice. Some people are committed, persistent and willing to address racism in positive ways and others are less so. That is the dilemma. The question remains of why the issue of racism does not seem to matter to some, or matter sufficiently to do something about it.

Explanations or justifications for this situation include lack of funding, inadequate knowledge and training and little time for discussions, resulting in it not being a priority. While perhaps genuinely believing that they are already practicing racial equality they often seem unaware of what is going on around them. They may not see the links between what they read about, hear and see and their role in perpetuating racism. For example, at conferences, seminars, meetings, advisory groups, training sessions and in staff teams, are organisers, leaders and participants aware of whether black and other minority ethnic people are present and, if so, in what capacity? Are they aware of whether equality issues are on the agenda and included in policies when they are relevant? Do they seek out opportunities to talk with and consult with black people? And are they concerned if no one is present who understands equality issues and can take a lead in bringing them to everyone's attention if appropriate?

While those with a national voluntary organisation or national or local government early years role have a specific responsibility to take the lead in addressing this issue, those more directly involved in early years practice with children have a similar responsibility. Both play key roles in determining whether and how racism is addressed in their work situations.

Parallel to this situation among many white people and some black people is a more general view about aspects of society. This view includes a belief that:

- Britain is largely a tolerant society
- existing inequalities mostly concern social deprivation that affects people from all ethnic backgrounds
- prejudice exists but it is mainly amongst ill-educated and disadvantaged people
- the law has largely got rid of wide scale discrimination
- if education gets it right for all, then this will deal with educational disadvantage
- making a big thing about racism will only make things worse
- people who make a big thing about racism don't really fit into or succeed in society
- the voices of black people often amount to special pleading.

It is against this background view that many people in the early years may perhaps try to balance current requirements about racial equality. In a sense there is a disjoint between some people's work and the rest of their lives.

This disjoint is reflected in the possible reasons for not addressing racism. It is likely that there is a multiplicity of reasons for this or for avoiding addressing it. Sometimes, there are difficult questions to ask ourselves, every one of us, whoever we are:

- What triggers our thoughts about racism?
- Does it exist where we live or where we work?
- Is it something 'outside' like the media, or 'inside' such as our own personal experiences? How does that shape our view? Is it serious?
- How do we feel when we hear people talk about racist experiences? Empathy? Embarrassment? Anger? Guilt? Something else? And why?
- And what are our instant reactions when we see people who look, behave or talk differently from us? Do we notice if nearly everyone is white?
- Do white people really feel an inbuilt privilege because of their skin colour? Who believes that they do? Does it matter?
- Should we worry if political correctness appears to stop us from making all children and their families feel included?
- Do we still need race equality legislation? How many people's responsibility is it to make sure that the law is followed in settings?
- Or is equality the same as diversity, which is already being celebrated?
- Do we need special knowledge to understand racism? And what should we actually say and do if a potentially racist comment is made by another officer, staff member or parent? Or a child? And is it different if all children, families and staff are white?
- What does it take to be the first person to take a stand against inequality? Or to pursue it if others seem less interested or concerned?
- Do we make a point of listening to what black people have to say?

Further points for reflection on the possible reasons for not addressing racism are given in Appendix 2.

This is hard, but it is the reality. The fact that it is hard does not mean that it is not worth doing. It is necessary, but support, advice and consistent messages are needed. It is specifically *not* about blaming anyone or making anyone feel guilty or inadequate. But there are many people over whom racism flows without a mark being made as to their role in perpetuating it or taking action to address it. There are many who believe that a softly softly approach is best, while making little effort to find other ways that are equally unthreatening but which might be more effective.

What is it that spurs people into action? It clearly includes a strong sense of justice, wishing to empathise with others, a responsibility as a citizen to one's fellow citizens, a knowledge that racism is unacceptable and a personal knowledge of the experiences of people subjected to it. But there is also some other intangible factor, difficult to actually ascertain, that is at play as well – something that many people are trying to grasp, something that recognises that the integrity of every single one of us is at stake if the forces opposing racial justice are not countered.

So what might facilitate a commitment to do something? Some people are fearful of possible reprisals if they take action and therefore may take the easier option of doing nothing. They need confidence to speak up because it is so often a taboo area to address. But it needs to be explicit that it is all right to ask questions about what they don't know and that they will not be blamed for doing so. This is so often empowering and just what is needed – to be given permission to take the first step. Considering the relevance of any of the above reasons, and those in Appendix 2, may be helpful. Making a checklist provides a structure to ensure consistency and legal compliance (see page 265 for suggested criteria). It should be a priority, when devising job descriptions and person specifications, to consider the criteria carefully and to include a knowledge and understanding of racism for key posts that involve policy-making, drafting documents or training. But taking the time to really talk through the issues together, wherever possible in multicultural, multiethnic groups and preferably on an ongoing basis and within a no-blame culture, is the model most likely to be successful. As is suggested elsewhere in this book, time given to such discussions over periods of time is likely to provide an important learning experience for everyone involved – an experience of mutual listening and understanding.

It's only a joke!

Humour is a very therapeutic thing to participate in, to give everyone an opportunity to relax, to laugh and to share it with others. Telling jokes, listening to them and reading them are a part of humour. But sometimes jokes are so blatantly ridiculing or belittling of someone or a group of people that, even though some people may laugh at them, others find them offensive. Overt racist jokes fall into this category – to most people they are not funny because they demean someone or a group of people. Telling and listening to jokes where a person or group of people become the negative butt of laughter at their expense because of who they are, are now generally seen as unacceptable.

However, there are numerous jokes about people, usually people other than themselves, that many people (who would not dream of making overt sexist, racist or other obviously offensive jokes themselves) do not see as offensive in any way. Such jokes are often seen as a way of poking fun at everyone, of putting them in incongruous situations, of looking at everyone's fallibilities and, by laughing at them, exposing them as a part of all of us. They are seen as an innocent way of having fun and claim that no one is hurt by them. There is often incomprehension to even consider the possibility that what has happened may be unacceptable to those who are the butt of the joke as there is no intention to hurt anyone in any way.

Others find the very concept of laughing at another person or group of people because of who they are makes them feel uncomfortable. They may see this as the thin end of a wedge where innocent laughter may, in different circumstances, become unacceptable ridicule on, for example, racist or sexist grounds. When they express this discomfort, however tentatively, the reaction is often to deny that this is in any way upsetting or offensive to anyone – that to suggest this is so, is just silly.

Comments like 'It's only a joke', 'Grow up', 'Get a life' or 'There are more important things to worry about in life than this' are made. There is an implication that the person does not have a sense of humour. Clearly concepts of humour and what is funny differ between different people.

Jokes about people are usually based on alleged stereotypes – things like being stupid, tight-fisted, greedy, lazy, mean, unrealistic, having inexplicable beliefs or even that they are too slow to understand a joke. In other words they are seen as different from the joke-teller. It is likely that every country has their own versions of these categories and who they apply to. Do people really believe these stereotypes and their frequent origins in history or have they just fallen into a category of being acceptable to joke about *precisely* because they are not really believed? Whether the jokes are acceptable to those who are made uncomfortable probably hinges on the answer to this question.

The context and purpose of jokes are both important. For example, when one group or member of a group shares a joke at their own expense, or the group's expense, with other members of their own clearly identified group, they appear to be seen as acceptable – the difference being that it is obvious that being a member of that group is not perceived as inferior by other members. In other words it is largely seen as all right to laugh at themselves. Such groups include those defined by ethnicity, gender or disability.

But the situation may be different or made more complicated when a joke is told by someone *not* of the group being joked about but at the expense of someone present who *is* of that group but who nevertheless appears content for it to be told. Any potential criticism may be apparently defused by such acquiescence. Explanations for this vary and may include:

- seeing genuine humour in some of the characteristics of their own group
- making an attempt to positively claim the stereotype of the joke
- seeing such jokes as part of life's humour and not taking it personally
- being so used to being vilified that they try to uplift themselves by joining in with those making the joke
- trying to win goodwill, compassion and a place in the pecking order from a majority who appear to be unconcerned about the effect on their feelings and self-esteem
- feeling alone and having little alternative but to laugh along, for fear of being ostracised as someone with no sense of humour, someone who can't take a joke.

Only the person or people involved know what they feel, whether they feel diminished, belittled, hurt or not – and whether it matters to them.

This all leaves those who find that jokes at others' expense make them feel uncomfortable, in a quandary. Are they being over the top in their reaction? Is it really worth making a fuss about? When is a joke not really a joke? Where is the line drawn between clearly and widely accepted offensive jokes and those that so many people laugh at? What is humour anyway?

Is it ever acceptable to laugh at someone else or a group of people because of who they are? Does it make any difference or make it better if a person belonging to the group of persons being made fun of appears to think it's all right to do so?

Do some jokes just encourage some people or groups to feel superior to others by distancing themselves from them, by establishing themselves higher up in the pecking order?

Case study 18

Joke?

Why did the chav get so excited after she finished her jigsaw puzzle in only 6 months? Because on the box it said 'From 2–4 years'.

Points for thought and discussion

- Did you laugh? If so, why is it funny?
- If not, why not?
- If it is funny (or not funny) is this because chavs are stereotyped as being ill-educated and therefore unfamiliar with educational resources?
- Are chavs so described only by non-chavs?
- Does any chav call herself a chav and, if so, would she be likely to find this funny?
- If you find it funny, do you feel good about this? Or a bit guilty?
- Would you find it funny if it used a black boy instead of a chav? Or a nursery teacher?
- Is there a difference? If so, what is it?

There are some questions that may help in analysing and resolving the quandaries created by this sort of situation in general, according to the circumstances pertaining at the time:

- Would the joke be told if it was known that a member of the group who is perceived to be the subject of the joke is present?
- Would the joke be written if a member of the group who was the subject of the joke might read it?
- How can it be known for certain that no one present or reading it is a representative of such a group or feels herself or himself to be one?
- Even if it is known for sure that no representative is involved, is it all right to relate the joke?
- Has the background assumption or stereotype about the people who are the subject of the joke been acknowledged? If so, is the joke still acceptable? Is the stereotype really seen as being the truth about the people or is it recognised as being, in fact, untrue and therefore acceptable to laugh because it is so clearly not true?
- Is it possible to explain away a joke to a subject of the joke without feeling some discomfort?

Legislation has drawn attention to the concept of unlawful discrimination on specific grounds leading to an increasing awareness that jokes about women, black people, religious groups, disabled people, people with learning difficulties and people from certain nationalities or ethnic backgrounds are hurtful, demeaning and should not be tolerated. The media are becoming more sensitive to the effect of such jokes and largely aim not to collude in them. But existing legislation does not address all groups – groups based on social or economic background for example. Examples might include 'chavs' (use any internet search engine to find general definitions and discussion) and other apparent stereotypes of working class people.

Using examples of jokes to illustrate the points being made is more complicated than might at first appear. There are so many and they are so varied that deconstructing them is problematic. But at the end of the day the answers to some of the questions raised are personal and differ between people.

Jokes should be instantly amusing and are not meant to be analysed to check if they are acceptable or not – this refutes the whole point of them. It is, however, important to give serious consideration to the principles involved with jokes in order to distinguish between those which are basically just fun from those that belittle others because of who they are or the groups to which they belong. Perhaps, once this is established, analysis will be unnecessary because this distinction has already been clarified.

Some principles arise from considering these issues.

- It is important to be sensitive to the possibility of someone being present who feels they are or might be the butt of the joke.
- Even if no such person is present the very idea of anyone being the butt of a joke or ridiculed because of who they are should be offensive to anyone concerned with equality.
- Where jokes are published or made to an unknown audience it cannot be known who the readers or listeners might be.
- You don't have to be a member of the stereotyped group that is being joked about to be upset by it and want to challenge it for your own integrity.
- The person who is being joked about may have had different experiences and opportunities in life from the person telling the joke – these differences call, not for jokes or pity, but for empathy and understanding.
- Something that is 'only a joke' may grow into something most would find unacceptable – the first stone is often 'only a joke'.
- Once such jokes are started they often become personalised.
- Some people will never be convinced that this is a serious issue – that does not make them right.
- Notions of such discussion of jokes all being 'political correctness' are not relevant – the issue should be about respect for others.
- If a child hears a joke about someone or some group of people based on a stereotype then, when he or she next meets a person from that group, they may find the memory and stereotype have remained.
- It is always better to sort things out by everyone talking calmly, openly and sensitively together within a no-blame culture than for people to take up entrenched positions in non-listening modes or for the media to become involved.

None of this denies the place of humour in society and its potential to be used in positive ways. Sometimes using 'funny' or awkward situations can illuminate prejudice and ignorance and help everyone to empathise with the experiences of a particular group – such situations may facilitate understanding but diminish no one.

But an important part of addressing unacceptable jokes and their discriminatory impact is to oppose them.

Terminology

The terms used when talking about racial equality issues are often the source of some anxiety and apprehension. People are sometimes reluctant to talk about this for a real fear of using the 'wrong' word, of causing offence or of displaying ignorance. It is important that everyone feels able to discuss such matters, that no-one 'knows everything' and that most of us are in a continuous process of re-adjusting our thinking and the terms we use.

Meanings change

Terminology changes with time. What might be acceptable to some people one day may, in a very short time, be less acceptable or unacceptable. For example, the term 'coloured' has been used by white (and sometimes by black) people in the past to describe others and themselves and is seldom intended to be offensive. It is still used by some older people or those who live in rural communities, often because they feel it is discourteous to describe someone as 'black'. This shows that it was not always seen as a negative term by everyone. However, it has a significant association with colonialism, slavery and apartheid that has made it come to be seen as a negative term, and it is not used as frequently now.

Other terms are racially offensive at all times and have always been seen as such by the recipient. Terms such as 'Nigger', 'Wop', 'Coon', 'Gyppo', 'Wog', 'Yid', 'Dago', 'Pikey', 'Paki', 'Kike' and 'Paddy' were and are racist in intent and hurtful to the recipient. They are unacceptable except when 'reclaimed' and used by members of the group, for example 'nigger' has sometimes been reclaimed by black people and is used between them. It should not be used by members of other groups.

The terms 'Caucasian', 'Negroid' and 'Mongoloid' derive from attempts to categorise people according to their skin colour and physical characteristics. There is no scientific basis for these divisions and they have no place in Britain today. It is interesting to note that Indians were included in the Caucasian category. This may go some way to explain the different historical attitudes of white people towards South Asians and black Africans (see page 42 for an explanation).

Terms used for talking about racism

The terminology used in this book applies to Britain. It may or may not be applicable elsewhere. Care should always be taken when using terminology in non-British contexts. Terms that are obvious to us may have a completely different meaning for people in other communities. For example, in Britain, although the term 'immigrant' means any person who comes to live permanently in a foreign country, currently it is often understood as referring to someone newly arrived here rather than referring to the generations of people who have migrated to Britain. The children and grandchildren of immigrants may be referred to as second and third generation immigrants, even though they were born in Britain. In some other countries the term 'immigrant' means people whose ancestors migrated there.

Many white people find it difficult to find the words for discussing racial issues. Sometimes they are afraid of using particular words for fear of offending someone and saying something that is apparently, but not intentionally, rude. Faced with the issue of a person's racial group or ethnicity, some white people may deal with it by trying to avoid using any specific words at all. This may be because they do not know many black people personally or do not feel comfortable enough to discuss such things with them. Knowing and interacting with them in work situations as colleagues is not equivalent to being friends and may limit openness and the asking of direct questions. (See page 87 for evidence about inter-ethnic friendship patterns.)

Different people, whether black or white, make a variety of choices as to which terms they like to use to describe themselves and others. Clearly some are unacceptable and are largely recognised as such. Others are the topic of differing opinions and, because of this, such differences cannot easily be resolved. It is important to understand that the use of any racial term often involves strongly held beliefs and feelings. There is consequently a need to be sensitive and adaptable.

Terms are constantly changing in their use and acceptability. Most will not be accepted by everyone: there are always some people who disagree with terms that are accepted by most other people. Some white people refuse to use the term 'black' for reasons varying from seeing everyone as human to being unable to see it as a political term. And many black people struggle to find a common language – perhaps the legacy of slavery and colonialism means that people want to find their own words for themselves. As a result some see the use of the word 'black' to describe them, as being unacceptable and offensive. This is just part of the way things are.

See Appendix 1(a) for some words used to describe people and (b) for some other terms in common usage.

What some terms really mean

The terms given in Appendix 1 are definitions and may have different meanings or are used differently when applied to real life.

No terms are agreed by everyone. The contradictions and conflicts that the use of many terms arouse in people must be acknowledged, even if they are not all understood. Very few terms are set in stone, fixed in meaning for ever. The continual changes in word meanings and interpretations, and the need to explore the issues around words, reflect the fact that the debate about race and culture is ongoing. It will always be so.

Black, black

The word 'black' is sometimes misused. It was first used widely in a positive sense in Britain in the late 1960s, when people of many different ethnic origins, but with a skin colour that was not white, wanted a term to describe themselves in order that they could present a more united front against the racism they all experienced. 'Black' seemed the most acceptable word – a political term (see page 8 for a description of the basic meaning of the terms 'black' and 'white' as used in this book).

Children and families from mixed race backgrounds (see Appendix 1(a) and page 191 for further discussion of these terms) may prefer to describe themselves as black. They are likely to be perceived as black even though they may define themselves as mixed race for categorisation purposes, for example in the census.

In the United States during the first half of the 20th century, the word 'black' was often used negatively and offensively. In the 1960s, there was a huge campaign to counter the entrenched internalised oppression that many black Americans had as a result of their experiences of racism over centuries; and to reclaim the word positively and particularly to stress the idea that 'Black is beautiful'. Perceptions of beauty are culturally biased, and have changed throughout history. It is hard to believe this now but many white people in the 1960s wrongly saw many black African and Caribbean people as inevitably ugly (this was tied to white people's own perceptions of superiority) and held the view that to have a black skin and particular physical features was undesirable and unfortunate. So the Black is Beautiful campaign was a vitally important campaign to enable people to rethink their ideas and accept that 'beauty is in the eye of the beholder' and not solely for describing white people. The concept of what is beautiful is learned, so it can be unlearned. (See page 137 for more discussion on concepts of beauty.)

Case study 19

The beautiful duckling

Judy, who is black, with brown eyes and cane-rowed hair listened to Helen telling the story of the Ugly Duckling. When he became a white swan, Judy asked if he was ugly beforehand because he was not white. Helen was shocked at her question. She said it was only a story but could not really explain why becoming white made him no longer ugly. Susie said 'But he is beautiful now!' Helen realised that there was more to this issue that needed to be addressed – positive concepts of blackness and further discussion with the children.

Points for thought and discussion

- What are the implications of this case study for people preparing to read or tell stories?

Everyone needs to be aware of the large number of negative ways that the word 'black' can be used and the number of positive ways that 'white' is used. For example, 'pure white snow', 'dirty black hands' and 'black mark'. For a child to have his hands described as 'dirty black' may reinforce black as being a dirty colour by definition. It is, therefore, likely to be hurtful. It also reinforces, in the ears of white children, the negative association of black and dirty – as if they go together. Using the expression 'dirty hands' is a sufficient description, no colour needs to be mentioned.

However, a lot of nonsense has been written and said about using the word black. In the 1980s, sections of the media and others cooked up stories about various antiracist organisations and local authorities, allegedly saying that they had banned terms like 'blackboard', 'Baa baa black sheep' or 'black bin-liner' because they would be offensive to black people. These stories were without foundation and were used to ridicule the organisations, making them appear to be extreme forms of thought police. However, they have been subsumed into urban mythology and are still widely believed.

There are many words and phrases such as 'blackboard', 'white snow' and 'black bin-liner' that are accurate descriptions and which make no value judgements, either positive or negative. It is absolutely appropriate for these things to be defined in this way. A sensitivity and a sense of reality and humour are needed here.

'Being black' or 'being white' is not just the fact of skin colour. It is not about 'being all the same underneath' the skin. While it is the same physically and physiologically, it is not the same experientially. It is about the whole experience of being black or white and the experiences that racism brings to each. So notions of being black or white being only skin deep are untrue – they are the accumulation of what racism means at a personal level and how they affect feelings.

If you want to know more

about the various ways in which the term black is defined, see Lawrence (2006).

Political correctness

Over recent decades there have been serious attempts to make language and terminology more relevant and appropriate to the circumstances of the time. Some people and much of the media, however, have treated these attempts with contempt. Furthermore, some of the language about racial equality has been adopted without a real understanding and commitment to it. Others have seen it as a requirement that they have to obey but do not understand.

Sometimes, people who are trying to use appropriate terminology are worried by accusations of being 'politically correct' (or 'PC'). This is usually done to undermine a person's confidence, even if it is done in a light-hearted way. Many of its origins are in the media-induced attacks, in London in the 1980s, on apparently being no longer allowed (that is, it being 'non-PC') to say such things as 'white or black coffee' and having to say 'coffee with or without milk' instead, as to use such word association was allegedly offensive to black people. These attacks were intended to demean people who were trying to address various aspects of racism. Such requirements were dubbed by the media as being ridiculous and PC nonsense. Indeed they were nonsense, because they were not founded on fact. No organisation had officially banned such word association anyway, although some individuals may have been trying to raise issues about terminology in their training courses.

Nevertheless this idea of political correctness still holds sway among some people, even today, and is used among those who wish to belittle attempts to use respectful, accurate and appropriate terminology. It still continually pops up in conversations or in the media just when it looks like it has gone forever. It is always important to try to use terms that acknowledge, value and respect people and everyone should be explicit about wanting to do this. Accusations usually come from people who do not whole-heartedly share this concern, are just saying it to appear superior or 'clever', to 'score points' over someone, put them down a bit, to isolate them by making them appear ridiculously oversensitive to nonsense or have not yet given the issue much thought. They should be ignored for the distraction from reality that they are.

Duncan Campbell defined political correctness as:

> *that masterful invention by conservative commentators of a problem which doesn't in fact exist.*

> (Guardian, 25 November 2000)

And Gary Younge describes it as:

> *one of those media constructs that gained currency but never acquired real meaning.*

> (Guardian, 23 January 2006)

 If you want to know more

about word association and political correctness, see Lane (2006a).

Sometimes it is useful to put the ball on the other foot, to turn the circumstances around, in trying to explain the effect of words to someone who is unable or unwilling to understand another viewpoint.

Case study 20

Two words will do…

A government officer was devising a form for ethnic monitoring purposes. He had decided to use the terms 'white' and 'non-white'. When another person drew his attention to the concept that this reinforced the idea of white as the norm and therefore non-white as being somehow a by-product of the norm, he said it didn't mean that and, anyway, he only had two spaces. After some discussion with him and others, the situation remained the same. Somewhat desperately he was asked, as a white man, if he would mind being described as a 'non-woman'. This analogy resulted in the full roll call of the census data being included on the monitoring form.

Points for thought and discussion

- How important is it to get right the way people are asked to define themselves on a monitoring form?
- Who should decide on how to describe people: an officer or the people being described?
- If the officer felt that people were being oversensitive, or had a chip on their shoulder, how would you respond?

See page 336 for a discussion of the term 'non-white'.

Nursery rhymes and political correctness

Despite the nonsense of some PC discussions there continue to be examples, often stirred up by the media, where some words or word associations are allegedly 'banned' and alternatives suggested. While these should be addressed individually according to the particular circumstances they sometimes involve early years workers who believe that, by doing this, they are supporting opposition to racism in practical ways. For example, there continue to be discussions as to whether to use the nursery rhyme 'Baa baa black sheep' with young children because it allegedly demeans black people. What is being misunderstood here is that the words of the nursery rhyme are being mixed up with the term 'black sheep' (of the family). It is only when a black sheep is seen negatively in this way that the rhyme is questioned. But the rhyme itself is in no way negative about black people because having black wool is not depicted as negative. And, because there are fewer black sheep than white sheep, they may be seen as having a special attraction in their rarity. In fact, the origins of the rhyme may be in the rarity of black wool and its consequent special value. Instead, when singing it, children could be told about the value of black wool at the time, and why it was so valuable. Although the term 'black sheep' (of the family) could be deconstructed in the same way as above, as being a special family member, it is not usually intended in this way and therefore needs to be challenged. This conflicting interpretation is confusing, only going to show the unpredictability of language (see page 46 for the role of the media in such issues).

It is so often the case that it is easier to talk about things with workers and children and find out their origins than to go through the minefield of apparently banning things that have been common currency for generations. This only upsets traditionalists and feeds unnecessarily into antagonism against people who are promoting racial equality overall. Their potential support may be lost if they feel their own culture is being taken away. It is always important to respect all cultures and to try to understand the origins and reasons for any differences between them. Of course there may be some situations, though rare, when it is perhaps appropriate not to use a particular rhyme where it, justifiably or not, offends some people. It is not the end of the world if a little compromise sometimes takes place in the interests of everyone. And this may eventually be of benefit to all. (For a discussion of concepts of beauty and nursery rhymes see page 137.) Talking through with children what nursery rhymes mean and sometimes introducing variations to balance any inappropriate perspectives is nearly always preferable to talk of 'banning' with all its negative associations of being 'taken over by alien cultures', even if it is never articulated in that way.

Culture

The word 'culture' is often used only to describe the culture of people who are black. It may be used, wrongly, to imply in contrast that white people are 'cultured', with the underlying implication equating the word to 'civilised'.

When white English people are asked to describe their culture, they usually find it difficult and may end up talking about top hats, queuing, roast beef, fish and chips, rolled umbrellas, Morris dancing, football and perhaps even booze drinking (see CRE website for survey of Britishness). They then realise that these things are not typical of the majority of English people. Similarly, most French people's culture does not include carrying strings of onions and not all Mexicans wear sombreros.

Cultural stereotyping is not only ridiculous; it is dangerous, because it makes assumptions that do not reflect reality. Everyone has a culture, or cultures, but it seems that only *some* people are required to define what their culture means for them. Most white English people just take whatever their culture is for granted and find it difficult to define in precise terms, whereas other white British people – the Welsh, Scottish, Irish – can clearly talk about their own distinctive cultures. Usually, only people who migrate to Britain are 'required' to describe their cultures so that they can be analysed, evaluated and accepted – or not. It is as if white (English) culture is hardly a culture at all, it is simply taken as the norm by which every other culture is judged.

Another concern is that the term 'cultural' is used as a reason either to condone or ignore behaviour (whether it is acceptable or not) or to not offer services. For example 'They don't use formal childcare because of cultural reasons'. It is always important to provide and explain information equally to everyone and to question the validity of explanations based on culture.

Diversity

When people call for diversity and link it to justice and equality, that's fine. But there's a model of diversity as the difference that makes no difference, the change that brings about no change.

(Angela Davis, US activist and academic, *Guardian*, 25 January 2008)

The term diversity is frequently used in an apparently positive way to acknowledge the fact that society is multicultural, multiethnic, multilingual and multifaith and that this is a good thing. Phrases like 'respecting or reflecting diversity' and 'valuing diversity' are common parlance in many documents. Without denying this acknowledgement, what exactly do these words mean? They are clearly intended to be positive but without spelling out what they mean in practice they are generally only placatory, as if acknowledgement is all that is needed. Unless it is explicit that identifying all the aspects of this diversity and ensuring that all the diverse parts are treated equally, or equality is implicit within the context of the text, then in a society where many people are treated unequally it becomes merely a palliative for changing nothing, for continuing as before. Furthermore, since it includes issues of age, gender, class and other aspects of society, it can be yet another way of avoiding addressing or prioritising race equality. Inequalities must be addressed before respecting and valuing diversity can be taken seriously.

I have been living in the US. If I had a gun, every time I hear the word diversity I would certainly reach for it. The US case shows that managing diversity is just basic code for business as usual.

(Paul Gilroy in Bunting (ed) 2005)

Ethnicity

Everyone belongs to an ethnic group. However currently the word 'ethnic' is often misused to mean any group other than white European.

There are links between culture and ethnicity, but ethnicity is more specific in its geographical origin, For example, people born in Nigeria may belong to Yoruba, Igbo, Hausa or other ethnic groups, and their ethnicity will remain the same wherever they move to. Culture is a more complex part of a person's identity. The culture associated with a person's ethnic origin will never be lost, but the same person's culture might develop in its complexity over time, particularly after emigration. A child coming to live in Britain from the Caribbean is likely to retain their Caribbean culture, but may also acquire a Black British culture. The role that the Caribbean culture will play in the child's future life will depend on a variety of circumstances.

Ethnicity should not be confused with nationality. The ethnicity of a child born to two white British people living in the Punjab will not be Sikh, it will be white European. A child born into a Sikh family who settled in London two generations ago will have British nationality, but their ethnic group will be Sikh, not white European.

There are, however, strong feelings about such terminology. Ethnicity is a more accurate term to describe a person's background than the non-scientific term race. But, in monitoring for ethnicity, simplification of the categories inevitably leads to suggested categories that are artificial for both black and white people. People should always be asked to identify how they describe themselves, rather than have an ethnic group ascribed to them by the person conducting the monitoring exercise.

Many people prefer to define themselves by their country or nationality or religion. But the concept of ethnicity is important. It is used in legislation. People undertaking ethnic monitoring need to be familiar with the arguments put up against it, so that they can prepare themselves in advance; affirm its power as a vital tool (despite some of its limitations) for identifying, challenging and removing racial discrimination; and make sure that appropriate services are provided (see pages 19 and 252 for monitoring information). It is also important to use the census categories in monitoring exercises, however unsatisfactory some people might feel they are. This is to allow a consistency of information across the country and across services, and so allow comparisons to be made, impact of services to be assessed and trends to be monitored. Any changes made to the census categories should take account of some aspects of dissatisfaction felt by people.

People from minority ethnic backgrounds are frequently and incorrectly called 'ethnics'. In Britain the fact that many visible minorities have a variety of brown or black skin colours and tones has led to the words being used as if they had the same meaning (that is, ethnic minority *equals* ethnic *equals* brown or black). Used in this way, the term 'ethnic minority' becomes an overall descriptive term rather than a term describing a proportion of people. Everyone has an ethnicity. And it is interesting to note the seldom-used complement to minority ethnic – majority ethnic.

It is important to be accurate about the ethnicity of a child – including the range of different ethnicities in the continent of Africa and Asia, and the difference between Africa and the Caribbean.

If you want to know more

about some aspects of terminology in the field of racial equality and the early years, see Lane (2005c and 2005e) and www.childrenuk.co.uk (October 2005).

Talking the same language

It takes a long time before specific meanings for terms are understood by everyone and used equally by them. Difficulties involved in coming to a common understanding are revealed when people from different countries with different histories and understandings of the world try to work together using a common language. For example, a European seminar looking at racism in childcare and education was held in England. Early on, one of the participants said she was unable to continue working in a 'racist hotel' (the venue for the seminar). She showed the others a sign in the foyer saying 'Only residents may use the lounge'. She had understood 'resident' to mean 'citizen'.

Another misunderstanding is where words are translated literally. For example, at an international conference for childminders the term 'black childminder' was initially used interchangeably with 'illegal' or 'unofficial' childminder, as in black market (incidentally, a racist term in itself; the phrase 'informal economy' should be used instead). (For further discussion of the term black, see pages 8 and 76.)

Sometimes people use terms or phrases that they have heard and repeat them without thinking about what they mean. It is important to consider what something really means before repeating it. For example, black dolls are sometimes referred to as 'ethnic dolls' or 'multicultural dolls'. 'Multicultural education' was intended to be about the cultures of all people but has often been hijacked as being only about black people. And setting up ethnic monitoring mechanisms that define categories as 'white' or 'ethnic'.

Are some groups really 'hard-to-reach'?

Osama bin Laden really **is** *hard to reach*

The term 'hard to reach' (or even 'harder to reach') is often used by government and others to describe some groups, their families and children, that are less likely than others to be using early years services (see Lloyd and Rafferty, 2006; and Barrett, 2008, for examples of these). They include, for example, families with disabled children; refugee and asylum seeking families; Traveller, Roma and Gypsy families; families living in poverty, poor housing or in distressing circumstances; and families from some minority ethnic communities. Such groups are often statistically underrepresented (compared to their numbers in the community) in early years settings, in the children's workforce, in parents' groups and as members of advisory, research and policy-making groups. In a sense, the term 'hard to reach' is correct in identifying those groups that are often perceived as being less familiar and easy to access, physically or socially, than some others; and perhaps as being seen to require precious and limited resources and time to ensure their inclusion. Whether these perceptions are true or not is important to determine – if they are not true then they are no more hard to reach than other groups.

It is vital that they are not stereotyped as a problem. For example, it may be that the systems already in place are not sufficiently explicit about including everyone. All families and children are equally entitled to what is available and therefore, unless they choose not to, should be equally represented, despite the difficulties they may apparently present and other pressing priorities. And, indeed, requirements of anti-discriminatory legislation make this a statutory requirement.

But the very use of the term is negative, reinforcing the concept that somehow such people are difficult, perhaps a problem, and that working with them might lead into unfamiliar waters. There may be hidden assumptions that the explanation that they are hard to reach lies with the groups themselves and that this justifies the less than serious attempts to include them. Any such assumptions, which see them as responsible for their apparent exclusion, may preclude examining the reasons why they are not included. They are problematised before contact is made. If they are perceived in this way, that is likely to influence the practice towards them and whether they are included on equal terms. It is therefore important to reflect on the terminology used so that any attitudinal barriers to equality are removed. If services can consider whether they themselves are 'easy to reach', some of the potential barriers might be more readily broken down. Might some groups themselves perceive services as hard to reach, so that the explanations for under-representation need to be examined? For example, do settings reflect all members and aspects of the community effectively, do services ensure that all families and children feel they belong and does everyone have equal access to what is available? In addition, some families may, for whatever reason, not wish their children to join an early years setting – there are, after all, other ways of spending one's early childhood. The reasons for this should, if possible, be sought to ensure that they do not include any discrimination or inappropriate curricular practice that might act as a deterrent.

There are, of course, other more positive ways of describing the groups identified. How about groups 'not yet reached', 'unreached', 'not yet included' or 'usually excluded'? Would these be better terms, thus placing the responsibility firmly on those whose duty it is to reach or include everyone equally? (For a discussion of the care needed when grouping apparently disadvantaged or non-participating groups of people together, see page 265.)

The English language is forever changing. The important point when using and discussing words for talking about race is to be continuously receptive and sensitive to the words that other people use and their reactions to ours.

3 How children may learn racial prejudice and the wider aspects of racism

The assumption, however implicit, that 3- to 6-year-old children are naive and guileless beings basically different in mental functioning and social activity from adults should go the way of the horse and buggy.

(Van Ausdale and Feagin 2001)

Just because we hope children will not learn to be racially prejudiced we must not delude ourselves into believing such hopes will be fulfilled and that therefore we need to do nothing about it. Every racist attacker was once a child.

He's only three…

A black woman, Esther, got on a London-bound train in the Cotswolds. She sat at a four-seater table, next to the gangway, beside a little white boy. His mother was sitting opposite him.

Almost immediately the boy started to push and kick Esther. She asked him why he was pushing her and he said he didn't like her sitting next to him, that he didn't like people like her and he didn't like her hair. His mother noticed what was going on but she did nothing. Esther told the boy that he didn't have any reason to think anything about her because he didn't know her, but he pushed and kicked her all the more.

Eventually she asked the boy's mother if she could please ask her child to stop what he was doing. The mother replied by saying: 'He's a child, he's only three.' Esther said she realised that, but as his mother, she was doing nothing to stop him. The mother then said: 'That's the trouble with you people, you've all got chips on your shoulders.'

Points for thought and discussion

What specific issues are raised in the example? What may have caused the little boy to behave in this way?

- Did his mother say that he was 'only three' because she believed such a young child could not be prejudiced?
- Can such a young child be prejudiced?
- Was the mother prejudiced herself?
- Were the child's actions 'natural' and, if not, where, how and when might he have learned them?

Whatever the answers to these questions they cannot detract from what it felt like for Esther to be subjected to such a demeaning experience.

Racial attitudes

It is an extremely limited exercise to attempt to challenge young children's attitudes while the material processes and practices that give rise to them remain in place.

(Connolly 1998)

We cannot ignore the power of our whole environment to influence and determine what young children are learning about people who are different from themselves.

It is difficult to know if the racial attitudes of children have changed over recent years as a result of changes in practice and the passage of time. And, of course, there will always be variations in their attitudes ranging from one extreme to another. Evidence from the Inquiry into the murder of Stephen Lawrence (Macpherson 1999) cites the racist attitudes of very young children being often confirmed during public hearings and stresses 'the need for education and example at the youngest age'. Recent anecdotal evidence from the Metropolitan Police also cites that children as young as four were involved in racist incidents – and we know that only serious incidents would come under the notice of the police.

Some people believe (and hope) that British society is becoming less prejudiced overall, particularly amongst young people and that the recent history of Greater London government and its specific policies on equality issues, together with London's ever increasing ethnic and cultural diversity, gives hope for the future. They suggest that London is on the way to being comfortable with itself in being multicultural and multiethnic. Furthermore, the existence of laws against racial discrimination may lull people into believing it is on the wane. But is this reflected in the way black and other minority ethnic families and their children experience early years services and settings? Against any optimism must be put the rise in antisemitism and hostility towards some groups of people, specifically asylum seekers and Muslims. And, compared with white

Europeans' experience, African and Caribbean people are 11 times more likely to be victims of racist crimes; Arabs and Egyptians 12 times; Indians, Pakistanis and Bangladeshis 13 times; southern and eastern Europeans 8 times; Chinese and Japanese 5 times; and Jewish people 3 times (*Guardian* 2005).

Somewhat surprisingly, a survey commissioned by the Commission for Racial Equality in 2004 showed that 94 per cent of white people had few or no friends from minority ethnic backgrounds (CRE 2004a), even though half of British-born black men and a third of Asian men have white partners (Alibhai-Brown 2000). And 10 per cent of London's population have identified themselves as mixed race (Livingstone 2006). It indicates a significant gap in inter-ethnic friendship patterns across society and highlights an issue on which efforts need to be focused. Real friendship, as opposed to just colleagues working together, provides a basic starting point for the removal of racism and a society more at ease with itself.

A question worth considering by white people:

How many black people do you think will come to your funeral?

Racist attitudes and behaviour don't just exist in a vacuum. They derive from the endemic racism in our society. It feeds them and nurtures them continually. That is why everyone must be aware of its potential and why it must be challenged at every point if the future attitudes and behaviour of all our children are to be at least non-racist or, preferably, antiracist. Racism is a worldwide phenomenon and the foundation on which racially prejudiced attitudes of any children may flourish.

Pretending to ignore racial differences between people, failing to address racist incidents and name-calling, not examining institutional practices and procedures to identify racial discrimination, and not considering the impact of racism on early years services overall (as well as on the whole of society), means that any work done with children about their attitudes and behaviour can only, at best, ameliorate the existing situation.

Case study 22

Outside in the inner-city

Asked when she felt racism against her if she was outside, Freda, a black manager of a Sure Start local programme in an inner-city area, said 'All the time'.

Points for thought and discussion

- What are the implications for black communities of the situation voiced by Freda?
- What are the implications for all workers in settings of the situation voiced by Freda?
- What are the implications for young black children who live in the area?

While some examples of racist incidents from several years ago are cited in this section, readers can assess for themselves whether similar incidents might occur now.

Research from Britain, the United States, New Zealand and Australia has provided evidence that children as young as two or three years old notice racial differences (see Further Reading). Two researchers also found that the failure to recognise children's 'blackness' damaged some black children's view of themselves and that children's racial identity is crucial for their successful development (Gay 1985, Maxime 1991).

The research shows that as soon as children are able to express what they are thinking, most of them associated negative or positive attitudes with racial differences – unless specific action to the contrary had been taken by those caring for them. Young children were 'racialised' before they went to primary school.

Using photographs of various black and white dolls as images of black and white people, the research shows that both black and white children as young as three or four years old were much more likely to prefer white dolls and white people than black children were to prefer black dolls and black people. Many of the white children showed a degree of hostility towards the black dolls. It is difficult to assess the true racial attitudes of young children, and using dolls is not an accurate test because they do not represent real people. Furthermore, a researcher needs to be objective and is therefore in no position to address negative attitudes should they arise, thus leaving any expressed negative attitudes unaddressed. This could be seen as colluding with such racist attitudes. And some children may say what they think the researcher wants them to say, what they think is expected of them – they may be influenced in their choices by who they see is valued in the society generally. Nevertheless, the choices made by the children in the research probably reflect the attitudes they met in their environments. Some were learning to hold racist attitudes and beliefs. Unless specific and ongoing action is taken with most young children to encourage the development of positive attitudes to racial differences, it is likely that from the day they are born, they are learning the beginnings of racial and often racially prejudiced attitudes – just as they are learning the beginnings of language. Children learn the language spoken by the people around them by being immersed in it as, too, they mirror the racial attitudes around them.

Children inside and outside many early years settings will directly observe the different roles that black and white people play. White and only a few black people are seen in positions of authority (except in a few urban areas); and many black people working in service industries have little recognition or status. At the same time as children may be learning racially prejudiced attitudes, these ideas are continually being reinforced and perpetuated by how they (and adults) perceive, interpret and make sense of the real world surrounding them. In this world many people from black and other minority ethnic backgrounds experience disproportionate poverty and disadvantage.

In the relative absence of black people in positions of power and authority in British society, there is little to contradict any assumptions that the reasons for racial disadvantage lie with black people themselves – that black people are responsible for their own circumstances. Unless specifically recognised as such, these racially prejudiced assumptions do not then allow consideration of the possibility of other explanations – for example, racism, poverty and disadvantage. Thus the outcomes and impact of racism become part of the evidence on which racist assumptions are based.

Research from the United States reveals that children do not only learn racially prejudiced or racist attitudes from adults but also from other children (Van Ausdale and Feagin 2001). This is important as it indicates, yet again, the power of the external environment on young children; and their position as agents for passing on such attitudes – they are able to analyse and are not just voids waiting to be filled. They may play an active role in the perpetuation of racial prejudice and racism. Clearly this has implications for practice.

Learning to be prejudiced

Case study 23

'Brixton, this is Brixton'

A group of white three and four year olds from a nursery in the south London suburbs travelled by overground train to visit a museum. On the way, they stopped at Brixton station. As soon as the announcement 'Brixton, this is Brixton' came over the tannoy, the children chorused 'Brixton! We don't like Brixton, do we?'

Point for thought and discussion

- Where and what might they have heard of Brixton, in what context, and why had they absorbed negative messages when they are unlikely to have had any personal knowledge or understanding of Brixton?

Children are learning all the time. They learn from the attitudes and values of the people around them, including other children. Attitudes, including prejudiced attitudes, are not inborn – they are learned. They learn them from everything that is around them, including books, dolls, toys, videos and posters, from adults, other children and the media, in the following ways.

What children see (and don't see) If children rarely see black people and mixed race families in their books, jigsaw puzzles and posters, they may learn that they are not really part of our society. On television, if they see few women or black people in status roles they may learn to think that only white men can be in these positions.

What children hear (and don't hear) If a child is with her mum and they meet a friend who refers to 'dirty Pakis', the child may receive the message that it's all right to use the word 'Paki' and that such people are dirty – unless someone immediately, or very soon afterwards, explains that the term used by the friend is completely unacceptable and that Pakistan is a country in the same way as England. If no one ever mentions black people and they do not live in their area, children may think that black people only exist on the television, live only in 'rough' inner-city areas, play football or do not live anywhere in Britain.

What children do (and don't do) If a white mother makes it clear that her daughter's black friend will not be welcome at her birthday party then her daughter is unlikely to invite her. The mother will not have the opportunity to get to know her, her daughter will feel uncomfortable and her friend is likely to feel resentful, unhappy, excluded and possibly not know why she was not invited.

From witnessing these sorts of situations, what do black girls and boys learn about their place in the world, and how might this affect their motivation, their attitudes and their behaviour? And what do white children learn about the world from everything that goes on around them?

The effects of racism on children

> *I reckoned that at least once every day since I was five years old I had been racially abused.*
>
> (Hanif Kureishi 2005)

Racial prejudice and putting it into practice are likely to be hurtful and possibly damaging to any child. As many children from many ethnic backgrounds are learning to be racially prejudiced it is important to work with *all* children on this issue.

The effects of racial prejudice and discrimination although damaging to all children, are different according to whether the child is a wronged person, a perpetrator or a witness (see page 219 for a discussion of the terms 'wronged person' and 'victim'). Although inter-ethnic prejudice may have some of the following consequences the power, in Britain, to cause the greatest damage usually lies with white people.

Aspects of racism very clearly affect many children from black and other minority backgrounds (and their families). For them, any form of racism:

- is hurtful and may interfere with their ability to learn by reducing their self-confidence and self-esteem, thus detaching them from seeing themselves as being able to participate successfully in the learning process
- may damage their concept of self-identity and make them believe that they are seen as inferior outside their homes
- may make them resentful and envious of other children who are not perceived as different
- may make them frustrated, upset or even angry at what they see as injustice
- can affect their behaviour, their motivation and their confidence
- may limit their access to high quality early years provision, appropriate resources and learning opportunities
- is likely to have a lasting effect on their education and life-chances.

Children from black and other minority ethnic communities need to learn that racism is not their fault and is not the result of anything that they have done. It is important to help them have a positive self-image. Sometimes black children who have been very strongly supported at home and have been given the skills to counter racism may powerfully stand up against it and appear resilient and confident in their own abilities.

Racism also damages white children. It may:

- lead them to believe that people from black and other minority ethnic backgrounds are somehow less human than they are
- blunt their sensitivity to others and reinforce false notions of their own superiority
- distort their perceptions of reality by failing to provide them with the full range of information on which they can make their own judgments, for example racism rejects some languages and lifestyles without offering the opportunity of learning about and enjoying them as different
- deny them the opportunity to meet black children and adults thus allowing them to grow up in ignorance about them – any curiosity about them may be already compounded by myths, possible tensions and fear
- lead them to ignore facts or opinions that have been contributed by black people, thus encouraging them to accept partial information as a basis for decision-making
- deny them the positive experience of learning about valuing difference
- prevent them from learning concepts of empathy to others – concepts that are fundamental to respecting and valuing one another
- compromise the possibility of their making a full contribution to society in the future.

There is almost no research on the effects of racism on white children. One piece of research done in the United States in the late 1950s showed that racially prejudiced seven-year-old children were significantly more intolerant of ambiguity than children who were not prejudiced (Kutner 1958). This means that they jumped to conclusions without testing ideas. They believed their solutions were the only ones possible.

It is important to take particular care to address the issue of some white children's often unconscious arrogance about who they are and their identity – their assumptions that they are superior because of their ethnicity and skin colour. This might be done by providing them with experiences demonstrating that a black child, or adult, can do some things better than they can (not because they are black but just that they have a particular personal skill) and that this is not a problem for anyone – that skin colour and ethnicity have nothing to do with it.

Being a witness to incidents of racial prejudice, discrimination and other aspects of racism is also damaging. It may:

- make children feel guilty and uncomfortable
- give them notions of superiority or relief that they were not the victims
- make them fear that they will be next.

In all these situations, any negative behaviour must be addressed and continuous work done to break down racial hierarchies, where languages, cultures, ethnicities, skin colours, physical features, hair textures and other aspects of people are ranked in an order of more or less worthiness, value and superiority or inferiority.

Misinformation, hostility, stereotypes and assumptions permit such hierarchies to persist and form the basis of racist attitudes. All need to be addressed by specific action to recognise both the hierarchies themselves and how to work with children to unpack them. Workers are unlikely to know what children really think about these issues and the attitudes of different children may vary. Given the embedded nature of racism in our society it is equally unlikely that children will not have been affected by it. Because of the insidious way that it percolates into children's lives it is important to work with all children, providing them all with opportunities to consider and evaluate their own attitudes and behaviour.

Work needs to be done on valuing differences so they are seen as just that – differences. Workers should work with perpetrators to enable them to reflect on their behaviour. Children and workers may sometimes, together, be able to take specific action against what happened. Both wronged children and witnesses can be empowered to say or do something. They can thus learn and understand about the principles of discrimination on any grounds and their responsibilities to do something to counter it. Furthermore, social class, gender and ethnicity often interact (see Chapter 7 on countering racism).

Embarrassed silence

Learned attitudes and values are influenced by the circumstances of the time and passed on from generation to generation, largely unconsciously. Some people may challenge them, others may change them. But because they are often so subtle and hidden, what is really being passed on is often unknown and unacknowledged. So it is only when there is a reason, a focus, for recognising or demonstrating them that they may come out into the open.

For example, in largely white rural or suburban areas, white children and the adults around them may never or rarely have seen a black person other than on television or in magazines. The sudden appearance of a black person on the street, in the shop or in the early years setting may then provide a forum for dormant racist attitudes to emerge. These attitudes may have been learned from a variety of sources but never previously expressed. In Case study 24, Yasmin Alibhai describes an incident that she witnessed.

Bedlam on the bus

On the 207 bus the other day, a white toddler filled the lower deck with piercing screams when a black man got on. 'He's black, Mummy, tell him to go away.' We sat throttled with tension as the mother tried to swat the youngster into silence. At some traffic lights, the man obligingly jumped off, the mother said the child was just being silly, and the passengers settled back into the comfort of that statement.

(Alibhai 1987)

Points for thought and discussion

- How might the toddler have picked up the information and attitudes that led to his behaviour?
- How might these attitudes affect his future life?
- What are the implications for settings providing for young children?
- What might the mother have said to the toddler when he voiced his anxieties?
- What might the toddler's family members have done earlier to prevent him from being anxious?
- Why might the black man have 'obligingly' jumped off the bus?
- How many of us would have the courage and the skills to deal with the bus situation in front of both the black man and all the other passengers, about whose attitudes we would be ignorant?

This example reveals the dilemma of what to do in circumstances when no one has ever talked with children about the differences between people. It demonstrates the need to prepare all children, wherever they live, to understand, know about and respect differences at a very early age. It also shows that in any situation – whether public or private – we need to know what action to take with children, with the person who has become the centre of attention (the victim, wronged person or target) and with onlookers.

Professor Patricia Williams, in her Reith lectures describes the dilemma of parents having to respond to a child's potentially embarrassing questions in public (Williams 1997). In these situations, parents may simply say 'sssshh', but a child is not restrained by manners. By saying 'sssshh', the message given is that there is something odd going on, something they do not understand. This may be reinforced when an adult doesn't answer properly or says that the subject is not something to be talked about. Alternatively, they may see it not as something having been said that is wrong but that they should speak more quietly.

Answering children's 'difficult' questions

It is important to be prepared to answer children's 'difficult' questions that perhaps cause some apprehension about an appropriate response. But, as Loris Malaguzzi (co-founder of the Reggio Emilia early education system in Italy) says, 'Children expect the help and truthfulness of grown-ups'. We should welcome children's questions as part of their developing intellectual curiosity and use them to better understand the reality of their lives. They provide insights into misunderstandings that require clarification, and inform workers about potential underlying issues and concerns to children. Questions may be personal, 'cheeky', philosophical, embarrassing, quirky, and possibly prejudiced – ones that challenge everyone's response skills. It is important to respond within a no-blame culture, not making any assumptions or judgements. Being knowledgeable, thinking constructively about and practising potential questions and answers with others beforehand are critical to the development of responses based on the key concepts of honesty and confidence. People working with children need to anticipate the sort of questions that children may ask. For example:

Why is Ahmed's skin dirty brown?

Why aren't you pretty?

Do you wear knickers under your sari?

Why does Barjinder have a hanky on his head? [Barjinder's family is Sikh and they like him to wear a *patka*]

Why can't I go to Basil's party? [Basil is white and the questioner is black]

Why does Selma's mummy have that black thing all over her? [Selma's mummy is a Muslim and chooses to wear a chador]

Do I *have* to sit next to Brian? [The children know Brian is a Traveller because one of the workers is a Traveller and has shown them photographs of his trailer]

Why does Syed's daddy wear pyjamas? [Syed's daddy is a Muslim and chooses to wear *salwar kameez*]

Can Yasmin take her scarf off? [Yasmin's family is Muslim and she chooses to wear a hijab]

Why can't Adu speak English? [Adu's family is from Sierra Leone and speak Mende]

Why has Eatel got pink feet? [Eatel is black]

What's that thing on Daniel's daddy's head? [Daniel's family is Jewish and some Jewish people cover their heads as a mark of identity and respect]

In order to answer some questions workers need to understand and know about some aspects of religions and cultures, often within a political context. They need to unpack the questions as to their real meaning. They need to be aware of other children present. They need to be sensitive to any incipient or overt prejudice and how to deal with it. Children can be very observant and perceptive. They need to be helped to understand the effects of their words on others in some situations and how they can hurt others. And sometimes it means a worker saying 'I don't know the answer but we will find it out'.

If you want to know more

about unpacking a particular incident concerning 'not being pretty', see Lane (2004b); and about questions and an exciting way of working with children to develop their first-hand experiences, see Rich and others (2005).

Skin colour

My son was killed because of the colour of his skin. This is absolutely terrible. We cannot change our skin colour.

(Mother of black teenager, Anthony Walker, murdered in Liverpool in July 2005)

It is indeed a terrible thing if anyone should even think about changing their skin colour for any reason whatsoever. No one, but no one, should *ever* have to think of changing their skin colour in order not to be attacked.

It is important to be able to describe and find the words for the actual skin colour tones that people have and not confuse them with the political terms 'black' and 'white'. The political terms white and black, although they describe some kind of skin colour differential, are not the same as the actual colours of different skins (see pages 8 and 76 for discussion of these terms). Finding the most accurate words for the variety of skin tones is challenging, but a stimulating exercise for both adults and children. Ideas may include a range from beige, golden, pinkish, light brown through to dark brown, indigo or black, although none of these are truly accurate because every skin has a kind of luminosity that makes accuracy of colour difficult to determine.

While describing skin colours may not be easy, most four year olds would be expected to tell the difference between a red and a yellow brick and usually to be able to name the colour. Babies recognise different people in their lives. So it should not be surprising that they can also *notice* different skin colours. Although over recent years more practitioners are talking about skin colour differences with young children, there is evidence that some people (many in established positions in society, including in education) still believe that very young children are incapable of noticing such differences. When this happens, this means that any prejudice based on skin colour differences is not addressed – it may be allowed to fester and possibly lead to discrimination against those whose colour is different as children grow older, thus following the possible beliefs of the older generation. In our society where racism is embedded, people whose skin colour is not white are far more likely to be subjected to racist abuse and violence than white people.

Furthermore, where skin colour is not discussed it may become a topic that is taboo, resulting in both children and adults avoiding it because it is perceived as something that is rude to draw attention to and makes people feel uncomfortable. What children may pick up from adults is the message that skin colour is an issue that they shouldn't talk about (and certainly not in front of adults!). Any discomfort is likely to originate from notions that some skin colours are preferable and, in practice, superior to others and that therefore to draw attention to them will only reinforce feelings of inferiority and superiority. Feelings might include somehow thinking that to have a brown skin is unfortunate and that it is kinder and better to say that 'skin colour differences don't matter'. This ignores the facts by pretending there are no important differences in terms of the way that racism often ranks different skin colours in a racial hierarchy, lighter tones being seen (wrongly) as more worthy and valuable than others.

'It was just a local edition of a universal fact: the enduring appeal of whiteness' – the response by a guide, Arun Pai, to a question as to why Indian advertising never depicted any human being with a skin shade darker than olive, when so many of the population, especially in the south, were by no means so light (reported by Ian Jack, *Guardian*, 14 August 2007).

This hierarchy of skin colour is found in many parts of the world, leading to some societies and individual families favouring lighter tones and some people even taking steps to bleach their skins. How can a person's skin colour be any measure of their worth? Such concepts are learnt and have no basis in fact. The ideas fly in the face of reality. It is vital that steps are taken to break into the cycle of perpetuating this hierarchy from generation to generation, a cycle that leads to people being valued quite falsely for their particular skin colour. Skin colour, as with eye colour, hair colour and texture, and body shape, is part of who all of us are. All skin colours are beautiful and add to the variety of people. By discussing the variety of skin colours positively, sensitively, openly and accurately, hierarchical notions can be dispelled and everyone encouraged to feel proud of their colour and respectful of that of others. It is vital that such action is taken in every setting, whether there is a variety of skin colours present or not – keeping a silence may merely reflect negative attitudes. Even in largely white areas there is a variety of skin tones though most people might describe themselves as white. Finding words to describe these tonal differences is not easy and, as with a painter painting a portrait, careful observation is important. Critical, also, is to share what work is being done with families, and the reasons why, so issues are raised at home as well as in early years settings.

Where children are surrounded by or are familiar with skin colour differences and see them and talk about them as part of everyday descriptions it can be clearly recognised that young children do indeed *notice* differences. The key issue is whether that 'noticing' is just part of a description of the people around them or one where negative values and attitudes become associated with particular skin colours.

Personal, but privately reported, examples of children as young as two openly, and as matters of fact, distinguishing between the skin colours of those around them in the way they talk and play, refute the concept that 'children don't notice colour'. Case studies 25 and 26 below are good examples of this.

Josephine's rainbow family

Case study 25

Josephine's mother is black and her father is white. Her mother recalls an incident when she was two-and-a-half.

'Josephine observed at the dinner table that I was "black". (She didn't use "brown" – she obviously knew that "black" was used to describe brown-skinned people.) I asked her about her father – she described him as "yellow" and herself as "orange". She evidently had a clear concept of the three of us having different skin tones but, as yet, no judgement.'

And Joshua, aged 22 months, clearly has long known the difference between his skin colour and that of his mummy and his daddy, as related in Case study 26.

Joshua's bear hugs

Case study 26

Joshua, aged 22 months, has a white mother and a black father. His mother said: 'When he was about one and a bit we started getting him to sleep more often in his own room – in his own bed. Until that point he mostly slept in the same bed with Mummy and Daddy and only played in his own room. From all the toys in his room he picked and still picks a brown bear and a white bear to take to bed with him. He calls them Mummy bear (the white one) and Daddy bear (the brown one). He even found amongst the numerous soft toys of various colours and descriptions a smaller light brown bear which plays with Mummy and Daddy bear and they all have big cuddles together and he calls the small bear Joshi bear.'

Points for thought and discussion

- Are Josephine and Joshua unique? Are they the only children who can recognise the colour differences and who they belong to?
- Why do so many people continue to deny that children notice colour? Why would they not?
- Does it have serious implications for the work we do with children? Or for the implicit criticism it gives of the society in which children grow up?
- Who and what forces in society maintain and perpetuate the myth that 'young children don't notice colour'?

Recognising this situation means acknowledging that racism is deeply embedded in society. It needs a strong political will to counter its insidious nature at all levels of society, from government to every early years setting. Joshua's story makes this link and identifies the responsibility for everyone.

The Points for thought and discussion, above, are ones that workers in the early years field and family members need to ask themselves if we are to begin to break down the ignorance that so often surrounds children – an ignorance that provides children with a head start in possibly learning differential values of skin colour, because no-one has thought to give them the opportunity to think otherwise. Because they are 'too young to notice'.

Joshua's powerful and poignant story should counter all the other stories in the media and elsewhere that children 'don't notice colour'. Young children *do notice* colour. The issue is not about whether they notice it or not, but about how their environment and the adults surrounding them involve them in making judgements about it. It is about recognising the early age that they notice and making sure that this noticing includes positive evaluation of the variety of colours. All the evidence points to the importance of talking with very young children in positive ways about skin colours as a vital way of countering other negative influences that so often surround them. This is not only a message for workers but for policy-makers, government officers and many people holding positions of power and influence in the education field.

It is absolutely essential that the myth about children not noticing skin colour differences is refuted. If we fail to take action children may grow up not hearing differences described as matters of fact, not talking about them, pretending this is not an issue when in their eyes and minds they can see and feel that it is. Adults and the media must take this issue seriously if we are all to work together to enable all children to learn positive attitudes to skin colour differences and recognise where negative attitudes come from. By doing this we can begin to break down the barriers that prevent us from acknowledging the deeply embedded racism in society and its implications for all of us involved in the early years.

But when children notice colour but adults do not believe that they do, the situation is serious.

Case study 27

Problem, what problem?

A setting in a rural area had few toys, jigsaws, dolls or books that included images of anyone other than white people. When the early years development worker from the local authority visited, she suggested that they get some more things to reflect today's multicultural British society.

Rather unenthusiastically, particularly because their finances were severely limited, the workers at the setting bought a black doll and a few books with illustrations of black people, and put them with the other things. None of the children played with the doll and only one chose one of the books. None of those working with the children played with the doll or read the books or encouraged the children to play with them. One of the workers with the children said: 'There, I knew it would be a waste of money to buy those sort of things for here.'

Soon after, Sunita, who is three and whose parents came to Britain from India, joined the group. On her second day Charlene, who is four and white, laughed at Sunita when she talked in Hindi and said she didn't like her because her face was 'nasty brown'. The same worker who had complained about wasting money said 'That's not nice' and distracted Charlene from saying more. She suggested to Sunita that she should take no notice.

The worker recounted the incident to one of the others, who agreed the incident must simply have been a clash of personalities as 'children don't really notice colour'. They decided to try to get Charlene to make friends with Sunita.

The two workers allowed their existing ideas to rule out the chance that Charlene was prejudiced against Sunita because of her skin colour. They were not intentionally unkind or uncaring. But their superficial response to the incident left Sunita to experience her hurt alone; and Charlene with no clear idea of exactly what was wrong with her comment and her laughter.

Point for thought and discussion

- How could the workers have addressed the situation in a more satisfactory manner?

Perhaps what some people actually believe is that skin colour differences are not important to young children – that children really don't distinguish between them and that they are of no consequence to them. This is not supported by the facts.

Patricia Williams, who is black, describes the damaging consequences of her black son's nursery suggesting that he was colour blind when he was not. It transpired that they had told the children that skin colour 'doesn't matter' and this led him to believe that the colour of things in general 'makes no difference'. By pretending that colour doesn't matter they failed to support her son by talking about his colour in positive ways. Racism definitely did matter to him and was allowed to be ignored by the white children and staff (Williams 1997).

Do some practitioners believe that because they see children as 'innocent' they think that a colour-blind approach is what is needed? Because racism is interwoven into the fabric of our society and skin colour is part of that, young children cannot choose to ignore it or forget about it. Therefore denying that children recognise different skin colours is equivalent to denying that racism exists.

Where young children have been given positive messages about the range of people's skin colours, they feel free to talk about them in the same way as they talk about other things. Unlike many other children and adults they feel able to say what they think. And they do.

Sweet talking

Ramiz, aged four, whose mother is of mixed-race parentage, was sitting with his maternal grandmother at breakfast. When she asked him what kind of sugar he wanted on his cereal. Ramiz said: 'I'll have brown sugar because I'm brown, and you have white sugar because you're white.'

Point for thought and discussion

- What does this story tell us about Ramiz, his understanding of difference and his attitude to it?

Skin colour is very important to children, and adults should never indicate that a child's skin colour 'doesn't matter'. Even if adults don't think it matters, children know it does. Dissembling simply ignores the facts of racism.

In recognising skin colour differences it is important not to make any assumptions about the colour of other immediate or distant family members. It is impossible to take for granted the skin colour of partners, children or any near relatives or distant ancestors. Both black and white people may have near relatives or distant ancestors whose skin colours are slightly or greatly different from them. Making assumptions about them may be embarrassing or lead to feelings of anger that assumptions about relationships have been made.

Granny Phoebe

Phoebe is the grandmother of David. She is black, David's mother (her daughter) is black, David's father is white and David also looks white. Phoebe takes and meets David from nursery. Family members and others responsible for children gather outside the nursery waiting to take them home. Gossip among some includes discussion of how much they are paid for meeting the children. One white woman asks Phoebe 'How much do they pay you?' She had assumed that Phoebe could not be related to David.

Point for thought and discussion

- Discuss the need for workers in settings to take care not to make assumptions about families and carers.

Children recognise skin colour differences. The question to ask is 'Why would they, or how could they, *not* recognise such differences?'

What happens when we don't talk about differences

Anything a child feels is different about himself which cannot be referred to spontaneously, casually, naturally, and uncritically by the teacher can become a cause for anxiety and an obstacle to learning.

(Paley 2000[4])

The following incident, although occurring some years ago, clearly demonstrates the still existent belief by some people that children are innocent of racist attitudes and 'don't notice skin colour'.

Case study 30

Photographic negatives

The headteacher of an all-white nursery school collected 14 photographs that portrayed black people in a variety of situations and in a respectful and non-stereotyped way. Her intention was to present them differently to two sets of children. With the morning children she would try to stimulate discussion by asking questions about salient features, other than those related to race, whereas with the afternoon children she would merely draw their attention to the pictures without asking questions and so presumably encourage a freer response.

Her hypothesis, that in neither group would there be reference to skin colour, nor indeed would any disparaging remarks be made, was fulfilled in the morning group, where experience was 'mediated' by the headteacher. The children didn't even make comments about a West African man, wearing sunglasses and traditional dress, except to refer to his glasses as being 'like Daddy's'.

However, with the afternoon group, the response was very different. The headteacher was not present and the children were observed and taped by a researcher who reported that after 3 or 4 minutes, the children began to make very negative and derisory comments about people in the pictures. The discussion was punctuated with cries of 'Ugh, Blackies!' Eventually, hostility reached such a pitch that the headteacher felt obliged to intervene and close the session.

(adapted from Jeffcoate 1979)

Points for thought and discussion

- Discuss the wisdom of conducting such an experiment without a skilled person present to lead the activity.
- How could the collection of photographs have been used with children in positive ways?

---

[4] This book includes pertinent observations about working with black children.

The incident reveals the fact that there are societal constraints, even on such young children, not to make overt racist comments in front of adults. They learn how to behave in certain circumstances, whether to comply with a moral code or just go along with what is conventional to them. They may be hiding from adults what they know is wrong racist behaviour. It shows that it is difficult to know, let alone be sure, what children are really thinking. The headteacher had not realised how the power of her presence had inhibited the children from saying what they really thought. If we do not know what children are thinking, it is easy to believe that they are the innocents we might wish them to be. It is easy to assume they really don't have any racially prejudiced attitudes. So, when adults deny the facts of racism, children try to hide their feelings about it in front of adults. Without the intervention of adults they are free of restraint and so their racist attitudes may be revealed. Denying the existence of racism, far from having the adults' desired effect of helping children to learn positive racial attitudes, may have the opposite consequences.

A more recent piece of research shows that children as young as four develop the ability to use mental control so as not to articulate their own ethnic prejudices in public (Rutland 2003). This suggests they were controlling their explicit ethnic bias in line with what is generally regarded as acceptable. This control increased as the children grew older.

Making opportunities to listen to children and finding out what they really think is important if workers are to be able to help children make sense of differences between people. Knowing what they think about such differences will enable workers to develop the most appropriate way to support them in learning positive and respectful attitudes to people they already know, to those they may not yet know and to those they may never know.

If you want to know more

see Miller (1997), Cousins (1999) and Clark and Moss (2001); and for a series of leaflets on listening to children, see McAuliffe (2004), including Road (2004), on equality.

What specific action can be taken to engender positive racial attitudes in children?

In addition to exploring our own attitudes, values and awareness, we can engender positive racial attitudes in children through:

- talking with children about racist incidents and concepts of fairness and justice at their levels of understanding and discussing what action, together, they might take (see page 231 for suggestions)
- sometimes shopping in shops that serve black communities
- taking part in local events that celebrate diversity in positive and constructive ways

- sometimes positively encouraging children to make friends with those different from themselves by providing real opportunities for them to do so
- taking all racist talk, from whatever source, very seriously
- being aware of the need to continuously work with children to develop and learn positive attitudes and behaviours to similarities and differences between people and introduce differences within an ethos of respect and equal value
- talking with children about how unfair assumptions and stereotypes can be
- discussing with children how different people do things that we all do, but in different ways – making tea, cooking, sleeping, sitting, dressing, washing, eating – according to their traditions and circumstances
- sharing stories with children, not only where fairness is seen to have won, but also where it has not, so that children can talk about the situation and what might be done about it (for an example of children taking supportive action, see the scene with Gurjit in the Persona Doll Training video (2004))
- looking for examples, with children, of elastoplasts appropriate to a variety of skin colours and birthday cards with pictures of children from a variety of ethnic and cultural backgrounds
- making sure that the art resources include colours that will allow children to select and reflect different skin tones
- thinking about what actions can be taken with children under the age of three (see the CD-ROM Lane (2002b))
- working with children using circle time or Persona Dolls.
- ensuring that we have prepared ourselves first – like putting a life jacket on as the plane goes down, so we are able to help a child.

Case study 31

Tight hold

A key worker was holding a nine-month-old baby on her hip when a Sikh man with a turban and beard came into the room. She clutched the baby closer than before.

Point for thought and discussion

- What message might the baby have received about Sikh men?

An exciting project is being pioneered in Northern Ireland in developing a strategy to help children to learn to respect differences. Research gave a detailed insight into the cultural and political awareness of young children aged three to six years old (Connolly and others 2002). The factors particularly shown to influence them were the family, local community and school. This highlighted the limitations of strategies aimed at addressing prejudice among children that do not incorporate the family and community in their remit. Based on social justice, equality, inclusion and accountability, the project aims to enable children to understand what it feels like to be excluded. Parents, teachers and the media are all involved in partnership with the Peace Initiatives Institute (Pii), based in the United States, and Early Years, a voluntary organisation responsible for developing early years work in Northern Ireland. The project is called Media Initiatives For Children (see website www.pii-mifc.org for details).

Unlearning racist attitudes

It is accepted that what men have learned they can unlearn.

(Bloom 1971)

While it is vital that children are provided with opportunities to learn positive attitudes and behaviour to differences between people, any already existing attitudes may remain untouched despite these opportunities. These may have been learnt from any of their earlier experiences and, if unchecked, may develop further as they grow up. As attitudes are learnt, they can be unlearnt.

'Unlearning' may be a difficult word to use initially, in the same way as any new word is. But it is important. If we have learnt something that is negative – such as racist attitudes – it is difficult to learn new and positive ones until we have got rid of, or at least recognised the existence of, the first ones. That is what unlearning means and that is why it is important. However, it is almost inevitable that some learned stereotypes and assumptions will remain at an unconscious level and possibly only pop up in specific situations. But recognising this process means that at least the stereotyping can be blocked and not allowed to influence future actions.

Case study 32

Fair cop?

One day Josie parked her car in a car park while she went to work. When she returned, a fair had arrived at the bottom of the car park. Her immediate thought, much to her instant shock, was 'I wonder if anything has happened to my car?' Her shock was at herself because she thought she had no negative attitudes towards fairground people – apart from going to fairs she had never met any personally. When she reached her car she found that it had a puncture. Again her thoughts were negative. Again she was shocked at her own reaction. But who helped her mend the puncture? The fairground people. She realised just how deeply ingrained were her attitudes, with no basis in fact or past experience, and that she had no knowledge of their origins or even that she held them until the incident occurred. Her negative attitudes were only triggered by the relationship of her car to the fair.

Points for thought and discussion

- How and where might Josie have learnt the assumptions that triggered her prejudice?
- Might it be possible to identify the source of the assumptions?
- Can one prepare oneself in advance not to make such assumptions?
- If so, how might this be done?

Specific and regular opportunities need to be taken to talk in positive ways about all skin colours, all physical features, all ethnicities, all cultures and all languages with particular emphasis on extolling, in detail, those aspects that may commonly be less valued and less familiar than others – correcting any common imbalances. Persona Dolls are one of the most effective ways of addressing dormant attitudes. By engaging children in the narratives and life stories of Dolls depicting situations and scenarios involving others, they are able to learn about differences in real life (see section on Persona Dolls, page 207). Circle time can also be used to consider these issues (see page 207). The key objective is to work with children to break down any racial hierarchies.

?

If you want to know more

see Brown (2001) and Persona Doll Training (2001 and 2004) videos and support packs.

Because addressing children's learnt attitudes and behaviour may impinge on the attitudes and values of their families it is critical that family members are involved in discussing and understanding why the work is being done and exactly what will be done with their children, so that they, too, may own the reasons for it. This is supported by the findings of the work done in Northern Ireland. The basis for action is the setting's policy for equality, which should already have been shared with families, and with which they should be familiar. The Race Relations (Amendment) Act 2000 places a duty on all provision by local authorities to prepare a race equality policy and action plan for its implementation. These documents should be consulted on with parents and carers, and should be published. (See Chapter 8 and Appendix 4 for information.)

Starting from the principle that every child is of equal value, it follows that the characteristics of every child should be equally valued. The rationale of the setting then follows on from this – most people know, when it is drawn to their attention, that these characteristics are not equally valued in our society so workers are providing an opportunity for the children to think about this in practical ways. Family members should be encouraged to participate in discussions with workers and attend sessions where work is done with their children if they wish to do so.

Careful planning is essential to avoid any potential hostility to, or misunderstanding of, the work and to ensure that all workers, family members, children and any governors, managers or committee members share and understand the reasons for it. It is also important, wherever appropriate and possible, to talk widely about why the work is necessary in order to defuse any potential antagonism from other sources, for example, the media. Because aspects of the process of unlearning negative attitudes are particularly sensitive it is important to:

- discuss the reasons for doing this work with all workers and family members and agree a programme of action, to be continually shared between them
- identify the factors/characteristics that need to be addressed and plan exactly how to work with children to redress any hierarchies and negative attitudes

- be alert to any perceived negative or positive attitudes towards the factors by children and take account of them in the work done
- consider how any changes or progress might be recorded in general terms to assess whether the work done is resulting in any positive change of attitudes
- continually be alert to, and respond to, negative attitudes
- not give up the work because changes in attitudes are not yet apparent – changes, if any, may take time to emerge.

(See Chapter 6 to see how this is an integral part of developing a policy for equality.)

Living in mainly white areas

If it's far from the eyes it's far from the heart.

(a saying in Portugal)

In Britain today there are very few areas that could genuinely be described as 'white'. Most areas have some black people living and working in them, and even in a county like Cornwall one per cent of the population is black or from another minority ethnic group – Travellers, Roma and Gypsies being the largest group.

There is considerable evidence that black people in rural areas experience racism as much or sometimes worse than in urban areas, but the impact is often different. Many teachers and even carers will deny that name-calling happens, and black and mixed race children living in these places often suffer in silence. The reason that many people say there is no issue of racism in white areas may be because there are no – or few – black people living there. The racist attitudes are lying dormant and stay there until black people come to live or visit.

> *Some manifestations of racism may be completely hidden from view. They exist in the form of absence. For example, there is the racism involved in ignoring its very existence; of sidelining it or of maintaining that it originates and operates only in inner cities, or only where there are black people.*

(Bhavnani 2001, p. 114)

One report describes the racist abuse experienced by South Asian primary school children in Norwich, but no one appeared to take it seriously. It was either not seen as a problem or not seen as a racial one (Akhtar and Stronach 1986). Three more recent reports vividly describe the extent of racism in rural, largely white areas – southwest England (Jay 1992), Norfolk (Derbyshire 1994) and Shropshire (Nizhar 1995). At a conference on rural racism in Plymouth in February 2004, organised by the Southall Monitoring Project and local groups, it was reported by the local group monitoring racist incidents that there had recently been a 900 per cent increase in racist incidents in the area.

Even the BBC's radio programme *Farming Today* produced a whole edition on rural racism (BBC 1996). It referred to a primary school headteacher who said that there had been no trouble with racism until M (a young black boy) came to his school. What he should have said is that no one noticed or acknowledged that racism existed in the area until M arrived.

It is obvious, really, that if there is no one present to be the target of racist attitudes, then it may appear that racism does not exist. It is less likely that anyone has heard anyone say anything racist to anyone or seen anyone do anything racist – unless they have seen it on television or read about it. However, it remains possible that children may have overheard adults making racist comments about what they have read or seen in the media, even if they do not yet understand its full implications. For example, any focus on the activities of some fanatical Muslims may have led a child to overhear a negative remark about them. Similarly, comments about asylum seekers may have been made in a child's hearing even if there are none living or proposed to be living there. Racist attitudes often fester particularly in areas where black and other minority ethnic groups of people are not visible, except through the media.

One small study, commissioned by the Home Office, examined the attitudes of 15-year-olds in community schools (schools where the local authority is the admissions authority, that is, schools with no religious foundation). It found that a third of pupils in a predominantly white school believed their ethnicity was superior to another; compared with a tenth of those in a majority Asian Muslim school; and fewer than a fifth in a mixed school (Holden and Billings, submitted 2008). Because the racial attitudes of pupils prior to attending the schools were not assessed, the apparent differences in the ethnic and religious compositions of the different schools could not be assumed to be the sole explanation for the differences in their attitudes – other factors, such as the racial attitudes of their parents and the ethnic composition of their home localities, may also have been relevant. However, the findings do appear to partly correlate with the amount of active racist activity in the respective communities, so that pupils in the predominantly white school had little ethnic variety to ameliorate any racial prejudices that they might have learnt.

Other research in primary schools shows that where at least a third of pupils were from minority ethnic backgrounds, their friendships carried over into secondary schools; and that day-to-day contact and friendships between children from different ethnic groups was more effective than forging links between different schools (Bruegel and Weller 2006). (Interestingly, a MORI project in 2007 found that those people who mix socially with others from different groups, rather than just at work, are far more positive about all aspects of integration and diversity than those who do not – CRE 2007a).

These findings have implications for taking positive steps to encourage children from different ethnic groups to mix with one another both within and between early years settings. But they also highlight the difficulties for workers in largely white areas, where few black people live, of knowing exactly what to do to address the development of racial attitudes most effectively. But the statutory duty under the Race Relations (Amendment) Act for many settings, and the moral duty arising from that for all non-maintained settings, to promote good relations between different racial groups remains, whatever the ethnic composition of the area.

There are examples of the experiences of white people travelling around or going shopping in their own largely white areas accompanied, for the first time, by a black person. The different and negative ways that they were treated compared to what they would normally expect was revelatory and a sobering recognition of the reality of racism in such areas.

Case study 33

Hitchhiking

Howard, who is white, often hitchhiked around his rural locality. When he was with Vaughan, who is of mixed race, no one offered them a lift.

Point for thought and discussion

- What light does this throw on experiences of disadvantage and racial discrimination in general?

Without any positive messages about racial differences, the slightest indications of racism may be all that young white children hear or see about the issue. These slight indications may build up to help form their attitudes. For example, the occasional or rare racist remark about people from black or other minority ethnic communities only has to be said once or twice in a child's hearing for the principle to be absorbed ('Well, Dad doesn't like them'). If the remark is more specific, what may be learned is a range of offensive attitudes, such as that 'they smell', 'they're all the same', 'they are dirty', 'they are taking over our country or our jobs' or 'they should go back to their own country'.

Case study 34

The Nigerian friend

A four-year-old white girl living in the north of Scotland, with no black families in the vicinity, was visited by her aunt, also white, and her friend, a black Nigerian man. When she saw the Nigerian man, the little girl asked if he was a boxer. When he replied that he wasn't a boxer she said 'Well you must have been in prison then!'

Points for thought and discussion

- How might the girl's perceptions of black men have been formed?
- What actions might the girl's family take as a result of what she said?
- What might workers, families and carers learn from this example?

The girl had learned something about black people from somewhere, even if she had not actually met a black person before. It was only the man's physical presence that provided a stimulus for her to articulate her idea. If he had not been there she might never have said anything to demonstrate her thoughts – her family might never have known what she thought, or believed her capable of such thoughts. Children are learning to make sense of the world around them – and in some cases they are learning to be racially prejudiced or make racist assumptions right under our noses, whether or not we have noticed it happening.

Some white people working with young children and living in rural, suburban or even multicultural areas do not yet see the serious implications of racism for their work and are reluctant to take positive steps against it. This is not necessarily because they hold overt racially prejudiced views or because they are unconcerned about racism when they see or hear about it in the media. It is usually because they:

- have not thought about racism being relevant in their area
- do not recognise the situation for those black people living in the area
- do not recognise their own position of privilege by being white
- may justify their reluctance by saying that black, Asian and other minority ethnic groups of people, as well as white people, may be racially prejudiced too – this does not make it right
- do not understand the need for early years services and settings to consider what needs to be done about racism
- do not recognise that young children may be part of the mechanism that keeps racial prejudice going and that young white children, in particular, may be part of the mechanism that keeps the wider aspects of racism going into the future.

If you want to know more

about young children and racism, see Connolly (1998) and Van Ausdale and Feagin (2001).

People working with young children in such areas should not fool themselves into thinking that there is no problem there. If anything, the work to be done is even more important in order to:

- give children a chance not to be influenced by racism
- help them to understand that our society is multicultural and multiethnic and, as a consequence, has a lot to offer if they are prepared to enjoy it
- prepare them for living in the wider society by extending their experiences to include positive aspects of diversity
- demonstrate to them what they will be missing if they do not take steps to enjoy the benefits of diversity
- help them unlearn any notions of white superiority that they may have already learned
- give them the skills to challenge inequality for themselves.

'Simple' images

Washbrook nursery in a southern English county had golliwogs in the toy box and portrayed on the curtains. All the children were white. The local development worker raised this matter with the leader suggesting that they were inappropriate for a modern nursery because they did not provide a positive image of black people and, because of the nursery's location, the children would be unlikely to see other images of black people. The leader said she wanted to have them and did not want to get rid of them because she loved them and had loved hers as a child. She claimed that the children in the nursery loved them too.

The development worker explained their origin in colonial stories and that they generally portrayed black people as 'simple' and childlike. She asked the leader what she would do if a black child came to the nursery. The leader immediately said that she would remove them. She clearly understood their damaging implications for black children but had omitted to recognise their potential effects on white children.

Point for thought and discussion

- What are some of the damaging effects of such images on white children?

There are important issues here. All people share a common humanity but all are different in some way or ways. There are differences, including those of culture, ethnicity, skin colour, language, faith (or no faith) and skills. But at the same time people influence one another and in many ways they depend on each other. There are examples of excellence and its opposite throughout the world. Most people long to belong somewhere and all need to be comfortable with multiple identities. And almost everyone craves to be treated equally in a world where justice prevails. All these factors have implications for early years settings and the provision of an environment where learning about this wide diversity is seen as a vital aspect of the education of all children.

Whereas those in multicultural and multiethnic areas of the country have ready access to much of this diversity, for largely white areas in towns or in rural areas, there is less. People living in such areas of the country may have little direct personal experience of people different from themselves in terms of ethnicity. Their attitudes are therefore likely to reflect their educational experiences, their family values and their interpretation of the media.

In some areas often (but not always) where racist organisations are prevalent, there is explicit hostility across a wide spectrum to black people, Travellers, Roma, Gypsies, asylum seekers and, increasingly, migrant workers, whether people involved know any personally or not. For early years workers who are trying to raise issues of racial equality in such situations, life can be very uncomfortable and difficult. It is the way that these issues are addressed – sensitively or not – that may determine whether people are willing to re-evaluate their thinking in the light of changing times. This is a critical and vital task, one that needs much care and support from local authorities and others, including national government. They need allies, practical support and strong leadership from the local authority in taking its statutory duties under the Race Relations (Amendment) Act extremely seriously (see Chapter 8). A national support network for such people would help to share strategies and support for each other.

Kim, Amanda and the Travellers

Kim's family runs the local village Chinese take-away in the southwest of England. It is very popular. When Kim is three years old she joins the local nursery class. She becomes friendly with Amanda, who is white. When Amanda is planning her fourth birthday party with her mother, she tells her whom she would like to invite. When she mentions Kim's name, her mother says she cannot come, as she is 'foreign'. Amanda is upset but doesn't say anything about it to Kim who, on the party day, is puzzled and a little disappointed as to why her friend did not invite her.

The school is aware of the requirements of the Race Relations (Amendment) Act – to promote good relations between people of different racial groups – and also of the Early Years Foundation Stage and Ofsted requirements on equality issues. The class makes a point of celebrating festivals from unfamiliar cultures even though there is almost no one attending the school who belongs to those cultural groups. This is not easy and the teacher and nursery assistant are aware of their limitations. They are not sure that they are celebrating the festivals appropriately. They do, however, try to include resources reflecting the ethnicity of the wider society even though it is not reflected in the immediate locality – some books, dolls and a few jigsaws. They have a beautiful Indian doll. Then there is another incident in the village.

A small group of Travellers buy a field from a local farmer and move their trailers onto the site. It is not known whether this is legal or not. The Traveller Education Service contacts the families and encourages them to send their children to school. But before anything is resolved, a group of people living in the village organises a petition to get rid of the Travellers. There is a lot of gossip in the local shop and in the pub against them and a considerable amount of racial abuse directed at them.

Two families, whose children attend the nursery and who live in the village, are very disturbed at both these incidents. They feel very strongly that it is wrong to call a young child foreign, especially when her family are British citizens, and that it is important to break down racial barriers rather than perpetuate them. One of the fathers has known a Traveller as a friend from where he lived before. Initially they seek the support of other people in treating the Travellers with respect and get some support. Eventually the Travellers move on and many of the villagers are relieved.

The two families regard the incidents in the nursery and with the Travellers as symptoms of the general attitudes in the village. They ask for a meeting with the headteacher to

Case study 36

discuss what might be done to prevent such incidents happening again and to help everyone to respect each other, especially the children, even if there are no other incidents. One suggestion that they followed up was to form a link with a school in a nearby multicultural town. They all recognised that there needed to be a lot of prior preparation with all the staff, the children and their families in both schools to ensure that they were all able and willing to share their lives with one another in a respectful way. After some initial difficulties the children looked forward to the visits and some children made significant friendships with one another and even visited one another's homes at weekends. It was the beginning of something that both schools saw as worthwhile.

Point for thought and discussion

- What are the main good practice points made in this case study?

The probability may be that in some rural and suburban areas and in some towns, white people in general may be almost unaware of the gulf between their thinking and that of many people who live in the reality of vibrant multicultural and multiethnic towns and cities. Such a gulf leaves fertile ground for myths to flourish, for blaming others for any perceived ills or thinking that racism is not an issue that need concern them. There are also likely to be others who genuinely do not hold racist attitudes but who may be totally unfamiliar with ethnic diversity and consequently lack the experience of relating with black people. They may use inappropriate terminology to describe people as a result of this unfamiliarity (for example, by referring to 'Christian names' or 'coloured people') and have no knowledge about their lives. Issues of racism may never appear to them to cross their paths.

Even in multicultural, multiethnic areas there may be settings relatively close together whose ethnic compositions are very different. Making links between them, with lots of relevant and informed preparation beforehand, may begin the process of mutual knowledge and understanding. All this takes time as the following quote shows.

> *We've got them for five hours a day and when they go home they're getting completely different messages. Things will only change if we make a difference to these kids and when they're adults they pass on the right messages. It might take a very long time. A generation.*
>
> (Alice Dunn, teacher at a school where radically different pupil populations were combined. TES 2007b)

Education work in schools and settings must take action to comply with their statutory duty under the Race Relations (Amendment) Act 2000 to promote good relations between people of different racial groups. But an early years setting (while possibly having this statutory duty as well, but certainly having a moral duty, reinforced by the local authority) is uniquely placed to raise issues of racial equality, not only with children but also by sharing this with their family members too. In largely white areas this may be the only work that is being done to counter the learning of prejudicial attitudes. As such it is a vitally important opportunity to influence future generations.

Raising the issues in such areas requires enormous commitment, sensitivity and understanding – but it is an incredibly important task to be undertaken. If the situation is allowed to continue unaltered, nothing will change. The cycle of learning racist attitudes will continue and discrimination will be maintained.

For further discussion of the issues raised in this chapter, see Chapter 7 on countering racism.

If you want to know more

about specific work in largely white areas, see EYTARN (1993a), Dhalech (2000), DfES (2004), Gaine (2005), Edwards and others (2006), and Knowles and Ridley (2006). For a description of development work in a largely white area, see Newbery (2006). For a paper with a particularly helpful list of practical suggestions for working on all equality issues in largely white areas, see Derman-Sparks and Ramsey (2003).

4 Learning from the past

Racism messes history up.

(Paul Gilroy, Introduction to *London is the Place for Me*, Honest Jon's Records, London 2005)

Where are you from? No, where are you really from?

(A question often asked of Ekow Eshun (and many others), artistic director of the Institute of Contemporary Arts. He went to Ghana (formerly the Gold Coast) and found one of his ancestors was a white slave trader (Eshun 2005))

What happened in the past is likely to have an impact on the present. Practices and procedures that had racist implications at the time may still have a legacy of influence now.

> **?**
>
> **If you want to know more**
>
> about the history of migration and about the contributions that migrants have made to Britain, see CRE (1996).

It is crucial to know about the past in order to understand it and to be in a position to prepare for the future.

Although some of the following examples may appear remote, it is important to consider whether they have resonance with what is happening today. Any resulting stereotypes and assumptions, unless re-evaluated, may remain entrenched long after formal practices and procedures have changed.

> **?**
>
> **If you want to know more**
>
> about the history of racism in early years practices and procedures, see the appendix in Lane (2006b), and Kwhali (2006).

Assessing developmental progress

When assessing the developmental progress of children, it is important to have some standards or norms by which each child can be measured on a range of factors. Children who are genuinely developmentally delayed need to be identified as early as possible in order to address the causes of the delay.

Until relatively recently most of these norms were devised using white, middle-class children as the basis. Some norms apply to all children, but others depend on the particular group that is being assessed. Different child-rearing practices and environments may result in different norms being applicable. In most cases, one type of practice is neither better nor worse than another – they are just different.

> **If you want to know more**
>
> by reading about a discussion of the variety of childhood experiences, child-rearing practices and the experiences of poverty and affluence in various places around the world, with mutual opportunities to learn from each other, see Penn 2006.

Culturally biased tests may lead to inaccurate assessments. It is therefore necessary to be aware, when assessing a child's development, of differences of upbringing and environment and to take them into account. For example, Orthodox Jewish dietary law forbids the eating of pork, and using a picture of a pig in testing recognition of farm animals may make a child feel uncomfortable.

Similarly it is important to be aware of the variety of child-rearing practices when testing a child, so ideas and items should be assessed for their cultural appropriateness before a child is tested for their knowledge and familiarity with them. Furthermore, unfamiliarity with particular experiences should not be assumed to indicate a family's lack of attention to visits and outings, educational experiences or appropriate ways to eat food. For example there are many cultures across the world where food is eaten with flat or soft bread rather than cutlery, just as Europeans would not expect to eat a sandwich or burger with a knife and fork.

The language of the test and the language of the assessor may make it impossible to accurately assess specific aspects of the Foundation Stage profile for children who are learning English as an additional language but who have not yet acquired the vocabulary to understand and answer the questions as well as they could in their home language. This may result in underestimating their knowledge.

Wherever possible, young children who are learning English should not be assessed by people who can only speak English using a test drafted in English. Such an assessment is unlikely to measure the child's abilities accurately.

> **?**
>
> **If you want to know more**
>
> about the Foundation Stage Profile, see the discussion in Houston and Gopinath (2003).

Books and research on child development

Until the late 1980s, books written about child development and child-rearing practices rarely credited the presence of people from a range of social and ethnic groups. They largely ignored people from black and other minority ethnic groups. If books did take account of them, it was mainly to see them as posing problems.

When researchers started to consider black and other minority ethnic children and their families, the messages that emerged were often negative and stereotypical. They failed to acknowledge the existence of racism and its possible effect on the development of young children and the interpretation of their behaviour. Nor did they make any attempt to examine the effects of racism on white children.

For example, a particularly influential book for nursery nurse students throughout the 1980s was *Child Care and Health for Nursery Nurses*. It had this to say:

> *West Indian children may appear to have a 'different' emotional make-up, and will cry and fight, laugh and love with equal energy. Their responsiveness to music makes it almost impossible for them to remain still when music is being played … Asian children may appear very passive and dependent on adults, as they are encouraged to be dependent and obedient within their families.*

(Brain and Martin 1983)

Such statements, while not being deliberately uncaring, could have led nursery nurses to allow black boys to dominate physical activities while giving them less access to cognitive learning skills than other children (see the examples in Case study 2 on page 16). Unless there has been some more recent specific in-service training and support, attitudes like this may still be around.

Other books and research publications drew false conclusions about families and parenting practices. For example, research conducted in Brixton, south London, to measure 'West Indian' children's development, wrongly concluded that they fell below the standard of white, urban working-class children in being disproportionately non-verbal in their communication, deaf, showing autistic behaviour and with poor motor skills (Pollack 1972). Using standards developed to measure the white English culture, their mothers were described as 'inadequate' and 'unmotherly'. However, the research failed to discover from the parents what behaviour they used to express their love and caring for their children, nor how they saw childhood and guided their children's development according to their values. In the absence of such evidence, conclusions cannot be drawn about parenting practices.

Another seminal piece of research in the 1970s identified the disproportionate number of 'West Indian' children being classified as 'educationally subnormal' in schools (Coard 1971 and follow-up, Richardson 2005).

In the same year Greta Sandler, a playbus organiser in Lewisham, also in south London, wrote to the Community Relations Commission (subsequently the Commission for Racial Equality) at their request stating her concerns about young African-Caribbean children (Sandler 1972). She was unaware of the Brixton research and its findings. From her observations, she said that many of the children were coming to the playbus and to nurseries in an environment that failed to take account of the reality of their lives, thus making it appear hostile to them. Many were traumatised by their experiences and their lives were seen by many white workers to be the result of deficient models of parenting. Sandler claimed that, like many other migrant children, they appeared withdrawn and sometimes mute. There were very few resources to reflect their cultural experiences and help them build their identities, and the fact that they were black was rarely taken into account. When an African-Caribbean worker was employed on the playbus, the children responded positively to her presence.

Taken alongside the Brixton research, Sandler's comments go a long way to offer an explanation of its findings. In Brixton, the children were assessed with little account taken of the fact that they were black, that few resources reflected their culture, that they had recently experienced migration, that they were environmentally and financially disproportionately disadvantaged and that they were likely to have experienced racism.

In a society where racism is embedded, black children are more likely to feel that they are accepted and belong when there are people like them who work with them; and where resources reflect them in positive ways. The importance of black children seeing people like themselves was visibly demonstrated when Sandler observed that African-Caribbean children responded in a more positive and comfortable way to workers in positions of authority who were also black, than to white workers. The children asked them for help more often and gathered round them at story time. Sandler managed to get a grant from the Community Relations Commission so that black childminders who helped on the bus could be paid as staff and attend a playgroup course at Goldsmiths College. She wrote a report about her observations for the CRE, which, subsequently, confirmed her findings in a research report of day nurseries in another London borough. Verbal reports (the only ones available) told of this research showing that it also drew attention to the differences in attitudes of staff to boys and girls, most of whom were black, and the stereotyping of black boys who were encouraged by white staff to play outside with bikes and scooters and were not encouraged to sit down and participate in any table activities. Black boys tended to be controlled from afar by shouting at them and seldom cuddled in the same way as girls.

Sandler voiced her concern that African-Caribbean children were being labelled. 'Evidence' showing that such children fell disproportionately below the developmental standards of white children was leading to them being disproportionately assessed as priority cases for places in social services day nurseries. Later research proved this situation to, indeed, exist (Van der Eyken 1984). This, in turn, led to the families being thought of as problematic and 'at risk', so many nursery workers, most of whom were white, came to see their place of work as a child protection environment.

At that time, because the general ethos was one of assimilation (see definition, Appendix 1), drawing attention to any differences between black and white children and their behaviour was perceived by some as racist. In other words, differences should not be noticed. While these findings may seem obvious now, at that time acknowledging differences was often perceived as controversial.

The above examples are cited, not in order to disparage or blame anyone, but in order to demonstrate the need to consider the actuality, the context, of children's lives when coming to conclusions about them. The implications of the findings, in terms of being part of a continuum into the present, are considerable and may contribute towards explaining the legacy and long-term consequences of negative experiences faced by some black children and their families.

In the absence of any reference to our multicultural, multiethnic society in most work published before the 1980s, anything that did address it, however inaccurately, assumed an undeserved authority. For example training courses, particularly for nursery nurses, widely used *Child Care and Health for Nursery Nurses*, despite its limitations (see above). It was only in 1989 that the Equal Opportunities Working Party of the National Nursery Examination Board (NNEB, later the Council for the Awards in Children's Care and Education (CACHE)) advised tutors that the book did not comply with the board's equal opportunities policy. To its credit, the NNEB wrote a detailed critique of the book citing all its many examples of racism.

In 1991, the Working Group Against Racism in Children's Resources (WGARCR) published guidelines about selecting and evaluating books on child development that addressed racism and its effects. It drew attention to the need to examine the issues critically from an antiracist perspective, to ensure that books reflect accurately the reality of British society and to consider what is 'normal development' in such a context.

Recent years have seen the publication of more positive books in this field. It is therefore important to consider not only the content of books but also to take into account the publication date. However, the text must not be *assumed* to address racism effectively just because it has been published recently. When evaluating books, it may be helpful to look up key words in the index and read the relevant text. For example, look for terms like: racism, race, race relations, culture, equality, equal opportunities, discrimination, attitudes and ethnicity.

Stereotyping and labelling had long-term effects on attitudes to child development, the consequences of which may still exist today. In considering some present day concerns, it is important to reflect on whether their origins lie in such early labelling and stereotyping.

If you want to know more

see Reynolds (2005) for a recent discussion of Caribbean mothering experiences.

Language

All that a child needs for the successful development of language is access to language.

(Edwards 1996)

Language change is inevitable, continuous, universal and multidirectional. Languages do not get better or worse when they change. They just – change.

(David Crystal, *How Language Works: How babies babble, words change meaning and languages live or die*, 2006)

Language is the main channel in which human beings share the contents of their consciousness.

(Steven Pinker, in the programme for the Cheltenham Literary Festival, October 2007)

There are 6,000 living languages in the world. Of these world languages, 96 per cent are spoken by 4 per cent of the people; and 60 have only one speaker. While, occasionally, a new language is born it is estimated that 50 per cent will die out by the end of this century (Crystal 2000).

It has long been accepted that all children living in Britain need to learn to speak Standard English so that they can function effectively in British society. But interacting with other English-speaking children has not always been recognised as one of the best ways for children to learn English as an additional language – more formal tuition away from other children was sometimes seen as the best way.

Knowledge about the variety of languages has often been limited too. Some people wrongly believed that 'African', 'Indian', 'Islamic' and 'Pakistani' were genuine languages. This led to situations where the issue of exactly what language a child spoke was not felt to be important. And children were sometimes reluctant to speak with their parents in their home language in front of people who worked with them. This perhaps indicated that the language was not felt by the child to be valued in the setting. Even very young children can feel the pressure of their peers and adults to conform.

If you want to know more

relevant details of 'other' languages in educational settings, see Edwards (1996).

In the past, some people thought that children should not be allowed to speak their home language in an early years setting. Apart from feeling a lack of control over the situation they saw it as interfering with or preventing the children from learning to communicate in English. Although there is no scientific evidence that this is true, and there has been research to show that on the contrary, being able to use both languages is an advantage in learning, some parents also believed this and put pressure on workers to support them. It was believed in Britain that bilingual children would not be as fluent in either of their languages as children who spoke only one language and that learning a new language when also still learning the home language would be confusing for a child. More recently, ideas of language acquisition have changed to acknowledge the importance of parallel learning of a new language at the same time as speaking the home language. In fact the vast majority of the world's people speak more than one language.

A friendly voice

Case study 37

Rashida is a nursery nurse in a nursery class of a primary school in a largely Pakistani area of a multiethnic town with a strong history of addressing 'multicultural and antiracist' issues over many years. She was born in Britain and speaks English, Panjabi and Urdu fluently. She is in her second year of studying for a foundation degree and is writing her dissertation on language issues, particularly encouraging *all* children to learn a language other than their home language at nursery age.

One morning the Pakistani parents of Saida, aged three, bring their daughter to the nursery for the first time. After they leave, Saida is quiet, a little disorientated and a bit mopey. Rashida starts to talk to her in Urdu and she immediately brightens up and over the next few days joins in with what is going on, supported by her common language with Rashida. After a few days, Rashida tells Saida's father that she has been talking with Saida in Urdu and how it has helped her to settle. His face falls. When she asks him if Saida speaks English he says she does. But, in Rashida's experience with her, she understands very little.

Saida's father obviously, and understandably, wishes her to learn English and asks the teacher, who is relatively newly qualified, to ask Rashida not to speak to Saida in Urdu. The teacher asks Rashida to comply with his request. Rashida feels compromised about her position and in a quandary as to what to do – comply with the request, fail to support Saida by speaking with her in Urdu, challenge the teacher's knowledge from her position of relative powerlessness or try to explain to her the needs of Saida and her knowledge of language acquisition – a difficult task when the teacher is meant to be aware of these issues.

The following points arise from this incident.

- Saida's father, quite rightly, wanted his daughter to learn English.
- Rashida had not been told what language(s) Saida spoke so was not prepared beforehand to deal with her needs.

- There was apparently no nursery/school policy on the importance of valuing a child's home language in the process of learning English.

- There appeared to be no sharing of information with the staff of basic details of the languages a child speaks and their level of English competence – even if it was collected when the child was registered in the nursery.

- Rashida's knowledge of Urdu was not perceived as important and an advantage for supporting Saida.

- The teacher clearly was unaware of the importance of valuing Saida's' home language or colluded with her father's request in spite of her better judgement.

- Rashida was put in an impossible position – knowing professionally what was best for Saida but, being in a less powerful position in the classroom, unable to put what she believed into practice. So one of the best ways for supporting Saida in learning English was thus limited.

- Saida's parents did not learn that the best way for their daughter to learn English was to value her home language at the same time – they were thus left uninformed about the well-established research evidence. If they had known this they might well have behaved differently.

- People such as Rashida, and those who work as bilingual assistants, need support and training to be able to manage situations such as this and to develop the ability and confidence to articulate their knowledge of best practice for children with English as an additional language (EAL).

- There just may be a lingering issue that, perhaps unconsciously, influences the perception that languages other than English are not so important, worthy or valuable. They may consequently be undervalued rather than equally valued – one of the ways that racism ranks languages in a racial hierarchy of value –instead of being seen as different but all equally capable of expressing what is intended.

This is just one example of the sort of situation that occurs in some settings. It is seldom that the motive behind such practice is anything other than laudable – they all want the child to learn English, but are misinformed about the best way to do this.

Point for thought and discussion

- What issues arise from this case study – for family members, for workers in settings, for the curriculum, for policy-making, for training and for support?

Case study 38

Speaking in many tongues...

Said grew up in Uganda. He learnt to speak English, Hindi, Gujerati, Swahili and some Arabic. When Idi Amin expelled Ugandan Asians he and his family went to Switzerland where he learnt German.

It is now well established that learning to be bilingual or multilingual is an asset, not a disadvantage, when learning English or any other language. The skills needed for one language, for example knowledge of grammar, can be transferred when learning another, however different they may seem.

?

If you want to know more

about the advantage of being bilingual or multilingual when learning a new language, read the Islington and Portsmouth local authority leaflets (see References); and about supporting children learning English (see DCSF 2007a).

Research shows that where people working with children value their home languages, the children's ability in other languages flourishes (Baker 1997 and Early Years Equality (EYE) 2005 for Mother Tongue posters). However, this is not always acknowledged, as the following example shows.

Case study 39

Battle of the languages

An early years setting had several South Asian children who spoke various Asian languages at home. They were only allowed to speak English in the setting. A South Asian helper, speaking three South Asian languages, was also forbidden to speak anything apart from English. The Ofsted nursery inspector explained that refusal to allow any other languages in the setting was not in the best interests of the children learning English, but those in charge said they believed what they were doing was right.

Learning a few or more words of a language that children speak is usually a solid gesture of support, and welcome to children and their families. And it can be fun. But care should be taken not to appear as if that is all that is needed. And for one or two communities their language is private to them and other people are not necessarily welcome to encroach upon it. However, it is important to teach children basic words like 'Hello' in a variety of languages and to build links with parents and families where there is no common language. A recognition that some families will not be able to read or understand English can be put into practice by translating, interpreting, making a tape or video, or providing English classes for them, according to their needs.

When some adults speak together in a language that others cannot understand, other adults may feel uncomfortable. Perhaps they think they are being talked about. Perhaps they feel excluded and powerless because they cannot understand it and so interpret the behaviour as rude. While this reaction is clearly a measure of the security and confidence they feel in each other's company and is therefore understandable, a sensitivity on both sides is needed. It also casts light on how children learning English as an additional language may feel when they first go to a school or early years setting. And, according to each person's personal experiences, there may be strong feelings about the rights and wrongs of speaking languages other than English in front of others. But no language should be forbidden to be spoken and there are times when sharing a language is comforting. However, when people are anxious about and lack confidence in relationships, not understanding what everyone else is talking about may feel alienating. Sharing explanations of what it feels like from both viewpoints leads to a better understanding and sensitivity as to what the issues really are.

Listening to an unfamiliar language is likely also to be a common experience of people living here who do not yet know English. So, where English-speaking people have had the experience of feeling uncomfortable as described above, it may help them to better empathise with what it might be like, for example, for an asylum-seeking parent to be surrounded by people speaking incomprehensible languages.

Are some languages more important than others?

The limits of my language mean the limits of my world.

(L. Wittgenstein *Tractatus Logico-Philosophicus* 1922)

As with other factors, languages are often perceived in a racial hierarchy. For example in Britain, French and Spanish (and, increasingly, Russian and Chinese languages) are generally considered more useful than Urdu, Hindi, Yoruba or Arabic. While French and Spanish are more likely to be taught in some schools, that doesn't mean that they are more worthy languages. They are just different from Urdu, Hindi, Yoruba and Arabic. We don't have to speak a language to value its importance and respect the people who speak it. Speaking a language and respecting those who speak it are not always the same thing. And Britain is becoming a country where many languages are spoken by many people, especially in urban areas. For example, it is estimated that at least 250 languages are spoken in London.

Where young children become aware of the hierarchy of languages – and they learn very quickly whether their home language is accepted, ignored or even laughed at – it can interfere with their learning of English. A person's home language is central to their sense of self, and belittling a child's language (or accent) is effectively an assault on who they are and what they stand for. It is likely to be the most powerful deterrent to speaking the language in front of others again. It also interferes with their confidence in learning English – the very thing that everyone wants them to be able to do. A similar result is likely to occur if those working with young children virtually ignore the fact that they are fluent in a language other than English. It is the positive and active valuing of a child's first language that facilitates the process of learning English most effectively.

Case study 40

Touché

Four-year-old Delroy laughed at Yasmin when she spoke in Panjabi. Susie, who is nearly five, touched Delroy's arm lightly and said: 'She's clever. She can speak English as well.'

Point for thought and discussion

Case studies 38, 39 and 40 show that children from black and other minority ethnic communities are often bilingual and multilingual.

- What are the advantages to all children of a multilingual nursery, where children's linguistic competence is valued and fostered?

Some languages are wrongly devalued because they do not have a written form. Others, such as Creole, are often seen as 'incorrect' forms of English. But Creole is a separate language with its own grammatical structure.

In places where there is no written form of the language spoken, or where there is a high incidence of illiteracy, there is often a strong oral culture, where story-telling to children is common – a valuable tradition that is less common among English speakers today. To communicate successfully in these communities, oral methods need to be developed and used. For example, the use of videos and tapes with Gypsies and Travellers may help families understand why early years education is generally seen as important, even if they decide not to avail themselves of it for their children. It may give them confidence to know that their children will be respected and valued in an early years setting. And story-telling is something that all children can enjoy.

What's so good about English?

It is important to realise that English has no linguistic advantage over any other language or dialect.

Every language has an equal ability to express human needs and ideas and any language can grow to include new words for new ideas. They all have rules for making words and for the way sentences are put together. There are no primitive languages.

Complex ideas can be expressed in all languages. Some have a greater number of words than others to describe something of critical importance to them. For example, the Inuit have a large number of words for different kinds of snow because it plays such a significant role in their lives, while Arabs and Bedouins have many words for camels, and computer whizzkids have lots of terms for computer software.

English is now viewed as the major language of the world, but this is not because it has any innate linguistic advantages – it is because English is the language of power in a world dominated by English-speaking peoples. This reinforces any notions of linguistic superiority held by white English people. It allows them *not* to have to make efforts to learn other languages and leads to assumptions that, in any case, others will just have to understand them. And, although an increasing number of white English people now speak other languages, it is still far from the norm for them to do so.

Everyone who speaks English does so with an accent, whether they are from Newcastle, Pakistan, Ghana, Glasgow or China, and whether they live in a Wolverhampton semi-detached house or in Buckingham Palace. Standard English is an accent. Of course it is important for everyone speaking English to be understood by other English-speaking people, but do white English people always make an equal effort to understand people speaking with different English accents? Do they listen to and hear what is being said in an Indian or Nigerian accent in the same way as they listen to and hear a Glaswegian or Geordie accent? And, if someone is difficult to understand, is the situation addressed or is lack of understanding blamed on 'foreignness'?

Many families, not only in minority ethnic communities, have members who speak languages other than English. Early years settings that take advantage of this diversity and put into practice this living experience encourage everyone to feel welcome and valued. For those families learning English as an additional language, welcoming words in their home language go a long way to helping the children, parents and those working with the children feel comfortable together. Where people working with children learning English also speak the home language of the children, there is an even greater feeling of security and understanding.

Words and pictures

Words, pictures and their associations often remain deep in our memories long after they have ceased to be commonly used. And dictionary definitions of words do not always accurately define or describe what they have come to mean in everyday usage. For example, in Britain the word 'civilised' – while not defined on racial grounds – is not usually associated with people of non-European origin. It has become loaded with connotations of what people of European origin are, even though the oldest of the world's civilisations were non-European (for example the Egyptians, other Africans and the Persians).

On the other hand, the word 'primitive' probably conjures up in the minds of many white people images and inappropriate language to describe black people, as living in mud-and-wattle huts, wearing grass skirts, often with painted faces and bodies, and performing strange rituals. The origins of this mythical imagery come partly from films and picture books that were printed earlier in the last century. Many of them are still around – some are still shown on TV, sometimes during school holidays – and they reinforce stereotypes that go largely unchallenged, perhaps because many people have no experience of what Africa is really like and perhaps because they feel no personal need to challenge them.

Terms associated with visual images can be very powerful on young minds. Words such as 'jungle', 'savages', 'war-dance' 'witch doctor' and 'mud huts' are loaded with negative value, are inappropriate and should not be used. Use appropriate terms, such as rainforest, or the name of the people (San, Asante, Yoruba, Shona, Zulu, etc.) traditional dance, traditional healer or herbalist, and traditional homes.

Other words in common usage may imply meanings that need to be questioned. For example, the words 'correct', 'proper', 'decent' and 'suitable' may, in some circumstances, express subjective personal opinions and not matters of fact. Is there a 'correct' way of speaking, for example, and what exactly is meant by a 'suitable' way to dress and who is a 'decent' person? And what does 'Sit or behave *nicely'* actually mean?

White English history and stereotypes sometimes distort perceptions of reality. For example, there are skyscrapers, glass-fronted offices and big hotels in most African countries but how many white people, who have never been to Africa, would picture this in their mind's eye? People live in various types of homes according to their needs, their economic situations, the weather and the environment – but are these measured in terms of an English perception of what is 'proper'?

Many white people's images of countries in Africa are wildly out of touch with the truth. If a traditional dance from Zambia is seen on television, performed for a particular special visitor, it may be no more typical of Zambia than Morris dancing is of England.

Most people seen in the media – in newspapers and magazines, and on TV – are white. Although there has been a significant improvement recently, children are still rarely presented with positive role models of black people in positions of authority. That is why it is important to have stories and picture books portraying a range of people in a variety of roles, chosen with care and with a critical eye to the messages being given by the illustrations.

After the destruction of the World Trade Centre in New York in 2001 and other acts of terrorism – most recently the attacks on London transport systems – Islamophobia increased significantly. Similarly, as refugees and asylum seekers sought sanctuary here, as a result of wars and torture in their own countries, hostility to them increased. And migrants legitimately seeking work as a result of extending membership of the European Union often experience taunts and abuse. All tend to be demonised.

Some words, although by a strict dictionary definition appearing to be neutral, are often loaded with negative associations. For example, the term 'asylum seeker' means a person who has crossed an international border and is seeking safety in another country. But it is often used in a pejorative way.

There are words that, when associated with other words, influence each other even when one of the original words is no longer there. For example, the term Muslim becomes negative when associated with 'fanatical' or 'fundamentalist' so that even when the first word is taken away the negative association remains. Similarly 'bogus', 'influx' or 'flood' when associated with 'asylum seeker', taints it.

If you want to know more

words and terminology, see Lane (2005c).

Sara Ahmed (2004) describes this as 'stickiness', being dependent on past histories of association that often work through concealment. As a consequence, the use of such terms needs to be carefully considered if they are not to have hidden meanings alongside their strict meanings. In contrast, though there are 'fanatical Christians', the word 'Christian' does not conjure up images of fanatical people.

Multicultural education

Most white people working with young children in the 1960s and '70s saw African-Caribbean, South Asian and children from other minority ethnic backgrounds as needing to assimilate into the rest of the community, for their own sakes. This meant that they had to change to fit into their new environment but no one else had to change the way they behaved. Two factors prevented people from assimilating.

1　People who move to live in another country seldom give up aspects of their own culture in order to 'assimilate'. Indeed they often maintain some of their cultural traditions long after people living in their countries of origin have moved away from them.
2　Society in general made it impossible for them to assimilate, even if they wanted to.

Inner-city areas, where most black families lived, were often seen by 'experts' as areas of social need. This was probably partly a result of the Plowden Report on primary school children, which identified social deprivation as a factor explaining the educational needs of children (Plowden 1967).

The report saw racial prejudice as playing little serious part in schools and that children accepted each other and ignored skin colour differences. But many people working with young children in urban areas saw that the real needs of black children were not simply about a failure to assimilate. So some workers with children set up mechanisms to support them by sharing cultures, such as learning to cook a variety of foods, using clothes from many cultures in the dressing-up corner and generally being friendly to each other. In educational terms this is usually called multicultural education and there was clearly nothing wrong with it in itself.

In the 1980s and '90s lots of excellent resources for young children were produced. Some, however, gave inappropriate messages to children. For example, as recently as the mid-1990s, a toy company produced a rag doll with a brown face, brown hands and brown feet. But the body underneath its clothes was white, with a join at the neck, wrists and ankles. What would a child playing with this doll make of this? Would he or she think that black people are really white underneath their clothes?

Some books and jigsaws reinforced stereotypes of black people, for example African-Caribbean men as bus conductors, Asian men as shopkeepers and African-Caribbean women as nurses. While these were positive images, they sometimes gave the impression that black people only ever did these jobs and were not likely to do anything else.

Multicultural education would have been ideal in a society where racism does not exist, but it could not even begin to address the underlying racist attitudes that many people held in Britain. The real problem was that it failed to touch on the way that racism ranked cultures in a racial hierarchy, some being seen as more worthy, and therefore more powerful, than others.

But, critically, multicultural education failed to take account of what black people themselves wanted for their children – to succeed in the educational system. Furthermore, while it extended people's knowledge about other cultures it did not necessarily change their attitudes. For example, a racially prejudiced child might visit a home corner that represented a particular culture. The child would certainly acquire information during the visit, but without support and the opportunity to reflect on what they had experienced, they would be left with the potential to use that information as ammunition against the people of that culture rather than the chance to gain real insight, knowledge of and respect for the culture and its people.

Multicultural education was initially seen as only being applicable in multiethnic areas, ignoring rural and suburban areas, and it largely omitted the cultures of white people. It set up the concept that the issue was about black people and where they live rather than about racism. It reinforced the notion that only black people have a culture. It was not until the publication of the Swann Report in 1985 that this perception was, in some areas, changed (Swann 1985). The report drew attention to the need to address multicultural education in all areas, mainly white as well as multiethnic. Interestingly, the term 'multicultural' does not usually include the differences and diversity of white people's cultures. It continues to render the term 'white' as being homogeneous and unproblematic. What is needed, and is now becoming more widely recognised, is a clear strategy for addressing racism – an antiracist strategy.

Lessons learned (and some not yet learned) in the early years field

Since the mid-1970s, there have been limited but continual and constructive changes in the ways that prejudice and discrimination in the early years have been tackled in Britain. For example, there were anti-discriminatory laws on sex and gender and race, and more recently on disability; and some positive aspects of the 1989 Children Act and its accompanying guidance with regards to equality, even though there was no coherent strategy to address it overall. These demonstrated not only the effectiveness of people who worked long and hard for changes, but a willingness on the part of national government to begin to take changes on board in legislation and policies.

Increasing numbers of organisations and individuals lobbied consistently for these changes, published books and articles, produced resources, organised training, conferences and discussions and by so doing raised awareness at a national level. For example, the Commission for Racial Equality published a book illustrating good practice and how some early years practice and procedures might be racially discriminatory and unlawful (CRE 1989). The Early Years Trainers Anti Racist Network (now Early Years Equality) was established and succeeded in getting the importance of addressing racism on the national agenda, if not yet into people's hearts. Since the launch of the national childcare strategy in the late 1990s, much more serious attention has been given by relevant government departments to what equality for children and their families means in practice. Equality is now seen in principle as integral to good practice though some critical aspects, specifically the acknowledgement of the facts of racism, are not yet being addressed (for details of government action for racial equality since 1997 see Lane 2006b; and for comments on government practices see Chapter 9).

At a more down-to-earth level there has been a huge increase in the availability of resources for children that reflect accurately the reality of our society. It is now possible to buy dolls that represent boys and girls anatomically and with a range of more realistic skin colours, although they less often represent a range of accurate physical features and hair textures. But although there have recently been more resources on mixed race families, they are still insufficiently represented.

However, racial equality is still largely seen as about black and other minority ethnic children and their families rather than the way racism impacts on everyone in our society – a 'problem' of urban towns and cities and not as an issue of concern everywhere. Considering the past may appear to have little relevance to early years practice in the 21st century, but the legacy of racism often remains deeply entrenched in present-day attitudes and behaviour that have implications for the work needed to be done today. That is why learning from the past should help to clarify what needs to be done in the future.

5 Thinking about racial equality

No one is born hating another person because of the colour of his skin, or his background or his religion. People must learn to hate, and if they can learn to hate, they can be taught to love, for love comes more naturally to the human heart than its opposite.

(Nelson Mandela at his inaugural speech as President of South Africa, 1994)

It is well established that people from black and other minority ethnic communities are largely disadvantaged and discriminated against. Many, but not all, are disadvantaged as a result of migration and other factors, often resulting in poor housing and living in poverty, and being discriminated against on the grounds of their skin colour, ethnicity, culture, language or religion. Evidence of the levels of poverty among minority ethnic groups shows that 65 per cent of Bangladeshi, 55 per cent of Pakistani and 45 per cent of Black African groups live in poverty, with Caribbean, Indian and Chinese groups all living in above average levels of poverty. Of all the Bangladeshi, Pakistani and Black African children, 50 per cent grow up in poverty; and Caribbean groups fare only slightly better (Platt 2007). Muslims face greater poverty than other religious groups.

Data monitored by ethnicity, concerning many aspects of early years services, is not yet sufficiently coherent to draw specific national conclusions despite the statutory requirements of the Race Relations (Amendment) Act. Local authorities and early years settings, however, should be able to access information from the census and other data. Although preliminary efforts are being made by government to get a picture of ethnicity in all aspects of the early years service, it remains somewhat ad hoc. In order to ensure compliance with the legislation and acquire a real understanding overall, a comprehensive analysis, by ethnicity, at all levels of the service should be undertaken.

?

If you want to know more

there are several useful early years publications that contribute to the issues raised in this book. Some have equality issues implicit. Others are about equality issues generally, about race equality in particular or about a specific aspect of race equality. They include: Derman-Sparks and the ABC Task Force (1989), Lane (1989), Creaser and Dau (1996), Early Childhood Forum (ECF) (1998), Brown (1998), Brown (1999), Vandenbroeck (1999), Richardson and Wood (1999), Essex EYDCP (2001), Dickins (2002), Richardson and Miles (2003),

Runnymede Trust (2003), NCB/Sure Start (2004), Baldock (2004), van Keulen (2004), Houston (2004), Daycare Trust (2004), Dickins (2005), Lindon (2006), Taylor (2006), Edwards and others (2006), Early Childhood Forum (ECF) (2007), Kahn and Young (2007), Bernard Van Leer Foundation (2007), and Glasgow City Council (2008). Looking at the issues raised in this book from a global perspective are: Garforth and others (2006) and Dell (2006). Useful, if largely school-based, websites include GTCE Achieve project, Multiverse and QCA Respect For All.

This chapter identifies some of the issues that arise when thinking about racial equality in early years services and settings.

Child-rearing practices

Nowadays notions of cultural superiority about child-rearing practices are less strongly held. The idea that there is one 'best' way to bring up a child is rightly being questioned. You only need to look back over the past 40 or 50 years to see how attitudes and practices have changed among and between groups. So long as a child is content and thriving most parents accept that there is no definitive right or wrong way to bring up a child and feel little pressure to conform to specific ways. They learn and value new ways of doing things from people of a different cultural background. From this premise it is clear that when we talk about treating all children the same we don't really mean that there is only one way to bring up a child – 'my way'. In practice, we treat them all differently in many subtle ways. What we mean is that we intend to treat them equally (see page 211 for discussion on this).

Bedtimes and sleeping

In the past, parents who didn't have their young children in bed by early evening were often regarded (by health experts, middle-class writers and other professionals – 'Tut tut, why aren't they in bed?) as inadequate or negligent. Few seemed to think that parents might enjoy their children's company or prefer not to limit their freedom. Black and working-class families suffered particularly from being wrongly seen as irresponsible in this matter.

Strict adherence to formal bedtimes is diminishing, and most children go to bed later than they would have done 20 or 30 years ago. More people seem to believe that within limits, as long as children have enough sleep and are ready for the following day, it does not matter exactly what time they go to bed.

Ideas about where a child sleeps are also changing. Learning from what people from a variety of cultures do has opened up discussion about the options available.

Food, meal times and eating

Thinking about food with children and planning activities about eating provides an opportunity not only to learn about the differences in worldwide culinary traditions, but also to learn about the people whose food is being discussed.

There are many different ways to eat food, all of which are appropriate to particular circumstances. Using chopsticks, just using a spoon or eating with one's fingers require specific dexterity and skills, although most children living in Britain will need to learn to use a knife and fork. It is a good experience for children to try different ways of eating and to be given opportunities to discuss what food and mealtimes are for and the need for sustenance and socialisation. The whole basis of which implements are used at mealtimes is culturally and socially loaded. Toast, biscuits, fruit, crisps and peanuts, for example, are eaten with fingers. Cake is mostly eaten with fingers too – except in certain posh situations when special little forks are provided.

What might be the consequences if a child, who is eating happily at nursery, is met with a cry of: 'Don't eat with your fingers, it's rude (or dirty or unhygienic or uncivilised)?' Other children may be left with the message that people who eat with their fingers are rude, dirty, unhygienic or uncivilised, however they may interpret that. The child herself may wonder whether her own family are the same. The likelihood is that she will become embarrassed about eating and reluctant to do so for fear of criticism or ridicule and apprehensive about how her family may be perceived by nursery workers. The legacy (from goodness knows where) that eating with one's fingers is only done by 'vulgar', 'coarse' and 'uneducated' people needs to be countered.

If you want to know more

about criticism levelled at eating with fingers, see the example in Lane (2005b); and about using food from diverse cultures in nursery settings, and examples, see McAuliffe with Lane (2005) and Lane (2005b).

Families arrange their meals in many ways, together or separately, at fixed times or when they are hungry. Some sit round a table, some sit and eat their food on their knees, and others squat or sit on the floor with or without a cloth on the floor.

'Good manners'

The concept of what constitutes good manners is probably well established in every society. It is so well established that whenever someone breaches the code of behaviour everyone 'in the know' recognises it immediately. This leaves those who are 'not in the know' ignorant of any unintentional offence that they may have given. And manners may be so routine that they become meaningless. For example, when you say 'Hello, how are you?' do you *really* want to know how someone is, or is it just an automatic phrase? If you don't know about queuing, you may attempt to go to the serving counter first. If you usually talk loudly with family members, you may shout on your telephone. In all such things there may be no intention to offend.

Manners, good or otherwise are programmed into children from a very early age – many young children in British society and in some other cultures are taught to say 'please' and 'thank you' almost from the day they are born, while others see this as over the top and unnecessary. They are taught that it is open and honest to look someone in the eye when being reprimanded and that to look down is to be devious and to appear unrepentant. But children from many other cultures are taught that it is disrespectful to look someone in the eye when being reprimanded, so they cast their eyes down. There is a phrase in Grenada, 'Don't let your eyes cross me!' Children who meet someone's eye in this situation – as a white British child might do – may be seen as rude, disrespectful or defiant. Similarly, a black child who casts her eyes down in Britain may seem insolent.

Body language patterns of behaviour are deeply culturally loaded. When building up empathy and understanding, it is therefore important to learn about the differences in body language and learn not to take offence or misinterpret unfamiliar behaviour.

This does not mean that accepted good manners should be ignored, but it does involve recognising and perhaps unlearning automatic negative responses to unaccustomed behaviour. A child who seems to be lacking good manners may simply have no knowledge or experience of certain learned patterns of behaviour.

If people do not take time to think about the way verbal language is used there is a massive opportunity for misunderstanding and misinterpretation, which may have serious consequences. Some languages do not have the words for 'please' and 'thank you'. Appreciation may be expressed in body language, built into the language or just accepted as being there without the need to say or do anything in particular. A Pakistani mother who says in English 'Coat, get it' to her child could be construed as rude. But the 'please' is implied in the changing inflections of tone, the body language and the facial features and the word order is a literal translation from Panjabi. There is no word for 'please' in Panjabi, and the Pakistani mother is speaking a language additional to her own.

Misunderstandings may also lead to irritation when adults speak in a language unknown to those around them. This may sometimes be perceived as being ill mannered or even rude, usually when there is no intention to be so (see page 124 for further discussion).

Identity and self-esteem

Children's sense of personal identity comes from many aspects including their name, sex, gender, skin colour, physical features, hair texture, position within the family and language. Their cultural identity includes their environment, who they interact with, the food they eat, the clothes they wear, the places they live in, the music they listen to and the spiritual values of their family.

The seeds of whether they are confident, proud and like themselves are sown very young and how others view them plays a part in this. What must it feel like if the feedback from the world is negative? What must it feel like if you do not see yourself or people like you represented anywhere? And what role does such negative feedback do to contribute to self-motivation? If children perceive they are not as valued as others because of their ethnicity or culture, this may impact on how they value themselves and others; and may go some way to explain the disturbing results of some research with young black children who appear to prefer white children/dolls when asked to choose who is successful, who they would like to play with or even who is most like them.

When children attend an early years setting some other influences come into play, influences that can promote or demote their self-esteem and confidence. The setting is in a key role to enable them to learn who they are, where others place them in that society and what they feel about themselves. They learn if and how their language, culture, religion, physical features or skin colour are valued.

The early years setting is therefore in a crucial position to influence a child's self-esteem. The aim should be to integrate, as far as possible, the cultures of all children with the educational learning process. Where the setting understands and values all the aspects of a child's cultural identity, the child is more likely to feel comfortable, at home and have a sense of belonging. Where the cultural values are alien or strange, the child is more likely to withdraw into a protective cocoon or, alternatively, to lash out in anger. Where children's cultures are loved they can more readily and openly love themselves for who and what they are, and are more likely to be motivated to learn from what the setting has to offer.

Lots of positive support for all children – about who they are, how precious they are, how much their culture, faith, language and skin colour are valued – promotes positive identity and gives positive messages to everyone that they all belong. Different lifestyles, for example those of Traveller families, all have something good to contribute to this diversity of life. For most white children there are many positive reinforcing images and messages around. But in a society where racism is endemic, it is particularly important to give positive messages about being black, being different (for example, being a Traveller, being Jewish, Polish or Irish) and learning to be, or being, bilingual.

All children's racial identities – their perception of themselves as belonging to a valued group as well as being an individual person – are important. But because so much racism is based on skin colour, it is crucial to reflect positive images and views about black children's personal and group identity in order to have a positive influence on their future academic success. White children's racial identity is important too and is largely reinforced by society generally, although those white groups who are subjected to xenoracism also need specific support. But in discussions about race, it is usually only black people who are seen as having a racial identity. Whiteness, which is part of the racial identity of white people, is rarely acknowledged. All children need to have positive identities and self-esteem to cope with fear, pain, confusion and the unavoidable aspects of life. This provides a stable core to their emotional health.

Everyone needs to feel good about who they are, to feel they really belong. Every child needs to be equally encouraged to be confident, to develop their intellectual curiosity and to expect to be able to contribute to our society in their future lives. It is particularly important to ensure that children who are members of groups that are already sometimes perceived and possibly stereotyped as being less likely to achieve academically are provided with opportunities to develop a lust for learning and to nurture their own self-motivation to learn to do so. Clearly children should not be identified individually as potential or future failures. All children should be expected to be trailblazers for fulfilling their dreams, dreams that are continually fuelled with high expectations of their future by the workers and family members around them. Furthermore they need to be helped to understand that their own personal contribution and dedication to their future success is a critically important factor in achieving it. And every child should be able and proud to say 'I know who I am and I like who I am.'

Some anecdotal evidence suggests that African-Caribbean boys may be more likely than other children to be singled out by some workers by being named, called out and reprimanded. Even though this gives them more adult interaction it is negative and may classify them as being badly behaved or unable to concentrate, thus interfering with their motivation for learning. Such stereotyping has implications for these boys in terms of expectations of their abilities and their behaviour.

Naming

Your name is your face to the world.

(Japanese mother living in USA 1998)

Changing a child's name without telling them is stealing from them; it's as if you are trying to wipe out their history.

(Pool 2005)

Most people are very particular that their names are spelt and pronounced correctly. Where young children from a variety of cultural backgrounds are involved this is especially important, but it takes time and commitment. Until recently, it has perhaps been assumed that where names are unfamiliar and seen as difficult to pronounce, shortened names or nicknames are acceptable.

But a name, like a language, is fundamental to a child's identity. If the name is unfamiliar, it is worth the small amount of effort to learn to pronounce it correctly, to understand the relationship between family and personal names and the order in which they are written or given. It may also require perseverance because some sounds are so unfamiliar to most English speakers that they find them difficult to pronounce. For example, with the Muslim name 'Tahir' (usually an Urdu word) the 'T' is pronounced for English speakers as a sort of mixture between a 'Th' and a 'D'. It is therefore difficult to write phonetically and has to be repeatedly pronounced in order to learn the new sound. Names often have religious or cultural connotations, so to pronounce them incorrectly may be particularly insensitive to devout families. And, clearly, it is incorrect to talk about the 'Christian name' of someone who is not

Christian, or refer to 'Christian names' in multifaith settings or where children do not belong to a particular faith at all. Instead, 'first', 'given' or 'personal' names may be more appropriate.

In recording a child's name the family name and first name should be identified as well as the sex of the child. Spelling names from the alphabet of another language may lead to discrepancies, with some children's names being recorded differently by their families in the English script but being the same in their own alphabet. It is therefore critical to discuss with families what they wish their child to be called, how the name is pronounced, how it is written and in what order. In some languages, the family name is written first and the given name, by which the child is called, is written last. It is also important to know the names of the family members because mothers and fathers may not share the same family name. Although there are resources on naming (Zealey 1995), the best basis for understanding the naming systems is to learn about them from family members.

The concept of beauty

No race holds a monopoly of beauty.

(Cesaire 1997)

In most societies there is a culturally and socially determined code of what is beautiful and many people, even within that culture, fall outside this perception of beauty. For white people, long blonde hair (and sometimes curly black hair), blue eyes, pink and white cheeks and certain physical features were once seen as the only recipe for perfection. The European perfection conformed to a European norm. The remnants of this are still around, for example in the large number of women (and increasingly men) who bleach or highlight their hair.

By these measures, there was no way that black people, particularly those of African or Aboriginal origin, could ever really fit into the European concept of what was beautiful, even if they wanted to. Many white people therefore wrongly saw black people as incapable of being beautiful because their skin colour and physical features did not conform to the European norm. Some white people even ranked people from black and other minority ethnic groups in a racial hierarchy of who they considered to be more or less beautiful. For example, women of Malaysian origin were often seen to be more beautiful than other black women. While black African, Caribbean and the original indigenous people of America, Australia, New Zealand and elsewhere were not seen as beauties in the eyes of these white people, these communities rightly recognised their own beauty. Even so, there are instances where the legacy of racism and colonialism may influence how different communities perceive themselves in terms of whatever is meant by beauty. (See page 76 for discussion of the 'Black is beautiful' campaign in the United States.)

The phrase 'Black is beautiful' campaign in the United States helped both black and white people see that black/brown skin colour, curly hair texture and specific physical features are beautiful. It was necessary for white people to reorientate their thinking as well as for those black people who had internalised their oppression. The climate has changed somewhat since then. Despite claims by black models that the modelling industry subjects black models to racism, there are more black mainstream models than before. Physical features other than skin colour, such as nose, mouth and eye shapes and hair textures, now often subtly determine beauty – an issue that is seldom openly discussed. This perhaps indicates some remaining apprehension in venturing into discussion of this particular issue.

Fairy tales and nursery rhymes, from Europe and elsewhere, should be used only when care has been taken to identify hidden (or not so hidden) messages of beauty. In 'Beauty and the Beast', the beast is usually depicted as black, while Rapunzel and Goldilocks are girls or young women with stereotypical blonde hair. These stories have a real place in fairy tale history, and present mythical, if perhaps old fashioned, messages for Europeans. There is no reason why such traditional tales cannot continue to be used as part of Britain's cultural heritage so long as practitioners are aware of their implications and take action to correct any apparent imbalances. So it is important to be sensitive in the use of such resources and consider the potential associations that children may make if negativity is largely about blackness and goodness largely about whiteness (see Case study 19 on page 76). A range of role models is needed and examples of beauty and beastliness (where appropriate) should be seen in all skin colours.

Because the concept of beauty is so culturally loaded and because everyone is unlikely to be considered equally beautiful in any culture, perhaps other terms could be used as well. For example, 'precious', 'lovely', 'wonderful' or 'unique' according to the circumstances – all new babies are precious.

But, as is demonstrated by the vast variety of ways that people present themselves or make themselves attractive, for example in dress, hairstyle, make-up and adornments, this variety reflects the wide range of individual opinions as to what constitutes attractiveness – a diversity of views that challenges any notions of conformity, even to what is beauty.

Observation

Giving time to observing what children do or say, who they relate to and interact with or who they do not relate to and interact with, what resources they access or do not access, is important. Listening to them in 'their world'; observing the gestures they make; the ways they play, dance and sing, are all part of observing them. And observing them both as individuals and as members of groups, including cultural groups, may indicate or reveal clues as to their thinking about where they feel they belong. It is an opportunity to consider patterns of activity and, by collecting apparently isolated bits of information together, create an overall picture that demonstrates more clearly the reality of individual or particular cultural or gender groups of children's experiences. What may not have been noticed before, when observed and recorded may indicate an issue of concern about equality and inclusion.

Do all children have equal access to the full range of learning possibilities and resources? Do they all feel equally able to take the initiative, should they wish to do so, to play with and relate to those who are different from them and are perhaps from different cultural backgrounds or genders? Do children generally welcome and involve all others equally in their activities? Are there particular activities where all the children are more likely to play together, for example at the computer? Are there any circumstances where cultural assumptions may be playing a part in the activities of boys or girls? If the answers to any of these questions have negative implications this does not necessarily mean that there is anything to be concerned about. But it raises an issue that needs to be considered – what the reasons and possible explanations for them could be. These may be personal – all children have preferences and needs for security and familiarity in their lives. Or it may be something that workers in the setting need to reflect on in terms of their practice.

There is absolutely nothing wrong with children and their family members feeling secure and comfortable with people who are familiar to them. It is helpful for children's sense of security, identity and home language development. Most people relate to familiarity. But in terms of the wider society and reducing tensions in the future, what happens in the early years may be the basis for a society that is more at ease with itself than at present. There may be an issue of concern if children in a setting do not form any relationships with those who are different from them or are not provided with opportunities or ever encouraged to do so. This may lead, in effect, to forms of exclusion – of excluding other children or being excluded by other children. Learning to appreciate and value differences between people can only be of benefit for community cohesion in the future.

One of the consequences of racism in our society is that children and their families may be less familiar with people from communities different from their own. If we, as a society, are to be in a position to break into this cycle of racism creating barriers between people, then helping young children to relate to one another, when their attitudes are forming, must be a priority. Early years workers have a responsibility to break down any potential barriers between people that result from this racism.

Schools and children's centres also have a statutory duty under the Race Relations (Amendment) Act 2000 to 'promote good relations between people of different racial groups' (see Chapter 8 on legislation); and schools also have a statutory duty to promote community cohesion under the Education and Inspections Act 2006. Non-maintained settings should also take note of these requirements (see section on local communities and society, page 156).

In terms of how family members, children and workers relate to one another when children are being brought or collected, observation may reveal patterns that indicate whether they feel comfortable with one another or not. As with children, there can be almost routine ways of getting by without communicating or reacting to those who are less familiar to them or of whom they are a bit apprehensive, and this may result in almost intangible barriers building up between them. These barriers may be part and parcel of their lives. Where families from a variety of communities meet in early years settings, bringing and collecting their children and taking part in their children's learning, there is a unique opportunity that has often been missed (an opportunity not so readily available in the later stages of their education) – an opportunity to learn about and understand one another. Many people observing families and young children in early years settings tell of different communities not fully communicating with each other.

If you want to know more

see Selleck (2006a) for an example of one of the many such observations in an early years setting.

Much has been written about the importance of observing children, including Drummond and others (1993) and Elfer (2005).

In busy early years settings it is difficult to find time for such observations but even a few minutes on a regular basis may be helpful in identifying things that may need to be considered. But taking the opportunity to observe for long periods will obviously be of benefit in understanding children's real experiences.

Establishing an ethos where children feel comfortable with differences from the day that they arrive in the setting is basic to this process – trying to do this later on when children are already established, particularly in their friendship patterns, may be more difficult than starting as we mean to continue. This might be explicit as part of the setting's policy for racial equality (see Chapter 6). Using Persona Dolls to support children in valuing differences will help them to learn to empathise and relate positively to such differences. It will also help all children coming new to the setting to feel that they belong equally. This is particularly important for Travellers, Roma, Gypsies, refugees and asylum seekers and the children of migrant workers. But it will also help children from all black and other minority ethnic families to feel they belong too because other children have been encouraged and supported in relating to and welcoming them (see Chapter 6 about making this explicit in the policy for equality).

Knowing about history and culture

We don't need to know anything about people from cultures different from our own in order to treat people equally.

Knowing about the history, culture and languages of people has little to do with not being racist. People can know all of this and still feel superior and be racist and vice versa. But not wanting to know or not being curious about these factors does not bode well for helping all children to respect and value one another. Learning about differences is part of sharing together, and to learn about others should be an important aspect of satisfying one's own intellectual curiosity. If the positive aspects of everyone's history are valued then it becomes easier to accept the wrongs that have been done in their heritages.

Knowing about a people's history in detail is less important than knowing about Britain's role in that people's history. Knowing something about slavery, colonialism and imperialism, about the origins of antisemitism and anti-Irish and anti-Traveller, Roma and Gypsy racism puts Britain's history into a context. It begins to explain how and why racism exists. It helps to explain how, in its various forms, racism started, how people tried to justify it and how, as a consequence, it became part of our society.

If you want to know more

about the history of migration to Britain and the contribution of such migrants, see Institute of Race Relations (IRR) (1982), Fryer (1984) and CRE (1996). For a discussion about how the understanding of racism has implications for respecting the heritage of children, see Walker (2006) and Lane (2007a).

However, conversely, in order to create an antiracist, inclusive ethos in the setting, it is important to reflect and value the histories and cultures of local and global communities in activities, resources, stories, displays and events.

It is important to find historical and cultural information from authentic sources – preferably from people themselves or, if that is not possible, from reliable resources. Children's families are the best sources for the home culture and lifestyle. But that doesn't mean that every family from that culture does the same thing. For example, some Indian families may eat fish and chips as often as English white people, and not every African-Caribbean family eats rice and peas. The best way to learn is to be part of a community, to genuinely want to learn and enjoy the variety of cultural aspects.

For information about the histories of different communities use material written by that community, if possible.

If you want to know more

by reading a discussion about what it is important to know about culture and religion, see Lane (2005d).

The outside environment of children is also important. It can be a way of introducing environments and gardens from a variety of cultural traditions to children. For an example of how this might be done, including in a nursery, see Wong (1996).

The role of parents and families in helping their children not to learn to be racially prejudiced

Throughout this book parents and families are seen as crucially important in supporting settings in countering racism. But parents and families (including grandparents) also have a role in ensuring that their own children learn positive attitudes to differences between people and that they are helped to unlearn any negative attitudes that they may have already learnt. Together with the workers in early years settings they are *co-educators* of children.

In the incident of the little Scottish girl who asked the Nigerian man if he was a boxer (see Case study 34, page 108) her parents may have been completely unaware that she had imbibed such information or where it had come from. There are many, and worse, stories of young children saying or doing things that their parents are shocked by because they themselves believe that they do not hold such negative attitudes. All of us need to realise the power of external forces on our children's lives that influence their attitudes and behaviour. This means recognising that holding positive attitudes ourselves is not necessarily sufficient to counter these wider forces (see Case study 43, page 163).

Parents need to consider how they might support their children both in learning positive attitudes to differences between people and unlearning any negative ones. Because they cannot know what their children may be learning (like the Scottish girl) they need continually to be aware and to take action to reinforce positive ideas and break down any negative results of racial hierarchies that may allow children to be ill-informed and develop racially prejudiced attitudes. By having play resources reflecting the wider society, by exploring multicultural areas with their children and investigating what they have to offer, parents can provide opportunities for discussing ideas with children and for finding answers to any questions they may ask.

If you want to know more

about talking with children about prejudice and discrimination, see Connolly (undated), for discussion.

Parents who enable their children to learn about a variety of cultures and lifestyles are preparing them to enjoy the feeling of belonging to a multicultural society in the future.

Multiculturalism

Multiculturalism is not about safeguarding self-contained ethnic and cultural boxes but rather about intercultural fusion in which a culture freely borrows bits of others and creatively transforms both itself and them. Far from implying that each individual should remain rooted in his or her own culture and flit between them, multiculturalism requires that they should open themselves up to the influence of others and engage in a reflective and sometimes life-enhancing dialogue with others.

(Parekh 2005)

Just to learn about other people's cultures, is not to learn about the racism of one's own. To learn about the racism of one's own, on the other hand, is to approach other cultures objectively.

(Institute of Race Relations 1980)

Multiculturalism thrives where racism is not present.

(Ouseley 2006)

There are sometimes misunderstandings about what the meaning of culture is – everyone has a culture in the same way as everyone has an ethnicity. So multiculturalism is about the cultures of everyone. There are continual debates about multiculturalism, what it is and whether it is a good thing and what the term means to different people. For example, in contexts mostly outside the early years field there is debate as to whether apparently encouraging and supporting cultural groups other than white groups to remain separate, through funding and other mechanisms (sometimes called 'culturalism') rather than pursuing their common needs, reinforces inter-cultural and ethnic divisions. Amartya Sen sees this 'plural monoculturalism', often determined by faith, as dangerous and divisive and advocates a need to rescue it from this interpretation (Sen 2006).

Institutional racism, developed as part and parcel of our society over centuries of colonialism and slavery, is the real issue behind most discourse on multiculturalism – the reality that ranks cultures (*all* cultures, including the various white cultures) in a racial hierarchy and reinforces racism. But the fact remains that we all live in a multicultural society. Whether all the component cultures are equal, whether they are encouraged to be separate, whether cultures see themselves as separate, whether racial discrimination is removed and what the consequent implications are for our society is the crux of the discussion. And of course there are cultural groups other than minority ethnic groups, socioeconomic and class groups, youth and religious groups – which, too, are part of multiculturalism.

But too often the good intentions of multiculturalism have led people to tiptoe on eggshells, rather than have the confidence to confront difficult issues (Matthew Taylor, reported in paper on multiculturalism by Birmingham Race Action Project 2003).

Discussions about multiculturalism usually include issues about assimilation and integration (see Appendix 1(b) for definitions). Whereas the aim of assimilation is a monocultural society, the aim of integration is a multicultural society. (It is interesting to note that, when issues of segregation arise, any local communities of white, Jewish, Arabic or Australian people are not considered. It is generally only South Asian people who are alleged to be segregated often, ironically, resulting from past housing policies, some of which were found to be unlawfully racially discriminatory.) The socioeconomic context and governmental policies are the determinants of how multiculturalism develops. But its ultimate aim must be equality. It must recognise the necessity of equality – equal dignity and equal respect underpinned by legislation. Without equality as the objective, different cultural communities may be set against each other in their struggle for recognition and acceptance (and funding) and thus marginalise and diminish the potential power of their joint opposition to racism (and poverty). A sense of social cohesion, a shared sense of identity and an open and positive interaction between cultures are critical for a multicultural society based on equality. That is why the early years need to play an important role in countering the racial hierarchies of cultures – and other factors.

If you want to know more

see Alibhai-Brown (1999) and Hall (2001) for discussions of multiculturalism; Sivanandan (2006) for a brilliant historical view of multiculturalism; Bourne (2007) for a defence of multiculturalism; and page 128 for a discussion of multicultural education.

Religion

The differences between religions raise some complex and different issues from those raised by languages, skin colours and ethnic groups. It is quite clear that each of the latter should be accorded equal value and treatment. While ideally this should also be the case with religions, the situation is much more complex. Some people respect the right of others to practise their religion, and believe that there are many ways to express a faith whereas others profoundly disagree with this. They believe that their religion is the only true one and that believers of other religions are wrong, or even sinners. There is consequently constant discourse about the interaction of religion, human rights and freedom of speech.

This book is not the vehicle for discussing the role of religion in society generally or particular religions in particular contexts. But early years services and settings need to take account of religious differences and consider the principles outlined below.

Principles to be considered in respect of religion

Discrimination on grounds of religion or belief in employment is covered by the Employment Equality (Religion or Belief) Regulations 2003, and in other areas by the religion and belief sections of the Equality Act 2006. In addition, if discrimination on grounds of membership of a particular religion disproportionately affects a particular national or racial group, this may constitute indirect racial discrimination and be unlawful under the Race Relations Act (see Chapter 8).

The setting must ensure respect for all religions, even though some people might find it difficult to respect all religions equally.

With regard to employment issues: Religious practices, requirements and needs should, as far as possible, be accepted. However this should not mean that some people do less work than others, contribute less or have fewer responsibilities, as a result of their faith.

Where particular religious requirements clash with the setting practice, this should be resolved, wherever possible, through negotiation. For example, an orthodox Jewish, Jehovah's Witness or Seventh Day Adventist worker in a setting that stays open until 6.00 in the evening may not be able to work after 3.00 on a Friday during the winter (people who are Orthodox Jews, Jehovah's Witnesses or Seventh Day Adventists may not work on the Sabbath which runs from sundown on Friday to sundown on Saturday). In this case, a shift pattern with other workers may be possible. Where it is not possible to negotiate a solution, other solutions may need to be agreed, even if they are less acceptable to some. For example, where a leader of a setting is required to be present at all times, it may be impossible to accommodate a member of a religion who is not able to be present on Friday afternoons during the winter. In order to be specific about what is required, an employer should provide a 'business case' for job applicants, in advance, that specifies the exact times of work when the leader should be present. The reasons for this requirement should be clear and the employer should have taken steps to ensure that no other solution was possible in the circumstances. In any potential claim of religious discrimination in an employment tribunal, the reasons may be needed to justify the requirement.

Nothing, however, should override the principles of equality of treatment for everyone. The issue of religious holidays may pose difficulties for the workplace. If religious holidays are given as days off to workers of specific religions, there will be inevitable problems to face as some people may end up having fewer days off than others, particularly those with no religion. It is impossible and inappropriate for the employer to decide which religious holidays should to be taken as days off and which should not. Solutions will need to be sought and negotiated according to the particular circumstances.

A principle of the acceptance of everyone's right to manifest their religion or belief should be the premise for any discussion of particular aspects. With regard to religious dress there are two guiding points:

- any dress must not interfere with the duties that a worker has to carry out
- it must not interfere with the safety of other adults or children, that is, it must comply with Health and Safety requirements.

This means recognising the importance of communicating with eyes and body language as part of the teaching and learning process (see National Union of

Teachers 2006 for information, although referring in particular to schools it contains a useful glossary of forms of dress).

With regard to practice in settings: Families and workers should be given opportunities to discuss any religious needs or requirements at initial meetings or inductions.

No child (or family member) should be discriminated against because of their family's religion (see religion and belief sections of the Equality Act 2006).

Children whose parents believe in any religion or no religion should be treated with equal care and concern.

Except in groups whose basis is on religious grounds, specific religious practices should not be observed as part of the setting practice.

No child should ever be required to practise a faith that is not their family's.

If a non-maintained sector setting is based on a specific religion, the existing overlapping aspects of the laws make the situation complicated with regard to admissions and any religious practices. Whether the forthcoming Single Equality Act will clarify this remains to be seen.

If possible, special diets for religious reasons should be made available in the setting. If it is not possible, families should be encouraged to supply their own prepared food. Where food is prepared on the premises, care must be taken about using separate cooking implements where required. Food that is unacceptable to a particular group on religious grounds must be kept separate from other food. It is better to provide vegetarian food (which is acceptable to all groups other than vegans) than be unable to offer a range of diets for children, at least on some occasions.

Where adults and children are unable to take part in certain activities (for example, celebrating a birthday, something seldom associated with any religious practice) because of their faith or belief, this should be accepted and, where necessary, explained to the others in positive ways.

As much notice as possible of forthcoming religious observances and festivals should be given by workers and families.

Trying to make religious issues as unproblematic as possible is important if the principles of implementing racial equality are to be achieved.

If you want to know more

about parental religious wishes, see Lane (2005f).

Religion and culture are often deeply entwined and may appear the same to an observer. Most white people born in Britain are likely to have a culture incorporating Christian values. Similarly, most people born in Bangladesh or some parts of Nigeria are likely to have a culture incorporating Islamic values. In addition, within each religion there are likely to be a number of different groups with different ways of interpreting the belief (Protestant, Catholic, Methodist, Baptist Christianity; Orthodox and Reform Judaism; Shi'a and Sunni Islam). This is inevitable, so that each situation arising in a setting where culture and religion are involved needs to be considered according to the particular issues. And what some people believe is religious is sometimes, in fact, cultural. For example, some Muslim families may object to quoting the rhyme 'Three little pigs' or visiting a farm with pigs, on religious grounds. According to Muslim academics there is no reasoning in the Qur'an to justify this, and it arises from the Islamic dietary laws – Muslims are forbidden to eat pork. However, where this belief is prevalent it is usually based on the traditional culture of the area from which the family has originally migrated. In those particular circumstances it does not seem worth having serious disagreements about something that can so easily be avoided. Talking it through with families may even make it possible for children to visit a farm with pigs. It is the mutual respect and understanding that are key concepts to be negotiated in nearly all instances where religion and culture play a part.

If you want to know more

read Draycott and Robins (2005) for an ecumenical approach to various religions.

It is this mutual respect and understanding that needs to be a part of early years practice. But sometimes an example applicable and readily understood from one's own culture clarifies and explains the strongly held faith of others.

Case study 41

Making a meal of it?

A Hindu student in a higher education institute ate her meals in the canteen. She explained that she did not eat beef but couldn't get the caterers to understand that just removing beef from a salad plate and replacing it with something else was unacceptable. Eventually, concerned about her health, her doctor gave the following example to the caterers. 'You have prepared a delicious Sunday lunch of roast chicken and vegetables and asked the visitor if that looked good. She agreed that it did. You then put a dog turd on top of it. When the visitor expressed some dismay at this action you said you would remove it. The visitor still declined to eat the meal.'

Such an explanation may facilitate an understanding of why people from some religious backgrounds as well as vegetarians may find meat and other food displayed on the same plate as totally unacceptable.

Consultation

There are several occasions when an organisation (for example, national or local government or an early years setting) needs to ensure that it is taking into account the views and ideas of everyone affected by their proposed work or actions or by a specific initiative. It is also an important mechanism in conducting a race equality impact assessment (see page 249). Consultation is complex because it usually involves a differential in power relationships between those undertaking the consultation (the consulters) and those being consulted (the consultees). Where the consulter has already drafted some paper for consultation, it is seldom that the wishes of the majority consultees will override any different wishes of the consulters. What it usually means is that consultee's views may ameliorate the pre-existing ones of the consulters. The situation is further complicated when consulters attempt to balance responses from organisations (who may or may not themselves have internal accountability mechanisms) and individuals (possibly with varying knowledge bases of the consultation issues), by giving them differing weights.

Where, however, the consulter is genuinely seeking information from consultees (for example, where a local authority is consulting about the sufficiency of childcare places) the situation is different – basic information is being sought. In devising a policy for equality, on the other hand, it is important that all the stakeholders are involved so that everyone can own it. This means that plenty of time and commitment should be given to the two-way process of formulating the policy and not just being asked to agree one that has already been decided. Talking things through and everyone explaining what is meant from their own perspective facilitates understanding and eventual agreement. It is pointless to devise a policy among a few workers that is rarely read or known about.

In listening to people and taking account of their views the principle should be that of the United Nations Convention on Human Rights – where every person's rights are acknowledged equally. This is a useful starting point where differing opinions are expressed. Clearly, when consulting on a racial equality scheme or policy (as required by the Race Relations (Amendment) Act 2000 – see page 247 and Appendix 4) everything should be in line with the equality principle. Any future schemes or policies on gender/sex or disability equality will also be in line with that principle. Sensitive, open and considerate discussions need to be the basis of any consultations where such differing practices are involved.

In many consultations the views of black and other minority ethnic groups are included in the overall consultation, but where their views are disproportionately different from the majority this may not be readily identified or known. This is similar to JK Galbraith's *Culture of Contentment* where the majority middle classes are 'content' to retain their material advantages (in terms of low taxes) in government decision-making at the expense of the less affluent whose views are perhaps known and whom higher taxes could benefit but, being in the minority, can be ignored (Galbraith 1992). The race equality impact assessment should identify any such disproportionate effect and indicate the need to address it.

Consultation is best when there are effective communication mechanisms already in place, preferably used on a regular basis and open to democratic accountability, sharing of information and, so far as possible, power-sharing. It is almost impossible to build an effective consultation process on the back of nothing. It should be part of something that is already ongoing, accepted and valued. In terms of the particular circumstances where people from black and other minority ethnic backgrounds are to be specifically consulted, the following principles might be observed.

- Wherever possible plan the consultation with appropriate members of the group(s) to be consulted.
- Ensure that all the groups to be consulted are identified and accessed, paying particular attention to those groups not yet usually included.
- Depending on the particular circumstances and consultation issues, devise a mechanism where everyone's voice can be heard/recorded.
- Ensure that men and women are equally consulted.
- Consider the most appropriate mechanism according to the urgency and importance of the task, the particular groups involved and the number of people/groups to be consulted.
- Consider translation and interpreting where relevant; written methods; meetings (but ensure that either everyone is present or there are mechanisms of accountability to ensure views are formally represented); venues and times of meetings (avoiding festivals and specific religious occasions); and interviews (ensure relevant language speakers).
- Where questions are involved, ensure that their implications are explicit, that relevant information is provided and that views are able to be represented.
- Build up confidence within communities so that consulters are familiar faces wherever possible.
- Have an understanding and knowledge of the cultural and religious backgrounds of consultees, preferably by using members of the relevant groups who are able to be unbiased in their communications.

Where groups are represented in a partnership with the local authority or other organisations, it is important to ensure that appropriate accountability mechanisms are set up so that the representation reflects the views of all members of the group as far as possible.

As with all consultations, it is important to give time to really listen to everyone, from whatever viewpoint, and equally from the perspective of the consulters and consultees. Consultations may be one of the mechanisms used to assess the impact of proposals, plans and policies on minority ethnic groups as required by the Race Relations (Amendment) Act and are required under the Childcare Act on specific issues (see Daycare Trust 2007 for a project about listening to black families).

Training and education

Training and education for racial equality in the early years is in its infancy with regard to its proven effectiveness. Whereas the mechanistic 'training' aspect is relatively simple and uncontroversial (for example, how to collect data monitored by ethnicity), the concept of education is more complex and problematic. It involves reflecting on practice, attitudes and values in a much wider sense and being open to changes as a result. Most courses incorporate both aspects.

The Race Relations (Amendment) Act requires all local authorities, in their race equality scheme, to make arrangements for training staff so they can comply with the general duty to promote race equality. Pressure from the DCSF reinforces this, together with the requirements of the Early Years Foundation Stage (inspected by Ofsted) and the Quality Improvement Principles (NQIN 2007), by expecting local authorities and settings to provide training so they can understand and comply with anti-discriminatory legislation.

Training and education for racial equality in the early years has changed over time from initially addressing English as an additional language through a focus on 'multicultural education' (largely consisting of promoting culturally appropriate resources to celebrate diversity, often through festivals), to beginning to address some of the practical implications of racism on children and their families in settings. These are important. But, although there have been significant improvements in much of the training and education about equality issues, seldom have any taken real account of the embedded nature of racism in our society and particularly its institutional implications for early years practice.

Research on interventions intended to remove the roots of racism, although not in the early years, concludes depressingly that most are unsuccessful (Bhavnani and others 2005). This is largely because most interventions do not address the causes of racism, how those causes are currently reproduced or the way powerful voices perpetuate them. The research indicates that successful interventions tend to be educational, aimed at improving knowledge and communication and strongly led. This suggests that courses in the early years need to shift their focus towards a basic understanding of inequalities and the ways that institutional discrimination works before embarking on curricular practice issues. Some courses are already beginning to adopt this approach but inevitably they are time-consuming and costly. However, short one-off sessions that do not address the underlying causes of inequality are very likely to be ineffective. When this happens organisers become frustrated at their lack of success – this encourages despondency and reluctance to embark upon such training at all. That is the dilemma for those organising courses with many pressing priorities, possibly little support or understanding from managers, little time and limited funding available.

The minimum levels for the assessment of practice are set by the *National Occupational Standards in Children's Care, Learning and Development* (NOSCCLD) (DfES 2006c) and the *National Occupational Standards in Playwork* (DfES 2006e). However, although they incorporate the principles of equality and anti-discriminatory practice, and in the NOSCCLD do this in an integrated way, racism and its institutional aspects are not covered.

?

If you want to know more

about the role of training and education in removing racism, see Bhavnani (2001); and for a strategic framework approach see the Anti Racist Teacher Education Network (2002).

Teacher education; early childhood studies and foundation degrees; courses in further education and the voluntary, independent and private sectors; the early years professional status courses; and the courses for the National Professional Qualification in Integrated Centre Leadership, mostly address aspects of equality but to varying levels of effectiveness, especially regarding racial equality. Included among the difficulties facing tutors and educators are their own varying levels of knowledge, skills, commitment and understanding; the lack of effective support and guidance available to them; and an insufficient knowledge of how to assess the effectiveness of the learning of participants. And the initial knowledge base and commitment of students range right across the spectrum, reflecting their own home and family experiences, their lives outside the home and their education.

Over the years, some voluntary organisations (notably the Pre-school Learning Alliance, the National Childminding Association and the Early Years Trainers Anti Racist Network, now Early Years Equality) have pioneered and developed training on racial equality, largely based on settings' practices. And the Council for Awards in Children's Care and Education (CACHE) published a guide on opening up access and qualifications for candidates from minority ethnic groups (Lane 1999a).

But overall there has been considerable reluctance for workers either to take part in or organise in-service training and education on racial equality, some senior officers even denying the need for it because, they claim, 'early years workers are not prejudiced'. One reason for this reluctance is the often hidden implication, to any requirement to take part in such training – that only people who are racist need training about racial equality. The fear of being called a racist may, understandably, be strong and foster resentment (see pages 48 and 66 for some discussion of this). That is why whole-setting or whole-staff training is likely to be more acceptable, thus manifesting a more overall professional approach rather than one that picks out individuals or groups of individuals for what may be perceived by some as 'therapy' or corrective training.

An obvious effect of not having the professional approach is that managers, leaders and others with influence may not see themselves as benefiting from training/education – they are often the powerful people who need it most. Furthermore, there are many people working in the field who are not part of a team or staff group – writing documents, standards, training materials and policies, conducting research and acting as advisors and consultants. They are not necessarily able to access training/education, even if they should wish to do so.

Until racial equality is integral to all policies, practices and procedures, training or support for people is essential if the critical work they do is to take account of this in positive and effective ways. The real difficulty to overcome is in enabling people to recognise for themselves, that they would be better able to ensure racial equality in their own work if they gave time to such training, support and open and honest discussions of the issues. Instead they so often assume that, in their position, they do not need it and that even to suggest it implies personal criticism – the whole concept is so often seen as threatening. Until everyone realises and accepts their own susceptibility to inequalities, that everyone benefits from training and discussion and that to take part does not undermine their status or credibility, training for racial equality is likely to be problematic.

But there are many other reasons for a reluctance to undertake training on racial equality. There may be a legacy of guilt-induced training experiences or a perception that training may be aggressive, irrelevant, negative or intrude into their personal situation. Participants may worry about questioning their own values, feel that their practice does not need changing or simply be uninterested. They may feel that they will be 'got at', found wanting or have their ideas challenged in uncomfortable ways and so seek to avoid it.

Some participants attend courses expecting just to be given tips as to what to do without having to engage actively or reflect on what the issues are (for discussion on this see Kapasi 2006). And, for some others, even attending a training course is a new experience.

Although some local authorities and organisations have addressed their own training needs for many years, most have done little if anything at all specifically on racial equality. For organisers (local authorities, settings, and training and education institutions and organisations) any reluctance may stem from:

- other apparently pressing training priorities
- a difficulty of finding effective trainers and knowing how to assess their competence in advance as there may be no accreditation of such training or trainers
- a difficulty in assessing whether apparently unsatisfactory training is due to the incompetence of trainers, inappropriately qualified or prepared participants, or reluctance or hostility on the part of participants to learn and participate actively
- a lack of knowledge and understanding of what should comprise such training
- unfamiliarity with the early years, specifically, on the part of some potential trainers
- the reluctance of some trainers to conduct training where previous experiences have encountered a hostile response from participants
- not seeing racial equality training as something that has to be built into the planning programme of the whole course from the start, so that it progresses through stages of understanding and knowledge
- reluctance or inability to pay for two trainers (compared with one trainer on other subjects) even where their value in terms of mutual support and other factors is recognised.

Although clearly good training for racial equality supports good practice generally, so far no training on racial equality in the early years has been independently evaluated to assess how effective it is.

The usual evaluation of training and education courses by requiring participants to complete a form at the end of the course, often anonymously, seldom provides useful and relevant information for trainers and organisers. Trainers generally do not assess participants' knowledge or commitment to equality prior to the course so they cannot realistically assess the success or otherwise of the course for particular people – the value-added effect. It is possible that completing an evaluation form some months after the course would be more likely to be helpful and indicate whether the objectives of the course had been fulfilled. And perhaps an open and honest discussion of the course with all participants towards the end of the course would reveal a more fruitful evaluation because it is immediate and spontaneous. This all reinforces the need for a comprehensive evaluation of training and education courses, of trainers and of their effectiveness in terms of removing unlawful racial discrimination and promoting equality of opportunity and good relations between people of different racial groups – the statutory duties of the Race Relations (Amendment) Act.

There is no clear model for racial equality training so individuals and organisations providing training and education have been struggling to develop appropriate courses to fulfil the need. Those aimed at fulfilling targets are seldom premised on a commitment to understanding how racism works in society and in early years services.

When procuring any training from external organisations or individuals, local authorities must comply with their duties under the Race Relations (Amendment) Act. This means advertising widely for all training bids; ensuring that all trainers, whatever the subject of their training, deliver training that complies with the legislation; that the training is equally relevant for all ethnic groups; that trainers reflect the ethnic composition of the local community; and that ethnic monitoring mechanisms are built into the whole process and outcomes (see CRE 2003a).

Everyone working in the early years field, including those in local and national government, needs to know about the amended Race Relations Act, how racism operates in our society and its implications for young children. They should all have opportunities for such training. This is of particular and obvious importance for inspectors and other assessors. For example, Ofsted inspectors need to be sufficiently trained to be able to inspect settings effectively on racial equality and understand the implications of the amended Race Relations Act, including for policies, admissions, employment and curriculum practice.

Resulting from the issues discussed above, it is clear that one-off ad hoc sessions on racial equality for people who have not had previous training or experience in this, however good they are, are much less likely to be effective (however that is assessed) than carefully planned courses, progressing over stages and conducted over a period of time. This is particularly so when workers from a wide range of backgrounds, qualifications and experiences come together initially with little shared understanding of their values, commitment or knowledge bases. Sessions that are part of a comprehensive course process within a no-blame culture, progressing step by step, addressing all inequalities and their causes initially and building up to specific issues about the various equalities, appear to be more widely accepted and lead to positive changes in practice. They are also more likely to defuse participants' anxieties that they might be confrontationally challenged about, for example, being racist. Such sessions provide opportunities among participants to build up a sense of rapport, an acknowledgement that this is often a sensitive issue because it challenges basic attitudes and ideas learnt over a lifetime and that individual participants are not alone in feeling as they may do. Creating confidentiality within a comfortable atmosphere – that is clear that the objective is not to 'judge' – with a shared commitment and the provision of an opportunity to discuss issues of common interest and concern on an ongoing basis, however testing to the facilitators, are critical components of positive changes in practice. Such circumstances have been known to result in the setting up of support groups, meeting regularly, perhaps with speakers on particular issues and providing a forum for discussion.

Training in this area can be a profoundly frustrating and disheartening experience for trainers and educators – effective training needs particularly committed, skilled and sensitive people and the active support and positive endorsement of organisers in recognising this. Because of the vulnerability of such trainers and educators in tackling sensitive issues it is usually more supportive where two trainers work together. This does have implications for funding, but it also offers the opportunity to have the perspective of trainers from different ethnic backgrounds. Where local authorities and other organisations organise or commission training and education on equality it is important that, wherever possible, an acknowledgment in person of the status accorded to the course and the seriousness with which such training is regarded and backed, is made explicit to participants at the beginning of the course. This means referring to legislation and explaining the moral basis of the rationale behind it – clearly and unambiguously and that a casual approach is unacceptable. Along with this should be an effective introduction of the trainers by the organisers to the participants so they understand the significance of the issues to be addressed. This will help to defuse any potential negative attitudes that such a course is really a waste of time.

One problem, particularly on initial training and education and early childhood studies courses where students are often white, young and inexperienced or in rural or suburban areas where people rarely meet black people, is the really basic lack of knowledge or experience of students to inform their understanding of what racism is. Although this points to the inadequacy of the National Curriculum teaching in schools and a lack of information being generally available, the situation facing tutors is difficult. What might be the triggers that alert such students to take responsibility to address racism as a fact of British society so that they want to take action about it in their future professional careers? (For some suggestions see page 26.)

There is a need for independent accreditation in the field of training on racial equality – both for courses and for trainers and educators. The apparent lack of effective training that addresses the key issues and leads to positive changes demonstrates this urgent need. The recent requirements of the Race Relations (Amendment) Act highlight this lack. There are a few people who understand what is needed – their knowledge and experience should be sought to consider the current situation and offer a basis for future training and education. Identifying effective training and providing training for trainers should be a priority for government if real changes in practice are to be made possible.

Not all is dismal and depressing on the training resources front however. There has been a huge development of good resources for children and for trainers. Nearly all national early years journals now include articles about various aspects of equality, including racial equality. And there are individuals and groups who work passionately to support such training. For example, Persona Doll Training has worked by using the Dolls to encourage children to develop concepts of empathy with others who are different from themselves. This training has been conducted all over Britain (as well as abroad) and has proved to be stimulating for workers who can see the results of their efforts in practical ways (see page 207 for further discussion). A very small number of organisations, including Early Years Equality, conduct training and organise conferences on racial equality for everyone and other voluntary organisations continue to produce some good training materials for their members and others.

However, most such training is about practice at setting level, which is very important because that is where children are, but largely ignores an understanding of racism and the institutional aspects that may have a profound impact on the life chances of workers, children and their families from black and other minority ethnic communities. All should consider the issues raised in this book including an understanding of the origins of racism and its present-day manifestations and implications. For example, the need for training on collecting data and monitoring it by ethnicity; identifying discriminatory and potentially unlawful admissions and employment procedures; how the under-representation of people from black and other minority backgrounds at all levels should be addressed; and how children can be enabled to unlearn any racist attitudes and behaviour that they might have already learnt. And all this should be within the context of the reality of racism.

Much more analysis and evaluation of the content of training courses for racial equality is urgently needed to ensure that the most effective courses are available. Training and education for racial equality in the early years really needs a whole book on the issues. In the meantime, the points raised here may provide support for trainers in planning what they might do.

If you want to know more

see Kapasi (2006) for an example of participative training; Selleck (2006a) for a local authority's training and development programme; Kapasi and Lane (2008) for approaches to training; and Lane (2006d) for a resources list to raise and support issues.

Early years settings and services, local communities, neighbourhoods and society

Making a positive contribution: being involved with the community and society.

(the fourth outcome of *Every Child Matters* 2003)

The world of the early years and, in particular, an early years setting, does not exist in isolation. It is part of a local community that, in turn, is part of the wider society.

In some urban areas of Britain people from many ethnic groups get along relatively amicably. Paul Gilroy calls this reality 'convivial culture' and compares it with other areas where racism and hostility (particularly towards asylum seekers, Travellers, Roma, Gypsies and Muslims) are prevalent and appear to be increasing under the cloak of anti-terrorism (Gilroy 2004). While there are some urban areas where multiculturalism and acceptance thrive, such lack of harmony elsewhere means many people are apprehensive about what might be happening around them. They may encourage their children not to talk to strangers, they are afraid of crime, particularly violent crime, and cannot accept that their fears might be exaggerated or imaginary. And many believe some of the myths about 'foreigners', dangers and potential terrorists that the media often encourage. At the same time there is an increase in racist attacks, including antisemitism, a rise in hostility to refugees, asylum seekers and other migrants, antagonism to some religious groups – particularly Muslims – dissension and sometimes violence between communities. There have been the terrible bombings on London's transport system and other so-far foiled attacks more recently. All these factors have implications for children and the world they will grow up to live in. Our society is, at present, experiencing many symptoms of not being at ease with itself.

What needs to be done to ameliorate or counter this situation? This is an important question to ask, not only of national government, but also of local government, organisations, communities, groups and individuals.

If children grow up in Britain as strangers to those who are different from themselves it does not provide for a future society based on equality. What role might settings play in contributing to a more contented society that benefits the present and future lives of young children? If we are serious about racial equality and children, our concern cannot just end at the doors of the setting.

To reach someone's soul, you have to have a social relationship, you can't just sit down in the cold world of legal jargon and settle the nuances of racism and what it does to the social and cultural fabric.

(Harry Belafonte 2007)

Understanding what it is like to really belong to a multicultural society means more than meeting and knowing people at work from a variety of cultural backgrounds or seeing them on the street. It includes friendships across ethnic and cultural boundaries, accepting differences between backgrounds as positive opportunities to learn more about our wider world and learning that such differences can be sources of enlightenment as well as things about which we can agree to disagree. It is about reorientating our thinking and learning to care about and understand each other across cultural backgrounds and boundaries, listening to people's experiences and perspectives and building up trust.

Something of this concept is included in the southern African term *Ubuntu*, meaning largeness of spirit and humanity to others. This was defined by Archbishop Desmond Tutu in 1999 as:

> *A person with* **ubuntu** *is open and available to others, affirming of others, does not feel threatened that others are able and good, for he or she has a proper self-assurance that comes from knowing that he or she belongs in a greater whole and is diminished when others are humiliated or diminished, when others are tortured or oppressed.*

It is about seeing an early years setting as a place to meet others, to make friends with people who are different from ourselves and to help to break down racial divisions. It is about acting 'towards one another in a spirit of brotherhood' (Article 1 of the United Nations Universal Declaration of Human Rights 1948). It is about recognising that we cannot educate people to be strangers to each other.

> *When diverse communities all stay together, are all engaged in making the decisions and, however poor they are relatively, are contributing to making decisions that benefit everyone, resentment, hostility and intolerance will be reduced and eliminated. That is contributing to building cohesion.*
>
> (Lord Ouseley at a conference on 'Racism, liberty and the war on terror' organised by the Institute of Race Relations, September 2006)

We need to take personal and collective responsibility to be proactive about ensuring that everyone is included, that everyone belongs, rather than just hoping that events that increase tensions and fears will all go away, lulling ourselves into a belief that it will not really affect or concern us. Where people go to work, where children go to settings and schools and where people live their daily lives, positive acts can be made to break down barriers or lack of communication – by individuals or groups. Rather than avoiding communication of any sort between those who appear to be 'different' for fear of not knowing what to do, what might be acceptable or what might be the implications, any person can take their own initiative to break down barriers between people. And there are instances where this is happening. But the urgency of the situation demands a more concerted and comprehensive effort at a variety of levels. There are clearly many agencies that are in positions to take action but, where families, workers and children are already involved together in their early years setting in ensuring equality, including racial equality, there is an almost unique potential for finding a voice to address this. In terms of the fourth outcome of *Every Child Matters* – making a positive contribution: being involved with the community and society – children as well as adults have a role to play.

> *If you smile at people they usually smile back – they lighten your steps and make the day better.*

There are, of course, many realities that already engender cohesiveness and break down ethnic and cultural barriers – a rapidly increasing number of relationships where the partners are from different ethnic backgrounds; a number of local campaigns involving people from different ethnic backgrounds on specific issues such as deportations or treatment of asylum seekers; as well as national campaigns about general and specific issues concerning racism, antiracism in education and racist murders and violence.

Early years services in local authorities are also in key positions to consider what they, too, might do to support settings and to identify and raise their role in promoting community cohesion as important where it is not already seen as such. In times of intense activity in the early years, thinking about the wider society and its implications for children's futures may seem an irrelevant luxury. But, in a sense, it is that very activity that should provide the impetus for considering what might be done and for planning activities. Services that see themselves as part of that wider society may wish to raise the matter as a shared responsibility that involves everyone. Viewed in this way the task is less daunting. Both settings and services, located in local communities, can work together and play a significant part in developing an awareness of, and responsibility for, fostering that sense of belonging for which most people yearn.

Some settings already see themselves as advocates for their local community, of belonging to it, rather than being an insular enclave within it. Such settings will be more likely to be aware of what is happening, or not happening, there. They will be alert and sensitive to tensions (both group and individual), to situations when particular communities feel threatened and where racial prejudice is open and overt. Not only will this give workers a clearer insight into how they might support vulnerable children and better reflect their needs in practice but will also give them the confidence to support families, to be strong and sensitive in countering racism and to know where to go to get advice and help if needed.

Providing opportunities for children to learn naturally about each other, playing together, sitting together, talking together, eating together, laughing and being sad together will give children insights into one another's lives, thus recognising and accepting each other's common humanity. The Early Years Foundation Stage supports this practice by suggesting that children be encouraged 'to choose to play with a variety of friends, so that everybody in the group experiences being included'.

Taking a lead from the early years setting where children have opportunities to learn to be open-minded and receptive to a variety of ways of doing things, workers, families and children can, together, be catalysts and precursors of ways of enjoying living together in the wider context of our society – a society where people from every ethnic and cultural community belong equally and can participate fully in what it has to offer. Workers and families can see that what has been learnt in the setting works for children.

We don't have to know everything about one another, or even like each other, in order to respect and accept each other. We can continue to live our lives as before and still value and respect those who live different lives to us. But getting to know one another and sharing common interests and experiences helps our understanding of one another better. There are different levels concerned with breaking down potential ethnic and cultural barriers – personal, organisational and work levels. Clearly personal friendships are likely to be the most long-lasting and secure. Organisational levels may provide an alertness and a framework in which to work. But, while work colleagues may appear to be integrated, if relationships are limited to work situations, where subtle barriers remain and do not extend outside, they are unlikely to be as secure as friendships.

Friendship is the single greatest antidote to fear.

(Chief Rabbi Jonathan Sacks, 'Thought for the day', Radio 4, 29 December 2006)

In areas where few people from black and other minority ethnic communities live the issue is, if anything, more urgent – the consequences of there being dislocated and troubled communities and individuals may eventually impact on such areas too. Lack of forethought about the implications of living in the wider society may leave settings unprepared for such situations. They also have a role to play in bridging the gap between the immediate reality and the future into which many children will live their lives. But even where the practice of linking up with different ethnic and cultural communities is not possible, then at least the principles of doing so should be raised with children and their families and practical work can extend their visions to the truth about society. For example, after careful preparation workers and families can visit their nearest multicultural areas in order to meet people and experience shops, places to eat and cultural activities less familiar to them than their own, not in voyeuristic ways or as 'culture tourists' but as people genuinely broadening their life experience. There are no simple answers to what is needed to be done and every setting and every early years service will have their own ways of thinking about it.

From September 2007, all school governors have been required by statute specifically to promote community cohesion and the well-being of pupils in schools (Education and Inspections Act 2006). Ofsted is also required to inspect for this. Some schools run children's centres and they are therefore also covered by this legal duty. Other children's centres run by local authorities, although not covered by the duty as they are not schools, should nevertheless consider it. And all children's centres should take account of their statutory duty under the Race Relations (Amendment) Act of promoting good relations between people of different racial groups and include 'promoting community cohesion' as integral to this duty. The principle of this duty should apply to all early years settings in the voluntary, independent and private sectors as well – good practice should be the same for all children and their settings. Practice Guidance for children's centres refers to children's centres as having 'a key role in promoting social cohesion and fostering positive relationships with their community'. It also says that 'opportunities should be sought to enable children and their families to mix with groups and individuals from a range of cultural and linguistic backgrounds' (DfES/DWP 2006) This reinforces the concept, together with the guidance to the early years foundation stage's suggestion to encourage children to choose to play with a variety of friends, that it is important for children to be encouraged to mix and play with children who are different from themselves (see page 139 for further discussion of this).

A cohesive community is generally defined as 'a community that is in a state of well-being, harmony and stability'. Guidance on the duty to promote community cohesion includes in its definition of community cohesion: 'working towards a society where there is a common vision, a sense of belonging by all communities and where the diversity of people's backgrounds and circumstances is appreciated and valued'. The Guidance identifies some of the barriers to this and includes useful information (DCSF/CLG 2007).

How do we enable local authorities and early years workers to consider their important role, for the benefit of all children's futures, of involving all children, families and workers in promoting social and community cohesion and in helping society to be more at ease with itself? The requirement to promote good relations between people of different racial groups should be an important starting point. While the following ideas may appear utopian to some, in view of the existing reality of our society and on the basis that every new idea has to start somewhere, the following suggestions are made.

What local authority early years services can do

▶ Raise the question of what role settings might take in supporting the lives of children by contributing to a future harmonious society.

▶ Ask how the support and development provided for settings might encourage them to see themselves as belonging to their local communities in practical ways. How might effective antiracist practice be linked with promoting community cohesion?

▶ Ask how the service might raise an awareness of this issue in the early years field generally – with settings, families and possibly with children – in benefiting all children's futures.

▶ Assess how the service might support settings in addressing this issue. Offer practical help. For example, the fourth outcome of *Every Child Matters* is 'making a positive contribution: being involved with the community and society', so how might children be involved?

▶ Consider whether having a written rationale about community activity would be helpful to settings. Should the race equality scheme and other early years policies include a commitment to consider these issues?

▶ Raise the question of what role the service itself might play, independently or in cooperation with organisations and settings, in contributing to the objective.

What early years settings (as well as working with LAs) can do

▶ Raise the issue of the role the setting might take, for the benefit of all children's futures, with workers, children and their families in contributing to a society, local community and neighbourhood being more at ease with itself.

▶ Analyse how the setting might engender an ethos of belonging to the local community, of being advocates for it and of everyone taking action to build friendships and community cohesion.

◆ Assess whether the setting's existing practice for racial equality provides a basis for addressing this appropriately.

◆ Assess what might be done in practical, sensitive and honest ways, as a result of good practice, to link the setting's work for racial equality with children to the promotion of a contented local community and the breaking down of barriers between and among different ethnic and cultural communities, both inside and outside the setting. These might range from:
  – smiling at people, having a friendly face and body language, making positive gestures of acceptance
  – learning how to say 'Hello' in different languages and when and how to use the words
  – taking positive steps to include people from different ethnic and cultural groups within friendship groups
  – learning about the lives of a diverse friendship group
  – making an effort to communicate with people who you do not usually talk to (workers, family members, neighbours and near neighbours, shoppers, shopkeepers in unfamiliar shops, on the street, in queues, at the bus stop, at clinics and doctors' surgeries)
  – making a point of attending and taking part in local activities where people from different ethnic and cultural groups meet – festivals, carnivals, celebrations, and community meetings.

◆ Where there are few people from minority ethnic groups, plan carefully prepared visits to the nearest multicultural town with a view to enjoying what it has to offer – shops, places to eat, buildings.

◆ Consider including a reference, in the policy for equality, to the setting's role in promoting community cohesion in the local community.

◆ Consider joining local campaigns supporting community members' experiences of discrimination and hostility.

◆ Involve children in thinking about their neighbourhood in a variety of positive, non-voyeuristic and practical ways.

Madeleine Bunting (director of Demos) makes some pertinent comments:

● *A comfortable multicultural society is not made in Whitehall, but on the street, in the school – in the myriad of relationships of friends, neighbours and colleagues. That's where new patterns of accommodation to bridge cultural differences are forged; that's where minds change, prejudices shift and alienation is eased.*

● *When did you last have a conversation with a Muslim in which you enjoyed each other's company enough for you both to change, even if only a small part, your minds?*

● *It takes more than tea and biscuits to overcome indifference and fear.*

(*Guardian*, 27 February 2006)

> **?**
>
> ### If you want to know more
>
> read a wider discussion of these issues in Lane (2006b), Lane and Ouseley (2006) and DCSF (2007).

Terrorism, trauma and tragedy

My friend Manzoor no longer wears his topi (Muslim cap) as it creates too much hassle.

There have been terror attacks on buildings and people around the world over recent years, perhaps the most memorable for children at the time being those of September 2001 in the USA and London in July 2005. There have, of course, been others. There have also been natural disasters, including the tsunami of December 2004; devastating earthquakes, including that in Pakistan in September 2005; and floods in Bangladesh, New Orleans and elsewhere. All of these may have troubled children in some way. Fear of travel, fear of potential suicide bombers and fear of what the future might bring are likely to have permeated their lives in some way. Children with families killed or hurt in natural disasters may wonder if it will happen to them. In order to even contemplate the future it is important to understand and accept that there are no easy answers to such tragedies. What may happen in the future remains unknown.

It is also important to allay any fears of children so far as possible by being open with them, comforting them and talking with them. Some may have been directly affected. It should not be assumed, because they don't appear to be affected, that they have not in some way experienced what has been going on. Opportunities for them to express their feelings and ask questions should be sought. At the same time opportunities should be provided for them to talk with each other about what they may have seen or heard about, to represent their feelings in whatever ways they wish and to act out their anxieties in a supportive environment. Workers should also encourage family members to talk with their children about what they may have seen and heard so they, too, can help allay any fears or help sort out any misunderstandings that their children may have. Where families and workers share information and feelings together in their concern for the children these form a basis for mutual support and understanding, a good foundation for any future activities together (see PBS parents website for suggestions for talking with children).

What happened? Nothing happened...

During the uprisings in London in the 1980s, many nurseries did not discuss with the children what had happened. Even though children may have heard sirens and witnessed fires, overturned vehicles and police and public confrontations on the streets for several days and listened to their families talking about it all, nursery workers felt it inappropriate to draw attention to this. By pretending that nothing had happened that was of concern to them, children were left with their fears unaddressed, their questions unanswered and puzzlement about the division in their actual experiences. Workers had not prepared themselves for such discussions. In 2005 a similar situation occurred in Birmingham, where in some schools teachers were apparently instructed not to discuss the Lozells disturbances with students or encourage them to talk about it among themselves (see John 2005 and page 51).

Point for thought and discussion

- What are the implications of this case study for professionals working with young children, both for the general curriculum and at times of news reports and possible local disturbances that will be upsetting for children?

The so-called 'war on terror' is likely to make Muslims feel more vulnerable than non-Muslims. In terms of terrorism, however angry people may feel at what has happened, any anti-Islam or anti-Muslim feelings in general must be addressed at every point, whenever they occur. Workers will need to watch and listen very carefully in order to support those children who may be being blamed by association, however subtly, for what has happened. They will need to be confident in their approach to all children, including those who are in any way expressing hostility to Muslim children and their families. Furthermore, children may be perceiving anyone who is not white as being Muslim and responsible for attacks.

Trouble in a turban?

A four-year-old white girl, Charlotte, on arriving at her playgroup said to one of the workers, Sonia, 'There are bad men outside'. When Sonia went outside to see what she had seen there was a group of Sikh taxi drivers wearing turbans talking together around one of their taxis. When Sonia told her mother what she had said she was shocked and said that neither she nor her father had ever said anything to her like this. Neither were they hostile to Sikh men. As a result of this the workers decided to talk more openly with the children in order to raise the issues involved in this incident and to try to identify the reasons why Charlotte had made the assumptions she had.

Point for thought and discussion

- What light does this throw on the requirements of the Race Relations (Amendment) Act for institutions to promote racial equality and good relations between people of different racial groups.

Some children who are perceived as being Muslim may have experienced hostility directly or know of family members who have been abused or attacked themselves. The need for them to feel valued and included in the setting is paramount. Sharing their fears and extending hands of support and compassion to everyone affected, in whatever way, is a positive way of countering any potential racial tension. Carrying on as if nothing had happened may only increase some families' sense of isolation and alienation.

We all need to acknowledge the fragility and chance of the origins of our beliefs so dependent on where we were born, its culture, any religion and our own family. Listening to each other and sharing our fears, our experiences and our stories may help to reaffirm our sense of belonging to a common humanity. Early years settings must remain havens of peace, support and empathy for every child and every family member. All of this demonstrates yet again the critical importance of preparation in advance for such eventualities and of thinking in practical ways about how to respond to children and their families.

If you want to know more

see, for practical support, Baig with Lane (2003), Lane (2005a, 2005g and 2005h), Hyder (2005), Adams and Moyles (2005) and the PBS Parents website.

It is only racism that holds all British Muslims responsible for the wrongs perpetrated in the name of their faith by a tiny minority.

(Paul Gilroy in a debate with Herman Ouseley, 2005)

6 Developing a race equality scheme or policy

Keep in mind always the present you are constructing. It should be the future you want.

(Alice Walker 1989)

The Statutory Framework for the Early Years Foundation Stage states that 'all providers must have and implement an effective policy about ensuring equality of opportunities'. Since 2007, all local authorities, as public authorities, must comply with their statutory duties under legislation on race, sex/gender and disability. These three strands should be incorporated into a single equality scheme or policy, although the actual way that this is done may vary. In terms of good practice the other three equality laws – age, sexual orientation, and religion or belief – should, where appropriate, also be included.

With regard to racial equality, local authorities must comply with the statutory requirements of the amended Race Relations Act 1976 (see Chapter 8 on legislation). This means local authorities having a race equality scheme; and maintained sector early years settings (including children's centres) having a race equality policy. Early years services and any partnerships will be part of the local authority's race equality scheme. As such they will be dependent on the authority generally but will need to ensure that their particular service takes account of the principles for racial equality. Both should have firm procedures and practices to ensure implementation. Early years services and partnerships should consult with all stakeholders about the scheme, for example families of young children from all ethnic groups and communities, particularly those known as not yet included, for example, Travellers, Roma, Gypsies, refugees, asylum seekers, other migrants and minority ethnic communities (see section on consultation, page 148).

Nursery classes within primary schools will be part of the whole-school policy although they should be able to contribute to it, bringing the distinct issues of the early years to the final policy; and other forms of local authority provision will have their own policies or be part of the scheme of the local authority. These should all comply with the strict requirements of the legislation and guidance.

Non-maintained sector settings are not covered by the statute but have for some time been required to have a policy for equality by the DCSF and this is inspected by Ofsted through the Early Years Foundation Stage. Such requirements should be seen as being consistent with the principles of the statutory duty – the moral principles and obligations to promote racial equality should apply in exactly the same way in terms of their commitment and responsibility to put racial equality policies into practice. The policy should be monitored for its effectiveness by the local authority (or EYDCP where relevant), backed up by training, support and, where necessary, sanctions.

This chapter focuses on a race equality *policy* for early years settings but many of the points raised apply also to the services that are required to produce a race equality *scheme*.

Having a policy for racial equality provides a framework for ensuring that all issues of practice and procedure are addressed. It enables workers, families and children to come together in a commitment to ensure everyone, whether already in the setting or potentially so, is fully included.

Developing a policy takes time – it is a process. It is more than just ensuring equality of access, opportunity and treatment for black and other minority ethnic groups. If it is to be effective it must take specific, regular and positive action (using the amended Race Relations Act where appropriate – see the section on page 244 of Chapter 8) to remove existing barriers to racial equality and include mechanisms to ensure that this is done. The provisions of the Race Relations (Amendment) Act stress that providers must actively promote racial equality.

It is not possible to be sure that a setting is practising equality unless it can be measured in some way. If we want all our children, their families and workers to be treated equally we need to think about everything that affects them and ensure practical mechanisms are put in place to demonstrate this.

The process of policy-making provides a forum for finding out what people think and an opportunity to discuss issues of concern to them. It also provides a way of addressing issues of contention in constructive ways. Even though everyone may not agree with one another the process should elicit a common information base on which people can consider the principles behind the policy.

Case study 44

Fairly equal…

The directors of an organisation whose objectives were focused on equality decided they did not need a policy for equality because 'everyone knows our job is about equality' and that somehow having a policy would indicate doubts about this. When provided with an opportunity to express their opinions, several junior workers cited instances where they felt people had not been treated equally. They wanted a policy in order to identify such instances formally.

Point for thought and discussion

- How important is having a policy for equality in promoting equality in an institution?

Because of the variations in any initial training, levels of support, understanding, commitment, resources and training provided by local authorities and others, many settings have only a minimal knowledge of what having a policy means in practice, especially some in the private sector. They are likely to be unfamiliar with the concept of devising an implementation programme or what monitoring entails. This is particularly evident where workers themselves have few relevant qualifications or educational experiences and where training opportunities are limited.

A policy for racial equality should cover everything for which the setting is responsible. It is not just a statement of intention and objectives, it must be accompanied by a detailed programme of what is to be done, how and when, and specific monitoring mechanisms to demonstrate that it is being put into practice. Otherwise it will merely be a paper exercise. The Race Relations (Amendment) Act requires public authorities, including schools, children's centres and any other provision organised by the local authority, to prepare an action plan as part of their race equality schemes and policies. The action plan must include a timeframe, and show how it will be monitored, evaluated and reviewed annually.

Both maintained and non-maintained sector settings will develop their own policies according to their own particular needs and circumstances. The time given to policy development is well spent if it is to be meaningful and owned by all the stakeholders. Settings will need to decide whether they want their policy to cover all equalities together or cover separate ones under a common umbrella. Both have advantages and disadvantages but, on the whole, a fully integrated approach is likely to win more adherents, even if the process of getting integration involves separate policies joining together at a later stage. It is more likely to ensure that everyone involved has a common understanding and acceptance of the various equalities, thus avoiding any competition between them. However, the Race Relations (Amendment) Act requires the race equality scheme or policy to be discrete, easily identifiable and capable of being separated from a full equalities policy or scheme in which it is a component and published.

It is really important to ensure that as many of the stakeholders as possible are familiar with the issues, understand their implications and are committed to implementing racial equality before writing the policy details. Learning to talk together and trust one another are critical to developing an effective policy (see page 56 for discussion of working within a no-blame culture). Although written prior to the implementation of the Race Relations (Amendment) Act in 2002, a detailed process of developing a policy for equality in early years settings is given in EYTARN (2001). Although it is preferable for the setting to write its own materials so that they are pertinent to the particular setting, there are lots of short articles and resources available on which practitioners can draw.

? If you want to know more

in general, see Lane (2003b); about the basic principles, see Pre-School Learning Alliance (PLA) (2005), Lane (2006d) and Kahn and Young (2007). Scanning through the references may identify other potentially helpful articles.

The advantages of having a policy for racial equality

While some people may feel threatened by the prospect of developing a policy – perhaps because they don't think it is necessary, they fear it may upset other people in the process or raise a hornet's nest where none was previously – there are real advantages to be had when it is finally agreed. In addition to the advantages listed in the publications cited above, a policy does the following.

⏩ A policy provides the opportunity for equality issues not covered by legislation to be considered and included – on grounds, for example, of social class or socioeconomic status, the variety of family backgrounds, culture, where people live, what jobs they have, whether they are employed or not, what they wear (including dress codes to comply with religious or cultural requirements) and what they look like – in terms of treating everyone with equal respect and dignity.

⏩ It provides support to back up and address potential family or workers' concerns about the setting's practice. For example, how far should a setting go towards agreeing to particular parental or worker's requests that may conflict with the policy for equality? (For further discussion see Lane 2005f.)

⏩ It ensures that time is given to the critical importance of discussions between everyone involved, but particularly among workers, in order to share ideas, identify disagreements and ambiguities, accept the differences between people and come to a shared understanding of the need for and rationale behind a policy for equality.

⏩ It builds up confidence to deal with the issues that are now out in the open and no longer lurking unidentified and unchallenged, and provides a framework for addressing them.

The role of an equalities coordinator in settings

In 2001, the DfES required all early years settings to appoint and train an equalities coordinator (ECO) to take responsibility for equality issues in similar ways to special needs coordinators (SENCOs). Area SENCOs were also appointed and funded (see page 270 for further discussion).

Currently there is a wide variety between authorities that have undertaken this task of ensuring the appointment and training of ECOs and those that have done very little or nothing at all. Rarely have they appointed an Area ECO. The differences in types of authorities in terms of being rural or urban do not correlate with those that have ensured the appointment of ECOs or not – urban authorities are just as likely or unlikely to have taken action as rural ones.

Some settings have taken the issue seriously and appointed someone with experience to undertake the task. Others have given the task to anyone prepared to do it regardless of their knowledge and suitability – some have appointed a person with minimal experience or training just because they are black, expecting them to have a natural understanding of the work. Training of ECOs and the competence of trainers vary greatly across the country. This unsatisfactory situation reflects the lack of commitment at many levels to address equality issues. It has implications for developing a policy for equality in settings and raises potential issues of conflict between the role of SENCOs and ECOs.

An effective ECO can provide a bridge between the early years service and workers in the settings when developing an equality policy as well as in its implementation and monitoring. An ECO can be a focus for: sharing information; collecting and disseminating it; identifying training needs; addressing, and liaising with, families not yet included in the authority's provision; explaining its rationale to family members; and liaising with the service on data collection and monitoring. Local support groups for ECOS should be a part of a support strategy from the service.

If you want to know more

about work in local authorities to support ECOs, Oxfordshire has provided a coordinated and practical training programme (see Selleck 2005 for details) and for a suggested job description/person specification for an ECO see Lane (2005j). For a video on the role of an ENCO and work with parents, see Wolverhampton Early Years Team (2003). (For information on ECO training done in Birmingham and Wolverhampton see Inspire training for ECOs.)

The process of developing a policy for racial equality

The statutory Code of Practice on the duty to promote race equality under the Race Relations (Amendment) Act gives comprehensive guidelines for the race equality policy (see CRE 2002a, Appendix 4 and Chapter 8).

The policy must consist of three parts: a policy statement about the aims and values; an action plan and programme for implementation; and a monitoring mechanism.

The policy must be a working document that establishes agreed values and objectives for equality, and one that is used as a source of confirmation of the principles of the setting practice. It must be monitored and reviewed annually, to evaluate how effective it has been in meeting the equality targets it has set, to check that the practices and principles are still appropriate, and to set new targets and actions if necessary.

Getting the race equality policy right is a priority where equality principles are seen as important. Several groups of people should be consulted and equally involved in the run-up to developing it. Settings should involve and consult with all people working there, the families and potential families using the setting, children, governors, management and committee members, and relevant and appropriate members of the local community. Families are crucial people to be actively involved in policy-making not only because they are powerful influencers of their children's racial attitudes and behaviour but also because their support is crucial to make the policy work in practice. It is an opportunity to engage them in ways of ensuring that their children are provided with positive racial attitudes, both in the setting and at home, and of getting their support for addressing the attitudes of families who may be less enthusiastic about this issue. There are various ways of consulting (see page 148 for discussion about consultation mechanisms, including policy-making).

The consultation and involvement process should include information about policies for racial equality (translated and interpreted where necessary and in audio-visual form where appropriate), that they are a government requirement, why they are essential, what they might mean in practice and how they are to be implemented and monitored.

A policy for racial equality should include the following.

A statement of intent about racial equality in employment and all services for young children in the setting. It should include everyone – white, Jewish, Irish and black people, people from other minority ethnic groups, mixed race people, Travellers, Roma, Gypsies, refugees and asylum seekers and other migrants.

An action plan to achieve equal outcomes in everything carried out by the setting, with timescales for how long it will take to achieve, who is to do it, who is to check that it has been done and any training and resource needs, including funding. It is usually advisable to agree a rationale on the reasons for the specific aspects of the programme in advance of writing it. For example, what racial hierarchies are, why dismantling them is important and how the process of doing this will be undertaken.

A mechanism for regular monitoring of the policy's effectiveness, including its implementation programme.

This will involve collecting and evaluating data monitored by ethnicity on all relevant aspects of the setting to identify any discrepancies or differential outcomes for different ethnic groups. The monitoring is to look at groups, not individuals (Lane 1998 and Chapter 8). For example, in terms of children accessing their entitlement to the curriculum, it is critical to examine (usually by careful observation) whether any particular ethnic groups (boys and girls separately) have less or more access to some of its aspects. Are bilingual children or children learning English as an additional language provided with the same learning opportunities as everyone else? And is the Foundation Stage Profile revealing any disadvantages or discrimination against any particular ethnic group of children? Could there be differences in achievement or other outcomes within particular ethnic groups, for example by gender or socioeconomic status, that may be disguised because data collection methods record ethnic groups as homogeneous? Are the ethnic groups so broadly defined that they are unhelpful, and cannot demonstrate the information a setting needs? An example of such monitoring would be when the category 'Black African' is used in areas where the achievement of children from asylum seeking communities cannot be distinguished from that of longer settled communities; or 'Asian' where Indian, Bangladeshi and Pakistani children are not identified separately. Issues of social class may be very important distinguishing factors in some of these examples. There needs to be:

- a race equality impact assessment (see page 249)
- procedures for promoting racial equality and addressing any inequalities
- procedures for removing or rectifying any racial discrimination found, and a commitment to doing so

- careful analyses of all employment recruitment and admission arrangements to ensure that they are not racially discriminatory and that all job descriptions and person specifications require employees to be committed to the implementation of racial equality in the early years
- a method for keeping effective records of children in the setting – including details of their full name, the name they are known by, date of birth, country of birth, any religion, diet, ethnicity (including mixed race), first language, first language of parents or carers, any other languages spoken at home, any experiences of previous early years settings, health, and attendance at a supplementary mother-tongue class, project or school
- a timetable for action on all the above
- a clearly defined allocation of responsibility for implementation of the policy at the highest employment level and for action at every level
- regular reviews of the policy, action plans and implementation programmes and monitoring mechanisms to check on their effectiveness
- a policy on racial harassment (see Chapter 7).

Some of the issues that may be raised in developing a policy are discussed below – the issues spelt out in each may overlap, so reading them all may be helpful. For example, developing a policy in mainly white areas may have similarities with 'working without support' and with 'families who disagree with the policy'.

If you want to know more

read a short introduction to the issues to consider in developing a policy (Lane 2003b).

The involvement of families in developing a policy for equality

Where friendly relationships with families are fostered, possibilities are opened up to remove barriers and to identify issues to share so that children can be as supported as possible – for example by providing important information about their cultural, ethnic and any religious backgrounds. Such relationships are fundamental to developing a policy for equality together. These early years are when the foundations of children's subsequent attitudes and behaviour are established. It is a period of intense learning for children and also a time when family members are most involved in their care and education.

Early years settings are one of the most significant opportunities in childhood where family members meet workers when taking and collecting their children, so initial and ongoing discussions about the setting's equality policy, together with these meetings, provide a considerable potential for interaction. Because of the closeness of family members with their children it is important to involve them as much as possible in understanding and supporting the work on racial equality done with their children – they are critical (but not the only) influencers of their children's attitudes and behaviour. Families can, together, learn about and experience communities different from theirs. Where workers and families work together for equality and share the reasons for doing it within an ethos of mutual trust, there is potential for changing any pre-existing racist attitudes and behaviour and for developing that sense of belonging to a group with similar objectives.

Case study 45

Debbie and Pria

The father of four-year-old Debbie, who is white and attends a nursery, was an active member of the National Front (an organisation based on racist ideology). The nursery did not have a policy for equality. One day Debbie was racially abusive to Pria, who is three and whose family had migrated from India.

The nursery headteacher first comforted Pria, saying they all loved having her in the nursery and that the comments Debbie had made were untrue. She then talked with and supported Debbie, explaining that what she had said was hurtful and was the sort of thing that other people in the nursery believed was unacceptable and wrong. She was very careful to make sure that Debbie knew that everyone thought that she was a valued member of the nursery. After some discussion they parted.

Later on Debbie came back to the headteacher and asked 'Does my daddy know it's wrong?' The headteacher realised the potential conflict that might have been caused in Debbie's mind. She spoke with Debbie's father about what had happened but he didn't really appear to understand and was hostile to what she was trying to do.

Points for thought and discussion

Several issues emerge here.

- If the nursery had had a policy for racial equality, these issues should have been addressed and discussed in the induction meeting. The policy on racist incidents would have been explained and the father given an opportunity to comment on it. The family could then have decided whether their daughter should attend such a nursery and the nursery could have talked about every family's responsibility to comply with the policy.
- Should the headteacher have used the word 'wrong' in this connection as it clearly implied that Debbie's father was wrong, thus reinforcing conflict in Debbie's mind? Would something like 'most people don't really want to call one another hurtful names' have been better?
- More activity about name-calling and hurtful remarks should have been part of the nursery practice.
- There is a near impossibility of avoiding Pria's hurt or Debbie's bewilderment in the absence of a strategy, including an explicit policy, to be proactive about such incidents.
- How can a setting balance an apparently racist father's beliefs with the nursery wanting to give his daughter an opportunity to consider another point of view on racist name-calling?

It is important to work with families to try to come to a joint understanding of what a policy should contain so that, together, they can all own it. Where children experience a set of values about racial equality in the setting and a different set of values at home they are likely to be confused. They may resolve it by avoiding it, they may make up their own minds and express what they feel or they may keep quiet perhaps puzzling in their own minds about what or who is 'right'.

In addition it is useful to have a basic policy on the responsibilities of both staff and children so as to avoid any cultural misunderstandings where families and staff may have unwittingly had different expectations of each other's roles – such things as times to collect and bring children, what to do when they are unwell and the settings responsibilities while the children are in their care.

Involving fathers in developing the policy in the same way as mothers and, possibly, other family members too is important. And it is particularly important to try to involve fathers who are not living with their children. Many are keen to be involved in their children's upbringing but may feel reluctant and apprehensive about taking a positive role in the setting's activities and in policy-making. Data from the 2001 census shows that more Black Caribbean, Black African and Mixed families are headed by a lone parent than white families. Taking specific actions to involve such fathers in as much of their children's early years experiences as possible, including in the setting and in policy-making, may help build up positive and mutually beneficial roles for the family members, even when they are not living together (see Guishard-Pine (2006) for research on men in black families; and Barnardo's Babyfather Initiative, encouraging responsible parenting among black men, especially those separated from their children, page 307).

Because all families are potentially an integral part of their children's learning process, developing a policy is an opportunity for them to be involved in considering their attitudes towards people from a variety of cultural, religious and ethnic backgrounds – to evaluate them within the context of the society in which we all live and to provide positive support about racial equality for their own children in their home lives. But perhaps the greatest opportunity, with the most rewards, is being involved in developing a cohesive and inclusive early years setting where children, their families and workers all take steps towards a shared objective of belonging and equality for all, both inside the setting and outside in the wider community. On this basis they can, together, develop a policy for racial equality that encompasses these factors and perspectives (see page 142 for a discussion about families helping their children to learn positive racial attitudes).

It may be impossible for every setting to comply with every family's wishes and, at the same time, maintain a set of principles about equality that give every child an opportunity to consider a point of view different from a family's racist attitudes and that protect children from racist abuse. And there is likely always to be the hope that taking part in the nursery's ethos of equality will perhaps enable family members to reconsider any previous negative attitudes. But sometimes it means saying something like 'Well that's our basic policy, which we have thought long and hard about. I hope you will give the matter some more thought. We do expect all our nursery community to adhere to the policy.' For a discussion on parental requests for practice that conflicts with the setting's policy for equality see Lane (2005f).

The majority of families who visit the early years setting for the first time are usually happy to discuss the policy for equality or the policy for racial equality in the context of looking at everything that is done. It is important to explain, at this early stage, exactly what it involves and to provide them with appropriate written materials as back-up. Ensuring that they know that there are regular opportunities for re-considering aspects of the policy and whether it needs to be updated, should be built into the induction process.

For families, the ability to see for themselves what goes on in the early years setting and to take part in its activities will demonstrate the value of being positive about differences. It is particularly useful if families work on tasks together with workers in settings, such as putting together the policy for equality or the implementation programme or examining resources. For example, families and those working with the children could, together, devise criteria for selecting resources.

Not all families have the same understanding of early years education and care. There are often distinct cultural differences and it is therefore helpful to give every family an opportunity to discuss ideas, share information and ask questions. This is particularly important where there is no common shared written means of communication or where some family members may be unable to read and write. Explaining what is being done and why, from the inside, will help families to understand, rather than feel that they are on the outside looking in.

To enter an early years setting where middle-class white values predominate must be daunting for those whose experiences are different. Creating an ethos where everyone feels they belong equally is very important. Only then can real trust and equality be put into practice, from which a meaningful policy for equality can derive.

Parents have many other commitments – work, caring for the rest of the family, personal lifestyles, celebrating particular festivals, observing specific religious duties or taking part in particular cultural events – that may influence their ability or willingness to contribute to the setting's activities. Although there are clearly exceptions to this, parents from black and other minority ethnic groups are more likely to live in low-income households than white parents (see page 131 for details). The pressures on their lives may therefore be considerable. According to the 2001 census African-Caribbean women are more likely to work full time, so they may find it particularly difficult to attend during the day. Some families will be totally unfamiliar with the concept of participation so will not come until they feel comfortable in their role. Others may be afraid of a possible 'Us and Them' culture, be in awe of any form of educational provision, or have had an unhappy school experience themselves. Some will attend regularly and others not at all. So long as everyone's needs have been addressed and all are equally welcome then all that can be done is to persist in trying to include everyone.

Letting people know that they are welcome requires continuous attention from the setting staff. It is important to ensure that the physical environment of the setting affirms that all communities are welcome and have a part to play. The displays around the setting should reflect a diverse community. Keeping a perpetual open door to all activities means that no particular group can become a clique or appear to be in charge, thus possibly excluding other individuals and groups. One significant measure that helps to include black and other minority ethnic group families is where the members of such groups are employed in the setting. For families where their children are learning English as an additional language, the employment of bilingual workers is particularly helpful.

Whatever happens and whoever attends, it must not be assumed that the people who attend ongoing discussions speak for the rest. Consultation must include all parents – none are representative of all others. This is as critical when a black person is a governor or member of the management committee as it is for a white person. Although black people are likely to have some experience of racism in common with other black people, they are no more likely to represent all black people's opinions and ideas than a white person would be to represent all white people's opinions and ideas. Full consultation should take place unless there is some formal mechanism whereby an elected delegate is accountable to the 'electorate' and where real discussion can take place.

There has been a lot written about the importance of parental involvement and partnership with services and settings both in the past and more recently, although few recent ones concern black and other minority ethnic families specifically (Kenway 1994, EYTARN 1995b, Ball 1997, Sure Start 2004a, NCB 2006, DCSF 2008b and, for an inclusive parent programme, see REU (now the Race Equality Foundation) *Strengthening Families, Strengthening Communities*). Particular efforts need to be made to ensure that all family members are involved in devising and re-evaluating the policy for racial equality and that the involvement includes being equal partners in the process. However, whatever happens, workers need to realise that, unless they are in exceptional situations, they are likely to have more power in the worker / family partnership than family members.

Working with families who disagree with the setting's policy for racial equality

While cooperation between families and settings is one of the surest ways to implement a successful policy for racial equality, people working with children must address racism even where families are unsupportive or hostile. Racism is wrong and must be worked against whatever the circumstances. This is supported by legislation.

Where a parent or other family member does not agree with the setting's policy for racial equality, further discussion may need to take place. There are principles about the policy, which are not negotiable, for example the fundamental *principle* of opposing racism is fixed, while the *methods* for countering it need to be flexible and open to new ideas.

Once a policy has been agreed, new parents will need to discuss it and endorse it if their child is to attend the setting. While parents should be given the opportunity to comment on the policy before their child attends, negative parental attitudes (or those of other family members) may be revealed during the induction. A dilemma arises if a parent refuses to accept the principles of racial equality, which can be summed up in three questions:

1   Should the parent's child be accepted into the setting to give them an opportunity to hear ideas that they may not hear at home?
2   Might the child's presence (and that of the family members) make it difficult and uncomfortable to be positive about equality?
3   More seriously, might the child or a family member say or do something that is hurtful to or about children from minority ethnic backgrounds and their families, whether such children are present in the setting or not?

Efforts should be made to explain the basis of the policy and the reasons behind it and new parents encouraged to participate in the activities of the setting to ensure that they are familiar with the practical implications of the policy.

When opposition to the policy persists, a decision about whether or not to accept the child into the setting will have to be made according to the circumstances. It is important to bear in mind always that people do change their minds, that they do sometimes admit that they had not really thought things through or understood what was meant and that a child, wherever possible, should be given an opportunity to reflect on what racial equality means in practice.

The situation is less serious if the principle is accepted but the methods are challenged. Such disagreements may encourage the setting to consider the methods they use from another point of view. The way a policy is implemented should always be open for discussion and possible changes.

If a family objects to a policy after seeming to have accepted it at first, this should be addressed by going back to the policy and talking about it together. For example, a mother might say that she does not want her son to play with dolls (let alone black dolls), or she might comment that there are too many black children in the setting. There is no simple way to deal with situations like this, but openly accusing this mother of being racist is unlikely to achieve anything constructive. The most important thing is to persuade her to reconsider, perhaps by reading something (Brown 1999, PLA 2001, Lane 2003a, Gill and Lane 2004 or a sample of articles listed in the references and in Lane 2006d); talking to someone else (perhaps another parent, a governor or manager); or coming into the early years setting to see and understand what is going on in practice. It is important, however, to state at an early stage that the policy of the setting is clear – that it values all children equally, and that the person with overall responsibility has every right to insist on the ethical values and principles of the setting being followed by the whole setting community – staff, parents and carers, and children.

Case study 46

Bad press

A mother of a child at a nursery attended a conference where a particular tabloid newspaper was described as fuelling racist attitudes towards asylum seekers. She blushed because it was the one read by her family at home. She went home and asked her husband why they read that newspaper. He replied that they had always read it. She began to think about the values that it was portraying and realised that, indeed, it constantly depicted people who sought asylum in Britain in negative ways. As a result she gave much more positive support to the nursery's work on equality issues and the family changed their newspaper.

Point for thought and discussion

- To what extent do you think the attitudes and understandings picked up by children in the early years stem from newspapers read and television watched by their parents and carers?

Working in these situations requires skill, patience and determination to overcome any apparent barriers – and it may take a long time to succeed. All those working with children need to practise dealing with a variety of complex situations (Elfer (ed) 1995, Lane 1999b, Lane 2001a, Gill and Lane 2004).

Developing a policy without support

Although every setting is required to have a policy for equality, many will initially only be minimal statements of intent. It is possible that some early years services will have neither real commitment nor have allocated resources to support settings, and inspections may not have identified a policy as a priority especially if the other aspects are satisfactory. In some settings a manager or leader may appear to be blocking progress in various ways, for example by prioritising other issues or never actually getting round to doing anything about it. Whatever the reasons for inaction, workers are often not in positions of power and influence themselves to devise a policy alone without the support of the manager or leader. Despite the legal requirements for a policy, the resources to monitor and ensure this are not yet in place nationally. In all such circumstances, therefore, it is only committed individuals, if there are any, who are then in a position to move things forward. They need to inform and prepare themselves so they are in a stronger position to raise policy issues in their own setting, for example by:

- identifying materials to support and train themselves
- seeking allies among other workers in the setting, in other settings, in the local authority, in national equality groups or elsewhere
- using persuasion, through discussion with colleagues
- encouraging others to read some basic articles, for example Lane (2003b)

- drawing attention to the possible sanctions if a policy and action plan are not produced, for example a poor Ofsted inspection report or criticism and possible identification by the local authority, legal action for non-compliance with the Act
- developing a rationale, based on legislation and DCSF and Ofsted requirements, for why a policy is needed in the particular setting, why it would be of benefit and linking it to all other inequalities – this could be used to seek support from the local authority to run a pilot project on developing a policy for equality that could be shared with others to encourage them with a practical example
- raising issues of concern at meetings
- raising the profile of the issues, and so putting pressure on reluctant managers
- asking for issues to be put on the agendas of the management committee or governors' meetings.

Examples of what racial prejudice is and how it may be manifested in early years settings are often useful methods of helping others to understand what it actually means to children and their families. Evidence from research about the early age that children recognise skin colour differences and how they may learn to put different values on them is also important. Real-life incidents and narratives from the setting are often more persuasive than theoretical analyses – and usually people's hearts have to be touched so that they realise the serious implications of what is being raised. It is important, too, to be clear about why it is necessary if the area is largely white.

It may be hard to find allies and to reject accusations of being eccentric or as having a chip on your shoulder. However, it is crucial to do both of these. Link up with other people working in the same way and join national groups that work for equality. Having this kind of support helps to maintain a realistic perspective on the situation.

People are often fearful of setting up a policy for equality. They are afraid of what it might entail and of the racism they might encounter, especially in largely white or rural areas. What they do not know or yet have the confidence to believe is that having a policy is actually likely to make life easier for them. A framework to refer to and an atmosphere of constant discussion reduces the fear of the unknown, and the process of policy-making helps prepare everyone involved to think about the issues through knowing and addressing the facts.

Sometimes people are anxious about tackling racism but are prepared to consider issues around other forms of inequality, for example about disability. This may be because it is seen as less difficult, threatening and emotive. It is also why an integrated approach to all equalities might initially be preferable to focusing on the particular issues of race. However, in public authority settings there is a legal requirement to have a discrete race equality policy. This should be part of a broader equalities policy, but must be capable of being pulled out, and must be published. In other circumstances black people may specifically want a policy to focus on race because their experience of an integrated approach may have meant that race was marginalised. Each situation must therefore be considered on its own merits.

In some situations, in order to place the particular race aspects in a broader context less likely to cause controversy, it may be a useful starting point to suggest having an initial policy on name-calling, all forms of name-calling on whatever basis. No one wishes their child to be called a name and everyone may agree that it is important to try to stop it. This cannot be done in an ad hoc way but only through a strategy where all families and workers support the objective (even though it may mean admitting some name-calling on their own or their children's part), incidents are recorded and follow-up work is undertaken and evaluated (for details of a suggested policy see page 234; the appendix of EYTARN 2001; and Lane 2001b).

Building up the policy and implementation programme slowly but surely, and checking on how it is going all the time, are the fundamental principles on which to operate. Obviously, rushing in without careful thought and planning would be likely to give trouble. But the policy can be seen as starting on the very first day that the first constructive discussions are held (videos and films may be helpful – for example, Jane Elliott's *The eye of the storm* and Persona Doll Training's *Celebrating diversity*).

Working towards a policy in mainly white areas

In mainly white areas issues of racism may be seen by some people as irrelevant. The misguided concept that such areas have no problem (because no black people apparently live there) is frequently voiced. But the problem is racism, not black people, and therefore it is all the more necessary to have a policy in order to dispel this myth as being irrelevant and potentially dangerous. The Race Relations (Amendment) Act requires the promotion of 'good relations between people of different racial groups'. So, even though there are likely to be few people from different racial groups living in the area, the responsibility to promote good relations remains. Because racism exists in white areas as well as in multicultural areas this responsibility should be taken particularly seriously. For evidence of such racism see Jay (1992), Derbyshire (1994), Nizhar (1995) and Henderson and Kaur (1999).

Apart from the need to address racism generally it is important to prepare children for living in our wider multicultural society whatever particular area they live in now. Living in a multicultural and multiethnic community means that resources for promoting good relations are more readily available, and there are opportunities for meeting people from a variety of cultural backgrounds. There is likely to be a variety of shops to use, places of worship to visit and multicultural resource centres for information.

But due to the absence of many people from black and other minority ethnic communities in mainly white areas, there are some very specific considerations to bear in mind when working with families and, possibly, with other workers. While some people will not have thought about issues of racial equality, others may hold racist views and have moved away from multicultural areas for that reason. Putting racial equality on the agenda nearly always involves one or two committed individuals who may struggle for years before seeing the rewards of their efforts.

If you want to know more

read a description of such an effort in Newbery (2006); page 106 for discussion of general issues about living in white areas; and EYTARN (1993a), Dhalech (2000), DfES (2004) and Edwards and others (2006) for issues about working in largely white areas.

Although the fact that nearly everyone is likely to be white has specific implications, the suggestions made under the section 'Developing a policy without support' (see page 177) may be useful here too.

Here are some additional suggestions.

▶ Read about the reality of racism in Britain, get facts on racial discrimination and be clear about what racism is and is not (see Chapter 2 and suggestions in Chapter 10 on essential knowledge).

▶ Be alert to how the media may influence the attitudes of people to those who are seen as different, particularly those who the media have sometimes demonised even when they have no personal experiences of them – for example, asylum seekers, Muslims, some migrant workers and Travellers, Roma and Gypsies.

▶ Attend training on using Persona Dolls with children – using such Dolls (see page 207) is likely to form an important part of the work with children in developing their concepts of empathy, equal value and respect.

▶ Be clear about why it is important and helpful, in principle, to have a policy – to provide a framework in which to work (a strategic approach rather than an ineffective ad hoc one) – and be able to explain the reasons for it, to identify what needs to be done in practice and how the involvement of families and children in devising it will help a general understanding and possibly provide potential support in making it work.

▶ Devise a rationale to underpin a policy, including notions of:
  – a shared humanity, similarities and differences
  – what sort of people we want our children to be (e.g. to value and respect each other?)
  – evidence from research on racism in white areas (see Further Reading)
  – how children learn to be prejudiced
  – the early age of attitude formation
  – how children may be damaged by holding racially prejudiced attitudes
  – how racially prejudiced children can become capable of valuing children and adults who are different from themselves if they come to live in the area or if they meet them in their future lives
  – every area aiming to have representation from minority ethnic communities, for example, refugees and asylum seekers as, even if the area is not multicultural and multiethnic, children may live and work in such areas in the future

- needing to act because if nothing is done to develop positive attitudes in children they may get negative information about black people from television and other sources anyway
- requirements for a policy from the Race Relations (Amendment) Act, Ofsted and DCSF
- the legal duty of the Race Relations (Amendment) Act to 'promote good relations between people of different racial groups' (see Lane 2004a and page 250 for some practical suggestions)
- establishing the commonalities and links between all inequalities and citing examples of these with regard to disability, gender, sexual orientation and socioeconomic situations.

▶ Share the rationale with other workers and take time to discuss it with them to gain their commitment and understanding. Try to identify people who will support the policy and ensure that they are present at initial discussions.

▶ Discuss any potential obstacles and difficulties that might arise and be explicit about the need to hear their views and ideas.

▶ Ask what might be involved in implementing the policy – consider examining resources, attending training and particularly the specific work that might be undertaken – using Persona Dolls, circle time, breaking down racial hierarchies and sharing these things with families and eliciting their support and cooperation.

▶ Find a solution to the lack of appropriate resources in the setting and of real finance available in the current financial year. The general resources and pictures around in the setting should reflect a diverse community, so that children see this as part of the world in which they live. Even where there is a total lack of resources reflecting our multicultural society and where there is no money to buy them immediately, it can still be possible to raise issues of valuing the differences between people. While it is easier to talk about skin colour differences if you have dolls with a range of skin colours, even white people have different coloured skin tones, hair and eyes. Used as part of the curriculum, these conversations can provide many starting points for discussions with young children. (See video Persona Doll Training (2004) for ideas and the section on play resources, page 204.)

▶ Consider and plan with workers the most effective way to embark upon the process of policy development – meetings with families, individual conversations, communicating in writing and having discussions on the basic values everyone wishes for the children (see section on developing a policy without support on page 177 and suggestions in EYTARN 2001).

Journey into the unknown

A development worker in a rural area suggested that workers from a few local settings might visit the nearest multicultural town some miles away one Saturday, visit some local shops and have a meal in an Asian restaurant. Many workers viewed this idea with horror and alarm – they would never dare venture into such a 'dangerous' area. However, a few agreed to join one another on a trip. They had a wonderful time, were delighted with what they saw, brought back some resources to add to their collection and came back full of excitement at what they had achieved. The next time such a visit was planned there was a clamour for places.

Points for thought and discussion

- How important is it for professionals to have an informed view of diverse communities?
- How important is direct experience of areas with diverse communities in informing understanding and breaking down any apprehensions?

Some of the principles and methods for working on the policy might include the following.

▶ Go in gently but with a firm understanding of why it is important to establish and implement a policy for racial equality. Be armed with lots of good examples of what the policy might mean in practice.

▶ Carefully plan and prepare all work with children in consultation with parents, children and those working with them. This means analysing and understanding the real reasons for wanting to acknowledge our multicultural society in as natural and positive a way as possible, perhaps by thinking and comparing how white people might wish their culture or cultures to be introduced to people from other cultures. A recognition and acceptance of our common humanity comes before celebrating our differences. All this may take time.

▶ Establish credibility as advocates for children, take time to talk with people about their views and try to explain and justify the reasons for working in this way before appearing to impose resources and ideas on children and their families.

▶ Everyone is to be equally valued, so every aspect of life in the setting has to be examined to ensure that this is happening.

▶ Consider starting with addressing identity and differences within the setting – in languages and accents spoken (include language and dialect or regional accent), skin colours (including among white people), hair colour and textures, and physical features. Celebrate the diversity of the people in the setting and in the community. Look at the diversity of lifestyle situations including work skills (being sensitive to those who do not have paid work and how some work may be considered more 'important' than others), celebrations, families and extended families (ensuring that all family situations and structures are seen as normal). Take care to value all and ensure that no-one is asked to reveal information that would embarrass them. Be aware that people from some communities, such as asylum-seeking communities, may be reluctant to give personal information because of their previous experience of persecution and fear of how such information might be used. Some others may have a strong sense of privacy. Involve parents and carers in building up a picture of a diverse setting in a diverse community (see section on celebrating differences and similarities, page 211).

- Once the principle of valuing differences in general has been introduced, work to help children value ethnic and cultural differences should be easier.

- Prepare workers in being able to address dissent about the policy in principle. Avoid appearing to contrive circumstances of a local multicultural society which fly in the face of reality and which alienates some people because they positively do not want to live in such a society. Affirm the local, regional, national and global communities, and show that the children will almost certainly live in a diverse community during their lifetime.

Employment

What struck me was that the black people I saw were not coming to the 'race' meeting but that they worked there every day

(adviser on racial equality attending a meeting on race in a city hall)

Employment is a critical issue for racial equality. Who works in a setting as paid employees or volunteers not only determines how good the opportunities for children to learn and develop their potentials are, but also whether all have equality of opportunity to access settings and to learn and develop positive attitudes and behaviour to differences between people. It is important for those responsible for recruiting workers and volunteers to be aware of legislation on racial equality and to be familiar with equality principles throughout the whole recruitment and selection process. This applies equally to both the maintained and non-maintained sectors. Furthermore employers need to be aware of their responsibilities under legislation to ensure that all employees comply with the law – they may be held liable for an act of discrimination by an employee, whether or not the act was done with their knowledge or approval (see pages 198 and 243 for examples of an employer's liability in a setting).

The local authority should be able to provide settings with data on the ethnic composition of the local population and also guidance on recruitment and selection practices and procedures with regard to equality and compliance with current legislation. Maintained sector settings will need to provide ethnically monitored data on employment to their local authority. Non-maintained sector settings will also need to have a policy on employment; and the early years service should be requiring data from the monitoring of the policy in order to evaluate whether it is non-discriminatory and effective. Ofsted also requires an equality policy to include employment practice.

In order to recruit a workforce that is based on principles of racial equality and able to ensure racial equality in all its practices and procedures, the following points may be helpful.

- Ensure that someone in authority (management, governor or personnel) is well versed on the amended Race Relations Act and is able to advise on the equality principles of recruitment and selection procedures (see Chapter 8).

- Consult with local community members and families about what data to collect on applicants for jobs and how to do it. The census may be used as a basis for comparison but other factors may also be important to record (see page 148 for information about consultation).

- In consultation with local community members and families, devise a rationale as to why it is necessary to collect ethnic data and to monitor it throughout the recruitment and selection procedures in order to identify any racial discrimination and ensure racial equality. Ensure that the rationale includes information on data protection issues (see page 252 for information about data collection and monitoring).

- Devise a flier to advertise a job with a prominent statement about being committed to ensuring equality, and with some information as to what that means in practice (for a guide to job advertisements see CRE 1993).

- Devise a job description that includes a responsibility for all workers to promote racial equality and identify and remove any racial discrimination.

- Draw up a person specification for the job that includes an essential requirement of commitment to ensuring the implementation of racial equality. Jobs at senior levels should also require knowledge, skills and understanding of the implications of ensuring racial equality. A criterion of commitment is essential as without it progress cannot be made – with that basic commitment it is possible to build up other aspects of what is required.

- Have a separate page for ethnic monitoring (and include gender and disability) to go with the application form as part of the application process. Include an explanation of the reasons for this monitoring.

- Advertise the job widely, using formal and informal ways of getting it known. Some jobs will be nationally advertised but all ways should be used for every job so far as possible – the media, local shops, places of worship, health centres, community centres and organisations, libraries, schools and other education places, local race equality councils, and distributing fliers in all localities.

- Ensure everyone involved in the recruitment and selection process is trained in the principles of equality in employment. Ensure that those involved in any short-listing or interviewing are competent to implement these principles in practice (see Darling and Hedge 1992).

- Plan any interview dates to avoid key religious occasions.

- Receive applications and record ethnicity on each.

- Organise any short- and long-listing to take account of the principles of legislation and guidance on racial equality, recording decisions by ethnicity.

◈ Prepare any interview procedures, including any questions or tasks to be completed. Assess commitment by devising specific questions such as 'What would you do if…' to elicit attitudes, practical experience, constructive analysis and critical thinking.

◈ Provide constructive, sensitive and carefully thought-out feedback to non-appointees.

◈ Analyse the ethnically monitored data to identify any apparent disparities of outcome in the whole process.

◈ Take action to remove any discrimination if identified.

◈ Consider whether any positive action should be taken to recruit people (both men and women) from specific ethnic groups in the local community who appear to be either not applying for jobs or not succeeding in getting them (see Chapter 8 on positive action).

◈ Reflect on the way the process worked in practice and discuss whether any changes should be made for the future.

See Lane (1999a) for suggestions on opening up access to qualifications and training.

Of course there is more to good employment practice than recruitment. A systematic approach to developing and maintaining good practice should include a policy for employment so that racial discrimination or harassment are identified and removed. Opportunities for promotion, training or other benefits, for example being invited to attend a management meeting, should be monitored. All of this is part of best human resources practice, and should be included in human resources procedures and referred to in race equality schemes and policies. Although the following publications may initially appear daunting, in practice the CRE material is easy to read, clear and practical. The basic principles of these publications should be known and understood (see CRE 2002a *Statutory Code of Practice on the Duty to Promote Race Equality*, CRE 2002b *A Guide for Public Authorities/Local Authorities*, CRE 2002c *A Guide for Schools*, CRE 2002d *Ethnic Monitoring: A guide for public authorities/local government*, CRE 2004c *Public Authorities and Partnerships: A guide to the duty to promote race equality*, CRE 2005b the *Statutory Code of Practice on Racial Equality in Employment*).

Establishing a multiethnic workforce

Evidence shows that workers from minority ethnic backgrounds in the early years workforce approximately reflect their composition in the population at large – about 8 per cent (Sure Start 2004b and ONS 2006). More recent surveys show there is generally a greater proportion of black workers in full day care than in sessional care – with 14 per cent in full day care in children's centres; 13 per cent in holiday clubs; 12 per cent in after-school clubs; 9 per cent in full day care other than children's centres; 6 per cent with childminders; and 5 per cent in sessional settings. There is a greater proportion of black workers in primary schools with a nursery class than those without – 8 per cent compared with 2 per cent (DCSF 2007b). (The situation of children from black and other minority ethnic backgrounds in provision similarly reflects this ethnic composition.) A recent overview of providers shows a slight increase in the percentage of black workers in full-time and sessional care but fewer childminders (DfES 2006c). Of course, in areas of high or low minority ethnic population the percentages will be different and should reflect those areas proportionately. London has by far the largest number of workers from black and other minority ethnic groups compared to any other area, with surprisingly few in the West Midlands. The data is not broken down into specific ethnic groups or their levels of employment. Furthermore, identification was assessed by managers and not by the workers themselves, who may or may not have correct data. It is always important that, wherever possible, people identify their ethnicity themselves. In an earlier survey, there were more people from an African-Caribbean background working in the early years than from a South Asian background (LGMB 1998). This is likely to be true today.

However, from anecdotal and other subjective information, it appears that workers from black and other minority ethnic groups are under-represented at senior levels of employment. Whatever the reasons for this – and some at least are possibly due to racial discrimination in the education and employment systems – to be a truly multiethnic workforce, black and white people need to be employed roughly in proportion to their numbers in the community, and equally at all levels reflecting the full range of work opportunities. Apart from the justice of this, black people (men and women) need to be seen as role models for both black and white children.

In mainly white areas, a multiethnic workforce is less likely to be achieved. But in other areas, realistic targets (relating to the ethnic composition of the local community for most jobs) for achieving such a workforce should be set. While it is unlawful, under the Race Relations Act, to set quotas (giving favourable treatment to a fixed number or percentage of the workforce) for employing people from particular ethnic groups, it is not unlawful to set targets to ensure that the aim of increasing the number of employees from minority ethnic groups is kept on the agenda. Target setting is important because if things just go on at the rate they are it will be decades or longer before the workforce accurately represents the minority ethnic population at all levels.

Further positive action can be taken to increase the number of employees from black and other minority ethnic backgrounds when there are very few or none already in the workforce, either by specific welcoming of such applicants in the recruitment procedures or by offering training specifically for such groups. Such action could be targeted at particular work, for example, that of senior managers. However, neither target setting nor these actions ever result in favourable treatment in the actual selection procedures for employment. (See section on positive action, page 244.) Before considering positive action to create a multiethnic workforce, existing black workers should be consulted as to their opinions. And it is crucial that the service or setting demonstrates that it is committed to such a workforce, for example by adopting as many aspects as possible of the suggested strategy framework for implementing racial equality across the early years (see Chapter 10). A setting that already puts racial equality into practice is far more likely to attract applicants from black and other minority ethnic groups to work there than one that does not do so. Advertising posts in places likely to be seen by them, going out to community facilities such as supplementary schools, religious and cultural organisations and meeting and talking with people directly, using local community languages to spread the word and passing fliers around are all things that could be considered.

After doing all these things no one should be discouraged if changes to the workforce do not occur immediately. Building up a reputation for being welcoming to all, for valuing the presence of children and adults from black and other minority communities in the setting and for being genuinely committed takes time. It may be that no one wants to be the first employee from a black or other minority ethnic group – a feeling of isolation or the risk of an unhappy experience may be too great to take. This is all part of the process of change. It reflects the historical legacy of centuries of racism.

Talking to (and consulting with) families from black and other minority ethnic communities may reveal circumstances that explain the lack of applications. Every avenue should be pursued. At the end of the day, the fact that the setting has tried hard, is a place where everyone is equally valued and respected may have to suffice for the time being. Keeping open minds and ensuring effective training is in place for all employees and volunteers should continue.

Once a workforce is multiethnic it should be a matter of priority to make sure that everyone has equal access to in-service training and support. Career progression should be open to everyone on equal terms. It is not enough to be satisfied with a multiethnic workforce if all decisions are made by white people. Even if this is so in the interim, there are ways of involving everyone in discussions, valuing everyone's contributions, learning from the experience of people from different communities and eliciting ideas and suggestions that reflect people's cultural and other experiences. This can be done informally or formally, by having regular agenda items to consider equality issues at meetings and ensuring that people are able to raise concerns in an atmosphere of trust.

Meeting together in ethnically specific groups

Sometimes black (or white) people working in early years services or settings may wish to meet separately from the others to discuss specific issues of concern to them. This may cause friction – some people feeling that they are being talked about and that the others are being given preferential treatment – but if everyone sees that discussions are exclusively for a positive purpose this should cause no anxiety. For example, black people may wish to meet separately to share their common issues in a context where they feel comfortable to talk about them with people who will understand.

In general, such meetings should be about empowering the participants as part of a short-term strategy with a concrete programme of action. In a small organisation such a meeting would be very unlikely to take place during work hours except at lunch breaks, for example. However many larger organisations encourage such groups as part of a programme of empowering groups unrepresented at senior levels, or as part of a programme of focus group meetings to get information for their own purposes. In these situations the meetings are likely to take place in work time, and be viewed as part of the workers' job. Workers from other ethnic groups may wish to have an equivalent time for meeting, and such requests should be considered according to the purpose and context of the meetings.

Sometimes managers or policy-makers may set up group meetings specifically to find out how different people are affected by an issue, and to get fresh ideas on appropriate provision, for example when conducting a race equality impact assessment. These would usually take place in work time.

A national group of black workers in the early years has been set up to represent their views in national policies (contact Early Childhood Unit, National Children's Bureau).

A framework to support a 'key person' approach

Close attachments in early childhood make a difference to a child's ability to live, love and learn.

(Selleck 2006b)

It is now well established that the maximum benefit to children's learning and well-being is where workers and families are fully involved, as far as possible as equals, in supporting children together. It is also essential that young children know that there is a 'special person' for them, someone who knows them and their family, understands their culture and knows about and can respond to their needs and is fundamentally concerned with their emotional well-being. Where the setting is organised so that there is this specific and special person (a 'key person') with a commitment to each child and their family, close and supportive relationships can be developed, relationships that may develop to overcome any possible cultural barriers. The way that this is done is critical – it must incorporate a framework across the setting that is understood by everyone, defines people's roles and sets up systems to ensure that this approach is managed effectively: for example, rotas to cover times when the key person is absent and ensuring that a second key person, in principle, is also involved with the child and family. Key persons work in pairs or 'buddies' with children and their families so that there is always someone who knows the child well when the main key person is off duty, sick, training or on leave. Such an approach would be part of the policy for equality, thus clearly defining the responsibilities of the key person to promote equality with each child and their family, and be laid out in their job description. Clearly each key person will be 'key' to several children, all of whom have a special relationship with that person.

Where a key person is involved with a group of children and is committed to this way of working, there is a specific opportunity to get to know the family members and to be able to learn about and address any particular needs with regard to their religion or culture or any disabilities. Building up such a rapport and consequent trust also facilitates communication about any racism that the family, child or worker may be experiencing, thus enabling greater understanding of each other's situation, together with the possibility of support in addressing it. This sharing makes it possible for every worker in the setting to also learn about the experiences of families from different minority ethnic groups so that, together, they can stand against any racism that may emerge either within the setting itself or outside in the local community.

The development of a key person approach is a requirement of the Early Years Foundation Stage and should be a priority for settings concerned about ensuring that families and workers get to know each other. Building up trust and confidence between them and thus facilitating a shared understanding of different cultural backgrounds and experiences should help create a relationship where issues of racial equality can be freely raised and addressed.

If you want to know more

see Elfer and others (2003) for a discussion about the relationships between key practitioners in early years settings and children and their families.

Taking account of groups that may not yet be included

One of the tasks for any early years setting, wherever it is sited, is for all workers, children and families to be prepared and to provide a positive welcome for any child who might join tomorrow. This means considering, in advance, everything that the setting does. Involving families in this should be part of developing a policy for equality and engaging them in thinking about the role of early years settings in helping the future society to be at ease with itself.

Including children and their families from differing backgrounds in the policy development helps to identify any specific needs they may have and to understand any particular difficulties that they may face.

But it is known that families from some minority ethnic groups are less likely to attend early years provision than others (see page 83 for discussion of the phrase 'hard to reach'). There may be many reasons for this including:

- not necessarily being in agreement as to whether early years provision would benefit all children, especially where racism is seen or feared to be present – keeping children away from this possibility for as long as possible, avoiding its potential until compulsory school age
- an awareness of the possible culturally inappropriate and ethnocentric provision available
- the cost of some forms of provision
- a tradition for mothers to remain at home, and to care for their children until statutory school age
- living in a remote area, far from any settings – this may affect Travellers, Roma and Gypsies particularly
- lack of trust in an unfamiliar system
- apprehension about a child being in an unfamiliar environment and venturing into unfamiliar territory when there is no legal requirement to attend
- the difficulties and complications involved in helping a child with a disability or special educational need to access a setting

- lack of information about early years provision generally
- fear of their child being the 'odd one out', different from everyone else and possibly teased.

Some families may just not want their children, for whatever reason, to attend an early years setting. While this may be so, it is important for both settings and services to ensure that all families are aware of the availability of such provision should they want it for their children. It is also important for settings (and local authorities), wherever possible, to ascertain the reasons why some families from minority ethnic groups do not take up places in settings for their children and to take account of these in their provision. Indeed, this is the very purpose of the race equality impact assessment required by the Race Relations (Amendment) Act. But it should not be assumed that such families are inadequate or do not care about their children's lives. Local authorities and settings will need to avoid any stereotyping when considering the sufficiency of early years places for families under the Childcare Act. A few projects examine the issues around families from minority ethnic communities, their circumstances, their access to and involvement in early years provision, making suggestions as to how this could be enhanced where appropriate.

If you want to know more

about some of the projects exploring the issues mentioned above, see Daycare Trust (2003), Hall and others (2004), Sure Start (2004a), Bryson and others (2005), Daycare Trust/National Centre for Social Research (2006), and Kazimirski and others (2006). Wolverhampton Early Years team also made a useful video about these issues (Wolverhampton Early Years Team 2003).

Some relevant issues for specific groups are considered below.

Families of children from minority ethnic groups having disabilities and/or special educational needs

Families that have a child with a disability or a special educational need often find accessing an early years setting difficult and complicated. Where a child is both from a minority ethnic group and has a disability or special educational need the situation can be compounded. Different cultural experiences of special needs or disabilities, different employment patterns of family members together with language and interpretation difficulties, often accompanied by disproportionate poverty levels, make particular problems to be overcome for such black and other minority ethnic families. While the principles, as discussed elsewhere in this book, remain the same for all children whatever their ethnicity or disability, it is important to be aware of potential situations facing such families. Some families, unfamiliar with the existing systems of supporting families and their children when they are disabled, may face bewildering circumstances. Asylum seekers and refugees may be particularly disadvantaged.

In thinking about ethnicity or disability, it is important to remember the needs of both at the same time. For example, the resources should reflect and include positive images of both black and white children with disabilities. And, in planning the curriculum, ensuring that the stories of people with a disability include black people as well as white people. The support of a key worker benefits such children and their families particularly, because of the close relationship and understanding built up between them. Settings needing advice or support should contact national, or any local, organisations working specifically with families with disabled children from black or other minority ethnic groups (see Include Me TOO and EYE posters, search the internet for websites, such as www.diseed.org.uk, giving possible contacts and other information; and for further information see Chamba and others (1999) and Dickins with Denziloe (2003).

Families and children with mixed race or ethnic backgrounds

> *Who I am is made up of lots of different things and shifts depending on the context and what questions I am being asked. Some things people find quirky about me, my liking for brown shoes is just one. My racial identity is also something of a talking-point to people. I self-identify as mixed race, not black. Not confused, not caught between cultures, not a marginal man. I am me. But getting to know me wasn't easy!*

(Bradley Lincoln, quote from an e-conference on mixedness and mixing, 2007)

Discussions about terminology often dominate talk about families whose parents are from different ethnic backgrounds (see Appendix I for discussion of the term 'mixed race'). This hijacking of discussion sometimes means that other issues are not raised. But Britain has a fast-growing mixed race (usually described as 'mixed heritage' in government literature) population. In a sense it is some measure of the possible lessening of racial prejudice among younger people in our society – that can only be a good thing.

According to the 2001 census there are just under three-quarters of a million people of 'Mixed' identity in the UK, the majority being British born – about 1.25 per cent of the population. Of all those in the UK describing themselves in the census as 'Black Caribbean men' and 'Other Black men and women', 40 per cent have a white partner; and of those describing themselves as being 'Black Caribbean women', 26 per cent have a white partner. Fewer men and women from other ethnic groups have white partners.

Research from the 2001 census shows that there are four times as many children as adults from mixed ethnic groups (Simpson 2006). (See Appendix 3 for a detailed breakdown (Owen 2006); for a succinct summary of 'Mixed' ethnic groups from the 2001 census see Bradford (2006) and Owen (2005)). Of these, 5 per cent of children are under five. The 2001 census was the first where mixed race people were able to define themselves as such – previously they had only the choice of 'black other'.

Nearly all of us belong to mixed backgrounds of one sort or another. But for some children the visible differences between their parents are more apparent than for others. They may have strong feelings about how they should be described. If one parent is black and the other is white they may learn, from society's values, that white is preferable. They may be referred to as black because that is how society perceives them, but may not feel that they are black or wish to be seen in any way to reject the heritage of their white parent. Not everyone, white and black, positively accepts mixed race families and their children. Rejection by both black and white people may isolate them into a group of their own, resulting in several layers of stereotyping, prejudice and possibly institutional racism affecting them. With the increasing number of mixed race families it is important for settings to take account of these issues. So, as far as possible, children need to have the identities of both parents recognised and understood.

Case study 48

Mum's fault?

Melissa's mother is Indian and her father is white English. They live on a suburban new estate. Her family is very loving. At four years old, she started at the early years setting in the area and was immediately teased there about her colour. She didn't tell anyone at home about the teasing but she spent a lot of time at home washing her hands and body to 'try to get the colour off'. She didn't talk to her mother for six months. When Melissa finally told her parents what was happening, they realised that they had wrongly thought that being a loving family would protect their daughter from feeling negative about her skin colour because of racism. Melissa had held her mother responsible for the pain she was experiencing.

Points for thought and discussion

- Discuss the implications of the fact that Melissa had suffered from racist abuse for six months, starting from the time she began in the setting, without anyone in the setting doing anything about it.
- Why might it have been her mother rather than her father who was held responsible for Melissa's pain?

An important piece of research into the educational needs of mixed race pupils provides information that is relevant for workers in early years settings (Tikly and others 2004). It points to key issues that early years workers need to understand and take account of in their own practice if they are to ensure that the experiences and needs of mixed race children are recognised and acknowledged in positive ways in their earliest years. Key findings included the following.

1   The attainment of mixed race White and Black Caribbean pupils was lower than the average for all pupils; that of mixed race White and Black African pupils was average; and that of mixed race White and Asian pupils was above average (see DfES 2003c for information about the achievement of such children).

2   This largely reflected the socioeconomic backgrounds of their families.

3 Mixed race White and Black Caribbean pupils' attainments levels were broadly similar to Black Caribbean pupils and they faced similar barriers at school.

4 This was partly explained by both groups being more likely to experience institutional racism, as well as possibly low teacher expectations of their abilities.

5 Institutional racism was often based on stereotypical views: that their home backgrounds were fragmented and that they had 'confused' identities. This confusion is rather on the part of those commenting on it, and may be due to the lack of understanding of 'mixedness' and the need to try to put people into their own fixed categories.

6 Mixed race pupils often experienced racism from teachers and from some of both their Black and White peers.

7 The particular identities of mixed race pupils tended to be invisible when they needed to be recognised and understood.

Early years workers therefore have a particular role to play in both adapting their practice to take account of the implications of these findings and in preparing mixed race children for their future schooling.

It is important for children to be clear from the start about who they are and who their parents are. Lots of positive talk about skin colour differences, about cultural differences and an understanding of how positive self-identity and self-esteem develop, will help children to feel good about who they are. Including their family members in the discussions, because they are all important to their children and need similar respect, is critical to building self-esteem in all families. So listening sensitively to parents and children about what they feel and how they wish to be described will help everyone feel valued and positive about who they are. However, the difficulties that some children may encounter in building self-esteem are demonstrated by the lack of many good resources – illustrations and stories – about or including mixed-race families or children.

There are several specific issues that arise for and around families of mixed race.

- If one of a child's parents is white, the family is often concerned that the early years setting will treat the child as black, and ignore the mixed race, or treat the child as white and make no attempt to address racism or provide a supportive environment.

- It is very important to maintain contact with the cultural roots of both parents. This is not always easy if one family lives in another country or the parents no longer live together. It is important to try and maintain contact with an extended family or community, even when they may no longer be in contact with that parent.

- Parents have to deal with the racism their children may face. Unlike families where both of the parents are black, a white parent may have less experience, knowledge or even understanding of racism – let alone any idea of how to deal with it. Having a black partner does not mean that a white person is antiracist, in the same way as having a wife does not mean that a husband is anti-sexist.

- White mothers in particular may have to face abuse and hostility from strangers. Research by a PhD student at the Institute of Education, London University, showed that most of these mothers experienced racial abuse in the company of their children (TES 2007c). They are sometimes seen as 'loose women' because they have had, or are having, a sexual relationship with a black man – another legacy of the evil of racism. Their children may witness this abuse.

Gary Younge describes this as 'one more attempt to pathologise black male sexuality – a titillating riff on the long-held myth of the untamed bestial urges that increase with the melanin colour' (*Guardian* 23 January 2006).

White childminders looking after black children sometimes also suffer from this – many have told of their experiences of racial abuse on the street. And a white parent of a mixed race child or white parents who adopt one may come to realise the reality of racism and the advantages of being white in society.

> *As a white person you don't have to think about being white, it's the norm. But once you have a mixed child you are no longer white. Suddenly the privilege you have simply by being white is taken away. It's a hard lesson to learn.*
>
> (Adoption worker quoted in 'Absent Voices' by Laura Smith, *Guardian* 6 September 2006)

- A white mother, whose partner is no longer around, may sometimes express her feelings of rejection by him in racial prejudice. This makes for a very confusing experience for her child.

- Sometimes, children of mixed race find that no child of any other racial group wants to play with them. Of course, this also happens to children who have two white parents or two black parents, but children of mixed parentage may feel particularly rejected because their parents may belong to the same racial groups as the children rejecting them.

- Some parents may have to face initial and possibly lasting racial hostility to their relationship from their own families.

- Parents may face questions like 'How black is the baby?' implying that to be too black might raise difficulties of acceptance. Where children from mixed race families have a range of different skin colours, the same questions about degrees of darkness may make everyone feel uncomfortable.

- Parents with children of a different skin colour from their own often have to face the surprise of others. The surprise suggests a suspicion that the children do not really belong to the parents and this can lead to disturbing incidents.

Case study 49

Passport parent

Melanie – whose father is white and whose mother is of mixed parentage herself – has fair skin and light-coloured hair. Soon after Melanie was born her mother began carrying Melanie's birth certificate around with her, as it was so often suggested that she was not Melanie's mother. These suggestions were sometimes threatening.

So it is vital to take specific action on the following.

- Multiple identities should be affirmed and treated as the norm, with *all* children and their families.
- Mixedness is a norm and should be affirmed with all children and their families.
- Children having more than one culture in their family should be made to feel proud of that fact and proud of both or all of their cultures.
- It is not appropriate, as often happens, to ask children if they are black or white (or whatever).
- Ensure that all children have access to resources showing a range of skin tones.
- Families should be involved in discussions about mixed race.

Mixed race families often report the positive changes they make to their own families. They often, for the first time, understand and try to address their own racism. They may all learn to be proud of their mixed extended family.

If you want to know more

for specific guidance about the early years, see Houston (2007). For further discussions see: Chambers and others (1996), EYTARN (1995a), Alibhai-Brown (2001), Ifekwunigwe (2004), and Joseph Rowntree Foundation (2008); the references to the above research; the CRE eConference website on Mixedness and mixing, 4–6 September 2007; and, in Useful Addresses and Contacts (page 312), see People in Harmony, and Intermix.

Travellers, Roma, Gypsies and mobile communities

The Traveller, Gypsy and Roma communities are diverse communities with many varying cultures, traditions and customs (see Appendix 1(a) for discussion). It is therefore important not to generalise about their wishes or expectations with regard to early years provision. Although all experience discrimination it is largely only Irish Travellers, Gypsies and Roma who are subjected to racial attacks and abuse. It is estimated that there are about 300,000 Travellers, Roma or Gypsies in Britain; 200,000 of whom live in houses, not trailers or caravans. A twice-yearly count of caravans and trailers is taken by the Department of Communities and Local Government but is subject to criticism as Travellers themselves are not involved and only caravans that can be seen or known about are counted. Local authorities are often relied on to provide information that may or may not be accurate. The term 'Traveller' generally includes English and Welsh Gypsies (some of whom may be Romany), circus families, fairground families (Showmen), Irish and Scottish Travellers (who sometimes call themselves Gypsies), Bargees, New Travellers and, more recently, European Roma. Some families, particularly from Eastern and Central Europe, regard the term Gypsy negatively and prefer the term Roma. Some Gypsies do not like being called Travellers. So it is always important to ask everyone how they prefer to be called.

Only Romany Gypsies (the largest group, who have been here since the early 16th century) and Irish Travellers have been defined in law as ethnic groups and are therefore covered by the Race Relations Act. However the needs of all Traveller families and their children, whatever their legal status in terms of the law, need to be taken into account in settings. The term Traveller is written with a capital 'T' to distinguish it from other travellers, such as commercial travellers. The word 'Gypsy' is also written with a capital 'G' as they are recognised as an ethnic group. The phrase 'travelling communities' is used to describe people who are, or who have been, associated with a traditionally nomadic lifestyle. As with most people, there is great variety in what travelling people call themselves.

Travellers have a long history of persecution and deportations. They, along with refugees and asylum seekers, tend to experience more hostility than any other group and have a high infant mortality rate. A recent poll in England showed that more than a third of adults admitted to being personally prejudiced against Gypsies and Travellers and reports show a greater level of prejudice than against any other group (Stonewall 2003, Mackenzie 2003/4). Most of the information about them had come from the media, which often appears to stoke up antagonism towards them. And people who challenge the hostility towards them are often themselves subject to abuse.

> Bett, a Roma woman, said she experienced a lot of abuse. Because it was an almost constant situation when she left the safety of her community, she said she dealt with it by giving the appearance of defiance and not caring, although she knew this would be interpreted as confrontational. Actually it never stopped hurting.

They are distinguished by their mobility, cultures and their connections with a travelling way of life. Those who are not living in houses or settled on sites are highly mobile and the number of moves that individual families make has increased since the repeal of the Caravans Sites Act 1968 (by the Criminal Justice and Public Order Act 1994). This removed the statutory requirement for local authorities to provide sites for Travellers and so left fewer authorised sites. This Act has exacerbated the situation, as police and local authorities now evict people more quickly from unauthorised sites, leading to an increase in the number of Traveller families who are in emergency housing, often against their wishes. Under the Housing Act 2004, housing authorities must assess the accommodation needs of Gypsies and Travellers 'residing in or resorting to their district' as part of the general review of housing needs in their areas (Communities and Local Government 2007).

Families who live in houses may still travel in the summer and retain their heritage values. This mobility has many implications for early years settings, not least the fact that all children in school are counted as part of the annual DCSF school pupil audit on a particular day, which may mean that a place for a Traveller child, who is absent on the counting day, is not funded. Usually, however, if a child is on roll but away because the family is travelling for work they are counted as if they are on roll. But, like other children, those who arrive mid-term may not be so readily accommodated. They have a strong family tradition that may partly explain their common reluctance to move away from other family members and from the tradition of travelling.

There is as yet no statistical data collected by government on the number of Traveller, Gypsy or Roma children in early years settings. The Foundation Stage Profile data on the ethnicity of all children in early years settings collected in 2007 should, if the evaluation is satisfactory, eventually provide this (see page 274 for further information). It was estimated some years ago that only about 20 per cent of Traveller children ever attend any early years setting (Ofsted 1996). One local education authority (LEA) reported that 29 per cent of Gypsy and Traveller children had received some form of pre-school education during the year (Ofsted 2003). This low percentage is partly because of the hostility they face; partly because of their nomadic lifestyle, evictions from unauthorised land and lack of familiarity with educational settings; and partly because of their distance from and lack of transport to settings. There is also a strong belief that education should be in the home with the family and that five is quite soon enough to attend formal provision.

It is therefore not surprising that, although the sample is small, the initial findings from the Foundation Stage Profile show that the lowest performing children are Travellers of Irish heritage and Gypsy and Roma children (see DfES 2005a). There are few resources reflecting their lifestyles in settings, they seldom have their cultural festivals celebrated, partly because they are little known, and are often seen as an afterthought when the curriculum is planned. It is critically important to ensure that their culture is reflected positively in the same way as the cultures of other groups as part of an inclusive curriculum. Seeking resources as an afterthought when a Traveller child arrives may only reinforce prejudice.

Workers need to see the statutory requirements of the Race Relations (Amendment) Act as providing a safe and supportive environment for Travellers of Irish heritage, Roma and Gypsy children backed up by the principles of the Early Years Foundation Stage. For children of statutory school age, there is funding from the government to support local authorities in their work with Traveller children. This is usually done through setting up Traveller education support services (TESS) within the local authority Children's Services, to provide a central team. Schools have the responsibility of providing education for all children; and TESS will help educational settings to carry out their duty in this.

In order to overcome hostility in early years settings, it is important to have a policy of respecting all children and being explicit about including Travellers, Gypsies and Roma. Resources reflecting Traveller culture should be available to children even if there are no Traveller, Roma or Gypsy children in the setting. The principle of preparing for the arrival of a child from any culture or background should be part of everyday practice. A policy involving discussions with families prepares the way for everyone to be equally accepted. Refusing to accept Romany Gypsy or Irish Traveller children to an early years setting because of who they are would be unlawful. Putting pressure on a setting not to admit such children, for example, by a parental petition, would also be unlawful.

Who wins?

An Irish Traveller family moved to a site near Green Street Pre-school. The chair of the management committee, Alison, feared that Irish Traveller children from the site might wish to attend the pre-school and that might cause settled families to transfer their children to another playgroup nearby. Alison told the leader of the group, Dulcie, not to accept any child from a Traveller family, if they applied to attend. She was to say that they had heard that Traveller children were very difficult to deal with and that she knew other children would leave if they accepted a Traveller child. They were therefore not willing to risk this happening so they were sorry but they would not be able to give a place to a Traveller child. In any case they were a bit short in numbers to make the group viable financially and to risk having children taken away because of a Traveller child might mean the setting would have to close.

Soon afterwards Aidan, who is four, and his father from the site came to the pre-school and asked if Aidan could attend. His father was keen that he go to school later on and wanted him to start learning as soon as possible. Although they had vacancies Dulcie, rather reluctantly and certainly with some embarrassment, said her bit. Aidan's father was upset but was too proud and humiliated to argue about it and so left.

Points for thought and discussion

The resultant situation would be as follows.

- If Aidan's father had decided to make a complaint of racial discrimination under the Race Relations Act, it is likely that a court would find:
  - that the pre-school had discriminated unlawfully against Aidan on racial grounds (Irish Travellers are a racial group under the Act)
  - Dulcie, as the leader, might have been responsible for that act of discrimination
  - Alison, as the chair, might have behaved unlawfully by instructing Dulcie to discriminate
  - the management committee, as employers, might have behaved unlawfully under the employer's liability section of the Act.
- Both Ofsted and the local authority would then need to consider the pre-school's situation with regard to registration and funding.

The spurious reasons given for the refusal of the place are irrelevant. Although there is some explanation for Alison's apprehension about other families leaving the group this cannot justify discrimination. The situation would have been different if the setting had had an equality policy that families had owned. In order to avoid families taking their children away if a Traveller child had been accepted it is vital that such a policy be put into place, discussed widely and understood by everyone. In order to avoid future situations where threats are made to take a child away from an early years setting if a Gypsy, Roma or Traveller child attends all, or a group of, settings might wish to consider devising a common policy on admissions or at least about admitting such children.

It is more likely that Gypsy, Roma and Traveller children will be truly accepted into a setting if a local authority early years service supports its equality strategy by referring to their particular needs in its race equality scheme. Furthermore, if the scheme requires all children to be accepted in a setting where there is a place available then, if Gypsy, Roma and Traveller or any other children are refused places because of their ethnicity, the service could decide to take action against the setting.

The local TESS usually knows where Travellers are sited. By visiting the site on a regular basis and in a sensitive manner, early years workers, in partnership with TESS, can become familiar to Gypsies, Roma and Travellers and also learn about their way of life. This might be the beginnings of sharing this experience with other children so all become familiar with one another – an important way of mutually breaking down barriers. Such communications may facilitate the process of Traveller children and their parents visiting the setting to see what goes on and possibly participate.

If children and their families come to understand that everyone has a responsibility to welcome one another, prejudice against Travellers may be reduced. Building on a common acceptance of difference and persevering towards this are important.

Local authorities, any remaining Sure Start local programmes and children's centres need to take specific action to identify Traveller, Roma and Gypsy children in their areas and encourage them, if they so wish, and in partnership with TESS, to attend a supportive setting. They need to support them in their travelling lifestyles in ensuring continuity by providing them with reports and resources that can be taken, when they travel, to other settings wherever they are living. Some authorities provide transport as many sites are far from other communities. Some have made videos about early years provision so that families can consider the issues at their leisure.

If you want to know more

there is a considerable amount of information available to support Traveller, Roma and Gypsy children in settings, to try to dispel myths about their lifestyles and the law (see websites of National Association of Teachers of Travellers and Romany Gypsies and Irish Travellers, Norfolk Traveller Education Service (1997) video, CRE (2003c), DfES (2003a), CRE strategy (2004b), Johnson and Willers (2004), CRE website for Britain's forgotten minority (2005d), the facts and myths (CRE 2005c), Marlow and Peck (2005), Cemlyn and Clark (2005), Tyler (2005), CRE (2006b), (2007) and DCSF (2008a). For more about cultural awareness training and activities, see Save the Children/DfES (2006) and for details of a comprehensive support project see Save the Children (2007).

Most local authorities have a local Traveller education support service that gives advice and support and there is a national magazine for Travellers (*Travellers Times*). Some local authorities produce specific guidance for Gypsy, Roma and Traveller children in the early years (for example, see North Yorkshire County Council 2001, Oxfordshire County Council 2003). A particular concern of workers and families when they move around is the consistency of children's experiences in different settings and how assessment using the Foundation Stage Profile can work in practice within attendance time limits. There is a similar difficulty for special educational needs assessments for mobile pupils.

Education – moving on

One local education authority has embarked upon a process of really involving Traveller, Roma and Gypsy families and children in education. It opened a pre-school project for young children and their mothers in a portakabin on the borough's official Traveller site, led by TESS, together with the site community organisation and the local Pre-school Learning Alliance. By building up relationships with families and involving the mothers in activities over a period of time, feelings of security were established so that they became more confident about their children going to school.

The process developed over time. Classroom assistants were recruited from the sites and trained and supported to work in classrooms. They work with all children but particularly with Traveller children, thus making use of their personal experiences of a travelling lifestyle and Traveller culture. They still live in vans on sites and travel during the summer months. This has built up a greater confidence in education generally and has been very successful.

A third project for early years has been created in an early years excellence centre where Traveller classroom assistant posts have been created and recruited from the Traveller community to encourage participation of Traveller children in early years education. All projects have been supported by the borough's Traveller Education Service and included involvement of its Traveller liaison worker. This is important in order to share current circumstances with regard to school attendance and avoid the possibility of on-site provision that only perpetuates a non-inclusive educational experience for children.

Points for thought and discussion

- How might you begin the process of involving Traveller, Roma and Gypsy families in early years settings?
- What might be the long-term benefits of early years provision for them?
- What difficulties might settings face?
- What difficulties might the families and children face?

These projects demonstrate the critical value of long-term planning to provide ongoing support for Travellers and their children. They began a process of building up positive relationships with families so that education is now seen by the travelling community as of benefit to their children and adults as well (see Miles 2006 for details).

Refugees and asylum seekers

Imagine you are five years old and fleeing your home and country taking just a small bag. You have ten minutes to decide what to take with you.

(Adapted from a speaker on asylum seekers from Salusbury World at a seminar in 2005)

Most refugees and asylum seeking families are here because they are fleeing from intolerable experiences in their own countries. They come from many communities, with a variety of skills, knowledge and experiences and seek temporary or permanent security in this country. Their children may have been involved in or witnessed situations that have given them cause to be anxious and distressed. Early years settings can provide them with a haven of peace, comfort, safety and support in adjusting to their new lives. They can begin to learn the skills needed to live in a new society – confidence, language and communication, especially if they are supported in learning English. In turn they may offer children and their families already in the setting an opportunity to see through a window into a world different from their own and learn from that new experience.

As with Travellers, Roma and Gypsies, asylum seekers, and to a lesser extent refugees, are among the recipients, from many sections of society, of the most racial hostility, prejudice and vilification of all minority ethnic groups. Their experiences on arriving here compound their already often traumatic experiences in their home countries. They are frequently hounded by the tabloid media thus fuelling the many myths about them and making them very vulnerable. Some British citizens, some of whom may also be vulnerable and with stressed economic circumstances, and others who are unfamiliar with people from any minority ethnic group, are readily susceptible to such myths. But more affluent groups, with less economic reasons to feel threatened by the presence of asylum seekers, whether they are housed near them or not, also express prejudice.

If you want to know more

see Lewis (2005) for further discussion on public attitudes; the Refugee Council (2005) for a very helpful pocket guide on the myths; page 46 for research on negative media coverage of asylum seekers; and, on readers' assumptions about them, Brown and others (2006).

Asylum seekers are subject to strict limits on benefits and where they may live and are often dispersed to areas where there may not be many people from their own community or speaking their home language when they arrive. They may then be re-housed several times by local authorities, into emergency housing. Many live in near-destitute circumstances (see Information Centre about Asylum and Refugees (ICAR) 2006). Their children may be frightened from their experiences and they themselves will inevitably be worried about their status and future lives. Helping all families to identify their common needs and countering the myths that may be preventing people from understanding what it is like to be an asylum seeker are likely to be important roles for workers.

The policy for equality, together with the legal requirements under the Race Relations (Amendment) Act, should be used to underpin the work to ensure every child's entitlement to equality in the Early Years Foundation Stage. Young children from refugee and asylum seeking families have the same rights to attend early years provision and have the same entitlement to early years education and care as other children in England. Challenging myths and providing a safe environment should be seen as part of the statutory duties under the Race Relations (Amendment) Act; and taking account of the suggestions in this book may help provide workers in settings with examples of what they might do to implement effective practice.

Refugee and asylum seeking families may be anxious about many things as a result of their experiences both in their home countries and since arriving in Britain. Although joining an early years setting may be of benefit to the family they may be unfamiliar with early years practice and, even if they do know about it, may be apprehensive as to how their children will be received and cared for. They may also prefer to have their children near to them in order to keep them safe, rather than expose them to unfamiliar early years provision. Knowing who lives in the local community, being aware of the arrival of refugee and asylum-seeking families and making efforts to contact them demonstrate valuable ways of informing them about the existence of early years services. Local community organisations can help with this, and in a dispersal area the local authority may agree to pass on information to newly arriving families. Providing advice and practical support to them is important if their children are to have the opportunities available to others. Regular contact with services already working in the local community (for example, health visitors) and refugee groups, as well as providing accessible information in a variety of languages, will facilitate communication.

A research project looking at the experiences of refugee women in accessing early years provision for their children in London revealed that lack of information and in appropriate languages was the main barrier. They had nowhere to turn to for support and when they did access provision it was often ethnocentric in its practice and resources (Barnabas 2006). This points to the need for more effective training, for more culturally sensitive settings and for them to be proactive in seeking out families and providing them with information in relevant languages so that they can decide for themselves whether they wish their children to attend.

Being part of a supportive and caring setting may help to alleviate some of their worries, help them to feel safe and secure and reduce their sense of isolation in an unfamiliar environment. It can also begin the process of healing and restoration often so desperately needed by children and their families.

Settings can also provide information and support about any particular needs that refugee and asylum-seeking families may have (including, for example, where to get appropriate help and advice with housing, benefits, immigration and health matters) so that the family feels that they belong with a group of people who are receptive and sympathetic to their circumstances and can be pathways connecting them to a range of services. In this way they may begin to feel a part of the local community. By involving refugee and asylum-seeking families in the activities of the setting other families can get to know them as friends, thus possibly countering some of the damaging stereotypes that abound and giving them an understanding of what it feels like to be dependent and financially constrained in a new country.

There are some excellent resources to help workers support refugee and asylum-seeking children. Some describe how war and conflict can interrupt the development of young children and how play and participating in early years settings can help restore their lost childhoods.

If you want to know more

read about an example of a project supporting refugees and asylum-seeking children and families on the Salusbury World website. For videos and support books see Hyder and Rutter (1998), Save the Children/Refugee Council (2001), Save the Children/Salusbury World (2004), Hyder (2005) and the National Refugee Integration Forum and General Teaching Council websites.

Migrants from Europe

With the enlargement of the European Community some people who have not previously had such opportunities are coming to Britain to seek work. Most are white and many have never before lived in a multicultural, multiethnic society. They are increasingly subjected to hostility because of their nationality – a form of racism called xenoracism that is sometimes reinforced by the media. Wherever they work this may be associated with an underlying fear of undermining local job security.

When they live in multicultural and multiethnic urban areas their lack of familiarity with and attitudes to such a society may be seen, rightly or wrongly, as racial prejudice. Their children may be as bewildered by the situation as children of asylum seekers (although with different histories). There is increasing evidence of prejudice against Eastern European pupils in schools as well as evidence of racial abuse by some Polish pupils of black pupils and teachers (TES 2007a). In such situations any evidence of prejudice or xenoracism, from whatever source, should be addressed in the same way as for all forms of racism. It again points to the need to be prepared, in advance wherever possible, to welcome any child who may arrive in the setting tomorrow and to be able to deal with any circumstances arising from that.

Working with young children

The policy implementation programme should provide details of the work planned with the children. This should cover all aspects of the curriculum and take particular account of the following issues.

Play resources

There is now a wealth of resources that reflect our multicultural society, although cost will influence what early years services and settings can actually buy. Resources to reflect a diverse society should not be seen as extra resources incurring additional cost: rather they should be purchased as part of ongoing good buying practice for the setting. But resources cannot create a positive view of society by themselves – it is the way that they are used and the way adults and children involve them in their play and curricular activities that are the critical factors of change. Alone they cannot counter racism – talking about issues is likely to be more effective in changing attitudes than having resources reflecting our multicultural society which no-one plays with. So the term 'anti-discriminatory resources', as sometimes used, is incorrect – no resources can be anti-discriminatory by themselves.

For example, if a black doll is bought but then ignored and not played with either by children or adults, the children may receive subtle messages that the doll is not 'wanted'. Instead of the doll helping to create a positive view of society, these messages may reinforce negative concepts about who is valued in society. Adults may also convince themselves that they are not really necessary, especially where all the children are white. They may allow themselves to assume there are cost implications, rather than understanding that the setting's resources should always be chosen to reflect a diverse community. If dual-language storybooks are the only multicultural resources in a white monolingual playgroup and nothing active is done with them, they cannot help children understand the reality of our multicultural, multilingual society.

The key to ensuring that everyone is valued equally is to consider carefully what the children might already have learned about people who are different from themselves. Those working with children need to know why appropriate resources are important, should be able to answer questions from children or their families and anticipate what the questions might be. For example, in answer to a question about why a worker is discussing photographs of black and white people in work situations with children, saying something like 'Well, I am only doing what I am told to do' hardly gives a message of understanding and commitment. A more helpful statement might be 'All of us have thought about this. We live in a diverse global community and we believe it is appropriate to include people who are different from us in everyday situations in our work with children.'

It is important to understand that even if families have migrated to live in Britain from somewhere else, they are here now, so it is life in Britain today that is relevant to the children, rather than the lifestyles of people in, for example, Asia, Africa or the Caribbean. This is not to ignore the heritage of children whose families have migrated here, it simply puts that heritage in context. Consequently, pictures of families from a variety of cultures who are living in Britain and doing ordinary everyday things in Britain are the real reflections of a multicultural society for children.

The existence of a properly implemented policy for racial equality will have prepared everyone – those working with children, families, the children and others – for such circumstances. They will have thought and talked about how to use a black doll and the dual-language books effectively. Those working with children will have thought about how they might respond to any questions that the children might ask. In this situation a child's reaction is more likely to be one of curiosity than of rejection, for example 'Why is the doll black?' or 'Why has Samidha's mummy got a red spot (a *bindi*) on her forehead?' The way adults use the resources is important in setting an example to children.

Involving families in organising workshops or discussions about resources is particularly important, as they are likely to acquire books and toys for their children at home. Those working with children and families can, together, devise checklists or guidelines for selecting them. Thinking about the criteria to be included helps everyone to understand why they are important.

Below are some guidelines on planning play resources.

- Ensure that a *range* of resources is available.
- Include a range of skin colours, hair textures and physical features in dolls and other representations of people and in book illustrations, jigsaws and posters.
- Know the correct names for cooking pots, musical instruments and clothes used for dressing up and how to use them.
- On pre-numeracy and science or technology activities, include materials that reflect the lives of a variety of people.
- Ensure that the resources reflecting our multicultural society are used actively, in positive ways, and not just left lying around. The way that resources are used by adults and children are critical for giving strong messages that they are a full part of normal, everyday learning activities.
- Provide accurate images of people living around the world, living in Britain and in the local community. Talk about people from all ethnic backgrounds who have contributed to the local and general culture, literature, sports, inventions and history in a way that young children can appreciate and understand.
- Provide photographs of people from various parts of the world as well as in Britain accurately depicting their lifestyles, houses, food, work, dress and leisure activities and talk about them in positive and respectful ways. Be careful to select those that represent life now, using accurate terminology to describe things and to counter typical stereotypes. For details of a campaign to counter stereotypes about women, see Equal Opportunities Commission (2007).
- Recognise that dolls are particularly important in children's play because they are objects to hold and express feelings about and in some ways represent real people, although it is almost impossible to get accurate representations of anyone. White children have plenty of role models of white people around them, so the accuracy or otherwise of dolls is perhaps less important than for black children, who have fewer positive role models. It is therefore essential that great care is taken to avoid stereotyped or 'golliwog-like' dolls that may reinforce negative imagery for all children. Dolls' clothes can reflect a variety of cultures.

Ensure that dressing-up clothes represent a range of cultures, for everyday and special occasions. Some should be kept separate because they represent particular special occasions and should be treated accordingly. Where miniature clothes are collected, they should be from all cultures and not just representing those of people from minority ethnic groups, for example, not just small-sized salwar kameez but also dresses, jelabas (long dress/coat), trousers, saris and shirts. Names of clothes and how, by whom and when they are worn should be known. For example, a head-covering provides a great variety – including a topi, scarf, hijab, bowler, busby, kippa/yamulka (traditional skullcap), panama, sombrero, cap, and gele (head-tie/wrap). Ordinary clothes in different colours can also be useful, for instance to illustrate that in the Hindu culture brides wear red, while white is worn by widows. Care should be taken to ensure that children respect and do not ridicule clothes from cultures other than their own.

There are several guidelines and checklists setting out criteria to use in selecting and evaluating resources that promote equality (Dixon 1992, WGARCR 1995).

Books, pictures and language

Looking at books and illustrations, and being read to, all play an important part in children's language development. They also provide opportunities to learn about scripts, their variety and the skills needed to write and read them. Some are written from left to right, some from right to left and others from top to bottom, some rest on an imaginary line while others hang from it. So the 'back' of an Urdu book is the 'front' of an English book and vice versa. The variety is yet another measure of the variety of people. Children and adults do not have to be able to understand the detail of the text in order to appreciate the script. Dual-language books help children to respect and admire scripts that are different from their own. When there is someone present who is able to read the second-language text alongside the English words, the diversity of language can be heard in practice (Edwards 1996).

Encourage all children to speak their home languages as well as learning English as an additional language. Seek advice and guidance about how best to help children to learn English. Where necessary, try to get expert support for the children's language development. Obviously, bilingual and multilingual adults have much to offer but everyone working with the children should reinforce the value of linguistic diversity in personal ways. Introducing languages, dialects, accents and scripts (including sign language, lip reading and body language) that are less familiar and knowing how they are written, read and understood is a way of breaking down language hierarchies. (See page 212 for a section on learning English.)

In these ways children are helped to recognise the skills needed and the advantages to be had from learning, singing, rhyming and speaking languages other than their own. There are many dual-language storybooks available. See Letterbox Library, and for guidelines on selecting books and pictures, see Working Group Against Racism in Children's Resources at www.wgarcr.org.uk.

Circle time

Circle time is a space within the day when children can sit down together in a circle to develop understanding and valuing of themselves and each other. It is facilitated by an adult. Circle time provides an opportunity for open discussion about any joys, sadnesses or conflicts that may have happened during the day, and for questions or issues to be raised in a way that is appropriate to the children's ages. It can be an opportunity to listen to the experiences of others and to express feelings about them. The discussions can be models for children to learn that differences can be positive, joys and sorrows can be shared, conflicts resolved peacefully, that talking about something can be empowering and that everyone has something to learn from others. Discussions may focus on something that has happened outside the early years setting, something that children have witnessed or seen on the television, or a local carnival. If such issues as terrorism or community conflicts arise, feelings can be expressed and shared and any particular concerns followed up later.

Children can be encouraged to talk with others or in pairs before contributing to the general discussion. This provides opportunities for less forceful children and for children learning English as an additional language to share their thoughts and be a part of the group ideas. Thinking about ways of ensuring that every child can participate, by encouraging a variety of ways of indicating they wish to say something – for example, by holding a pebble or by putting their hand on the shoulder of the child sitting next to them – may promote listening and may reinforce an approach that supports every child's contribution equally.

Some rules need to be agreed for circle time, for example, rules about not interrupting, and about accepting comments, feelings and ideas with respect. Circles can be big or small depending on the circumstances. Children are usually able to express what they think if they feel confident and free to contribute their thoughts in a supportive atmosphere.

Persona Dolls

The process is largely about putting students into the shoes of someone else and understanding that person's position, rather than looking at a situation from a single prejudicial perspective.

(Susan Denton-Brown talking about the School for Peace in Israel for Arab and Jewish children, *TES* 2006)

Another way of addressing specific issues and encouraging personal, social and emotional development, emotional literacy and well-being and the valuing of a variety of cultures is to use Persona Dolls. To enable the children to bond and identify with the Dolls, each is given its own individual personality, life history, family and cultural background, likes and dislikes – its persona. The aim, in the hands of skilled workers, is to develop children's ability to empathise, appreciate and feel the hurt that prejudiced attitudes and discriminatory behaviour can cause and, crucially, to develop the skills they need to be able to stand up for themselves and others when faced with unfairness and prejudice. (For a specific discussion of this, see Derman-Sparks, 2004.)

For example, they can learn to feel the hurt inflicted on a friend if they are called names. They are also enabled to express their feelings within a supportive environment. Through their identification with the Dolls, children are helped to see the injustice of the situations being presented to them in the stories and are motivated to think of solutions to the problems the Dolls 'tell' them about. Being in the role of decision-makers and problem-solvers helps boost self-esteem and confidence.

The story-telling sessions encourage children to feel good about themselves and their own cultural and family backgrounds while at the same time respecting, valuing and learning about the cultural and family backgrounds of the rest of the group. Talking about the similarities and differences between themselves and the Dolls can help children understand that being different is not something to tease or harass each other about. Asking open-ended questions like, 'If you saw what happened to [the Doll's name] what would you have done?' helps develop children's ability to empathise and encourages them to talk freely about their experiences, feelings and to make up their own minds on issues of fairness and unfairness. Children can thus learn befriending skills and what it feels like to 'walk in someone else's shoes'.

Persona Doll stories can be woven around incidents that have arisen during the day, either inside or outside the setting. For example, if there has been name-calling, a story could be told about what this means – for the hurt person or for the name-caller, but obviously not citing individual children. It helps to focus children's minds and thoughts on a person, at one step removed, so it is not threatening and may cause a child to think and reassess her or his attitudes. To be able to participate in the discussion and to think critically children need to have the appropriate words in their vocabulary and to understand their meanings. Words such as fair, unfair, respect, hurtful, not true, can be introduced through the stories.

Stories can encourage children to express the prejudices and misinformation they may have absorbed and that otherwise might have remained hidden. Practitioners can then tell stories that give correct information and help the children think about their ideas and attitudes. Comments during a story can highlight the need for an issue to be the theme of another story.

The settings children attend may be the first places outside their families where they meet people or are introduced to Dolls representing people different from themselves. Encouraging critical thinking in children and providing them with the skills to appreciate these differences helps them to grow up with a concern for others and recognise and respond to unfairness.

It is important always to be respectful of children's opinions and acknowledge their ability to learn to respect the views of others – to give them credit for this ability to empathise, and to show understanding and caring behaviour (Alderson 2000). These skills can be developed when working with Persona Dolls.

Children may develop empathy with others in many small ways when they are just toddlers but in the early years children are mostly preoccupied with their own feelings and need help to understand the experiences and feelings of others. As children develop they need support and practical guidance to help them to see the world from another's point of view. Adults can support the development of empathy by offering children scenarios in their play, in stories, as well as talking with them about real encounters with other adults and children so as to help them 'stand in another's shoes'. By talking to children about feelings, their own and other people's, they will become more able to identify and express their responses to the words and deeds of others, as well as being better able to imagine how others will respond to what they do and say.

Persona Dolls and their stories provide an exciting, effective, enjoyable and non-threatening way to implement antiracist policies and practice and are particularly effective when used as part of an anti-discriminatory and culturally appropriate curriculum. Training on how to use the Dolls is being run very successfully in many parts of the country (Brown 2001; Persona Doll Training video and support pack 2001, Brown 2008).

Other resources may be used in the same or varying ways as Persona Dolls. For example, empathy dolls are used to develop inclusive practice and support emotional literacy with young children (Dawes 2006).

Celebrating and responding to festivals

If an early years setting wishes to celebrate or respond to the various cultural and religious festivals in our society, workers need to ask some searching questions about their current and future practice. They need to be clear about the difference between religion and culture – everyone has a culture but not everyone has a religion or faith (see Lane 2005d.)

It is important to think how (or if) celebrating festivals counters racism.

- Which festivals and cultural events do we currently celebrate? Do we know and understand what these celebrations really celebrate? And why do we celebrate any festivals at all?

- Do we consider less familiar festivals? Do we include those celebrating white British cultural traditions? And how do we celebrate events without seeming tokenistic or paying only lip service to them, especially if there are no children or families from that culture or religion to help us? Or what if it is a religion that we do not practise or one with which we profoundly disagree?

- How do we ensure that we value each culture and religion equally – especially when most of the children in the setting are from a majority culture and religion?

- Does celebrating festivals reinforce the view of aspects of different cultures as exotic in some way, rather than ordinary, but special, experiences? Are there more everyday, ordinary, common-or-garden things that we can do to learn about each other?

- Are we able to give equal respect to acknowledging the cultures and religions that make up our society (for example, through Christmas, Easter, Diwali, Eid-ul-Fitr, Rosh Hashanah, Chinese New Year, Hanukkah and Guru Nanak's birthday)?

- What does celebrating a festival tell us about a particular lifestyle or culture? For example, does celebrating Diwali tell us anything more about Indian Hindu life and culture than celebrating Christmas tells us about English life and culture?

⬧ Might we consider celebrating other events acknowledged by the United Nations system? For example, International Mother Language Day (UNESCO 21 February), International Day of Families (UN 15 May), Universal Children's Day (UNICEF 20 November).[5]

These are complicated interlocking questions that may baffle us. People will have different answers to the questions. Even so, there are fundamental principles that should be behind our practice in this area.

⬧ People from all cultures and faiths should be equally valued and respected.

⬧ It is important to value the people whose culture is being celebrated and not just see culture in isolation from people.

⬧ Everyday and ongoing value and respect for difference (and similarity) is more important than what we do on special occasions.

⬧ We need to involve all families in what we do, while bearing in mind the principles and commitment to racial equality.

⬧ Acknowledging, respecting and celebrating a religion is not the same as believing, practising or participating in it.

⬧ We cannot celebrate a particular festival and the lives of people whose festival it is and then do nothing about those people for the rest of the year.

⬧ If parents object to celebrating particular festivals, it may be because they do not understand. Open and honest communication between workers and parents may help to resolve such difficulties.

⬧ There is no one way to be – there are lots of ways, all equal.

Any festival that is celebrated must be celebrated as authentically as possible. In multicultural, multifaith areas the resources for accurate implementation of the celebration are present or readily accessible. Where this is difficult, for example in a largely white or specific suburban area, are there other ways that children can learn about, and value, people from a variety of cultures? If they don't do this, if they only celebrate their own festivals, how will they learn that other people (those not living in their area) also have festivals that they celebrate? But it is likely that some people from cultures other than their own already live in the area – an examination of the variety of cultures among white families may be a starting point for this.

In such areas it is essential for staff to prepare for any celebration of any culture which is unfamiliar to them by visiting the teachers' centre or multicultural resource centre, or contacting specialist organisations such as the Shap calendar of religious festivals, religious organisations, local faith communities, and talking to relevant people to get accurate and appropriate resources, information and advice. Most areas have a town somewhere near where people from minority ethnic communities live, shop and celebrate their festivals – visits to such places have been known to be

---

[5] A list of International Days, observed by the United Nations system, is available from UK UNESCO National Commission, www.unesco.org/general/eng/infoserv/db/days.shtml

enjoyable ways of breaking down preconceived ideas about multiethnic communities (see Case study 47, page 182 for an example of this). Accepting that the celebration may not be perfect is part of trying to get it right. Evaluating the resources used, after the events, is critical in operating open-mindedness and thinking how the celebration might be better conducted next time. (For sharing how families and nurseries celebrate Chinese New Year, Diwali, Eid-ul-Fitr and Hanukkah, see video from Child's Eye Media.)

Celebrating differences and similarities

We sometimes hear people working with young children say that they 'treat all the children the same'. On reflection this is unlikely to be true. We rarely treat any child in the same way as another, because they are all different from each other and require and deserve treatment to reflect these differences. Parents of more than one child will realise that, in practice, they do not treat their children in exactly the same way – they deal with them in the most appropriate way according to each child's personality, capabilities and needs. What they usually *do* is to treat them all *equally*. That means that they receive equal access to things that are important, but not necessarily in an identical way.

When people say they treat children the same, they probably mean that they think they are equally important and wish to give them equal chances. But if children really are treated in the same way, it is likely that some children will not have their needs and differences acknowledged. For example, providing food that is familiar to most children but unfamiliar to some is treating them all the same, but the effect is that some may find it easier to manage than others.

There is a need to think about differences very carefully so that 'different' is not seen as 'bad' or 'wrong'. Professor Steve Jones made this point in his 1991 BBC Reith Lectures:

> *People look different. Difference usually means classification; and it is only a tiny step from classifying people to judging them.*

(Jones 1991)

We can value differences and similarities by talking about them, by discussing our different skin colours, hair textures and colours, eye, lip and nose shapes, temperaments and abilities, as well as our common humanity, our concern for others, our need to eat and sleep and our need to be loved. We can also learn to respect other differences, for example the different places where we live, the types of homes we have, the amount of money we have, whether we are quick at learning things or not so quick, whether some of us who are not so quick have other skills and attributes that can be valued, whether we are extrovert or introvert, whether we dress like everyone else or differently. Most of these issues are culturally loaded. Some value-judgements, such as which people are beautiful or attractive, are particularly culturally subjective and require great sensitivity when discussed (see page 137 for discussion about beauty). Perhaps we should get away from the whole concept of beauty and, instead, talk about glorious children who are secure in that knowledge, and see others as glorious too.

All children (and adults) should treat others, and be treated, fairly. Children enjoy playing games, they (nearly always) have a home, but they have a variety of family structures and family members. They all wear clothes but they are different for different occasions. Most of them see films and videos at home, but they may be very different. This range of similarities and differences is more obvious in multicultural areas, but in largely white areas children may also have a range of similarities and differences, and they can form the basis for talking about differences and similarities in society at large.

It is important not to pretend there are no differences. Of course, we are all human beings but we are all different from one another. It is a good thing that there are differences between us, adding to the variety of our experiences. But our differences do not mean anyone is of less value. When differences are not acknowledged it is often because those differences are not valued equally with the cultural norm. And we all have similarities – finding out what they are is important for children.

Differences between us extend our knowledge of the world, they put us all in perspective and enhance our lives.

Learning English

> *How can one ignore a child's first language?*
>
> (Winnie Gulsin, early education advisor for EAL, Kent LEA)

About 10 per cent of pupils in schools in England have a language other than English as a home language. In an English-speaking country, it is obviously important that every child should be or become proficient in speaking and writing English if they are to function to their best ability in their future lives. This does not mean that their home languages are less important to them – they should all be valued in settings and the advantages of speaking several languages acknowledged. Helping children to learn English or any other language is a skilled task. In the maintained sector, guidance and support should be sought from any local English language support service. Support for bilingual pupils in the teaching of English as an additional language (EAL) is usually funded through the ethnic minority achievement grant (EMAG) from the DCSF. Recently this grant has been local authority formula-funded, based on ethnic monitoring of achievement in the local authority. It is largely devolved to schools, thus leaving less support centrally in the local authority.

Although there is usually effective and ongoing support for children in the maintained sector, this support seldom extends to the voluntary, private and independent sectors except where specific arrangements have been made. This is illogical, as the need for support exists whatever setting a child is in. As both the Statutory Framework and the Practice Guidance for the Early Years Foundation Stage refer specifically to the needs of children learning English as an additional language, this anomaly between the statutory and non-statutory sector needs to be addressed as a matter of urgency (DfES 2007a). To make the issue more problematic, a survey by the Teacher Training Agency in 2004 found that only about a quarter of newly qualified teachers felt adequately trained to cater for bilingual pupils. It is even less likely that workers other than teachers will feel sufficiently prepared for this demanding role.

Children needing English support may range from families where it is not spoken at all at home or where the child only hears the home language spoken (although others may speak English) to where the home language and English are spoken alongside one another. Increasing numbers of families from the enlarged European Union are working here as well as asylum seekers thus adding to the number of languages already spoken. Children acquiring English may be referred to as bilingual but many speak more than two languages or dialects so are more accurately described as multilingual. Their families may or may not be literate in all the languages spoken.

In the same way as learning English can be described as learning 'an additional language', so too can learning languages other than English. For example, for children whose home language is English, learning Spanish, Greek, Swahili, Russian or Hindi can be described as learning an additional language. Where *all* children have the opportunity to learn a language other than their home language, the benefits of multilingualism become the norm and children can share the experience of learning a new language with each other. They can *all* learn that learning another language is more than just learning about how to speak it – it is also about learning languages with different backgrounds and communities and with different understandings, new sets of social conventions and ways of life. It is therefore important to open up the whole concept of linguistic diversity with children so that hierarchies of language can be removed.

Young children learning English are still learning the foundations of their home language. At the same time, like other children, they are entitled to access the curriculum. Learning English is most readily acquired by listening to and being with English-speaking children and adults, although extra one-to-one support may assist the process.

But there may be barriers to learning that limit this – for example, an unfamiliar and unintentionally unwelcoming environment and with adults in unfamiliar roles so that children lack confidence. Care needs to be taken to break down these barriers and to develop a trusting and supportive way of working and being with the children. Friendly words and body language, smiling faces, supportive gestures and paying attention to what a child says are all part of welcoming a child – in many ways no different from welcoming any child but particularly important where a child may feel isolated by language. Providing space for a child to listen, to learn and to observe are all part of the process of a child tuning in to language. This process may result in a child being silent for a while. But it is important to be aware that, although there are sequential but flexible stages in the learning of English, including silence, children need continual reassurance and should not be left alone to pick up language as if by osmosis. They need continuous vigilance over them as to whether they are feeling secure with that sense of belonging that makes learning much easier. Having appropriate resources reflecting the child's life and cultural background will provide an environment of comfort, familiarity and support. It will facilitate a sense of belonging for the child. (See page 216 for suggestions for linking children speaking the same language in a buddy system.)

The role of bilingual classroom assistants working in nurseries can be crucial, both in providing a probably multiethnic but certainly multilingual workforce and in providing access to the curriculum for children learning English as an additional language. This has been a lifeline for many children. Critically and significantly, most of the settings employing bilingual workers are in centres with well-stocked resources, often providing the only effective access to resources for teachers and other workers in their areas. These centres have often been the focus of antiracist work in local authorities as well as being some of the very few places where black and bilingual staff have been employed in significant numbers.

Some families believe that their child will learn English more readily if they do not speak their home language in the setting and are required to communicate only in English. This is a mistaken understanding of how languages are learnt. Workers need to be familiar with the principles of the existing research that demonstrate the importance of valuing and maintaining the home language in the process of learning English. They need to feel equally confident in explaining this to family members. (For short practical, though limited, guides for parents and workers on the issues, see Islington (undated) and Portsmouth City Council (undated) leaflets and DCSF 2008c.) See also Case study 37 on page 121 for issues about valuing the home language of a child.

It should be a priority that children hold on to and develop their home language. Not only is valuing their home language critical for learning another language but it gives a strong message to everyone that home languages are important for all of us, children and adults. It is an opportunity to be quite clear that any racist attitudes to languages are unacceptable. In a society where even very young children may have been aware of racist attitudes generally, such positive valuing builds up confidence, an important aspect of learning. And, because learning a language is much more than learning a vocabulary and grammar, it is vital that children are supported in their personal, social and emotional development as well as in the actual language learning. Confident children will more readily make friends and start to use the language so that they can access the range of activities that enable all children to develop their language skills. And there can be shared laughter along the way!

Case study 52

Meat or no meat

Asked at lunchtime if he, Sarjit, wanted 'meat or no meat' he replied 'No, Sarjit!' (thinking they were trying to say his name and had got it wrong).

Both those working with Sarjit and Sarjit himself feel sufficiently confident in the ethos of the setting to know that in learning a language you sometimes get it wrong and that this is not a problem for anyone. It is a situation where shared laughter and the likely misunderstandings in the learning process can be fun, release potential tensions and demonstrate a mutual confidence in working and sharing together – not laughing at someone but laughing with them and the situation.

Family members may be anxious at leaving a child in the setting who does not yet speak English; and feel vulnerable if they have insufficient English to ask relevant questions or explain about their child's needs. Workers living in urban areas are occasionally also likely to have experienced what it is like not to understand the conversation of those around them – an experience that gives an insight into what a form of dislocation and disempowerment feels like. Sensitive communication with the family, through body language and gestures if there is only a limited formal vocabulary, helps reassure both the child and the family that he or she will be cared for and nurtured. Finding some survival words on basic needs and expressions or someone who speaks the language helps build confidence. Where there is a key person approach he or she is a critical link between the child, the setting and the family.

If you want to know more

see NALDIC (1998a), Siraj-Blatchford and Clarke (2000), Elfer and others (2003), Dryden and Hyder (2003), Kenner (2004), Drury (2007) and Portsmouth EMAS and NALDIC websites.

Everyone supporting one another – everyone belonging

Anyone can re-hash the well-established practices of multiculturalism, but the real measure of inclusion isn't what you embrace already. It's about how much wider your arms can reach.

(Huw Thomas, head of Emmaus Catholic and Church of England School,
Sheffield, *TES*, 27 October 2006)

Everyone needs support in new situations:

- children not yet speaking English
- children who are newly arrived (in the country as asylum seekers or refugees or new to the setting)
- children perceived as different by other children
- adults newly involved in settings or services
- both adults and children who need to be encouraged to be welcoming, supportive and inclusive of others.

While some individuals may be inclusive as a matter of course, others may be less so. In any case it is the individual actions as part of the whole ethos that comprise inclusion. Being explicit about practice with children, their families and workers helps to identify the responsibility of everyone to recognise and participate in making an inclusive ethos a reality.

Aspects of an inclusive ethos might include:

- developing a buddy system for children to support other children in unfamiliar or difficult situations – a buddy can be allocated to any newly arriving child, as a positive welcoming action
- linking a new child or parent or family member with another who speaks the same language
- linking family members from different cultural backgrounds to share experiences and befriend each other as part of the setting's commitment to addressing barriers between cultures
- having positive welcoming and farewell procedures and events when children, their families and workers newly arrive at or leave the setting, as models of friendliness, kindness and empathy – building up confidence, solicitous expectations for their future and continuing support if that is wished for
- in effect, setting up a network to identify needs and support within this ethos
- devising mechanisms for monitoring the effects of such an ethos.

Looking out for one another is a good way of learning to be antiracist.

If you want to know more

see Kapasi 2007 for an example of what being antiracist in playwork means in practice.

Responding to emotions – a case study

One early years setting tried to address emotional reactions to racial equality issues by creating a no-blame culture with the families, their children and those who work with them (see page 56 for discussion of a no-blame culture). It started with the manager recognising that issues of racism were getting in the way of developing a policy for equality and were difficult to discuss without people getting uptight and defensive. The issues included the fact that some black families were being criticised for not collecting their children on time, some Asian families were not joining in parents' activities and there were some families who appeared very resentful at the presence of children from asylum and refugee families. Emotional responses prevented everyone from arriving at satisfactory solutions to the problems that were being discussed. After a series of meetings, the manager suggested that they all try to think about discussions around racism solely in the light of their responsibility to the children and that this might be facilitated if they made positive efforts to work within a no-blame culture. This had three fundamental principles.

1 Everyone was to try not to react negatively to criticism from any source.
2 No one was to blame anyone or feel self-righteously superior.

3   There was to be absolute acceptance that everyone makes mistakes, everyone can learn from them, and that learning and change only happen when people do not feel under threat or threaten someone else.

(This last point is a parallel with the way that children learn – they cannot learn effectively if they are fearful or insecure.)

After some adjustment and time, everyone in the setting supported the approach and began to work together using the three no-blame principles. For example, a black key worker felt a white mother was avoiding her, even though the worker had a particular responsibility for her child. She felt the white workers encouraged this by taking over her role with the mother. Instead of complaining about it to the manager, as she might have done in the past, the black worker felt able to talk openly with the white workers concerned. She started by trying to look at the situation from the mother's point of view, by asking the other workers to consider the following questions:

- Was she (the black key worker) doing something that might be affecting the mother's relationship with her?
- Was she as welcoming as she might be?
- What might be the mother's perception of the key worker's relationship with her child?

All the workers then looked at the situation from their own point of view, asking themselves:

- How did the black key worker perceive the behaviour of the white workers?
- How did they perceive her?

Having considered these issues together, they were able to make suggestions as to the way forward. The white workers accepted the vulnerability of the black worker partly as a result of her experiences of racism elsewhere. They also accepted that they might not have sufficiently encouraged the mother to talk with her key worker (the black worker). This was due to their efforts to be helpful to the mother, rather than to any negative view of the black worker. The black worker accepted their genuine wish not to take over her role and that, because of past experiences, she had perhaps misinterpreted their actions. To clarify matters, everyone agreed to reinforce the setting's policy for parents to discuss their children with their key worker whenever possible.

Of course, the black worker's analysis that the white workers were colluding in racism could have been correct. If that had been the case, the setting's workers would have had to face the issue in the same cooperative spirit.

Another positive effect of the no-blame policy was seen when a four-year-old South Asian girl said to one of the white workers, 'You don't like us, do you!' After some discussion with the girl (including who she meant by 'us'), the worker realised that, at story time, she rarely heard Asian children's answers to questions about the story she was telling. This was mostly because they didn't indicate that they had something to say. The worker thought about it and acknowledged three apparently unconnected things:

- most of the Asian children in the setting sat at the edge of the story-telling group
- she only ever involved the children who indicated that they wanted to contribute
- these children were sitting near her in discussions about a story.

By thinking objectively about the day-to-day reality of the children's experiences and of her own practice, the worker was able to see the situation from the South Asian girl's perspective. To her, it had appeared that the worker didn't like Asians. In a racist society where even a little girl may have experienced or heard about racial hostility, it is understandable that she had interpreted the worker's actions in this way. The worker understood this and, without being defensive, she was able to change her practice and try to vary the places where the children sat, be more receptive to how they indicated that they wished to contribute and how they asked questions.

What came out of the whole no-blame process was a development of trust, empathy, cooperation and greater happiness in this early years setting. The whole ethos changed towards a place where people listened to each other without taking offence, where constructive comments were given and received positively, where respect and understanding became the natural order of the day and where children, those working with them and families all clearly benefited. This change in relationships made the development of a policy for equality a positive process rather than one to be endured with little real commitment to its objectives.

For those wishing to establish a no-blame culture, it is a good idea to suggest that people work within existing teams or existing work relationships. The principle behind the culture can also be fostered with children, for instance during circle time (see page 207).

7 Countering racism and dealing with racist incidents

Doan let nuttin pass.

(Jamaican saying)

All forms of racism should be countered wherever and whenever they occur. Every incident, whatever form it takes, demeans the perpetrator (even if they are not aware of what they have done or are part of, others may be witnesses) and damages the target. Where the wronged person is a child, it is vital that every one of us takes action to protect their vulnerability and ensure their life's opportunities are equal to others. The particular form of racism needs to be identified and then dealt with in the most appropriate way according to the specific circumstances pertaining at the time. Some forms can only be countered by state action, others by laws, organisations, institutions, and groups of people or individuals. The objective, to remove it or stop it, needs to be kept firmly in mind. But, at the same time, it is sometimes particularly crucial to take careful account of the sensitive nature of addressing it in ways that engender an awareness and acceptance rather than resentment, resistance or denial (see Chapter 2 for detailed information on racism, and other examples discussed throughout the book).

The term 'victims' of racism is sometimes problematic because it may indicate that such people are incapable of defending themselves, are somehow passive, weak or defenceless. The term 'wronged person' may be preferable in certain circumstances, focusing responsibility on the perpetrator rather than the target. But, similarly, perpetrators who are young children may as yet be unaware of the implications of what they are saying or doing – they may be merely reflecting what they have seen or heard, even if they intend to be hurtful. It is seldom that blame is appropriate. Perhaps referring to what they have done by de-personalising it may be less threatening and more susceptible to reflection.

Racist incidents between young children range from an incident with perhaps no intention or knowledge of being hurtful or damaging, through more harmful incidents of name-calling, physical rejection (for example, not wishing to hold someone's hand who has a different skin colour or culture), pushing someone away, teasing, excluding, ganging up against someone and even violence. Recipients may experience a range of reactions ranging from feeling unhappy, bewildered, hurt, upset, anxious, marginalised, unwelcome, a lack of self-confidence, worthless, as if they don't belong, powerless, resentful to angry. Perpetrators may not even be aware of what they are doing (unwitting) or may experience a range of feelings from success, guilt, knowing they have done something wrong, revenge to power. This imbalance of power replicates the power relationships in the society.

Institutional racism and racial discrimination

Careful and watchful observation, analysing and evaluating the implementation of race equality schemes and policies – using ethnic monitoring, race equality impact assessments and the law where relevant – should identify both institutional and other forms of discrimination or provide data on differential outcomes or disparities that can then be examined. Early years services and settings should have systems in place to monitor employment, including promotion and access to other benefits (for example, training, attending external events, careers advice) and all other aspects of the service and setting. The systems should include procedures to deal with racial harassment and guidance on identifying and addressing racial prejudice and racist incidents. Children's activities should also be observed, on a regular basis, to ensure that, wherever possible, every child has equal access to the full range of learning opportunities. Any differential outcomes observed may be a result of procedures which have the effect of discriminating against some children. It is these procedures that are described as institutional racism, and which are most often the result of institutions previously not having examined their outcomes, policies and practices. However, differentials could be the direct result of racial discrimination. Constant vigilance and alertness, on the part of everyone, for any potential or existing discrimination should be an objective.

Case study 53

Who's the boss? Who notices?

One day Jonathan, who is white, took a moment to look at the early years workers in the department of which he was the head. Because the overall ethnic composition roughly reflected that of the outside population he had not previously given much thought to racial equality matters – in departmental meetings many black people were present. It was the first time he had really considered its ethnic composition in relation to what work each person was doing. His local authority is part of a large metropolitan conurbation with a significant minority of different ethnic groups living there. Apart from Felicity who is mixed race and heads the development workers' team and Ranjit who is a member of the training group, everyone above the lower administrative grades is white. It began to dawn on him that his department should by now be employing more black people at higher levels. This worried him and he set in process mechanisms for finding out the historical facts about recruitment in the department. On getting the information, he could not understand how he had not noticed what was going on before – he took action, together with the human resources department, to remove past potentially discriminatory procedures, open up channels of discussion with the workers and decide to take some positive action, under the Race Relations Act, to correct the obvious imbalance.

Point for thought and discussion

- What are some of the actions Jonathan could have taken to improve the situation?

Racially prejudiced attitudes, racist incidents and racial harassment

Indications of racial prejudice may not always be perceived as such. Indeed it is important always to pursue such indications with a view to ascertaining the reasons for them. For example, a child may react negatively to a culinary tradition other than her own by saying 'Yuk' – this may mean a lack of familiarity with any food not seen or eaten before or, more seriously, a reaction to food associated with people from a particular ethnic or cultural community. Care is always needed in following up such reactions to differentiate very clearly between a child's natural apprehension and racial prejudice.

Most authorities, including education, police and statutory and charitable bodies, now use the definition of a racist incident from the Stephen Lawrence Inquiry:

> *A racist incident is any incident that is perceived to be racist by the victim or any other person.*

The intent and perception of the perpetrator are irrelevant; it is the nature of the incident, the context in which it takes place and the hurt it causes that determine whether it is racist or not.

With children, racist incidents vary from one-off name-calling, through refusing to hold someone's hand or sit with them, to sustained bullying and serious physical violence. A target may be present or not, and incidents of racist graffiti, distributing racist literature, telling a racist joke or making a racist speech are all racist incidents. While very young children are unlikely to be involved in these latter incidents, adults in the local community may be. It is important to feel confident to take appropriate action to address all racist incidents from whatever source they come.

Comments may be made unwittingly by anyone with little thought being given to their implications. Consider how seemingly innocent comments by adults may be hurtful, with no deliberate intention of being so. For example, describing someone's skin as a 'nice light colour' (implying somehow that lighter is better) or saying that skin colour 'doesn't matter' (however well intentioned) – although it will probably not be noticed by a child it may upset a family member. Such comments may reveal prejudice or a misguided understanding of reality (see page 95 for a discussion on skin colour).

Young children of all ethnic groups may hold racially prejudiced attitudes but not necessarily have ever behaved in an overtly racist way. It is important to be alert to such attitudes if they are expressed verbally, by body language or in any other way, and to talk with children about this in appropriate ways. Work might be done using Persona Dolls or circle time as well as ongoing work about respecting differences and breaking down racial hierarchies. Where such attitudes are noticed from other workers or family members they, too, should be discussed, using the policy for equality as a basis for discussion. This is likely to be a very sensitive issue, one that calls for tact, particular interpersonal skills and working within a no-blame framework. It is an area where workers might benefit from practising with one another to ascertain the most effective way, if there is one, of talking to someone who has expressed or indicated prejudice, enabling them to understand its implications without feeling, or being made to feel, personally inadequate.

It is also important to be alert to instances where children are learning positive attitudes to differences so that everyone is comfortable with expressing them. An early years setting can be a place where there is not just the absence of negative attitudes and behaviour but also a place where positive attitudes and deeds of support and the promotion of self-esteem are just part of everyday practice. Such settings might be havens where children watch out for each other, where they are alert to other's feelings and where they take responsibility for caring for each other both in words and actions. This foundation will enable them to view the world outside the setting with critical eyes and prepare them to take their part in a society where caring about those they know extends to caring also about those they do not yet know, the world of their future.

Where racial prejudice leads to a racist incident it should be taken equally seriously whoever instigates it. Action should be taken with the perpetrator, the wronged child and any witness or witnesses. All such incidents are hurtful and potentially damaging to the wronged child. They may react by being defiant and brazen in all they do. Racist incidents are also damaging to the perpetrator, and if they are not challenged will give them, perhaps unconsciously, unjustifiable notions of their own power and how to exercise it; encouraging in them concepts of the acceptability of causing hurt rather than empathy, respect and value for others. Witnesses may feel uncomfortable, possibly feeling a bit guilty because they were relieved that they were not the victim or that they did not know what, if anything, to do. Action should be taken as soon as possible with all children involved, with priority being given to the wronged child in sensitive and supportive ways and avoiding appearing to dismiss the incident as trivial. It is important to reassure the child that it is nothing they have done that justifies such behaviour. Great care should be taken to avoid a perpetrator feeling *personally* rejected but making it clear that what has been *done* was hurtful, unacceptable and wrong. Understanding and reflection might be assisted if it is explained that everyone sometimes does wrong things. Talking through the incident together, without making an unnecessary meal of it, may help resolve any antagonism. Similar support should be given to any witnesses. Again, work with Persona Dolls or in circle time should be planned to follow up such incidents.

Racial harassment occurs when incidents accumulate to target an individual or group – extending individual incidents to be perhaps more organised. Continually ridiculing or belittling someone because of the language they speak or continually and inappropriately 'picking on them' may constitute harassment. The way people practise their faith may lead to harassment, particularly among adults. Harassment among children should be dealt with as above. Where harassment of adults is involved it may be unlawful (see Chapter 8 on legislation).

It is vital that everyone takes all racist incidents and harassment equally seriously whoever the perpetrators are and whatever their ethnicities; and it is vital to be seen to be even-handed towards them all.

Anti-racists have to be consistent, not only from a moral point of view but because our enemies use it against us when we aren't.

(Editorial, *Searchlight*, January 2006)

Racist incidents among children in early years settings tend to be around name-calling, casual thoughtless comments and reflections of what they may have already heard or seen, and peer group relationships. For example, a child calling another child a 'blackie'; or referring to South Asian people (and sometimes anyone who is not white) in passing as 'Pakis', 'those people' or saying 'they smell'. Sometimes a child may say something completely contrary to what family members think, thus reflecting the powerful influences of the world outside. It is also important to acknowledge that instances are not always directed at someone personally – there may be something said or done with no obvious recipients present and no concerned witnesses to counter it (see Case study 23 for an example of nursery children passing through Brixton, on page 89). Whether there is a target present or not, further action should be taken as suggested above.

Peer group relationships are also very important and influential with young children.

Syed and Ripon

Case study 54

A group of white and Caribbean boys are playing together. Syed and Ripon hover near them but do not join in. Nothing is said overtly but they are effectively excluded from joining in by the behaviour of the group in subtle ways – closing ranks physically, virtually ignoring Syed and Ripon and only having eye contact with one another, thus indicating that 'we don't want you here'. Syed and Ripon eventually drop away. The white and Caribbean boys appear to be unaware of either their behaviour or its consequences.

Points for thought and discussion

- What exactly is going on in this interaction?
- How can the white and Caribbean boys be helped to understand what they are doing?
- How can workers observing this best effect access to the group for Syed and Ripon?

Perhaps Syed and Ripon need to be supported to have the confidence and skills, including verbal skills, to gain access. Perhaps the group would learn something from participating in working with Persona Dolls so they can think about what it might feel like to be on the outside rather than the inside of a group. They could be encouraged to suggest what might be done so that everyone can join in equally or at least acknowledge one another's presence.

Racist incidents including ongoing racial harassment, on the other hand, may be hidden under apparently acceptable behaviour. All of those working with young children should keep a particularly watchful eye on how they behave together. Sometimes it is only careful vigilance that identifies what is really going on in an apparently happy play situation.

Case study 55

Playing outside; feeling an outsider

Most days Shenaz tried to be near Jennifer, one of the members of staff who supervised children's outside play in the setting. Jennifer always welcomed Shenaz, who appeared a little shy and nervous. At the same time she encouraged Shenaz to play with a group of girls who she seemed to have played happily with on several occasions.

One day, Jennifer took Shenaz over to the group, who apparently welcomed her. Jennifer then moved away and returned unobserved, only to discover that the apparently happy play involved Shenaz being teased and pushed about. The girls were calling her a 'Paki' and saying that she ate 'smelly food'. The behaviour was quite different from what it appeared to be from the other side of the play area.

Points for thought and discussion

- What are the implications of this case study for staff training?
- What are the implications of this case study for day-to-day nursery practice?

On other occasions early years workers may be so involved with their own immediate situation that they fail to link it with what may be going on outside the setting.

Case study 56

Racism writ large

An early years setting on the outskirts of a town had three black children. Two of them were siblings in a Nigerian family. The staff were becoming increasingly concerned that they were not settling in and that some of the white children were ridiculing them because of their appearance and because they spoke Igbo together. They asked an adviser to visit. As she walked along the building next to the setting she noticed racist graffiti, written large, on the walls. When she mentioned it to the people working with the children, none of them had seen it even though they all walked by it every day. The Nigerian children's parents also walked by it every day.

Point for thought and discussion

- Might there have been any links between the graffiti and the situation of the Nigerian children in the nursery?

Immediate responses to racist incidents

In some racist incidents it may be unclear as to whether the perpetrator perhaps did not understand what they were saying or doing, and had absolutely no intention to be hurtful – or deliberately racist. In such cases care is needed to sort out the intentions before taking any action. Even where there are clear indications of an incident with racist implications, care should be taken in making an appropriate response. Special care must be taken with children to find out exactly what happened, was heard or was said, to avoid any possible misinterpretations, any mishearings or misunderstandings. Practising and thinking about such situations beforehand is an important element in responding appropriately and effectively. But whether or not an appropriate response to the perpetrator is made, a child who has been the subject of a racist incident must be given support and comfort immediately or as soon as possible. However, no racist incident should be ignored, because the effect is the same, whatever the intention.

An example of responding to an incident, with no apparent wronged person present, is described in detail (Cook and Lane 2002/2004). Two white girls stirring food in a wok, when asked what they are doing, say they are 'playing Pakis and cooking poo'. Such incidents may be the result of thoughtlessness, but they have definite racist overtones. The young children may not necessarily have had a deliberate intention to be racist or demeaning to others (although they might have). Nevertheless, the implications are as serious as if they were intentional.

Any incident where an adult, for example, tells a South Asian child that she is 'not eating properly' when she is using her fingers or describes an African child's hair as difficult, fuzzy or kinky, needs to be dealt with immediately to maintain the child's self-esteem. In these cases, the child would need immediate support in the form of a positive endorsement of the value of eating with fingers or a happy, open discussion in positive ways of all the different types of hair that the world's people have. Circle time or Persona Dolls can also be used to raise issues like this.

However, this sort of incident also requires an approach that will enable any adult involved to really examine their own thinking and to make positive changes where necessary. Countering or challenging racist incidents between adults or from an adult to a child may be difficult because, understandably, the person involved will be unlikely to welcome it. They are likely to feel threatened, embarrassed and defensive. Should the event be ignored? Should it be dealt with at a later date? And was it really racist or are things being read into what is innocent? There are no easy answers. A criticism in public for being racist is unlikely to help, as none of us responds well to being humiliated. No one likes having an accusing finger wagged at them even in private, let alone in front of others – it is more likely to mortify them, make them feel blamed and shamed and consequently alienate them.

> *One of the worst experiences of my life was when it was suggested that I had behaved in a racist way. It comes back to haunt me even now.*

(Feelings expressed by a worker who was active against all forms of racism)

How would any of us wish to be told that what we had said or done was unacceptable? If an adult is made to feel bad in this way, their self-esteem and their ability to think clearly will diminish. This will prevent them from being more thoughtful, rather than help them towards it. If the same person is presented with the issue sensitively and in private without being blamed, they are more likely to remain confident and be willing to look at the concern raised in an objective manner.

However, the balancing view is that others may have overheard the incident and, if nothing was said or done about it at the time, may have thought it was of no consequence, that it was acceptable or that some people were unchallengeable. This quandary will need to be addressed at the time of the incident and appropriate action taken according to the circumstances and the persons concerned. It reinforces the need for guidelines in following up the setting's procedures for dealing with racist incidents.

Whatever is decided and done at the time, a clear approach is needed afterwards, one that stands back and assesses what has happened in a wider context. Obviously the staff member must be made aware that such behaviour will not be accepted in the setting. So an individual and hopefully supportive discussion is needed in any case, perhaps where experiences are shared on the basis that everyone has probably done something unacceptable at some time or other. It is important that this is not seen as punitive or humiliating but what happened was one of the inevitable consequences of living in a racist society – and recognising and accepting that some people have just never had an opportunity to seriously reflect on these issues. Such situations are extremely difficult to handle without engendering feelings of being punished – feelings that are the least likely to be conducive to reflective thinking and more likely to result in defensive behaviour, even if it is hidden from others.

But there may also be other issues to consider, including whether other staff might behave in similar ways. It may raise the issue of whether there is a need for training. Rather than requiring only the person concerned to attend training on these issues it may be that all the staff would benefit and learn from a training course that they attend together. Whole-staff training, where everyone participates, listens and learns, is likely to be far more long lasting and effective than picking one member of staff out for special measures. It raises the question of how training about racism can be acceptable to participants when the implication is likely to be seen that people needing training about racism are, by definition, racist – a quandary in its own right (see Training and education, page 150 for further discussion).

Ideally an aim should be that there is an ethos where people can say things to each other in a mutually supportive way. Most of us sometimes say things that we have not really thought through. The aim to bear in mind, after supporting the wronged person (child or adult), is 'What is the most likely way of addressing this situation so that the person concerned will listen, understand and consider changing their behaviour?' Creating an atmosphere where issues can be addressed openly, in a no-blame atmosphere, is discussed on page 56.

Countering racist attitudes from young children is very different from dealing with the racist attitudes of adults. We know that children have not yet had the opportunity to consider other information and points of view so the situation needs to be addressed particularly sensitively and the age and understanding of the child taken into account. On the other hand, when there is a clear racist intent, it is necessary to be specific in condemning the action.

Many racist incidents are accidentally overheard. They are not addressed specifically to the person who overhears them and might be said confidentially between colluding white (or black) people who would not have said or done what happened if a black (or white) person had been present. Racist name-calling may occur between black or between white people. Anyone who overhears such things has to judge how best to deal with the incident, and whether to leave it until later, respond to it immediately or, on occasions, let it pass in favour of planned activities in the setting to educate, raise awareness and change attitudes. However, in the case of racist incidents witnessed by other children, these must be addressed immediately. Ignoring them would make the wronged person, the perpetrator and the other children believe that such behaviour was all right, and that the adult seeing it agreed with it.

The principle is that such an incident should not be ignored especially when it involves the early years setting itself, except in specific circumstances. For example, according to the circumstances, someone who overhears a racist comment might counter with one of the following statements, taking care not to appear confrontational, superior or 'holier than thou':

- I'm sorry you think that.
- I don't agree with you.
- What makes you think that? / What makes you say that?
- That's not my experience.
- Please do not include me in that.

However, responding by saying something like 'That's not nice – how would you like to have that happen to you?' does not deal with the key point. Whether or not the person would mind the incident happening personally is irrelevant. While helping someone to empathise with being a target of racism is important, it is not the same as not wanting it to happen to oneself. It is the perpetrator's action itself that needs to be seen as wrong and unacceptable.

In all public authorities, including settings such as schools, there is a requirement stemming from the Home Secretary's recommendations following the Stephen Lawrence Inquiry, to record all racist incidents and report to the local authority on the number of incidents and the number in which follow-up action is taken. Settings in the voluntary, independent and private sectors, while having no statutory responsibility to record racist incidents, should demonstrate good practice and commitment by doing so. They should also regularly monitor such records and relate them to the action taken to address them (see page 234).

(For specific advice on dealing with racism, although written some time ago, see EYTARN (1993b) and, for a brief description of 'political correctness', see page 77.)

It happens all the time!

Case study 57

Something for nothing

Freda, a white woman, buying something in a shop with her child waited in a queue while a South Asian family, a man and woman, struggled over paying for some goods. There was a lot of questioning from the shop assistant in a very supportive way and it took some considerable time. When Freda got there she complimented the assistant in being so helpful and how good it was that she had taken such care. The assistant whispered 'Well "they" always want something for nothing don't they!'

Points for thought and discussion

- Was this racist and hypocritical – acting in one way but having negative attitudes behind the action?
- Was there a genuine issue about the way people from different cultural backgrounds negotiate shopping?
- Was Freda being patronising in complimenting the shop assistant?

Another example of being incorporated into racially prejudiced conversations is at the bus stop, where we hear things and chat, perhaps with young children present.

Case study 58

Bedside manner

A stranger made this remark to a mother with her child at a bus stop.

I'm just going to the hospital. I hope I don't have one of those foreign doctors again – they don't speak proper English and I don't like them touching me.

Points for thought and discussion

Acknowledging the presence of a child at these incidents is important, as is doing something about it before the moment has passed.

- How should one respond so the children don't get racist messages and what is an appropriate response when the bus is just coming over the horizon?

Racist jokes

People who tell a racist joke sometimes don't see it as racist. They may sometimes say the people about whom the joke is told don't mind. Whether this is true or not, such jokes often reinforce damaging stereotypes. It is important to say something at the time or as soon as possible afterwards so that the teller is able to go away and think about it without feeling personally under attack and consequently defensive – trying to get someone to think about what they have said, rather than humiliating them in public (especially when he or she has been so upfront about the joke). If the joke is overtly and intentionally racist it is, in some ways, easier to deal with by being explicit about disagreement. The teller knows it is racist even if they don't care (see page 70 for more discussion about jokes).

Name-calling

Name-calling is now widely recognised as being one of the most damaging and hurtful things that happens to young children. All forms of name-calling are totally unacceptable, however innocent they might seem. Name-calling picks a child out, usually because they are different and often potentially vulnerable in some way. Although such incidents are now generally being taken more seriously than previously, children have often suffered this kind of abuse in silence, not even daring to tell their families what they were going through. This protective silence, the dread of telling on others, has often prevented adults from realising the full extent and pain that some children experience.

Case study 59

Anthony Walker

Gee Walker, the mother of the black teenager Anthony Walker murdered by white racists in Liverpool in 2005, said she wished she had done or said something at the time about the racist names that her children were called. She said it was down to all of us to join together about racist name-calling and not to turn a blind eye

(BBC *Woman's Hour* 3 February 2006)

Point for thought and discussion

- How important is it not to turn a blind eye when we see racist abuse happening?

Name-calling is always unacceptable and always wrong. Personally insulting names like 'Four Eyes', 'Big Ears', 'Fish-face' or 'Fatty' are hurtful and offensive.

Elizabeth was always called 'Fatty' at school. Forty years later a school friend asked how this had affected her. She replied 'I remember it every day'.

While totally acknowledging this type of pain, name-calling has particular implications for black children. When a black child is ridiculed for being black, the child's family and whole ethnic community are also being made fun of. So the effect is over and above specific personal insults. It is therefore important to recognise the particular anguish that a black child may go through, while at the same time dealing with every incident of name-calling in a similar manner. There are some similarities here with name-calling about girls where their mothers, other female relatives, and girls and women in general are also implicated. However, compounded by the history of racist violence and oppression, racist name-calling is especially severely damaging and threatening (see page 19 for a discussion of this).

Because name-calling resonates with most family members – no one wishes their own child to be name-called, whatever the name – it is one of the issues about equality around which all families, workers and children might unite. Together they can own the need to do something about it.

Discussing name-calling, considering its hurtful and damaging aspects and committing themselves to do something about it, is a process that involves everyone, irrespective of their own particular backgrounds, genders, abilities or ethnicities. It is a way of engaging everyone around a common purpose that may lead to a more ready acceptance of the need to address racism in its wider sense. It involves everyone equally in accepting that their own child may be a name-caller or a recipient of name-calling. This means acknowledging the responsibility for doing something about it by taking action with the children, together with workers in the setting. Crucially it must involve everyone working together within a no-blame culture (see page 56). It must involve the acceptance by everyone that incidents are acknowledged; and that they are recorded and monitored to assess whether subsequent work done with children reduces specific forms of name-calling and name-calling overall. Various methods of addressing it may need to be tried, for example using circle-time, Persona Dolls, stories, role-play and discussions, both one-to-one and in groups. This all means developing a policy to counter name-calling as part of the setting's policy for equality.

If you want to know more

read the suggestions about a policy on name-calling in the appendix of EYTARN (2001) and in Lane (2001b).

How do we know if children have hidden racist attitudes?

Children often mirror the attitudes and behaviour of the adults around them, including in their settings. They are also alert to the sensibilities of adults by sometimes keeping from them any negative attitudes they may hold. (See Case Study 30, page 101 for an example of this.) But how can we counter such attitudes if we do not know about them? Working on the principle that there are many attitudes that need to be unlearnt, using Persona Dolls may reveal attitudes that can then be addressed. While clearly settings should be places where expressed racist attitudes are unacceptable, dormant attitudes may still exist despite action having been taken. Each setting will need to decide how best to address this issue. Providing an atmosphere and situation where a child feels able to articulate their attitudes without censure may be problematic. This is because if they reveal negative attitudes the lack of censure may indicate to the child that there is nothing unacceptable about such attitudes – a situation contrary to what might be the ethos of the setting. But providing space and opportunity to discuss attitudes with an individual child within a no-blame culture, where questions may be asked and answers accepted, may give time for a child to reflect on what has been said. These situations need to be very carefully and sensitively conducted – not imposing personal ideologies nor indoctrinating children but nevertheless making the points about everyone being equal and that racist attitudes are hurtful, damaging and demeaning. Group discussions should usually be avoided because they risk hurtful prejudiced attitudes being expressed in another child's presence.

It is essential that families are fully involved in understanding and supporting this work. This means explaining why it is important for all children to be provided with opportunities to respect and value those who are different from them and eliciting the support of their families to do this. If possible it has to be a shared activity where similar messages are given, both in the setting and in children's homes, in order not to in any way subject a child to the stress of family and workers having conflicting ideas.

Families should be involved before approaching this sensitive issue – in the same way as their involvement is advocated in the development of the policy for equality – so they can have time to consider and reflect on the issue. The aim should be for families and workers, within a context of acceptance, to be able to feel included and comfortable in sharing and discussing their feelings and opinions together. This is an issue for workers to discuss, always remembering that people can change their attitudes even when there is an apparent impasse.

Procedures to counter and prevent racist incidents

There should be clear procedures in settings for countering racist incidents in situations where there is a perpetrator and a wronged person, whether they are children or adults. It may be inappropriate to use the word 'wrong' to describe an incident – this will all depend on so many specific circumstances pertaining to that situation and that child or adult. The incident may be verbal or physical. Approaches for addressing incidents where adults are responsible have already been touched on. While the following suggestions address incidents where children are involved, they apply equally to adults.

After identifying an incident as racist – whatever its level of severity – the first priority is to comfort and support the child who has been targeted and to make it absolutely clear that nothing he or she has done justifies it. The following steps can then be taken, taking great care to be sensitive to all the emotions likely to be involved.

1   Make sure that anyone listening to, overhearing or witnessing the incident understands that what was said or done was hurtful and unacceptable.
2   Support the child who has said or done something racist while, at the same time, making sure that they know it is hurtful and unacceptable and that it will not be condoned. Explain why. Take care not to undermine the child's self-esteem by ensuring that the incident itself, and not the child herself or himself, is dealt with. Try to tap into their concepts of empathy to what it feels like to experience racist

behaviour and, where appropriate, consider raising this sort of issue in circle time or by using Persona Dolls. This is a difficult path to tread and everyone will have their own ways of doing it as sensitively as possible. Few of us wish to deliberately hurt someone else's feelings or offend them. But doing nothing is not acceptable either.

3   Where appropriate, talk together about the incident with the perpetrator, the wronged person and, where necessary, any witnesses.

4   Follow it up with whatever strategy is necessary to prevent it happening again, according to the circumstances and the incident itself. Work with children, workers and family members, as appropriate.

It is vitally important to provide children from all ethnic backgrounds, who may experience racist incidents including racial harassment or name-calling, with the skills to deal with them. Black children in particular may have few positive or useful alternatives in reacting to these forms of racism, and there are three common negative responses.

Children might ignore them and pretend they have not happened, bottling up the pain inside themselves and possibly appearing not to care – and some time in the future this may burst out in anger.

They might respond by calling names back. But there is no racist abuse against white children (and adults) that comes anywhere near the offensiveness that children from black and other minority ethnic backgrounds might experience. Calling someone 'Honky', 'Whitey' or 'Chalkface' are mild terms compared with 'Wog', 'black bastard', 'Coon' or 'Paki'. These latter words are loaded with historical and offensive implications. In any case the argument may be that to return words in kind is to stoop to the level of the perpetrator.

They might lash out physically, and then may be blamed for being aggressive or violent. There is plenty of anecdotal evidence that when children do lash out, it is because they are at the end of their tether and that the incident is the last in a long line of unaddressed incidents: the straw that breaks the camel's back.

Sometimes the experience for racially abused children is to be reprimanded or punished for retaliating, with little recognition or understanding of what harm it does to them or of the cumulative effect of such situations. Where no adult notices what is going on, the only real alternative for children is to tell someone what is happening. A child can only safely tell in a setting where others will take responsibility and do something constructive about it, where they will be comforted and their pain acknowledged, and where they will not subsequently be victimised. It is no good a child reporting something if an adult says 'Oh, dear, let's just try to forget it, shall we?' or 'Just ignore it', or if the adult tries to divert the issue or make amends by suggesting everyone does a jigsaw together.

So to make telling possible, workers (and family members) need to make it clear to children, by the most appropriate method possible, that they will listen to them, that they will understand their hurt and experiences of racism (however they choose to define that word) and will do their best to stop it happening again. Children need to know where adults stand about these issues. They will also feel supported if they know that they are not alone, that other children will recognise their pain and hurt and stand up for them. One suggestion for older children is to have a particular time – it could be called 'bubble time' – when a child wishes to tell an adult something that is upsetting for them and collects a token (a bubble) from a particular worker and says who they want to talk with. That worker then liaises with the person the child wishes to talk with, who then talks with the child. This removes the need for the child to approach the worker out of the blue.

Similarly, adults in work situations need to make clear to other adults that they will take issues of racism seriously and, where appropriate, take personal action and provide support to anyone subjected to it.

Children should also be encouraged to learn that they, too, have a role to play in taking responsibility to tell adults when they witness any form of unkindness, racial abuse or name-calling. Young children can be encouraged to recognise it happening to themselves and others and to tell an adult, without going through the feeling of believing that they have betrayed a member of the group. If they can be helped to see that both the wronged person and the perpetrator will be supported, they may be more willing to come forward.

Children can also learn about taking the matter into their own hands through assertive responses, and empowering themselves.

Case study 60

The visit to the pet shop

Children from the nursery visited a local pet shop. The owner asked them which nursery they were from. When they told him he said 'Oh that's where nig-nogs and dumbos go, isn't it?' Their teacher remonstrated with him. But back in the nursery the children decided to write to him, with the help of the teacher, saying how upset they were at his comment. On receiving the letter he was very contrite, closed his stall on the market for the day and came to the nursery to talk with the children about how sorry he was and showed them some of the pets he had. The children had been empowered by their action. The teacher also learnt how important it is to check visits out in advance. And the pet shop owner learnt something very important too.

Point for thought and discussion

- From this case study, what kind of ethos and education do you think is promoted in the nursery?

Children also need guidance and support about how to respond to racist incidents. They could make use of all the following forms of self-defence:

- strong self-esteem
- a clear understanding that the problem is with the racist perpetrator, not with the wronged person

- the ability to use different forms of response – for example, 'I like who I am' (a Traveller, Roma, Gypsy or refugee) or 'I'm black and strong' (or South Asian, or African or African Caribbean according to the circumstances) or 'I am white and strong'.

All three forms of self-defence are most effective if families and workers work together to provide the children with the tools of their defence and the confidence they need to use them.

Having a policy on all forms of racist incidents and name-calling

There are obvious advantages in having a policy already in place to deal with name-calling and other racist incidents, one that is owned by families and discussed with them prior to attending the setting.

Case study 61

'Just joking'

Ropers Corner Playgroup has developed a specific policy on name-calling. On Tuesday morning Janice, who is African Caribbean, is completing a jigsaw with Krutika, who is Indian. Krutika accidentally knocks the jigsaw and upsets the pieces that Janice has put into place. Janice says, jokingly, 'Oh, you are just a silly Paki!' Anna, a worker in the playgroup, overhears this comment and talks with both children about it in a supportive way but making it clear that such words are unacceptable and, even if Janice did not intend to do so, what she said may have hurt Krutika's feelings.

She records the details of the incident in the name-calling incident book and at the end of the session tells Janice's mother and Krutika's father what had happened. Because they have both been involved in devising and agreeing the policy they accept what has happened (though Janice's mother is disappointed about what her daughter has said and insists it had not come from her) and agree to talk with their children about it when they get home. Anna arranges to tell a story to a group of children with a Persona Doll soon afterwards, using the same principle of what had happened but with a different example, so that Janice would not feel personally identified.

All workers continued to be watchful and listen for any other name-calling. At the end of the year no 'jokey' name-calling had been heard again and name-calling of any kind had nearly stopped.

Point for thought and discussion

- What features of good practice in addressing a racist incident are shown in this case study?

All children and adults need to be part of a system that has policies, procedures, responsibilities and monitoring systems in place to counter racism in general (the policy for equality); and has detailed policies on countering racist incidents, name-calling and harassment in particular. Everyone working with children, all the children and their families should know about them, understand what they are for and, wherever possible, have ownership of them themselves (never assume that a child who harasses another has parents who don't care; they may strongly support the setting's policy and be unaware of what their child is doing). Consistently raise issues of valuing and respecting everyone. Deal with every incident as part of the procedures identified in the policy.

The Stephen Lawrence Inquiry defines a racist incident as any incident that is perceived to be racist by the victim or any other person. Settings that are part of a public authority have legal obligations to record the number of racist incidents which take place, and the number in which follow-up action is taken. These must be reported to the local authority, which then reports the aggregated numbers to the Audit Commission. No individual institutions are identified and it is the governing body that is required to report the figures to the local authority.

Some people think that if a large number of racist incidents are reported, this will reflect badly on the institution. In fact, the opposite is the case. Since no establishment is isolated from the outside society, there are always likely to be incidents. Higher numbers show that the incidents are being picked up and dealt with by staff, and that the children know what to do – they know that they are wrong and they trust the staff and tell them.

Record all incidents and monitor them on a regular basis to check whether any patterns emerge and whether any particular children are perpetrators or victims (or harassing others or being harassed) and whether particular issues need to be addressed. Describe what happened, where it took place, details of the ethnicity and age of the child(ren), what action was taken to support the wronged child and the perpetrator, and how the families are to be informed about it. Identify any future work that needs to be done with children or their families to ensure that what has happened does not recur.

After a racist incident, take the opportunity to talk with children, to explain that what happened was unacceptable and emphasise that what a person does, not who they are, is what matters. Talk with parents about what their children are doing or being subjected to, and seek their support in dealing with it in an organised way. Sometimes hurtful name-calling can lead to physical violence, where the depth of the hurt may not be sufficiently acknowledged (see the checkpoints in Finch 2000).

A specific policy on name-calling may be an effective way of engaging everyone – families, workers, children and visitors – in getting rid of *all* forms of name-calling, racist or otherwise. Working together in this way may enable all to share the pain and damage to children of such name-calling. It may, in addition, help formulate and get acceptance of other policies for equality because the principles have been established. A suggested policy strategy is available (see appendix of EYTARN 2001 and Lane 2001b).

Government Advice on countering racist bullying, which includes the early years, is available (DfES 2006d). Although people in the early years may prefer not to use the term bullying with reference to young children, it is used in this Advice as an umbrella term, part of a continuum through schooling generally. For a very helpful, comprehensive booklet about dealing with and recording racist incidents see Essex County Council (2007).

Assessing the impact of what we do – recognising, celebrating and evaluating positive changes in children's racial attitudes

Everyone hopes that the proactive work they do with children to promote racial equality will have some effect – that the work done has an impact on their future behaviour as they grow up to be adults. Can we find out what works? What might be the mechanisms?

This may be something that takes years to be able to measure accurately and would require careful, sensitive research methods. And we can only assess changes in individual children if we assess their attitudes and behaviour before work is undertaken with them – and perhaps also the attitudes of their families – as well as afterwards, possibly at varying stages of their lives. This is a daunting and long-term task. Perhaps the best we can hope for is that, in general, attitudes and behaviour will be more positive in the future and certainly in those of the younger group of people who may have experienced early childhood practice for racial equality. But how could all the other factors influencing children as they grow up be taken into account? It would be difficult, except by very careful analysis, to identify the particular effect of specific early years work with children on their adult lives.

But, where action is taken with children to learn positive attitudes and behaviour to differences and to unlearn those negative ones that they may have already learnt, it is worthwhile sometimes reflecting on whether there are any indicators that we might be able to identify. Is there anything that we can observe (about workers; about family members, and from families from minority ethnic groups specifically; from all children, and from children from minority ethnic groups specifically) that provides us with any evidence of the effectiveness of our work? Something that we can celebrate?

The answers to these questions will depend on many factors and the circumstances pertaining at the time. These might include the amount of time given to observing children and the period of time over which they are observed, the length of time a child has been in the setting and the skills and experience of the workers (see page 103 for a description of a project about respecting differences in Northern Ireland).

However, the absence of demonstrable proof of effectiveness should be no deterrent to what must be, by any measure, good practice and in the ultimate best interests of all children.

When discussing racism and young children some people might get the impression that they are all inevitably racially prejudiced, while others will deny the possibility of racist attitudes in young children. One of the purposes of this book is to identify any racist attitudes and behaviour and make suggestions for rectifying them. But not all children are prejudiced and some, perhaps having once been prejudiced, are learning not to be so. They have had opportunities in the care of effective and aware workers and family members to learn positive attitudes to people who are different from themselves or to unlearn those negative attitudes that they may have previously learnt. This is a cause for celebration, celebrating that changes *are* possible and that individuals or groups of workers and families *can* make such changes possible.

It is critical to maintain that feeling of hope and of achievement. Otherwise how can workers keep the faith that what they are trying to do works in practice – that the day-to-day, day-after-day reorientating of children's vision to acknowledging and welcoming our diverse society does change their lives for the better. Of course there will always be people who say that it is not for the better because they themselves are imbued with racist attitudes. But by any serious objective measure the elimination of racial prejudice in children's lives is a good thing.

But it is not only the *removal* of prejudice that is a cause for celebration. Enabling children to demonstrate friendship by standing by one another in the face of prejudice, or for other reasons, provides children with a sense of security, reinforces loyalty and prepares them for dealing with the stresses and strains of adulthood. And it is not only by standing by friends that they may learn, but standing against injustice wherever they see it, even if the person subjected to injustice is not their friend or is someone they do not know. These skills are one of the bases for the development of a future society where we all look out for one another and care for one another even when we do not know one another or agree with one another – our common humanity is being acknowledged.

So what are the measures that we might look for where children have been helped to work and think in this way? What does a setting's practice look like when children have been working to develop positive attitudes and behaviour to those who are different from them? And what do we look for in their attitudes and behaviour? Workers need to ask themselves these questions and try to identify aspects of practice that appear to work and manifestations from children that it has worked, manifestations that are measurable in some way. Perhaps specific criteria need to be considered. For example, in considering the words children use about others, identifying words that range from positive to negative so an objective evaluation can begin to be possible. From this they may be able to build up an evaluation of practice over a period of time. This would ideally mean identifying what the situation was before such work started. Is this possible?

Many suggestions have already been identified in this book – they might also include observation of:

- the words and terms children use, especially those used to describe people
- the welcome they give to others
- their relationships with those who are different from and unfamiliar to them

- their self-confidence in multicultural groups
- their acceptance of one another
- their expressions of friendship
- the way they describe themselves and others, their languages, their skin colours, not just in words but in body language
- the way they deal with conflict and dissonance
- the resources they chose to play with and how they play with them
- their caring attitudes and support and empathy for others
- their lack of negative attitudes and behaviour towards those who are different from them
- their open-mindedness and receptivity to others, new ideas and challenges
- the way they stand up for one another and against unfairness
- the way they work through uncomfortable situations and take responsibility to do it.

By developing a picture of existing practice and actions it should be possible to be in a position to evaluate an early years setting for its effectiveness in putting antiracism into practice.

The local authority should be an active partner in this for it is in the interests of everyone that effective practice is highlighted and made available to others. Work in this area is new but beginning the process of questioning is where it should start.

8 Legislation for racial equality

Law is an agent of change.

(Lord Justice Sedley, Discrimination Law Association conference,
December 2005)

there is respect for the dignity and worth of each individual and mutual respect between groups based on understanding and valuing of diversity and on shared respect for equality and human rights.

(General Duty of the Commission for Equality and Human Rights [EHRC],
Equality Act 2006)

All equality law should be about respect for human dignity.

Over the past 40 years or so there has been a considerable advance with regard to addressing aspects of racism nationally. Since the Race Relations Acts of 1965, 1968 and 1976, there has been increasingly specific legislation about racial discrimination and promoting racial equality – the Race Relations (Amendment) Act 2000; European legislation on racial discrimination; and the Equality Act 2006 setting up the Equality and Human Rights Commission. Also having implications for racial equality are the Children Act 1989, the Children Act 2004, the Childcare Act 2006, the United Nations Convention on the Rights of the Child 1989 (particularly Articles 2 and 29), and the Human Rights Act 1998.

Present legislation also covers discrimination on grounds of sex and gender and disability in similar ways to that of racial discrimination. Recent European legislation includes employment law covering discrimination on grounds of age, religion or belief (including lack of religion or belief) and sexual orientation. The Equality Act 2006 extends this cover for religion or belief and sexual orientation to goods and services.

The Race Relations Act 1976

Laws against discrimination cannot change people's attitudes, but they can change people's behaviour.

Although in 2000, the Race Relations (Amendment) Act amended the existing 1976 Race Relations Act (RRA) to place a statutory duty on public authorities to promote racial equality in all their activities, the provisions of the original 1976 Act are in force and are important as the basis for the current amended legislation.

The RRA covers early years services including via its provisions on education, employment, local authorities, training, services, public functions and advertising. (For an historical perspective on the laws against racial discrimination, see CRE 2005a.) This law – together with requirements, guidance and policies from the Department for Children, Schools and Families (DCSF); guidance from the Qualifications and Curriculum Authority (QCA); and inspection arrangements from the Office for Standards in Education, Children's Services and Skills (Ofsted) – provides a framework for local authorities and any partnerships, voluntary, independent and private organisations, elected members, officers, policy-makers, lawyers, administrators, trainers and providers to plan and operate a service which is based on principles of racial equality. Details of codes of practice and guidance on racial discrimination and the duty to promote race equality in employment, education and other matters are available from the Equality and Human Rights Commission (EHRC) (see website www.equalityhumanrights.com).

The RRA defines the forms of racial discrimination that are unlawful. It does not cover every form of racism but is specific about types of discrimination and the circumstances in which they might occur. Only people belonging to a racial group, as defined under the RRA, are covered by the legislation.

In the RRA, a racial group is one that is defined by reference to race, colour, nationality, citizenship or ethnic or national origins (Jews, Sikhs, Romany Gypsies and Irish Travellers are covered, among others). Discrimination on racial grounds means discrimination on the grounds of race, colour, nationality, citizenship or ethnic or national origins. (Note that the grounds do not include religion, culture or language.) In 2003, an important new aspect to the definition of indirect discrimination and a new definition of harassment came into force under the Race Relations Act 1976 (Amendment) Regulations 2003.

The RRA identifies four forms of discrimination.

1 **Direct discrimination** – Section 1(1)(a). This means treating a person less favourably – on racial grounds – than another person is, or would be, treated in the same or similar circumstances.

> *For example*, it would be unlawful to refuse a child a place in an early years setting simply because they are black, white or an Irish Traveller.
>
> It would be unlawful to give a child on the waiting list of a setting preference solely because of their racial group, even if the aim was to reflect the ethnic composition of the community or to have a multiethnic group of children.
>
> It would be unlawful for a setting to set racial quotas for children or reserve places on a racial basis.

These provisions apply to all settings, no matter what the reason or apparent explanation for the action.

Harassment – Section 3A. The definition of harassment, brought in by the Race Relations Act 1976 (Amendment) Regulations 2003, applies when discrimination is on the grounds of race, ethnic or national origins. Harassment on the grounds of colour or nationality could amount to less favourable treatment and may be unlawful direct discrimination.

A person harasses another on the grounds of race, ethnic or national origins when he or she engages in unwanted conduct that has the purpose or effect of:
- violating that person's dignity, *or*
- creating an intimidating and hostile, degrading or humiliating, or offensive environment for them.

For example, it would be unlawful to create an atmosphere of ridicule and make mimicking noises whenever workers communicated together in their home language.

2　**Indirect discrimination** – Section 1(1)(b). This has two forms and occurs when:
　i)　a provision, criterion or practice, applied equally to everyone, puts people from a particular racial group (based on race or ethnic or national origin) at a disadvantage because they cannot comply with it. This will be unlawful unless it can be shown that the provision, criterion or practice is a proportionate means of achieving a legitimate aim.

For example, it may be unlawful to operate a waiting list on a first-come-first-served basis, giving preference to the child whose name is at the top of the list. Those at the bottom of the list are likely to, disproportionately, include people newly arrived in the area, those who are unfamiliar with the system of waiting lists and how early years services and settings work in practice, those who do not know that early years settings even exist or are available to them and those who do not understand or read English. Such people will include Travellers and Gypsies, people who have recently moved into the area and people whose home language is not English and are relatively recently arrived in the country, especially if they are from countries where early years services are minimal. Waiting lists are important to indicate who might wish to attend the setting but admissions should be open, fair and objective.

Another example might be an insistence that girls wear skirts, which may disproportionately affect Muslim girls who are required by their culture and faith to cover their legs. While Muslims are not covered under the RRA as a racial group, they may be largely from a particular nation – for example Pakistan or Bangladesh – that is covered.

ii) a requirement or condition, applied equally to everyone, has a disproportionate adverse effect on people from a particular racial group (based on colour or nationality) because they cannot comply with it. The requirement or condition will be unlawful unless it can be shown to be justifiable on non-racial grounds.

> *For example*, it may be unlawful for a setting, where all the staff are white, to ask them to find out if anyone they know would like to fill a job vacancy (word-of-mouth-recruitment), if this disproportionately disadvantages possible applicants on grounds of colour.
>
> *Another example* – it may be unlawful to give preference, formally or informally, to applicants to an early years setting who live in a particular catchment area, if this unjustifiably excludes an area where, disproportionately, asylum-seeking people or people of a particular nationality live. This might include people from Somalia, Zimbabwe, Poland or Albania.

Acts of indirect discrimination may be lawful if they can be shown to be justified. For example, an early years setting advertises a post for an Urdu-speaking nursery nurse. The requirement that the post holder can speak Urdu is indirectly discriminatory against people who are not from a Pakistani background as fewer non-Pakistani people will be able to comply with the condition. However, the nursery may be able to justify the condition on the grounds that the nursery is in an area with a large Pakistani population and such a worker is needed to best meet the needs of the children using the nursery (extract from Kahn and Young 2007).

Customs, practices and procedures that may have been in place for a long time, and were never intended to discriminate, may nevertheless have an indirectly discriminatory impact on particular racial groups.

This form of discrimination is important because it reveals examples of practices and procedures where there was never a specific motive to discriminate but which, in practice, have that effect.

3 **Victimisation** – Section 2. A person is seen as being victimised if they are treated less favourably than others in the same circumstances because it is suspected or known that they have brought proceedings under the Race Relations Act or given evidence or information concerning such proceedings, or alleged that discrimination has occurred.

> *For example*, refusing a child a place at an early years setting because their parents had previously complained about racial discrimination in the setting would be unlawful.

4   **Segregation** – Section 1(2). Segregating a person from others on racial grounds alone, constitutes less favourable treatment.

For example, grouping children at mealtimes or for play activities according to their racial group, and for no other reason, would be unlawful.

There are other sections of the RRA that are also relevant to early years services and settings. They include:

- discriminatory practices
- instructions and pressure to discriminate
- aiding unlawful acts
- advertisements
- associations
- charities.

For example, regarding pressure to discriminate, it would be unlawful for the person in charge of an early years setting to put pressure on a college not to send them a student on placement who is of a different racial group from the children. It would also be unlawful for parents to organise a petition for a setting not to accept an Irish Traveller child. The reason for the pressure is irrelevant (Section 31).

It would be unlawful to instruct the person responsible for allocating work experience placements for students not to send someone from a particular racial group to a specific placement (Section 30).

Specific areas where discrimination may occur are defined in sections covering employment, education, services (including early years organisations and settings not covered by education), public functions, and vocational training (see CRE 2005b for statutory code of practice on racial equality in employment and EHRC website for other publications).

For example, the legal responsibility for any discriminatory act or conduct by a worker or agent rests with the employer unless he or she can show that all reasonably practicable steps have been taken to prevent them. For example, if a caretaker of a setting responsible for booking rooms in the evenings or weekends when the setting is not open, refuses to book a room (or makes excuses not to book a room when there is a vacancy) for a South Asian women's group, the employer (the management committee or local authority according to the situation) could be held responsible for that act of unlawful racial discrimination. An employer may be held liable whether or not the acts were done with their knowledge or approval and may extend to a worker's behaviour in a work-related situation, for example, a nursery party (Section 32).

A legal duty is also placed on public authorities to have due regard to the elimination of racial discrimination and the promotion of equality of opportunity and good relations between people of different racial groups (Section 71).

Exemptions from the Race Relations Act

There are a few ways that the RRA permits discrimination on racial grounds. These are strictly limited and specifically defined. They are intended to moderate the consequences of past discrimination and disadvantage, to encourage and make known to applicants that they are welcome to apply for jobs or training, or to address certain situations where being of a particular racial group is important – for example, having special (but temporary) needs such as the need to learn English. They include:

- employers and other persons encouraging people from under-represented racial groups to apply for work or providing training for those groups
- recruiting a person from a particular racial group where being of that group is a 'genuine occupational requirement or qualification' as specified under the Act
- taking action to meet the special needs of a particular racial group in regard to their education, training or welfare, or any ancillary benefits, according to the particular circumstances and other actions. (See below for the particular definition of 'special needs'.)

Although these forms of action are lawful it is never lawful to favour any particular racial group in the actual recruitment and selection process for employment.

In early years services and settings the exemptions listed in the points above might be used in the following circumstances, and are addressed in the sections of the Act shown in the headings. Some examples of positive action are given in Lane (1999a).

Taking positive action

It is important to take positive action, in its widest sense, if the consequences of both present and past discrimination and disadvantage are to be addressed, for example, with regard to the serious under-representation of workers from black and other minority ethnic groups at senior management levels throughout the service (see pages 260–265 for further discussion). Failure to do this may result in such consequences and their implications for racial equality remaining for many future decades.

Training for particular work – Section 37

Any person or group under this section may provide members of a particular racial group with access to training for particular work or encourage them to take advantage of it, so long as people of that racial group have been under-represented in that work at any time within the previous 12 months. For example if there were very few people of Bangladeshi origin either working in playgroups or pre-schools or trained in playgroup or pre-school work in the area, and someone or some group wanted to offer training in such work specifically for Bangladeshi people so that they were qualified to apply for such work, that would be lawful. It may be lawful to offer transport and childcare specifically for this group of people.

This might be a way of ensuring that Bangladeshi children were supported by Bangladeshi people as well as providing a role model for people from other racial groups, where this was appropriate.

Encouraging applicants into employment and providing access to training for particular group of employees – Section 38

If an employer wants to have a multiethnic workforce that reflects the ethnic composition of the local community, or wants to convince (or try to convince) potential employees that applicants from the racial group in question are really welcome, then the employer can lawfully advertise this fact. The advertisement can state that applicants for work are particularly welcome from that racial group, but only if that group has already been under-represented in the workforce at any time in the previous 12 months.

The exemption only provides a level playing field with regard to applying for jobs, so that under-represented groups are specifically mentioned and encouraged but they do not get favourable treatment at job selection.

Under this section an employer is also able to provide training for employees from certain racial groups who, within the last 12 months have been under-represented in particular work in their employment, for example, at senior levels, which would help fit them for that work.

Special needs – Section 35

This section permits action to give people of a particular racial group access to facilities or services to meet their special needs in regard to their education, training, welfare or any ancillary benefits.

Special needs, under this section of the RRA, are not the same as special educational needs in education law. Special needs under the RRA are usually defined as being needs 'that are either different in kind from or are the same as, but greater, than those of the rest of the population' and are assumed to be temporary. (This definition is from Section 11 of the Local Government Act 1966.) For example, an early years project could be organised specifically for children from refugee or asylum seeking communities, belonging to particular racial groups, to address their recent experiences and to help them come to terms with their new lives in Britain.

Care needs to be taken in using this section of the RRA to ensure that the needs really are 'special'.

Other exemptions

These exemptions are not about taking positive action, but address specific situations.

A genuine occupational requirement or qualification – Sections 4A and 5(2)(d)
i   Genuine occupational requirement (GOR)
    An employer may lawfully discriminate on the grounds of race or ethnic or national origins if he or she can show that the use of a GOR is a reasonable means of achieving a legitimate aim.
    (The GOR definition was brought in by the Race Regulations 2003.)
ii Genuine occupational qualification (GOQ)

The original GOQ exception is now only available in relation to discrimination on grounds of colour and nationality, for instance to:

a) achieve authenticity in a dramatic performance or similar entertainment or in modelling or photographic or artistic work
b) achieve authenticity in bars and restaurants
c) provide personal services to particular racial groups defined by colour or nationality, which only the person of the same colour or nationality can do most effectively.

If an early years setting has a significant number of children from a particular racial group and few or no people of that racial group working with the children, it might be seen as important or helpful to the children to employ someone of the same racial group to support their particular needs. For example, it may be a good idea to employ someone who speaks the same language as the children. An advertisement for such a post can state that someone who speaks that language is required, and it would not be a breach of the RRA to do this because the condition is not on racial grounds (anyone of any racial group is able to learn and speak any language). However, care should be taken to ensure that the requirement is not indirectly and unjustifiably discriminatory (see page 242).

The desire to employ someone of a particular racial group on those grounds alone must be considered under Sections 4A and 5(2)(d) of the Act in order not to be discriminating unlawfully.

If all (or nearly all) of the people working with the children in an early years setting are white and a large percentage of the children are of African-Caribbean origin, the organisation may wish to employ an African-Caribbean worker to support the children in a way that only an African-Caribbean person is able to do effectively. Young black children – who are growing up in a society where they experience some forms of racism – may feel more comfortable with a person who seems familiar to them, particularly if they are upset. That sense of familiarity may only be provided by someone of the same racial group who understands their culture, home life, dialect or language and family relationships. Employment of such a person could therefore be seen as conducive to the children's welfare.

This in no way suggests that white adults in this kind of early years setting would not be kind and supportive to a black child. Instead, there is a sort of parallel with the way that young children, when upset or hurt, may run to their parents even when other familiar and kindly adults are around. However, the fact that racism exists has to be taken into account when understanding how a black child might perceive a situation and might react. In distress, they are perhaps more likely to seek comfort from a black adult, who is similar to their family members, than a white one, however supportive the white ones are.

It is not possible to determine, in advance, whether such an exemption would be possible under the law – only a tribunal could decide that. An employer would have to show that the example met the requirements of either the GOR (in relation to race, ethnic or national origin) or GOQ (in relation to colour or nationality). So it is critically important to assemble all the facts, together with the relevant arguments, about why only a person of a specific racial group could do a job effectively. In the case of the GOR an employer would have to consider whether it would be a reasonable means of achieving a legitimate aim before advertising the post under Section 4A; and in the case of a GOQ under 5(2)(d), whether the post could meet any of the criteria laid down in that section. Advice can be sought from the Equality and Human Rights Commission (EHRC) or from a racial equality council. However, employers are strongly advised to seek their own independent legal advice on these issues. (For further discussion see CRE 1993; and the statutory code of practice in employment CRE 2005b.)

Employing nannies – Section 4(3)

It is unlawful, when recruiting someone to work in a private household, for example as a nanny or an au pair, to select someone on racial grounds, except on grounds of colour or nationality. Under the Act, working in a private home is not the same as working in the world outside the home.

Membership of associations – Section 26

An organisation of more than 25 members that has a constitution which regulates admission to membership, is allowed to restrict admission to a particular racial group, so long as it does not refer to colour.

For example, an Irish, Pakistani or Jamaican group or a synagogue could set up an early years setting only for the children of its members. It could lawfully refuse admission to children whose parents were not members of the organisation.

The Race Relations (Amendment) Act 2000

This Act amended the Race Relations Act to ensure that the law is not only concerned with racial discrimination but also with a duty on public authorities to take specific actions to ensure racial equality is put into practice. It makes it unlawful for any public authority to discriminate, directly or indirectly, in any of its public functions, with limited exceptions. It also places a positive duty on public authorities to promote race equality when carrying out its functions and implementing its policies. It does not cover the private sector.

Discrimination is one measure of inequality but the absence of discrimination does not necessarily mean that racial equality exists. For example, a local authority that only employs white people in a multiethnic area may not be discriminating against black people because none actually apply to work there. But it could not be said to be ensuring racial equality in such circumstances unless it had ensured that it had done everything possible to recruit, maintain and support black people in its workforce. Building up policies, practices and procedures that require such an authority to take action to achieve an objective of a workforce reflecting the ethnic composition of the local community at all levels is a mechanism to promote racial equality. Such things have to be monitored to assess whether the objectives are really being put into practice.

The General Duty (the race equality duty) under the amended RRA is a set of obligations, consisting of three parts where all public authorities must have due regard to the need to:

- eliminate unlawful racial discrimination
- promote equality of opportunity
- promote good relations between people of different racial groups.

This means that public authorities (including local authority schools, children's centres and any other provision organised by the local authority) must consider racial equality in everything that they do – they must make it central to their work. To do this they are given some specific duties as well. For example, local authorities must publish a race equality scheme; and early year settings in the maintained sector and children's centres must publish a race equality policy and an action plan and monitor, by their racial group, all their employees and all applicants for jobs, promotion and training. Local authorities and early years development and childcare partnerships (EYDCPs) should ensure that settings in the voluntary, independent and private sectors comply with the principles of the general and specific duties. Even though they do not have a statutory duty under the Race Relations (Amendment) Act, the principle must be that the children in their care should be treated equally to those who are covered by the duty.

In commissioning (procuring) any training or other goods, facilities or services (the supply side), they need to ensure that opportunities to bid for this are made widely available to all ethnic groups. In particular, they should ensure that training on any topic promotes racial equality, where appropriate; and that any training on racial equality, specifically, is effective and conducted by trainers who are experienced, knowledgeable and have a real understanding of the issues involved, including the law. Using these procurement powers provides an important lever for change.

Local authorities have the responsibility for monitoring employment in maintained sector schools and settings and children's centres, rather than the organisations themselves, and should require information for monitoring from all other settings as well. This should then be analysed and evaluated.

Public authorities have legal requirements to comply with the duty when working in partnership with other organisations. A partnership is a single body that brings together representatives of different sectors and communities to pursue common aims. Local authorities will need to ensure that the partnerships with which they work reflect the ethnic composition of the local community as accurately as possible. They will also be expected to develop an equality strategy, ensuring equality of access and opportunity and anti-discriminatory policies, procedures and practices in all aspects of the service and the settings. Advice on this, which is also relevant for voluntary and community organisations, is available (CRE 2004c). Specific guidance for the voluntary sector in their work with public authorities is also available (CRE 2005e).

Race equality impact assessments (REIAs)

Early years services and settings need to assess the possible impact on particular racial groups of any decisions, policies, practices or procedures they may make. This is a statutory duty for public authorities and should not be seen as onerous or somehow irrelevant in the early years. It is a way of ensuring that the service or setting treats everyone fairly and identifies any existing or potential adverse impact on minority ethnic children and their families. It is about pre-empting the possibility of what is done, or proposed to be done, affecting some minority ethnic groups unfavourably. Without this any unintended consequences might remain unknown, thus possibly unwittingly perpetuating disadvantage and discrimination. The assessment is a useful tool for planning what action to take to ensure racial equality and must be published. While this duty clearly covers maintained schools, nursery schools and children's centres, the principle of considering the impact of actions in the non-statutory sector of early years provision on minority ethnic children and their families applies equally to them. As with public authorities it is an important tool for planning, reviewing practices and involving communities.

The process of carrying out an REIA for services and settings should include both:

- making a list of the functions and services on offer or provided
- going through each one to see if there is any adverse impact on black and other minority ethnic children and their families.

This means examining the ethnically monitored information to see if all groups have equal access to services and equal outcomes from them. In the absence of such data it involves taking account of any anecdotal information or impressions that people may have, as a result of the consultations, about any differentials in access or outcomes – without quantitative ethnic data this may be all that there is initially to begin the process of identifying any differential outcomes. It must include consulting with and involving the local communities as to their experiences and perspectives – both present and potential users. This will improve mutual confidence between communities and services or settings, thus engendering opportunities for support and facilitate the setting up of the most appropriate provision.

Having acquired a REIA it will help to identify any needs in planning policies or new services. It will help to distinguish between existing good practices and those that may need reviewing in order to remove any inequalities of access or outcome. And it will flag up any need to set up ethnic monitoring systems to continue the process of reviewing any objectives in policies and action plans and identify if any re-prioritising is necessary. Of course, after the assessment, monitoring the effects of actual practice once it is in place must be maintained. (See www.cre.gov.uk/duty/reia/index.html for step-by-step guide on when and how to do this.)

A paper, commissioned for Sure Start, on implementing racial equality by taking account of the requirements of the Race Relations (Amendment) Act 2000 is in Appendix 4 (Lane 2004a). It covers all relevant aspects of the legislation. A publication on standards in schools has principles that are relevant to the early years (CRE 2000).

Specific concerns in implementing the General Duty in the early years

One aspect of the General duty that is often particularly difficult for settings, particularly in largely white suburban and rural areas and in some towns, is to implement the third part of the General duty – to 'promote good relations between people of different racial groups'. 'Good relations' means: equally valuing and respecting differences; avoiding stereotypes and cultural assumptions; unlearning any negative attitudes and behaviour; taking steps to learn about each other's cultures, languages, faiths and ethnic backgrounds; being open-minded and friendly, supporting and caring about each other; sharing commonalities; and taking action to remove inequalities between each other, as individuals and as groups. It also means taking action to consider how to break down barriers between communities, both inside and outside the setting, and encouraging children to play with others less familiar to them (see page 156 for further discussion). In a multiethnic area, resources are readily available and people from at least some minority ethnic groups live there. This is not so in some other areas. Suggestions about what to do have been given throughout this book and in the sections on mainly white areas (pages 106 and 179) but focusing on this particular part of the duty may be helpful.

Practical suggestions might include the following:

developing a whole-setting approach of common values and respect together with families, within a non-partisan, balanced context, with space for feelings and where everyone feels equally valued, safe and secure. This is essential in order to be able to help others. It must also include ensuring that the setting and everyone involved in it, are prepared for any child who might arrive tomorrow to be welcomed, see themselves reflected in the resources, valued, treated equally, feel they belong and have any needs addressed

engaging with families and seeking their support for any planned work so there is a common understanding of the principles behind it

working with children using Persona Dolls to develop concepts of empathy with people who are different from them (see page 207)

examining the variety of hand skin colours between children and adults (the variety of skin tones among so-called white people is significant and demands careful thought as to the words used to describe them – whose is like whose, taking care not to reinforce a racial hierarchy of darker or lighter tones), hair colours and textures and other physical characteristics, being careful that they do not feed into racist assumptions and, if they do, being prepared to know how to deal with the situation

conducting a language audit with extended family members including earlier generations, to identify and affirm linguistic diversity

including information from a variety of cultural and ethnic backgrounds (ensuring that it is understood that all are equally valued members of our society), regularly and sensitively, and making positive and respectful comments about people

reflecting a diverse society, where people look different, have different lifestyles, and speak different languages, in the setting's resources, including in posters, the media, books, jigsaws, and dolls

providing resources which include positive role models from different communities, along with their stories and histories

providing opportunities for children to talk about their attitudes on a one-to-one basis with a worker within an atmosphere of active and positive support for anyone who is subjected to negative attitudes (whether they are present in the setting or not) but making it clear that such attitudes are hurtful, damaging and do not contribute to happiness generally [Note, group discussions should usually be avoided because they may involve hurtful prejudiced attitudes being expressed in another child's presence]

supporting the development of caring attitudes to others and discussing examples of where people help each other

making time available to talk about relevant incidents in the news to provide some sort of understanding commensurate with children's ages, using Persona Dolls where appropriate

encouraging children not to blame others, whether the apparent others are present or not

being clear about the nature of the range of racist incidents, knowing how to address and record them, and in local authority provision, following the statutory recording and reporting procedures

watching out and listening for any name-calling or harassment and dealing with it constructively, sensitively and immediately, supporting both perpetrators and recipients, even where no apparent victim is present

talking about peace and being positive role models for peace

practising talking about political and current events among workers prior to talking with families and children

fostering peace-making, talking together with children and adults about concepts of fairness and justice and practicing how to challenge their opposites within a no-blame culture

embracing and promoting non-violent approaches to perceived injustices to achieve a harmonious society

considering the influence of the media, their effects on families and taking steps to counter misinformation wherever possible

seeking active ways to dispel misinformation about different faith communities, Muslims, Islam, refugees and asylum seekers and other migrant communities and Travellers, Roma and Gypsies

ensuring that any open discussions only take place when *everyone* has carefully thought through and understands the implications of an equality policy within a firm value base that they can all relate to.

It is necessary to be confident and informed to answer questions and pose others in order to counter racist and Islamophobic attitudes and behaviour. There are many people, not necessarily with strong racist ideologies, who nevertheless ask such questions as 'Why do we allow these people to come here and try to change our culture?' or make statements like 'I don't mind them being here but I don't have to like them as well'. Addressing such questions by a balance of non-aggression while not being sympathetic to their sentiments are important skills to acquire.

Monitoring commitment to the Race Relations Act

Legislation against racial discrimination cannot work in a vacuum. Evidence has to be identified in order to prove any discrimination so it is important to keep this constantly in mind when promoting racial equality. Although anecdotal or impressionistic information may be the starting point of beginning to identify actual evidence, continuous data collection will show up any apparent discrepancies or inequalities of outcome and ensure that any discrimination can be identified, rather than suspecting it is occurring but having no database to prove it one way or another.

Coming to terms with the details and implications of the amended RRA is not easy. Legal action should never be taken without a real knowledge and understanding of the legislation. Advice is available from the Equality and Human Rights Commission and local racial equality councils.

To ensure that a commitment to racial equality is being put into practice, information should routinely be collected on the ethnic origins of people working in the early years service and settings, including their levels of employment, and of children in settings, and compared with that of the local community. Data needs to be collected for a national monitoring of racial equality objectives and must therefore be consistent with any national requirements, such as the use of the census categories. Locally, however, additional data may be seen as important to collect to reflect local circumstances – including languages spoken, any faith or belief, community group involvement or any country of origin prior to migration.

Data on job applicants should be collected alongside the job description and person specification, with information about all stages of the selection processes, job offers, promotion, access to career opportunities, training and any other benefits. Ethnically monitored data should be collected alongside the admission criteria on applicants for places (admissions) in early years settings, selection processes and offers of places in the settings. This data should be analysed to check whether any racial groups appear to be less successful at any stage than others. Any discrepancies found do not necessarily mean that unlawful racial discrimination has taken place, but they do mean that the reason(s) for such discrepancies should be examined (see Lane 1998). Be aware that certain groups within particular ethnic groups may perform differently from the rest but, overall, present a picture where there are no apparent discrepancies. For example, socioeconomic differences within an ethnic group may be disguised by an apparently equitable overall result or gender differences overall may disguise the fact that one gender within an ethnic group is achieving better than the other. Whereas collecting data on socioeconomic status is at present problematic, data on gender should be collected and evaluated to identify any specific gender differences within one ethnic group. For useful information on admissions, although school-based see DfES 2007b.

The publication on ethnic monitoring by the Commission for Racial Equality is aimed at public authorities and is therefore relevant for early years services (CRE 2002d). For settings it may perhaps appear initially overwhelming. It does, however, cover all relevant aspects of what is required although in more detail than is appropriate for some settings. But workers will be able to find sections relevant to their own circumstances. Such documents reinforce the need for someone at the local authority early years service level to be familiar with what is required and to be able to support workers in settings to conduct ethnic monitoring effectively.

When assessing childcare sufficiency, as required under the Childcare Act 2006, local authorities will need to ensure that they consult with minority ethnic groups and conduct a race equality impact assessment on families from minority ethnic communities of their provision, as required by the Race Relations (Amendment) Act (see the Guidance, DfES 2007c). The purpose of the race equality impact assessment is to assess the impact of the function, policy, service or procedure on minority ethnic communities, to identify any existing adverse impact. A race equality impact assessment must also be conducted on proposed new or changed provision at the planning stage, to make sure the new provision will not have any adverse impact on minority ethnic communities.

Local authorities must also comply with their public duty. This means ensuring that all settings comply with the three parts of the general duty. Not only quantity but also quality and equality will need to be assessed before a sufficiency can be regarded as compliant with the law (see Appendix 4 for details of the duty). Furthermore, issues relating to the needs of children and their families from black and other minority ethnic communities will need to be carefully taken into account. These may not be the same as those for the usually larger white community although some of these may include Gypsies, Roma, Travellers, asylum seekers, refugees and other migrants who may also have specific needs. In terms of 'needs' in the sufficiency assessment, 'freedom from racism' might be seen as a need for parents and children from minority ethnic groups. Clearly comprehensive data will be required in order to ensure that early years provision caters for all families equally, whatever their ethnicity. Methods of consultation with families from black and other minority ethnic communities will also need to be carefully and sensitively devised (see page 148 for discussion on consultation processes).

Members of local black and other minority ethnic communities should be consulted about collecting ethnically monitored data and the terminology to be used, bearing in mind the reasons for collecting it and any need to compare data nationally. Extreme care must be taken in explaining data protection issues, why the data is being collected, how it will be collected and stored, who will have access to it, what it will be used for and what will be done about it if any discrimination or under-representation is revealed. Collecting individual ethnically monitored data should always, wherever possible, be done on a self-identification basis (every person defining their own ethnicity) – anything else is open to incorrect information. It is important to take specific account of children from mixed race backgrounds and identify them as such, including their particular heritages. This is because, partly due to their increasing numbers in our society, their specific identities need to be acknowledged and reflected in the provision made, and because there is evidence in their later schooling to show that they are not having equal outcomes from services.

Collecting and analysing data will only reveal patterns of differences in outcome and access between different ethnic groups, it will not show whether a particular individual is being discriminated against. This can only be done by comparing their particular circumstances with someone of a different ethnic or racial group. This may be done by seeking information from that other person, the person(s) alleged to have discriminated or by taking out a complaint, under the RRA, in an employment tribunal or in a county or sheriff court.

Some early years workers, family members and others are reluctant to collect ethnically monitored data on children, on workers generally or identify themselves by ethnicity. They explain their antipathy as being that they do not wish to label people, that they are all human beings or that it appears intrusive into their personal lives. The reasons for reluctance usually arise from not understanding the reasons for collecting and monitoring such data. It is not about identifying individuals but about identifying whether groups of individuals are not being treated equally. Even where discrepancies are found it does not necessarily mean that discrimination has occurred – there may be totally justifiable reasons for such discrepancies. Monitoring is the only way to demonstrate that racial equality is being put into practice or identify where it is not.

Some people who have come from countries (for example, South Africa prior to the abolition of apartheid) where racial discrimination was rampant and where identity passes had to be carried, may fear that monitoring is used to discriminate rather than to identify differentials in outcome, access or gaps in service. Additionally, people from refugee and asylum seeking backgrounds may be fearful of the reasons for collecting information on them. Such fears seldom arise from prejudice or from hostility to the wish to treat all children equally – none of these reasons indicate that equality is unimportant to them – sometimes it is the very opposite. It is therefore important to be very clear about why monitoring is necessary.

If there is a policy for racial equality it cannot be known whether it is being put into practice unless it is measured and assessed to see if it is being effective. A policy alone may not remove any discrimination. In order to measure whether the policy works it is necessary to collect, analyse and evaluate ethnic data.

> **?**
>
> **If you want to know more**
>
> there is schools-based information on ethnic monitoring with implications for early years settings in the DfES consultation (2005c) and DCSF Standards site www.standards.dfes.gov.uk; for a discussion on the pros and cons of ethnic monitoring see CRE (2006a); and for further details when working in partnerships see Renewal.net

The weaknesses of the amended Race Relations Act

While the amended Race Relations Act has made significant differences to the range of possibilities in addressing racial discrimination and promoting racial equality, there remain persistent limits and barriers to ensuring racial equality for everyone.

The legislation is a limited tool for addressing racism, among the reasons for which are the following.

- It is difficult to prove discrimination and get evidence that compares the experiences of people from other racial groups.
- The law in this area is increasingly complex and without sufficient training and experience not all tribunal chairs and county and sheriff court judges will have a proper understanding of racial discrimination cases.
- Cases take a long time to pursue and they are stressful. Legal advice, support and advocacy are often not readily available and rarely free. It can be a lonely business in taking up cases of complaint. Legal aid is not available in tribunal cases, so more funding and support are needed.
- Although public authorities are covered by the general duty under the Race Relations (Amendment) Act, private organisations are not.
- Insufficient funding and enforcement powers result in a lack of knowledge of the requirements of the law and a reluctance to take account of it.

If more people understood the RRA better they would realise its creative potential. They would know that comparative data is an essential part of proving discrimination and that a threat of using the law can be a powerful tool for complainants to use against respondents in getting equal treatment. In some ways, the RRA is in its infancy and its potential is untested. The fact that the resources allocated for enforcement of the RRA through the Commission for Racial Equality were insufficient, particularly with regard to enforcing the statutory General Duty, reinforces the need for preventative action to be taken so that enforcement does not become necessary. It is not yet known whether the Equality and Human Rights Commission (EHRC) will fare any better in this regard.

9 Government requirements and policies for racial equality

There is nothing in the Government's 'Choice for parents, the best start for children, a ten year strategy for childcare' that could not have been written had the population been exclusively white.

(Josephine Kwhali in 'Colour neutral: The absence of black voices in Early Years', *Race Equality Teaching*, Spring 2006)

The paper is 'white' in every sense of the word. 'Black and Minority Ethnic Children' are disposed of in three paragraphs that take up half a page in a 116 page document.

(Comment by Professor Gus John on the government's White Paper, 'Higher Standards, Better Schools for All', published in October 2005)

In the field of early years, national and local government departments are largely responsible for organising the way that settings ensure the well-being of children.

The present situation

Is this as good as it gets?

The recent unprecedented, comprehensive and strategic expansion of the early years field, supported by legislation, has created huge opportunities to address decades of neglect. While there are clearly some serious concerns about some aspects of the expansion the general direction and commitment are to be welcomed. Integrating all aspects of the service and developing a strategic approach to the whole sector has made it possible to get away from operating ad hoc methods in early childhood and raised the potential for developing a strategic approach to implementing racial equality. The government should be congratulated for opening up this possibility.

In the process there has been a whole raft of government documents and changes, some of which, for the first time ever, refer to issues around racial equality. This is a significant achievement in itself and so it is tempting to assume that racial equality is now firmly on the national early years agenda. In a sense the issue is on the agenda but the reality of the implications of its implementation is not. How racism impacts on the experiences of workers, children and their families from black and other minority ethnic backgrounds, is seldom a part of government documentation, policy and changes in the early years field.

There has been significant progress in terms of identifying the importance of equality of access and opportunity for black and other minority ethnic groups (and some gestures towards recruiting more into the workforce) and anti-discriminatory practice. Valuing diversity and respecting languages, cultures and faiths are also cited as hallmarks of progress, even where 'respecting', 'valuing' and 'diversity' are not explicitly defined. But the failure to implement the statutory requirements of the Race Relations (Amendment) Act and also to address potential and existing racial discrimination, has resulted in racism remaining mostly firmly entrenched. This omission has particular implications for identifying institutional racism in the policies, practices and procedures of national and local government, their agencies, related organisations and in early years settings.

Here are some examples.

- Equality of access to, and opportunity in, settings cannot exist if racist attitudes, stereotypes and assumptions (however unconsciously held) pervade the curriculum; if admissions arrangements are not widely advertised and applications monitored by ethnicity; or if employment and recruitment practices both in services and settings are not examined and effectively monitored.

- References to equal opportunities and valuing differences, acknowledging cultural diversity and multiculturalism, although important, are less meaningful in the context of a society where such things as skin colour, ethnicity, culture, religion and language are already ranked in a racial hierarchy of more or less significance and worthiness.

- Without effective monitoring procedures for identifying discrimination and a strict implementation of the requirements of the Race Relations (Amendment) Act, institutional and other forms of racism may remain unidentified.

- Advocating respect for diversity, without spelling out equality for every group comprising that diversity, may be relatively meaningless.

- Devising documents for consultation on various issues without taking account of racial equality issues, or setting up seminars or advisory groups without taking account of their ethnic composition or their members' knowledge of how discrimination and its institutional aspects work in practice, may result in key omissions from such documents or in results that fail to take effective account of racial equality.

- Not realising that the involvement of constructive and knowledgeable black and other minority ethnic people and others with specific equality knowledge, in initial discussions, facilitates a better understanding of racial equality issues by everyone and leads to documents more representative of the needs of all groups.

- Suggesting that racial equality implications are added in at any consultation stage, subsequent to initial drafts, means that they are more likely to be marginalised and not incorporated into final documents.

◆ Without effective training and understanding of the amended Race Relations Act and its implications for racial equality, inspections, assessments and research may not identify and address manifestations of racism.

◆ Without an effective approach to enabling children to unlearn any racist attitudes and behaviour that they may have already learnt, such attitudes and behaviour may remain entrenched into their future lives and subsequently affect other children and adults negatively and maintain the reality of racism in society.

◆ If training and education for senior posts (for example, leaders of integrated centres, early years professionals and teachers) do not facilitate knowledge and understanding of racism, they are unlikely to be able to ensure racial equality and comply with the amended Race Relations Act

◆ If legislation is not enforced and local authorities are not required by government to ensure racial equality in practical ways then those who are least committed may do little.

The consistent reluctance by government to take a lead in recognising and addressing racism means that much of the good work being done with children in settings remains largely a palliative. The whole power of racism has not been addressed and dismantled. While clearly government action alone is not the answer, it should and could play a critical part. It's like protecting just one plant in a storm of locusts. It's worth doing but it doesn't solve the basic problem.

There are, of course, examples where committed groups and individuals, in both the statutory and voluntary sectors, have taken specific action to address this wider issue of racism, through training, documents, policies, information and discussion forums. These individuals and groups have tried to effect changes within the existing parameters of policies and documentation by analysing them carefully and identifying where antiracist work can be undertaken. But, in general, they are isolated and their relative powerlessness means that the wider facets of racism and its institutional aspects remain largely intact. It does mean, however, that there is an increasing number of people who are determined to effect changes, organise themselves and exert their influence. There are oases of effective work, supportive groups, committed and pioneering individuals, enthusiastic practitioners and people in national and local government gnawing away at obstacles to racial equality. For a discussion about some of the reasons why the necessary changes have not occurred see page 66 onwards.

The fact that there is no consistent national government policy and practical support for the work needed, results in it being mostly marginalised. In a crucial sense it is this absence that is the vital missing link to ensuring that early years services and settings are fundamentally based on racial equality principles.

Although the Race Relations (Amendment) Act 2000 requires local authorities to be explicit about promoting racial equality, it is too soon to assess whether there have been any significant changes as a result of its enactment. In any case, voluntary, independent and private sectors are not covered by this legislation so it is only by the specific commitment of a local authority to incorporate them into its orbit of requirements, through contracts and funding arrangements, that changes will be possible. But anecdotal evidence does not indicate that systematic policies and procedures are yet in place.

Racism still exists in early years services and settings and acknowledging its relevance and its implications is the first step to removing it. A lack of understanding rather than any deliberate intention sometimes covers an apparent unwillingness to begin the process of such acknowledgement. Institutional racism, in particular, remains a difficult or unacceptable concept to grasp and accept at all levels, from national government to practitioners in settings.

A specific issue of concern is the lack of time made available for some people in positions of authority and power to familiarise themselves with current issues of racial equality and to listen to the voices of black people in society at large. While some workers in settings and early years services are becoming more informed about these issues by attending seminars, conferences and training, reading articles and discussing them and relating them to their practice; some government officers, policy-makers, researchers, academics and others drafting documents, training materials, national standards and policies may be less so. Recently there has been a surge in the number of articles, videos and other resources covering a range of racial equality issues for workers in the early years field and wider, which others may not access or have the time or commitment to digest. This has opened up a potential gap between who is writing and reading documents on racial equality and who is not. It is critical that people in positions of authority are as familiar with the principles and current thinking about racial equality as are an increasing number of workers in early years services and settings. It is vital that they are not cocooned in a world where they do not meet or talk openly with black people, do not take account of their ideas or of the reality of living in a multicultural and multiethnic society in planning policies and do not ensure opportunities to discuss racial equality are available.

Another area of increasing concern about implementing racial equality is that of the appropriate representation of workers from black and other minority ethnic communities at all levels in the workforce and in training and education, and effective consultation with them on government advisory groups and on policies, guidance, research and other aspects of the early years. Data on representation should provide evidence of any racial inequality and be the basis for taking positive action under the Race Relations Act and complying with the requirements of the Race Relations (Amendment) Act.

Although some ethnic groups are under-represented overall in the workforce and in training and education (for example people from Bangladeshi and Pakistani communities), most minority ethnic groups appear to be disproportionately in low grades and under-represented at senior levels. In the Childcare and Early Years Workforce Surveys of 2002/3 (Sure Start 2004b) and the subsequent Childcare and Early Years Providers Surveys of 2005 and 2006 (DCSF 2007b), managers identified the ethnicity of workers but not the level at which they worked. The fact that workers were not themselves asked to identify their own ethnicity reveals another area of concern, and possible assumptions, about the validity of the survey. (See page 244 for further discussion of workforce under-representation.)

This inevitably means that they are less likely to be included in discussions, on advisory groups, in planning training programmes and in consultations at the national or local levels. Their absence at national and regional forums is also noticeable. Their voices are therefore not heard.

While clearly both black and white early years workers have much in common, the specific voices of each need to be heard where there are differences or gaps of information between them. Whereas some white workers have a real understanding of racism their voices cannot replace those whose day-to-day experience it is and who are able to articulate it effectively. It is important for constructive and knowledgeable black voices (and the voices of others concerned with racial equality) to be heard in all groups and not just during consultation periods, but from the beginning, when documents are in the process of being drafted. Not only does this mean that their ideas are considered and included where appropriate, but such occasions and discussions often provide a previously unknown and unacknowledged opportunity for both black and white people to really listen to and learn from each other. This inevitably facilitates overall understanding. Whatever the explanations for this absence it is vital that the voices of workers from black and other minority ethnic groups are heard and listened to if racial equality is to be implemented in practice. Both national and local governments need to ensure that they take this seriously. There is therefore an urgent need to take action to address this situation by taking positive action, if necessary, and complying with the Race Relations (Amendment) Act to rectify it. For further discussion about the lack of black voices see Lawrence and Lane (2006).

Recently, as a result of concerns about this issue, a national network of early years workers from black and other minority ethnic backgrounds has been established (for information contact the Early Childhood Unit of the National Children's Bureau).

While no one doubts that nearly everyone in the early years field genuinely wishes to ensure that racial equality is fully implemented in principle, the above issues, together with some others, form a pattern that should be a subject of urgent debate about the reality of practice.

Government practice and racial equality

it is the continued popularity of traditional notions of childhood innocence that constitutes the biggest obstacle to the development of a successful and comprehensive multicultural antiracist strategy among infant children.

(Connolly 1998)

Since 1997, with the development of a national comprehensive childcare strategy, there has been a huge explosion of legislation, reorganisation (including new forms of provision and children's information services), innovation, documentation, guidance, research, training, reports and funding emanating from a variety of government departments. Barely any aspect of early years services and settings has remained untouched by this colossal rethinking process. It represents, on the whole, a significant change for the better for all young children, including many children from black and other minority ethnic communities.

Documentation on the early years, some with implications for racial equality

This is not the place to provide a detailed analysis of all the recent documents that have emanated from the government and whether they are relevant to racial equality. (A list of the most significant ones is given in Appendix 5.)

Legislation with implications for the early years is defining and developing a framework on which a strategy for racial equality could and should be based. The Children Act 2004 integrates children's services, thus providing a structure for a strategic approach instead of divisions between them. This should include inspecting and monitoring for racial equality by the Joint Area Reviews (JAR) with a report and action plan showing how to rectify any inequalities. The Childcare Act 2006, in requiring local authorities to secure a sufficiency of childcare places in settings to meet the needs of working parents and then conduct regular assessments of that sufficiency, will need to incorporate the needs of families and their children from black and other minority ethnic groups in their assessments and consult with them about any concerns that they may have. They will need to ensure that settings themselves address racial equality and any family needs seriously. Ofsted inspections should be critical factors here. As a result, gaps in mapping the supply to the real demand should be identified. For guidance for local authorities on the quality and appropriateness of provision for children from all ethnic groups, see DCSF (2007a).

Both these Acts mean that local authorities, Ofsted inspectors of settings, and inspections by the JARs, will increasingly need to take comprehensive and strategic account of racial equality issues and concerns, including the race equality impact assessment on the functions and policies of settings, and any new proposals, as required by the Race Relations (Amendment) Act. In principle this strategic approach should provide an ideal and unique opportunity to ensure that racial equality is integral to the national childcare strategy. It remains to be seen whether this proves to be so. Much will depend on the skills and commitment of individuals. But without the understanding of what is needed the future is not yet hopeful. Unless those with the political will, together with the power to make it happen, 'get it', then this opportunity is unlikely to be taken.

The majority of the documents implementing the national childcare strategy are framed around the five outcomes of the Green Paper proposals in *Every Child Matters* (DfES 2003b) – being healthy, staying safe, enjoying and achieving, making a positive contribution and economic well-being. These are important outcomes that could mostly be effectively incorporated as the basis of the suggested framework and strategy for racial equality in early years services and settings (see Chapter 10).

However, without effective monitoring and evaluation as to their relevance for, and impact on, children and their families from black and other minority ethnic groups, it will be difficult to assess whether racial equality is being implemented in practice.

Although *Every Child Matters* and most subsequent documents could have some implications for racial equality, none effectively addresses the potential barriers to such equality – the structural and institutional aspects of racism which may prevent it. Documentation seems to deal with culture, an important subject in its own right, rather than with racism which is the greater determinant of equality. There is also an inconsistency of approach across the range of documents, making coordination to ensure racial equality impossible. A few even omit key references to equality generally or racial equality at all. There is silence on the need for ethnic monitoring to assess the impact of policies and procedures on black and other minority ethnic groups – required under the Race Relations (Amendment) Act. There does not even appear to be an authoritative statement on racial equality, including discrimination, institutional racism and the amended Race Relations Act, which would be an umbrella cover for all government documents. It is as if racism did not exist, as if society is racially neutral, as if a completely colour-blind approach to society was being adopted, that there was no ethnic diversity and laws do not have to be obeyed. There are frequent mentions of the aim to ensure all children can benefit from early years support and childcare and that this means ensuring the particular needs of ethnic minority groups are met. But a critical need for such groups is to get rid of the barriers caused by racism. Yet this is not mentioned.

There is abundant evidence of how discrimination in all its forms acts against black and other minority ethnic groups, not least from the findings of the Stephen Lawrence Inquiry Report that the government itself set up (see CRE website and others). But the statutory requirements of the Race Relations (Amendment) Act in the early years field seldom get a reference. The hard reality of what is needed to be done by government in practice is largely missing. Whether this is due to a lack of knowledge and understanding, a failure of determination to tackle the task, a fear of the consequences (a media backlash?) or no true commitment is an enigma. Although no justification, government departments need ministerial authority for much of their documentation – without this, departments may be limited in what they can do.

For example, the important consultative document on the Children's Workforce Strategy (HM Government 2005a), clearly having an intention to ensure that people from black and other minority ethnic communities are represented in the workforce, fails to mention or address how racial discrimination and the racism of society might be barriers to such representation. It does not refer to the statutory requirements of the Race Relations (Amendment) Act and the need for ethnic monitoring. Nor does it mention the fact that representation must be at all levels, which at present, it clearly is not. In the face of such limitations it cannot be sufficient just to reiterate the need for more workers from minority ethnic groups without examining the barriers to this within a historical context. While there have recently been welcome improvements towards racial equality in training and education programmes, in recruitment practices and in service delivery, for a children's workforce to be representative by ethnicity, clear and explicit changes need to be made in all of these as part of a comprehensive strategy for racial equality. The Government's response to the consultation document asked the Children's Workforce Development Council to explore, with the Children's Workforce Network, the potential for extending current data collection to establish a baseline assessment of ethnicity (gender, age and disability) at all levels of the workforce (DfES 2006e, para 1.21). But this is anyway a statutory duty under the amended RRA and therefore mandatory. (See Appendix 6 for a critique of the Children's Workforce Strategy consultation, and Lane 2005i for a full response to the DfES on the consultation document.)

This issue of the under-representation of some black and other minority ethnic groups in the workforce is serious. The CWDC has made some attempts to address it and the DCSF has identified it as a concern in its race equality scheme (DCSF 2007c). But, the issue of the general under-representation of all such groups at senior levels is neither being seriously acknowledged nor addressed, although identified in a DCSF research report (Craig and others 2007, see page 277 for details). Large conferences across the country are still being held where few or no black delegates attend, reflecting the reality of the situation and indicating that this is an on-going issue which successive strategies have not yet engaged with.

Perhaps now is the time for a wider strategy with the responsibility firmly within the CWDC's remit and incorporating the DCSF race equality scheme – but extending to a radical new approach incorporating the whole education service, schools, training and education (including foundation and early years degrees/early years professionals and leadership courses) and within local authorities. Such a strategy would take concerted action, using the positive action sections of the Race Relations Act, strategic advertising, robust ethnic monitoring and, crucially, involving and consulting with black and other minority ethnic groups and workers themselves. Standards would include requirements to implement anti-discriminatory legislation and recruitment targets would be set.

Another important document identifying the common set of skills and knowledge needed for everyone working with children is sensitively written and refers to the importance of knowing about current legislation, but does not mention racial discrimination as a part of this knowledge (HM Government 2005b). Although it identifies 'relevant legislation' including most that are important (in an annex), it fails to identify either the amended Race Relations Act or the Sex Discrimination Act. Similarly disappointing is the action plan for the ten-year childcare strategy that says nothing about racial equality, minority ethnic groups or discrimination (DfES/DWP 2006a).

The Early Years Professional National Standards, while including important practice issues about equality, do not mention anti-discriminatory legislation, ethnic monitoring or the need to identify, understand and remove discrimination (CWDC 2006a). Familiar and important phrases about taking account of diversity, valuing difference, promoting equality, inclusion, children's rights and anti-discriminatory practice are threaded through these and other documents from the CWDC (CWDC 2006b and c). But unless those devising and implementing training fully understand the practical implications of these, as well as including legislation and ethnic monitoring mechanisms to identify any discrimination, they may be relatively meaningless. In contrast the National Standards for Leaders of Children's Centres are specific about complying with 'discrimination legislation', although there is no mention of monitoring (DfES 2007d). It is important to be explicit about this.

After so much significant legislation, so much evidence about the discrimination and disadvantage facing children and their families of black and other minority ethnic communities, all in the context of rising tensions in our society and elsewhere, how is it possible that so many documents are inadequate? It may be difficult to fully appreciate the importance of being explicit about racial equality. It may appear obvious that the general points made will automatically include all members of society equally or that there is no need to identify discrimination because there are laws against it. But this is not the reality, however much we may wish it to be so. The reality is widespread racial discrimination and institutional racism and a frequent failure to recognise or accept that this is happening. Until this is faced, the promotion of racial equality and the elimination of racial discrimination must be both explicit and implicit in all government documentation and commissioned work.

All of the above unsatisfactory situations might have been avoided, if there was a will to do so, by devising a short checklist to consider equality issues when drafting any document or commissioning research, advisory groups, training or training materials. A checklist would include ensuring:

- compliance with anti-discriminatory legislation (including ethnic monitoring and conducting race equality impact assessments)
- recognition and understanding of the facts and reality of racism on whatever is being addressed
- that the implications of addressing racial equality are made explicit *as well as* being threaded through documentation
- the appointment of people knowledgeable, skilled and with an understanding of the subject and issues being addressed
- consultation with relevant black and other minority ethnic and equality groups
- appropriate representation from black and other minority ethnic groups (at all levels)
- the inclusion of those knowledgeable about equality issues in the work to be done
- equality principles are enshrined in first drafts
- any apparent differentials in access or outcomes between ethnic groups are questioned and any possible explanations sought before finalising reports and documents
- appropriate and consistent terminology is used
- the meaning of terms are made clear before they are used.

On the positive side, however, guidance (Sure Start 2005a and a revision in DfES/DH 2006) on the organisation of children's centres demonstrates an integrated as well as a specific approach to working with families from minority ethnic communities. These demonstrate some real progress in the understanding of those writing such documents.

Being black is not equivalent to being 'at risk'

A perhaps relatively minor point, but one that needs to be considered however, is that in some documents, in an attempt to draw the attention of local authorities and others to the apparently poor outcomes for the children of some families and their need for additional support, many groups are listed together, some of which are clearly disadvantaged and others which may or may not be so (Sure Start 2005b, the revision DfES/DH 2006 and DfES 2007e). Among the groups listed are families from minority ethnic communities. It is important to understand that although, as with other families, some minority ethnic families may be disadvantaged, it must never be *assumed* that they are all disadvantaged. Labelling families in any way, however unintentional, may lead to unwelcome and unfortunate results where the implications of racial discrimination are not identified. While recognising the praiseworthy and vital intention of not stigmatising any family, it is perhaps unhelpful to lump groups together in this way but to make the point that many families of all backgrounds may at various times in their lives need support – this means seeing everyone as individuals and responding to each family's particular circumstances at any moment in time.

This point is made explicitly, although not entirely consistently, in the toolkit complementing the guidance for 'reaching priority and excluded families': that provides information on data collection, planning and useful checklists for the identification and targeting of such families – it asks if *services* are 'hard to reach' for some individuals. It refers to families who may 'feel discriminated against because they are from Black and Minority Ethnic communities' (Together for Children (tfc) 2007).

The term 'at risk' has similar connotations to 'disadvantage' and is no more applicable to families from minority ethnic communities than those from majority ethnic communities. Perhaps this issue is one particularly for training – to help people understand the effect on families of the disadvantages that factors such as poverty, imprisonment and being asylum seekers have – and the implications of this for their work as professionals. When needing to identify specific groups that may, for whatever reason, not be accessing provision, then perhaps particular groups that are nearly always likely to be disadvantaged should be targeted. Children from minority ethnic families do not fit here in the same way. That does not mean that they should not be targeted – they should, but not because they are assumed to be disadvantaged. The experience of racism has significant implications for minority ethnic families and explains much of what may be perceived as non-involvement.

Everyone has to be aware of various groups in order to consider them and assess if they are accessing provision – and if not, why not – not to *require* them to attend but to ensure that there are *no barriers* to their attendance. Perhaps some criteria for making such judgements would be helpful. And it is critical always to remember that the term 'minority ethnic families or communities' includes a variety which, apart from their joint experience of racism, may have very differing experiences, backgrounds and needs – they are not a homogeneous group.

For some time the DCSF and the former DfES have been concerned at the low take-up of childcare by some minority ethnic families, specifically those from Gypsy, Roma, Pakistani, Bangladeshi and Black African families. Their early race equality schemes (RES) defined such families as 'disadvantaged' or 'hard to reach' (see text above and page 83 for discussion on the use of these terms). The updated RES (DCSF 2007c) and the Single Equality Scheme (SES)(DCSF 2007d) both determine to 'promote engagement' and consult with parents of children from minority ethnic communities and community groups and evaluate their experiences and publish the findings in order to address the low take-up (see DCSF 2008b for leaflet on welcoming everyone). This is a positive move away from possibly perceiving them as problems. Disturbingly the text of the SES links the 'resulting impact' of the low take-up with low achievement, a link which is as yet unproven. Their other aims include:

- closing the attainment gap between minority ethnic children
- ensuring that local authorities take account of their statutory duties to assess and secure sufficient childcare and improve outcomes for children, using advice in guidance on the requirements of minority ethnic families (DCSF 2007e)
- improving information about childcare, children's services and parenting support
- using children's centres to reach out and engage 'hard to reach' communities – funding is available to local authorities to employ two outreach workers in centres serving disadvantaged communities
- creating a more diverse ethnically and culturally sensitive workforce, working with the Children's Workforce Development Council on under-represented communities
- publishing guidance on working with Gypsies, Roma and Travellers
- disseminating the findings of development projects.

While these are important issues there appears to be no significant recognition of the potential for racial discrimination or the wider aspects of racism as barriers to racial equality. Issues raised elsewhere in this book need to be taken into account if the worthy objectives of the schemes are to be satisfied effectively.

Guidance on practice in settings

In terms of practical support for settings and their specific work with children there have been significant documents supporting racial equality. The Training and Development Agency for Schools (TDA, formerly the Teacher Training Agency) published audit materials for the Foundation Stage (TTA 2004) and guidance and resource material for raising the attainment of minority ethnic pupils (TTA 2000). The *Curriculum Guidance for the Foundation Stage* (QCA / DfEE 2000) and *Birth to Three Matters: A framework to support children in their earliest years* (Sure Start 2002) provided support for practitioners wishing to address racial equality. They are sensitive, reflect the expertise of the practitioners involved in writing them and take account of equality issues consistently. Compared with any earlier documents these demonstrate a significant and refreshing breakthrough that should bring credit on all those who wrote them. Concepts such as 'mutual respect', 'being alert to injustices', not being excluded because of ethnicity, discussing differences and learning that others have different views from theirs all contribute to a new way of government thinking.

The accompanying CD-ROM includes articles about racial equality (Lane 2002b).

Such positive support at practitioner level was heartening, although yet to be included was the concept of enabling children to unlearn any negative attitudes that they may have already learnt, a vital part of the other side of the equation of treating all children equally. Nor was there any indication of the effects of racism in the wider society on the curriculum itself (see Houston 2004 for an antiracist approach to the Foundation Stage curriculum).

The *Early Years Foundation Stage* (EYFS), set up under the Childcare Act 2006, coordinates both documents, together with the National Standards on day care and childminding and is due to be implemented in September 2008. The EYFS is statutory for all early years providers who are registered with Ofsted. The consultation document (DfES/DWP 2006b) drew comments for a racial equality perspective to be both implicitly and explicitly addressed in the final publication. Specific comments also stressed the need for a principle on equality; a separate section on the acknowledgment and detailing of the implications for early years practice of the embedded racism (and other inequalities) in our society; and for a comprehensive training strategy to support this and to avoid prejudiced attitudes and behaviour being perpetuated into adulthood (for example, see Ouseley and Lane 2006). The government's response to the consultation, although somewhat muddled in its understanding of the term 'inclusion', indicated that the concept of adding a new principle was being considered 'to cover the importance of not excluding or disadvantaging children because of ethnicity' (DfES 2006f). However, the final publication does not include a specific principle or a specific section about equality – nor does it specify sufficiently the requirements of the amended Race Relations Act (DfES 2007a).

It does, however, build on the very positive issues identified in the earlier documents with solid, sensitive and many very welcome points made throughout, reflecting the positive experiences of practitioner influences in the writing of its contents. Although this is not the place to elaborate on the details, the particular positive aspects of the statutory framework include providing and promoting equality of opportunity and anti-discriminatory practice, removing or helping to overcome barriers for children, having regard to arrangements for reviewing, monitoring and evaluating the effectiveness of inclusive practice, working together harmoniously and a duty to include anti-discriminatory legislation. Guidance refers to supporting children's understanding of difference and of empathy by using props such as Persona Dolls, encouraging children to choose to play with a variety of friends so that everybody in the group experiences being included, being alert to injustices, and unlearning discriminatory attitudes.

These are particularly important as they provide opportunities for everyone to accept both that children do indeed learn their attitudes when very young and that the society in which they grow up fosters racially prejudiced attitudes unless specific action is taken to counter them. This points to the need to identify and address racial hierarchies of such things as culture, language, ethnicity, skin colour and religion. While there has been a shift to ensure that racial equality issues are both implicit and explicit in the detailed practice, the absence of a principle and section on equality results in the barriers to racial equality remaining unidentified. An opportunity has been missed – there is no *strategy* to counter racism or other inequalities either in the early years framework or practice document.

Without this strategy, which must incorporate training (initial and in-service) and job selection procedures, practitioners may or may not understand what is needed and why. They may be reluctant to take this seriously. As with every practice document the implementation of racial equality depends on the knowledge, skills, understanding and commitment of practitioners – they are absolutely key to putting it into practice. Similarly the knowledge, skills, understanding and commitment of inspectors are key to identifying where racial equality is *not* being put into practice. Despite the great advance with the EYFS there remains still a long way to go before racism is effectively addressed and before all practitioners put racial equality into practice in settings. For examples of the factors impacting on practitioners, supportive and otherwise, and both inside and outside the setting, see Lane (2007b).

Further material (with draft status), standing alongside the EYFS material on observation and assessment, is available for local authorities to raise outcomes for low-achieving children (DfES 2007e). As with the Children's Centres Practice Guidance it identifies a list of groups of families who may be at risk of poor outcomes. The same points as those made above about the reasons for not lumping apparently disadvantaged groups together are equally relevant here.

The government has set up specialised training courses for early years professional status and leaders of integrated centres; set up early years courses in further and higher education institutions, including for foundation degrees and early childhood studies; and devised National Occupational Standards. It also requires local authorities, under the Childcare Act 2006, to plan for the delivery of the EYFS and to set up training to support its implementation. This is certainly a strategic approach. Ultimately, whether the EYFS ensures that racial equality is put into practice in settings will depend on whether all those involved understand what racism is and how to counter it. This includes all local authority and voluntary organisation planners, course content designers and planners, trainers, leaders, governors, managers and heads of all early years settings, practitioners (including childminders) and inspectors. Everything hinges on them – their commitment, understanding, knowledge and skills. Unless everything is explicit in terms of countering racism, whether the EYFS delivers racial equality for all children and their families will depend on these people. Similarly, apparently appropriate terms in the EYFS depend on every individual's interpretation of their meaning in practice.

But curriculum documents themselves cannot address the wider issues of racism alone in the services and settings – for example, legislation, employment, admissions and all the policies, practices and procedures – and are only some aspects of the legislative requirements for racial equality.

Documentation and research on racial equality with early years implications, and on early years with racial equality implications

In terms of the government's identification of priority issues to ensure the inclusion of black and other minority ethnic groups as integral to the childcare strategy, research has mainly focused on identifying the barriers to equality of access to childcare for families and the implications for their participation in the labour market. As part of this a pilot study on promoting inclusion was commissioned. It made several specific and important recommendations none of which, so far as is known, has been implemented (Sure Start 2004a, see Appendix 7 for details of recommendations). This indicates a serious failure to understand the importance of beginning to take action to develop a strategy for racial equality. This should include addressing the following key issues. (For documents specifically on racial equality and / or early years, some of which are school-orientated, see Appendix 8.)

Requirements, standards and inspections

Since 1998 the early years sector of the DfES (DCSF), now called the Sure Start, Extended Schools and Childcare Group, has issued planning guidance and set targets for local authorities and EYDCPs on equality issues. Starting from a minimum level these have, year on year, placed increasingly more detailed requirements on them and on settings, including equal access and providing for the needs of communities such as Travellers, refugees, asylum seekers and children learning English as an additional language.

Specifically, EYDCPs were required to ensure that they had 'effective equal opportunity strategies which are monitored at least annually and that they ensure that all settings identify and train someone to take responsibility for establishing and implementing the setting's equal opportunity strategy by 2004' (DfES 2001, Target 21). Such people have been variously called equal opportunity named coordinators (ENCOs), equal opportunity coordinators (EOCOs) or equalities coordinators (ECOs) (see page 168 for further discussion). But, in the absence of effective monitoring by government, local authorities have varied in their compliance with such requirements, some taking them seriously and others hardly at all. For example, the appointment of equality coordinators in settings and the required training of them are very patchy. At the time coordinators for special educational needs (SENCOs) had considerably more specific requirements, funding and tighter timescales in place for appointing them than ECOs and also for the setting up of networks of Area SENCOs to support them. There have been repeated calls for Sure Start to require local authorities to appoint someone to coordinate, train, advise and support all the setting equality coordinators at area level in the same way as for Area SENCOs. The government has chosen not to support this important and practical suggestion. The logic of the call seems irrefutable, particularly in order to require those authorities that have done very little. Despite the requirements of legislation, the commitment to remove racism and the fostering of a future harmonious society cannot be left to individual local authorities to decide whether or not to take action.

The DCSF devolves many of its responsibilities to local authorities but continues to inform them about current issues. While local authorities may receive guidance from government, it remains up to each to determine the priority given to implementing racial equality in practice. This is somewhat mitigated by their statutory duty to ensure racial equality under the Race Relations (Amendment) Act as well as the responsibility of settings to devise policies for racial equality. But some evidence points to the fact that the education sector is less likely than other public authorities to comply with its statutory duties (CRE / Schneider Ross 2002). And, because the voluntary, independent and private (non-maintained) sector is not covered by this statutory duty, it remains up to each local authority to devise appropriate mechanisms to ensure that they themselves require compliance in principle. In 2008 all settings will have to comply with the Early Years Foundation Stage and the requirements for registration and inspection under the Office for Standards in Education, Children's Services and Skills (Ofsted). It is likely that some local authorities and settings will take the issues seriously and others, unless required to do so, will not. It remains an issue of critical concern that ethnic and gender equality are given less specific government mandates than for disability and special educational needs, important though each of those are.

If you want to know more

about the Education sector and its statutory duties under the Race Relations (Amendment) Act, see CRE (2003b).

For more on the government's position on racial equality in the early years, see Lane (2006b).

Under the Childcare Act 2006, local authorities are required to secure and assess the sufficiency of childcare in their area. They also have to comply with their general duty under the Race Relations (Amendment) Act to conduct a race equality impact assessment on their services. This assessment identifies whether all groups have equal access to services and equal outcomes from them. It identifies where there are gaps in services; and where proactive steps need to be taken to ensure that the services are appropriate, and all communities know about them and can access them. Ofsted inspectors should take account of whether settings are compliant under all three parts of the general duty. The local authority sufficiency assessment (which must consequently be regarded as looking not only at quantity but also quality including equality) can itself be assessed for compliance.

Over recent years, Ofsted has gradually become more aware of the importance of inspecting settings for racial equality. A simple 1990s document laid out the parameters of what this might mean (Ofsted undated). In the past there has been a variety of inspection mechanisms for the different types of settings in the maintained and non-maintained sectors – childcare, funded nursery education, combined and school inspections, each requiring different levels of detail with regard to racial equality. These ranged from little in-depth analysis to requirements for significant understanding and information. From September 2008 all early years settings and services are inspected by Ofsted and must meet the requirements of the Early Years Foundation Stage and the amended Race Relations Act. Since 2005, inspections have to take more account of settings' own perceptions of their competence by being required to complete a self-evaluation form which plays an important part in the inspection itself (Ofsted 2005a). The information required has to be continually updated and evaluated, incorporating and taking account of the five outcomes of Every Child Matters (ECM). From

September 2008 the self-evaluation will encompass questions and evaluation on a wider range of race equality, inclusion and diversity issues.

The judgements made depend on the ability of the inspector to assess the implementation of the EYFS in practice and whether the requirements are being fostered effectively and appropriately within the very different contexts of schools and settings – ranging from an all-white school to a multicultural, multiethnic, multifaith and multilingual pre-school and to a childminder. Although Ofsted is providing more effective training on racial equality, where inspectors are inadequately trained, experienced and supported to be in a position to fully understand how to assess these issues, they may be unaware of their implications. In such inspections the reality of the assessment on racial equality becomes relatively meaningless. Furthermore there have been concerns that if all requirements other than for racial equality are judged to be satisfactory, then inspectors who have had insufficient training may find the setting standards/requirements satisfactory overall. Lack of support means they are insufficiently confident and competent to make adequate judgements about racial equality.

These concerns are serious. In its final report, the Commission for Racial Equality recommended legal action against Ofsted on the grounds that it had failed in its duty to promote race equality – the poorest record on race of any public regulatory body (CRE 2007c). Unless the inspections are rigorous, it is difficult to distinguish between a report where there is clearly good practice on racial equality and the inspector has the ability to judge this and a setting where the practice does not address racial equality but the inspector does not have the ability to identify this. For example, unless inspectors understand the amended Race Relations Act they will not be able to assess whether an admissions or employment policy is potentially discriminatory and unlawful. Until all inspectors are familiar with the methods of judging racial equality effectively the inspection reports on this subject remain unreliable. This has implications for local authorities using Ofsted reports when assessing childcare sufficiency and racial equality.

The EYFS provides a framework, if somewhat limited, for checking whether all ethnic groups are accessing the learning opportunities equally as required by the legislation. Inspectors have to be able to make these judgements, even if some are more knowledgeable about racial equality issues than others. In general, inspectors of the maintained sector have been better trained so that they are able to address the issues with confidence, taking account of a supportive publication on inclusion in schools (Ofsted 2001a). A report of recent practice in schools might also have relevant aspects for the early years (Ofsted 2005b).

Ofsted itself, in the 2006 consultation on its race equality scheme, identified the lack of specific training on racial equality for inspectors under the, then existing, framework indicating a need for more emphasis and consistency on specific reporting. A later race equality scheme consultation document stated that a desk-based study was being conducted of how well Ofsted reports on equality and diversity issues in childcare (Ofsted 2007a). A further revised race equality scheme consultation document states that it is committed to 'even further training' to ensure judgements on outcomes for children are the very best that they can be. In particular, it aims for inspectors to demonstrate a good understanding of all aspects of race equality and have the necessary skills to inspect and report accurately on them. The impact of training is to be monitored regularly. It reports that a survey of a few settings in 2007 found significant barriers to learning included inadequate support for children in the early stages of learning English and that local authorities were insufficiently prepared to support children from families of 'minority ethnic heritage', especially recently arrived refugees and asylum-seeking families (Ofsted 2007b). (This reinforces the need to make support for children learning English equally available to all children regardless of the type of provision they attend – see page 212 for further discussion).

These statements, together with some anecdotal experiences of practitioners and others from elsewhere, reinforce the need for careful recruitment procedures to ensure that inspectors are only appointed when they already have the knowledge and understanding to be sufficiently skilled (or where the training provided will give them the necessary skills) to be effective in inspecting for racial equality. Monitoring of all inspections requires skill and detailed knowledge of the amended Race Relations Act by inspectors – this is an essential part of the evaluation of whether inspectors are competent to inspect the implementation of race equality.

The National Occupational Standards for national vocational qualifications (NVQs) at the various levels apply to workers already in post – for early years, the National Occupational Standards in Children's Care, Learning and Development (DfES 2006a) applies. Workers register for NVQs with an awarding body and are assessed by an assigned assessor according to their underpinning knowledge of the relevant issues and the evidence of their existing skills in the workplace. Equality issues are integral to the Standards and qualifications but, as with Ofsted inspectors, the judgements made by assessors will depend on their individual knowledge and experience and their understanding of racial equality in particular.

All leaders, early years professionals and teachers in settings should be fully qualified to implement the amended Race Relations Act, to identify unlawful racial discrimination and to know what an effective ethnic data collection and monitoring system is. They should be able to understand and recognise the endemic aspects of racism that both allows many children to learn racist attitudes and behaviour and prevents black and other minority ethnic children from achieving their potential and feeling equally comfortable, valued and respected in society. The concept of 'unlearning' any existing racist attitudes, while present in the EYFS, should be an integral aspect of their practice. A specific key area encompassing all equality issues and including the government agenda on community cohesion, as well as issues being addressed in all other key areas, could address the above issues of concern in the EYFS and Standards. It could perhaps be called *Building an equal society.*

Assessment and research

For some time there have been concerns about the low achievement levels of some ethnic groups of children in schools, particularly Gypsy Traveller pupils, African-

Caribbean pupils (including those with one parent who is African-Caribbean or African) and pupils from minority ethnic groups, especially those in mainly white schools). (For further information, see the standards site of DCSF – www.standards.dfes.gov.uk/ethnicminorities/raising_achievement.) It is important that levels of achievement of children should be assessed accurately and by using accurate and appropriate measures. Any assessment measures and the process of assessment itself should be as free of cultural bias as possible and conducted by those who are competent to do so and who understand the role that stereotyping and cultural assumptions may play.

Assessment by the Foundation Stage Profile (QCA/DfES 2003, DfES 2005a) at the end of the Reception Year, of a representative ten per cent sample of children measuring progress against the early learning goals, indicated that Irish Traveller, Roma, Gypsy, Pakistani and Bangladeshi children and children whose first language is not English underachieved. Black African and Black Caribbean children, although to a lesser extent, also underachieved. This data correlates almost exactly with that of those children who have free school meals. There is no substantial evidence that these findings have changed to any great extent subsequently. However, although the data is now improving, according to research and colleagues at the DCSF responsible for such data, they should be treated with some caution due to the small sample size of some ethnic groups. In 2007 data was collected for the 100 per cent sample and results will be published when they have been analysed. Local authorities may have more comprehensive information on their areas; and the local authority level sample size is more likely to be statistically valid. The information also needs to be considered in the wider context of the achievement of bilingual children: children who are learning two languages at the same time, or who come from a home where they have been cared for by adults speaking a language other than English, may take longer to be perfectly proficient in both – but in the longer term their achievement will have benefited.

In 2003, when the Foundation Stage Profile was first conducted, research based on the previous system (the QCA Baseline Assessment scales) suggested that teachers received limited and variable training and that the moderation of results between local authorities was patchy (DfES 2005b). This is also likely to be true for the Profile to varying degrees across local authorities. However, annual reports from the National Assessment Agency (NAA) indicate that the quality of local authority moderation is improving year on year. But concern remains that where teachers doing the assessment are inadequately prepared for the task, much of it resulting from observation, there is a potential for stereotyping and making cultural assumptions. This reinforces the need for local authorities to ensure that teachers conducting such assessments are appropriately trained to avoid these consequences – various interpretations of the assessment process may result in inaccurate or inappropriate judgements of a child's competence. This is especially potentially problematic when issues of culture and belief are being assessed as workers may have different perspectives on them. There needs to be an agreed meaning and interpretation between workers on such issues before any assessment is recorded. Unless these issues are addressed in the context of careful observation of children, together with the involvement of their parents (particularly when children go on extended visits abroad), the judgements may lead children to be recorded falsely as lower than reality.

There have been some concerns that assessors of children learning English as an additional language may not be able to make valid judgements unless the assessor speaks the child's home language. There are also issues about the sample size and the language in which children learning English as an additional language are assessed for their levels of development (other than for competence in English where the assessment is conducted in English). Recent guidance, however, shows that all the scales other than for communication, language and literacy can be assessed reliably and accurately through the child's home language by a practitioner unfamiliar with that language (NAA 2007). There are only a few scales in the communication, language and literacy assessments that must be assessed in English and thus require bilingual assistance. The Profile handbook suggests that assessments of such children can be made using the home language but relevant interpreters may not always be available. Again any concerns revolve around the availability of competent interpreters who are familiar with the process of assessment and whether all local authorities are able to offer such skills.

While the Early Years Foundation Stage is explicit about ensuring that no child should be excluded or disadvantaged because of ethnicity, culture, religion or home language the issues raised above need to be considered seriously if this principle is to be implemented in practice. Settings should plan an inclusive learning environment so that all children are able to develop fully and be assessed accurately and appropriately. Furthermore, local authorities have a statutory duty under the Race Relations (Amendment) Act to assess the impact of their assessment procedures on different minority ethnic groups. National government should also monitor whether local authorities are complying with their duties.

Although the validity of data from a few local authorities prior to the introduction of the Foundation Stage Profile has been questioned, it showed that African-Caribbean children, under the former baseline assessment (conducted when children entered primary school), out-performed all other ethnic groups; although their achievement levels declined rapidly through all the subsequent key stages (Gillborn and Mirza 2000). Some local authorities now report that African-Caribbean children achieve highly at Key Stage 1 (KS1). One large urban authority (previously collecting ethnic data under the baseline assessment), however, reports that African-Caribbean children, previously outperforming all other ethnic groups at baseline assessment, performed less well than white children when the Foundation Stage curriculum was implemented (Gillborn and Warren 2003). This suggests that the Foundation Stage curriculum, or the way it was implemented or assessed, had benefited white children more than African-Caribbean children.

While acknowledging that some group has to achieve the highest level and that progress in data collection and teacher assessment may be ongoing, these apparent discrepancies and contradictory pieces of information clearly need further analysis. This has implications particularly for the serious and well-documented underachievement of some black and other minority ethnic pupil groups in their later schooling. Foundation Stage Profile results showing the underachievement of some minority ethnic groups point to the need for accurate data collection; and effective training of those doing the assessment using the Profile on children from a variety of cultural backgrounds and an analysis of the potential influence of the language of the assessor on the results. An examination of the role of the early years in children's future attainment levels from all ethnic groups would provide indicators for effective practice in potentially countering any subsequent low achievement levels. For a charter to address concerns about the achievement of black Caribbean boys see NUT (2007).

If you want to know more

about assessment, see NALDIC (1998b) (although it refers to baseline assessment, the principles are the same); and Houston and Gopinath (2003).

Where any research or reports involve children and their families from black and other minority ethnic groups it is always important to ensure that those commissioning, conducting and writing them are familiar with the cultural backgrounds and childrearing practices of the families and have an understanding of the impact of racism on such communities. Furthermore they need to be aware of the potential cultural bias in any measures used in assessment as well as of stereotyping and ethnocentric assumptions in the assessment process itself. For example, there may be some words used to describe children and their families and circumstances that may have different implications for people from different cultural backgrounds and in particular situations – words such as 'cooperative', 'suitable' and 'motherly' may have a variety of interpretations and manifestations.

There are concerns that some research and other reports may have taken insufficient account of these principles. While maintaining objectivity, researchers and report writers must be alert to these factors and be open and receptive to questioning when any apparently negative results are found. In such circumstances any possible valid and alternative explanations of the results should be sought from appropriate members of the relevant communities before coming to final conclusions. Failure to do this may reinforce notions of cultural deficit, which may be replicated and perpetuated unwittingly in other subsequent reports and research, including those by other people, based on such possibly questionable findings. For example, research methodologies to evaluate such aspects of children's lives as their home learning environment, intending to assess the opportunities in the home for offering learning opportunities to children, while apparently worthy and measurable, may be inappropriate to the families of some minority ethnic groups. In some families there may be more opportunities for all family members to talk and share ideas together regularly than for others. There may be more story-telling in some families than in others. There may be other ways of providing learning opportunities that are not included in the assessment. Research reports have indicated an awareness of the need to be sensitive to the possibility of cultural stereotyping and using inappropriate measures of assessment when researching children and their families from minority ethnic communities (Sylva and others 2007, Millennium Cohort Study 2007). While accepting that it is necessary to assess the important learning opportunities provided for children at home, it cannot be assumed that the accuracy of the measures used applies equally to all families. Furthermore, any suggestions or indications that responsibility for ensuring positive learning outcomes lie partly with the homes, rather than equally with early years services and settings, may detract from their responsibility to take action to reach out to minority ethnic families, to ensure equality of access, to provide a culturally sensitive environment and support families facing disadvantage and possible discrimination.

?

If you want to know more

see Brookcr (2002) for research into the home learning environment of Bangladeshi families, the ways that parental teaching at home may remain invisible to children's school teachers and the need to question potentially ethnocentric concepts of such things as 'play', respect for adults and the conceptual differences between learning at school and learning at home. For a critique of early years aspects of the Equalities Review interim report for consultation, see Livingstone (Mayor of London) (2006).

A research report, *Sure Start and Black and Minority Ethnic Populations*, in evaluating the effectiveness of Sure Start Local Programmes (SSLP), makes strong criticisms of the lack of an overall strategy to address how they might involve black and other minority ethnic families in the programmes (Craig and others 2007). The findings have significant implications for children's centres and the way they work with families from such communities. The report makes the points that ethnicity is strongly associated with poverty and other factors relevant to the aims of Sure Start and that, despite their common experience of racism (both individual and institutional) and discrimination, there are considerable social and economic differences between the various minority ethnic groups. Particular findings include:

- the treatment of ethnicity as an important element of the work was largely absent, as was the need for an awareness of the requirements of the amended Race Relations Act
- a lack of effective ethnic data collection and monitoring, using carefully considered ethnic categories, both locally and nationally to evaluate the effectiveness of work done and the crucial role of such monitoring
- a need for a wider community development role in addition to outreach work, together with the recognition that this takes time and that work with some groups takes more time than others if it is to be effective – this is related to an often 'colour-blind' approach which is largely discredited and indicates a need for more understanding of difference and diversity
- the necessity for an appraisal of the need for variability in resource allocation
- an uneven use made of interpretation and translation work
- the need for a review of employment practice to ensure more black and minority ethnic workers at senior levels
- a need to emphasise the role of SSLPs in promoting community cohesion

- though taking account of local independence, there is a need for more notice to be provided and taken of national and local guidance, literature and research findings.

The detailed report elaborates on many of these points, with some suggestions for action, and should be important reading for leaders of all settings, including children's centres. The findings of the National Evaluation of Sure Start research show that the effects of SSLPs are positive for white families, negative for Black Caribbean families and have no effect on other ethnic groups (Sure Start 2008).

A report on listening to black and minority ethnic parents about childcare may be helpful (Daycare Trust 2007). A House of Commons report confirms that overall Sure Start Children's Centres have not yet sufficiently met the needs of some minority ethnic communities (2007).

Qualifications, training and education

The national childcare strategy highlighted what was previously called the 'under-fives muddle' – including a multiplicity of qualifications and training without an overall framework of progression or coordination. The task of addressing this is formidable. It is essential that equality, including racial equality, is integral to future arrangements and planning. Over the last two decades training and education for work with young children has taken some steps to include aspects of racial equality in their programmes. For example, training courses in further education colleges validated by various bodies, courses run by voluntary organisations and courses in higher education all, to varying extents, addressed racial equality. Courses run by the Pre-school Learning Alliance (PLA), the National Childminding Association (NCMA) and the Council for Awards in Children's Care and Education (CACHE), in particular, took the issue seriously. For example, guidance on opening up access to qualifications and training for candidates from minority ethnic groups was published by CACHE (Lane 1999a). But, however good the course structure, the knowledge and understanding base of the tutor or trainer was inevitably critical to its effectiveness.

National standards, occupational standards, inspection frameworks and other government requirements all contribute to what training courses need to include. But if they themselves are inadequate then, unless there are inspired and innovative trainers conducting courses, the training based on them is also likely to be inadequate. The relatively new courses – including foundation degrees; early childhood studies degrees; and courses for managers and leaders, early years professionals and leaders of children's centres – unless carefully monitored and evaluated, may vary in the way they address racial equality issues. Those planning and organising these courses need to have the knowledge, understanding and skills to ensure that effective approaches to racial equality are included. They need to be able to counter some of the simplistic ideas that some workers have, for example, that people in the early years cannot play any part in perpetuating racism because they love all children. It is clear that there is an urgent need to recognise the severe lack of expertise across the country as to what constitutes effective training for racial equality.

Those who plan courses may be unaware that they do not necessarily understand or know what is needed in terms of addressing the racism in society and the role that early years workers can play in countering it. They may not know what they do not know.

If people do not understand issues of racial equality how can they make decisions on the appropriateness of bids to conduct such training? The need for urgent action to train people and to train trainers on effective ways of working for racial equality needs to be a government priority in order to comply with the requirements of the Race Relations Act. Independent accreditation of trainers and of courses should be part of this priority. Failure to address this important issue may result in inadequate training, frustration and reluctance to address the issues at all.

The need for a national government strategy for racial equality

It is important to recognise and acknowledge the positive changes that have occurred – to remember the successes and not dwell on the failures. Most legislation and policies are beginning to be part of a coherent whole – a comprehensive early years agenda for children and their families, a strategy. Most of the key issues for racial equality that need to be addressed have already been identified, if not by government; even if they have not yet been acted upon.

Many of the national early years organisations themselves have addressed racial equality in their various ways and are committed to its principles. For example, the national Early Childhood Forum (ECF) (a coalition of nearly all the national early years organisations concerned with the well-being of children from birth to eight) has its own strategy with five central areas of work to form the policy agenda. They include 'Championing children's rights and entitlements' and 'Addressing inequalities and valuing diversity' (ECF 2006). What is now needed is action by government, both national and local, together with organisations and settings to implement all that has already been identified as critical for racial equality. 'Getting it' is a pre-requisite for the action to be effective.

Changes in the way that racism is approached, though still insufficiently comprehensive and strategic, have come about through, for example:

- an increasing national government commitment through, for example, requirements and targets, policies, regulations and inspections, standards, research, publications, training, guidelines and support
- legislation
- books, dissemination of information, training and resources through journals, videos, conferences, seminars and the distribution of pertinent articles
- the development of specialist groups campaigning against racism, meeting with key organisations and drawing the attention of government to the need for action
- national early years groups and organisations incorporating issues and concerns about racial equality in their training, organisation, work, research, publications and practice

- the inclusion, by national training and education bodies, of discussion about racial equality in syllabuses and training materials
- the development of methods for evaluating resources and a vast increase in the availability of appropriate resources for children and practitioners
- organisations producing resources to support specific groups
- black and antiracist groups continually identifying and reinforcing what needs to be done
- the development of training and education strategies to counter racism
- individuals thinking about and raising the issues
- networking on a large scale.

However there is, as yet:

- little action against racial discrimination or the wider aspects of racism, using existing strong legislation
- no overall, comprehensive strategy to address racism in the early years or even a real understanding of what racism is, particularly institutional racism
- no making of links at national government level between issues of racial equality in the early years and the government's national respect, integration and community cohesion agendas
- no independent assessment of the effectiveness of training and education on racial equality either at initial or in-service levels
- no independent assessment of the competence of trainers to train/educate on racial equality issues
- no independent assessment of the competence of inspectors to inspect for racial equality either in the maintained or the non-maintained sectors
- no accreditation scheme for training and education in relation to racial equality
- no national guidance and support for local authorities or settings as to how to develop practice for racial equality.

Despite these gaps and reservations there is now a serious potential and structure to devise, support and implement a national framework for racial equality in the early years, including an understanding of racism – a strategic approach. All that is needed is the will at national level to begin the process of implementing it. A checklist for all work, as described on page 265 would be a start – a truly Sure Start.

As a contribution to this strategy a comprehensive analysis and critique of recent government documents, policies, legislation and guidance is essential in order to identify what has been omitted and what is now required. This should be supported by a comprehensive mapping exercise of all the positive and effective work done for racial equality in all sectors. In the meantime, for an analysis of the government's position on racial equality in the early years see Lane (2006b).

Monitoring as fundamental to the strategy

Strategies are important in order to define what needs to be done. But it is also important to ensure that what is planned has in fact been implemented, and implemented effectively. Ethnic monitoring is essential to assess this and the statutory duty under the Race Relations (Amendment) Act requires ethnic monitoring. In many ways such monitoring in the early years field is in its infancy – very few local authorities or settings really know how to do it. Ensuring that outcomes are equal for all ethnic groups is proving difficult for people to measure. The National Evaluation of Sure Start (NESS – Sure Start local programmes) indicates the struggles that workers have in determining what to monitor, how to do it and how to evaluate any findings (Lloyd and Rafferty 2006). Of the programmes that submitted reports, nearly all of which were in areas with a high representation of diverse minority ethnic communities, most used the 2001 population census as the basis for their data collection. Even so there was an inadequate consistency in the ethnically monitored data collected, some appearing to see black and other minority ethnic groups as homogeneous and others using a variety of terms for ethnicity. There was a low level of response from the programmes to issues concerning black and other minority group usage and involvement, indicating a lack of knowledge about the whole mechanism of monitoring – the data collected was seldom effectively evaluated or even properly understood. There was little overall understanding of issues such as representation from diverse ethnic communities, for example on partnership boards and staffing, or of what racial equality might mean in practice.

Whilst it is important to use the census categories as a basis for monitoring by ethnicity, to be able to have consistent comparators, it is important for the categories to be expanded to identify and quantify significant local communities. Without this, local authorities and settings are unable to use the date to identify the needs, access to services and outcomes from services for their local communities.

This raises serious concerns for the future evaluation of racial equality and the inclusion of children and their families from black and other minority ethnic communities equally in the children's centres now being set up in every community. Sure Start local programmes, neighbourhood nurseries, early excellence centres, nursery schools and other settings are the precursors of children's centres – the evident lack of training and education and support for workers across a range of racial equality issues, including ethnic monitoring mechanisms, should be of major concern to everyone. The failure to address racism in so many of the policies, practices and procedures identified above does not bode well for these new centres, aiming to provide seamless, holistic and integrated services and information for everyone equally.

It is clear from everything discussed in this text that nothing short of a full scale revision of the whole national childcare strategy to take account of racial equality must be a priority. In this priority, training and education must rank very high. (For the text of a talk given at a conference about government documentation and racial equality see Lane 2007c.)

10 Planning for racial equality across early years services and settings

Despite the many obstacles and occasional push backwards, I believe that we have no choice but to continue working towards an equitable early childhood and primary education system for all. The children have that right and the world needs it.

(Louise Derman-Sparks in *Race Equality Teaching*, Spring 2006)

The laws, policies, practices and procedures of the country impact on national government departments, agencies, organisations and on local authorities, which, in turn, impact on early years settings and all who are involved with them. All have implications for each other. In principle, most of the structures are already in place for a strategy for racial equality to be implemented in practice. However, until the political understanding ('getting it') and the will are there to ensure this is done – as already indicated – the specific responsibility to implement racial equality is likely to be absent.

This chapter, however, focuses particularly on the issues that early years services and settings need to address in order to plan for the implementation of racial equality. The issues that ministers, national government and departments, agencies and organisations also need to address are identified elsewhere in this book or in other documents (see Lane 2006b). But in order to be effective, whether the issues are at ministerial, national or local government levels or in settings, it is essential to have a strategic approach encompassing all documentation, activities and decision-making. Anything other than a comprehensive strategy is unlikely to address all the aspects of racism that may be a part of the service or setting practice and procedures.

Racism is only one aspect of inequality – but it is usually most effective if all inequalities are considered as integral even if the specific components are analysed separately. In this context the term 'inclusion' may provide an overall focus for considering all inequalities as part of an integrated approach to equality generally.

The following definition, devised by the national Early Childhood Forum in 2003[6], may be helpful in working towards this objective.

Inclusion is a process of identifying, understanding and breaking down the barriers to participation and belonging.

Leaflets describing and elaborating on the various parts of this definition, including children's rights and entitlements, are available (ECF 2005 and 2007). As are articles describing how setting leaders might lay the foundations for inclusion (Lane with Owen 2004/2005).

While an integrated approach to all equality issues is critical to an understanding of their similarities and differences, this chapter concerns itself specifically with racism and racial equality as a part of this inclusion definition. It introduces a framework approach, a strategy, that encompasses the issues and concerns that need to be addressed in order to implement racial equality across the service and settings. Each component of the framework needs to be considered in light of the government's Every Child Matters priority outcomes, some of which may be more applicable than others. For example, references to:

- fear of racist abuse, emotional hurt and name-calling relate to *'being healthy'*, affecting emotional well-being
- racist incidents and feeling secure about racial identity relate to *'staying safe'*
- removing discrimination relates to *'enjoying and achieving'*
- taking action to understand and belong to the local community relates to *'making a positive contribution'*.

However, some aspects of racial equality do not fit easily into any of these outcomes. For example, being treated equally and having a sense of belonging to a setting are more specifically positive factors, requiring specific action to be taken with children, because of the racism embedded in our society, than any of the outcomes of Every Child Matters. And institutional racism is unlikely to be removed by just addressing the five outcomes. The situation is similar for other inequalities. At a series of conferences in 2005/2006 held to consider the above definition of inclusion, 'Participation and Belonging', Sue Owen (the director of the Early Childhood Unit of the National Children's Bureau) identified a sixth outcome as:

'being equal – feeling that you belong'.

(DfES/NCB 2005/2006)

This is an important additional outcome to the other five and is more likely to incorporate all those factors about equality that do not fit readily into any of the original five outcomes. It should be used where it is not obvious how the other

---

[6] The national Early Childhood Forum is a coalition of professional associations, voluntary organisations and interest groups aiming to bring together partners in the early childhood sector to debate issues, celebrate differences and develop consensus to champion quality experiences for all young children and their families.

outcomes apply to the particular situation. Settings can provide a shared sense of belonging for everyone.

The importance of early years services and settings having a strategic approach to racial equality

Countering racism and ensuring racial equality in the early years is a process, not a one-off activity. It must be strategic and planned for in order to be effective. An ad hoc approach, where some aspects of early years services and settings are addressed but others are not, results in failure to dismantle racism overall, ignores the interlinking mechanisms that continually reinforce it and leads to frustration for those who want to implement antiracist practice but appear to be working in an unreceptive environment.

Sometimes, however, the task of even getting equality issues to be discussed at a minimum level appears impossible, let alone having a comprehensive strategy. This is perhaps more likely to occur in largely white areas where racist attitudes may lie dormant and unrecognised and lassitude about these issues prevails. Perhaps this apparent dormancy is only ever specifically expressed in hostility to Travellers, Roma and Gypsies who often live and work in rural areas, to asylum seekers who are dispersed there and to the increasing number of migrant workers who may be doing temporary agricultural or horticultural work there. But sometimes racist attitudes may be vehemently expressed against particular groups, for example towards asylum seekers, even when none are present in the area. It is also possible that some people may have moved from towns and cities to such areas in order to avoid living in a multicultural community. But the hidden negative attitudes to black and other minority ethnic groups may remain entrenched. Committed individuals, who may be working in such unreceptive environments, then have to begin to plan a strategy (using legislation and government requirements) to build up support in the service and settings by organising discussions and training seminars and raising the issue on every possible occasion in order to identify allies to work with them (see page 106 and 179 for issues on working in largely white areas).

Appointing someone to organise development work on racial equality (and other equalities) should be a priority for all early years services; and in large authorities a team of people is necessary.

Legislation plays a critical role in ensuring that racism is addressed. But this relies on those involved in policy, development work, training and research knowing about the law and having it continually in their minds in all they do. Very few people are yet sufficiently aware of their statutory duties and responsibilities under the law to ensure racial equality is integral to their day-to-day work, let alone having a moral duty to promote it.

Because government has not taken a strategic lead in ensuring racial equality in the early years it means that some services and settings fail to recognise racism as an issue for them at all. While some may take action anyway, whether there are laws and government requirements or not, others may await such requirements before they do anything, pay only lip-service to them or be unaware of the need to take any action at all. But while some address racism in sensitive and constructive ways, there are only a few who really understand how it works, know what needs to be done to counter it and are able to put it into practice. There are many who have not addressed racism seriously and a few where ignorance or even hostility prevail.

As a consequence, putting the elements of what needs to be done into an overall context – a strategy – may be helpful. A strategic approach across the whole early years service and settings may help identify and focus on what action needs to be taken to ensure racial equality is put into practice everywhere. How local authorities and settings take account of the five (and suggested sixth) outcomes of Every Child Matters and frame the strategy around them will depend on the particular circumstances of each. This strategy is offered as a guide in delivering racial equality.

If you want to know more

see Gopinath (2004) and Selleck (2005) for developing a strategy for equality in Cambridgeshire and Oxfordshire respectively.

A suggested strategy for racial equality

Although in the future there may be a comprehensive strategy for equality (all equalities) it is likely that each strand will need to be developed first and the common aspects identified later.

The overall objective might be:

_____ [insert name of local authority] early years service and all settings will work to provide racial equality in employment and in all services for workers, young children and their families.

This objective should be the basis of a strategy for racial equality that encompasses all those factors that disadvantage and discriminate against anyone involved in early years services and settings. These factors often reinforce one another and may also overlap. For example, a black mother with a disabled child living in a high-rise block just outside the catchment area of a setting she would like her child to attend, may feel she experiences discrimination but cannot identify whether it is on the grounds of ethnicity, gender, social class, poverty, lone parenthood, her child's disability or a mixture of some or all of these factors. Considering her situation from all possible aspects – using the inclusion definition – may help to reveal whether, and if so where and how, discrimination is taking place. Action can then be taken to remove any unlawful discrimination. Any discrimination that is outside the scope of the law or any disadvantage resulting from historical, structural or any other circumstances may require specific solutions, according to the particular situation.

Local authorities organise themselves in a variety of ways, allocating their roles accordingly. Despite the government's approach in unifying all early years services, some authorities retain a partnership, some work with maintained and non-maintained settings together and others work separately. In order to ensure the implementation of racial equality, the race equality scheme, policies, practices and procedures of the local authority early years service and the settings need to be examined overall and every aspect analysed, including differentials in outcome from and access to services. This process should be one part of the race equality impact assessment. Evaluation in this way will make it possible to identify the following.

1   Whether any racial discrimination may exist.
2   If so, how it operates.
3   What solutions are most likely to remove it.
4   What resources and training might be needed to do this.

This strategic or framework approach, backed up by legislation and other government requirements, means that there is a real chance of effecting change, of removing racism and of implementing racial equality across the local authority early years service and settings. But the political will to ensure that it is done is an essential part of success.

Areas of responsibility within the local early years service need to be identified. The local authority's published race equality scheme is required to identify all the local authority's functions and policies, and their lead officers, so information on the early years service may be readily available. These functions are reinforced in the associated action plan.

The early years service is responsible for the employment of its workers, policy and decision-making, training, advice, development and support, administration, and the implementation and monitoring of the settings' policies. Although some aspects of some settings' organisation may be organised centrally each is ultimately responsible for its activities. These include policies, employment, involvement of any volunteers, the arrangements for admissions, the curriculum, assessment, children learning English as an additional language, translation and interpreting, and family involvement.

Any strategy aimed at countering racism by addressing identified concerns needs a clear framework. The framework should have key elements, or components, each of which addresses particular areas of responsibility. These components interlock like links in a chain, they are dependent on each other and are designed to address responsibilities and their implications. For example, in terms of curricular resources, the links across a whole early years service might be:

1   aiming to ensure that the resources in all settings are culturally appropriate and support antiracist practice
2   devising criteria for evaluating those resources

3   appointing appropriately qualified workers to monitor the use of the resources across the service
4   ensuring that all settings are aware of the criteria for evaluating their resources and the process for monitoring their usage
5   appointing or training suitable trainers
6   training workers in settings so they know what to look for when evaluating their resources
7   including funding for this kind of training in the budget
8   sharing the information and learning acquired widely
9   considering whether a centrally based resource centre for studying, borrowing and training about resources might help in sharing advice and good practice.

These interlinked issues will be supported by others, for instance the need to establish monitoring mechanisms to ensure that resources are checked regularly. Family members, and others involved, may also be encouraged to share the principles and process of what it means to provide their children with appropriate resources for play. The links are endless.

The components in the race equality action plan (which is part of the race equality scheme or policy) should define and describe what needs to be done, when and how it is to be done, who is to do it and how it is to be checked to ensure that it has been done effectively. In order to do this, specific mechanisms are needed to enforce and support action.

Commitment is the key. Trying to implement racial equality without commitment will not work. Individual people at every level in the service will determine whether it works or not.

A framework of interlinked components

In this book three components of an overall framework have been devised. Other frameworks with fewer or more components could be adapted from the one here. (For a comprehensive overall detailed framework see Lane 2006b.) The requirements of the law and policy-making, already discussed in earlier chapters, come after the framework.

The framework is written in some detail, but this does not mean that every part is of equal importance or that every item should be dealt with immediately. It is a framework to work towards and is intended to be helpful. Every early years service and early years setting is unique. Because there are many common issues in the service and the settings in general they have been grouped together. Occasionally, whether a particular issue is appropriate to the service or setting will need to be considered. To be effective, the framework should be adapted for each situation but should keep the basic principles in mind. While the objectives may be idealistic, realism must prevail. It takes time to reach the ideal.

Essential knowledge

To implement a framework for racial equality effectively, workers in the early years service and settings, including those working with children, will need to have some knowledge and understanding of the issues listed below. Some issues will require someone to have more specific and detailed knowledge, for example, legislation. Many of these issues are dealt with throughout this book and, where appropriate, cross-references have been provided for discussions on a specific issue.

The law

- The Race Relations Act 1976 including statutory duties, the concepts of direct and indirect discrimination and positive action (see Chapter 8).
- The Race Relations (Amendment) Act 2000, including the general and specific duties; the race equality scheme, policy and action plan; race equality impact assessments; ethnic monitoring; and procurement (see Chapter 8 and Appendix 4).

Facts about racism

- The facts of racial discrimination, disadvantage and poverty in Britain today (see Modood and others 1997, CRE website, Cabinet Office 2003, Donnellan 2006, Platt 2007, CRE 2007b, CRE 2006a, CRE *Catalyst* email newsletter 2005 onwards, 1990 Trust Blink website, Institute of Race Relations website, and other sources).
- The history of ethnic diversity and British racism and the legacy it leaves today, including in largely white areas of the country (see IRR 1982, Fryer 1984, CRE 1996, IRR (undated) *HomeBeats*, Bhavnani 2001, Walker 2006, Kundnani 2007 and Chapter 2).
- How institutional racism may affect the service and settings (see page 33 onwards).
- The effects of racism on children (see page 90).
- How racial attitudes and behaviour are learnt and how they might be unlearnt (see Chapter 3).
- How racial hierarchies, including those of language, culture, skin colour, physical features, religion and ethnicity develop and how they can be broken down (see Chapter 3 for discussion).
- The way that cultural assumptions, stereotypes and adult expectations may limit children's equal access to the full range of learning opportunities and resources and affect outcomes from them (see page 14).
- The nature of racist incidents, harassment and name-calling and how they might be addressed and countered (see Chapter 7; EYTARN 2001, the appendix; Lane 2001b; Cook and Lane 2002/2004; Essex County Council 2007).
- See the Institute of Race Relations *IRR News* for a free independent weekly email bulletin on race and refugees; and the Britkids website on race and racism.

Practical issues

- Antiracist practice in early years settings (see Persona Doll Training 2001 and 2004 video and booklet; Brent EYDCP 2001a video/booklet on the Foundation Stage; Houston 2004; and Britkids website, which is school based).
- Effective policy-making, writing implementation programmes, collecting data monitored by ethnicity and evaluating it; consultation with families (see Chapters 5, 6 and 8; and EYTARN 2001).
- The role of effective training in the implementation of racial equality (see page 150 and Persona Doll Training 2001 and 2004, page 207).
- The importance of using appropriate terminology (see Appendix 1 and page 74).
- The issues involved in groups working together, of solidarity, of respecting a variety of opinions, establishing an atmosphere of trust and empathy, ensuring that the views of all families are heard (see page 53).
- Establishing a no-blame culture which addresses issues of racial equality so that others can understand and accept the need for change without feeling guilty or uncomfortable in discussions (see page 56).
- Countering racism and dealing with racist incidents (see Chapter 7).
- Information on the ethnic composition of the local community and other related matters (from the local authority racial equality section; census data; and the Pupil Level Annual School Census (PLASC) data on the attainment of pupils from different ethnic groups, from the DfES Standards website).

Working with children

- Ways of helping children to unlearn racially prejudiced attitudes and behaviour, and to learn positive attitudes to racial differences (see Chapter 3; Brown 1998 and 2001; Persona Doll Training videos 2001 and 2004; and van Keulen 2004).
- The importance of helping children to be critically aware of the world around them and how this can best be achieved.
- What to look for in assessing children's learning resources on racial equality issues (see page 204 onwards).
- The advantages of bilingualism and multilingualism and learning to be bilingual; and the current methods of teaching and learning English as an additional language (see pages 120 and 212).

Working with families

- The vital role that family members play in the development of children's racial attitudes, with a consideration of how best to involve them, in complementary ways, in working together towards all children having positive racial attitudes (see Chapter 5).

Working to help society be more at ease with itself

- The important role that workers, family members and children involved in services and settings can play in breaking down barriers between people in the local community and working towards a reduction of tensions in our society (see page 156).
- All workers considering what role an early years setting might play in the local community.

Taking a strategic approach to the implementation of racial equality

This approach includes a framework of components and some of the mechanisms by which to implement it.

Framework of components

The objective may be written as follows.

_____ [insert name of local authority] early years service and all settings will work to provide racial equality in employment and in all services for workers, young children and their families.

The linked components needed to satisfy this objective might include the following.

1   All members of the local authority early years service and any partnership should be involved in, and committed to, devising, implementing and monitoring the race equality scheme. Responsibility for developing and supporting the work of early years settings to implement racial equality lies with the service, including training, advice, sharing of relevant information and resources and monitoring of policies.

2   Everyone working in the local authority early years service and settings, and all children and their families involved in the settings, should be treated with equal concern.[7]

3   Strategies should be developed to support all children and adults in:
    a   learning positive attitudes and behaviour to those different from themselves
    b   countering any negative attitudes and behaviour to differences that they may have already learned
    c   promoting race equality.

---

[7] The term 'with equal concern' was coined by Greta Sandler and used in the Guidance to the Children Act 1989.

Mechanisms for implementing the framework of components

1   The process of developing a scheme or policy for race equality should ensure that everyone working in the service or setting, management, governors, committee and elected members, family members and relevant members of the local community are:
    a   involved in devising, implementing and monitoring its scheme or policy for race equality and
    b   committed to its implementation and to monitoring its effectiveness.
2   All aspects of the local authority early years service and settings should be free of unlawful racial discrimination, comply with any statutory duties, promote race equality and aim to counter other forms of racial discrimination that are not covered by the law.

Implementing the framework for racial equality

Early years services and settings should be safe places free of discrimination and harassment where everyone is treated with dignity, valued and given equal respect and concern.

Policies, procedures, practices, programmes and any curriculum changes take time and thought. The important thing is to start the process.

The workings of the framework as a whole need to be considered by key people responsible and involved in organising the local authority early years service and the settings. For those working in settings, it is worth identifying the components that relate most to the working situation. Think about the points that need most immediate attention (not necessarily the easiest ones) – and who might be able to help with them – within the context of the whole framework.

Component 1

> All members of the local authority early years service and any partnership should be involved in, and committed to, devising, implementing and monitoring the racial equality scheme. Responsibility for developing and supporting the work of early years settings to implement racial equality lies with the service, including training, advice, sharing of relevant information and resources and monitoring of policies.

Responsibility for ensuring that racial equality is implemented in practice lies with every person involved, but particularly with the managers, heads of service and other leaders. Opportunities need to be provided for everyone to share ideas, talk through what is involved, attend training and be fully involved and consulted on the development of the scheme (see Brent 2001b for an example of a simple equality audit).

Part of this responsibility is to ensure that all families, including the families of black and other minority ethnic communities, are fully, effectively and appropriately consulted and their views and wishes incorporated into the scheme in line with its objectives.

Look at the Sure Start website for references to materials, advice, documents on equality (www.surestart.gov.uk).

➧ Ensure that leaders demonstrate their responsibility to promote racial equality and good race relations.

➧ Ensure that all workers know about, understand and are committed to the race equality scheme or policy.

➧ Ensure that all appointments in the service include, in a person specification, an essential requirement to be committed to the implementation of racial equality; and, for senior appointments, in addition, a requirement to also have the knowledge, understanding and skills to implement the race equality scheme.

➧ Consider the implications of any legislation and DfES/DCSF, Ofsted, QCA, TDA or other government requirements for racial equality. For example, the implications of race equality impact assessments and procurement measures.

➧ Consider whether representation of any partnership or local authority early years service reflects the ethnic backgrounds of the local community at all levels. If not, take action to address this.

➧ Make sure there is an action plan for implementing the service's race equality scheme or policy – to cover who does what and over what timescales; and to define outcomes and monitoring mechanisms, resources available and ongoing consultation methods.

➧ Ensure the race equality scheme includes procedures for dealing with racial harassment of staff, and that these are part of the organisation's human resources policy and procedures and have monitoring mechanisms.

➧ Ensure that at least one member of the service fully understands race relations legislation and takes responsibility for racial equality, including consultation with families from black and other minority ethnic groups, procurement and leading on the race equality impact assessment, for example in assessing sufficiency (and quality in terms of racial equality) of childcare places. Develop links with the appropriate section of the local authority to share information, relevant issues and experience (for example, local authority Children's Services, Equality Services).

➧ Establish a database. Collect data monitored by ethnicity on all aspects of the service – all levels of employment (all stages of the recruitment process, promotion and access to benefits); monitoring of settings (all stages of the admissions and employment recruitment procedures, children present, hours attended, all workers at all levels, potential future users in the local community, racist incidents; and governors, management and committee members.

➧ Monitor and evaluate this data regularly and identify any disparities and inequalities and possible racial discrimination.

- Devise procedures for removing any inequalities found.

- Consider taking any relevant positive action under the Race Relations Act to address any under-representation or disadvantage of particular ethnic groups in the service or setting's workforce at all levels and, if necessary, set targets to be achieved by that action.

- Collect information on the service given to settings (training, support, development, advice and resources) about racial equality issues and devise mechanisms for monitoring its effectiveness.

- Review the race equality scheme or policy, action plan, implementation and monitoring methods regularly.

- Ensure that space at meetings is given for issues of concern about racial equality to be raised.

- Regularly identify and use sources of support, information, advice and training, and make them available to all workers in the service and in the early years settings.

- Establish a resource and training base of relevant materials to inform, stimulate discussions and provide examples of anti-discriminatory practice for settings to access.

- Consider and plan for any training needs and recruitment in order to implement the scheme or policy and the strategy for achieving it.

- Identify any training needs about racial equality in the settings and provide or support such training.

- Encourage governors, management and committee members of early years settings to reflect the ethnic composition of the local community and to support the setting's policy on racial equality. Regularly review this.

- Consider how the service might initiate and support action among its workers and in settings to address issues of building up positive community cohesion – a statutory duty for schools (including children's centres run by schools) – and removing barriers between communities.

- Try to build up an ethos of constructive communication, solidarity and trust between workers within a no-blame culture.

- Budget for and commit resources to implement the race equality scheme or policy. Ensure that the institution has appropriate buying procedures for resources and procurement.

Component 2

Everyone working in the local authority early years service and settings, and all children and their families involved in the settings, should be treated with equal concern.

This means ensuring that everyone is treated with equal value and respect and with equal regard for their feelings and beliefs. Ensuring that every worker has the opportunity to express any concerns about racial equality whenever they need to, with shared objectives, a sense of solidarity, and within an ethos free of blame and fear of the consequences.

With children it means thinking particularly about every child as an individual and ensuring that each child's needs are addressed. It means examining everything that is around the children – the adults and other children, resources, the overt and hidden curriculum – and ensuring that each child has equal access to the full range of learning opportunities. It requires more than simply making sure everyone has appropriate resources, it is about making sure that everyone's specific and general needs are addressed and that a watchful eye is kept on every child to check that they have access to all the learning resources and activities available and to which they are all equally entitled.

The principles and objectives of the scheme or policy for racial equality are the same, whether the area is largely white or multiethnic, although some of the detailed practice may be different.

For settings

- Examine resources. All resources – including toys, books, posters, dolls, play materials, jigsaws, puzzles, miniature play people, colouring and art materials, paper and games – need to be examined to ensure they are free of stereotyping, reflect all members of our society accurately, in all walks of life and do not ignore some completely, do not portray communities as exotic, and any images tell the same story as the text.

- Translate and interpret information, where appropriate, for families who do not speak or read English. Find out where to get material translated into other languages and how to access an interpreter. Consider becoming involved in making a video for families who may not read English, for example, Traveller, Roma, Gypsy, migrant workers, refugee and asylum-seeking families.

- Value differences and similarities positively. Organise projects to talk about, look at, illustrate, recognise and equally value the range of different skin colours (including among white people); hair colours, textures and styles; and eye, nose and mouth shapes. Talk about concepts of beauty and show that every child is glorious. Ensure that all young children are secure in the knowledge that they and their community are valued. Make sure a range of crayons, paints and paper colours is available for children to use in artwork to reflect skin tones. Be positive about people who are different from others as well as those who are similar.

- Encourage children to view differences as just that. Avoid reinforcing the message that people who are different from themselves are exotic, rather than being a part of our world.

- Acknowledge the reality of multicultural, multifaith (or no faith), multilingual and multiethnic Britain on a regular basis and not just when festivals are being celebrated.

- Have high expectations of every child, free of stereotypes. Analyse practice, observe children and record what they do and how they relate to adults to ensure that each is expected to succeed intellectually, socially, physically and emotionally.

- Enthuse all children with the excitement and joy of learning, to become thriving learners.

- Encourage all children to be open- and broad-minded, to share experiences together and to feel comfortable within and between each other's cultural backgrounds, supported by workers demonstrating these aspects.

- Encourage all children to be proud of their cultural backgrounds as well as wanting to value those of others.

- Actively ensure that all children's self-esteem is promoted by positively valuing them personally, their cultural and ethnic background, their skin colour and their families. Make it clear that all this is treasured in the setting.

- Allow and encourage all children to play all roles. Ensure that particular roles are not always perceived as only being able to be performed by a child of a particular colour or ethnicity. Children accept each other in make-believe roles, and indeed the modern theatre has seen many black Hamlets, and acclaimed performances of Henry V, Henry VI and more by black actors. It is important to include stories from a variety of cultures, so that the heroes and heroines come from different backgrounds.

- Observe and monitor children's interactions. Watch carefully what children do and say to each other to ensure that racially prejudiced remarks or behaviour are identified and addressed. Observe who is included and who is excluded and deal with anything that is excluding anyone on racial grounds.

- Deal with all racist incidents of racial harassment, however insignificant they might seem. It may range from unwittingly saying something offensive, to making offensive racist remarks or even racist physical abuse or violence.

- Devise a policy against harassment (see Chapter 7).

- Be constantly aware of how easy it is to jump to conclusions, to make assumptions about a person or people. For example, regarding how people spend their leisure time, what time their children go to bed or what clothes they dress their children in to come to the setting.

- Think about what terminology is used in the early years setting. Check that it is not reinforcing racist attitudes and behaviour and that it is not offensive to anyone. Create an atmosphere where people can say what they find offensive and why, and where other people will listen to what is said with respect and not resentment or a defensive reaction. Listen carefully to what children, those working with children and family members say and, where appropriate, deal with any offensive terminology in a sensitive and non-threatening way.

◆ Consider the variety of child-rearing practices. Find out as much as possible about the range of child-rearing practices used by families in the early years setting and elsewhere. In thinking about them and discussing them with colleagues, consider their role in the variety of cultural groups and assess what others can learn from this variety. Use the information to begin to break down racial hierarchies of what are often believed to be the 'best ways' to bring up children.

◆ Consider the overt (explicit) and the covert (hidden) curriculum. Examine whether there are any differences between what is overt and what might be more subtle influences in the curriculum. The resources, the adult–child, child–child and adult–adult relationships, and what is not said or not done may give covert messages to children about who is important and valued in the setting and elsewhere.

◆ Consider the ethnic composition of the children and the people working with them. Does it reflect the ethnic composition of the local community at all levels? If there are discrepancies, is this due to factors that the early years setting needs to address? For example, are the vacancies for jobs and places in the setting widely advertised? Are the selection and admission criteria fair? Is it necessary to take some positive action to rectify any discrepancies?

◆ Observe, monitor and evaluate which children are doing what. Consider whether every child is, in practice, having an opportunity to learn from and experience all the aspects of the curriculum to be able to develop the full range of learning skills. Observe and record what every child does on a regular basis. Evaluate the access that each child has to the curriculum.

◆ Observe and evaluate adult–child, child–child and adult–adult relationships. Not everyone can relate happily to each other, neither children nor adults. But every adult and every child must be treated equally. This means observing, with open minds, the way everyone relates to each other, to ensure that this is being put into practice. Recognising and accepting that no one is perfect and that everyone finds some aspects of life difficult, including life in the early years setting, is important. This is not easy to do and is likely to be best done in practice when there is a no-blame culture.

◆ Observe and listen to children and their worlds and whether children of the same cultural group appear to stay together and seldom play with or relate to children of other cultural backgrounds – try to find out why. It may be because of a common cultural understanding and sense of belonging to that group, but it may be because they do not feel welcome, accepted and valued by children of other cultural groups. Their previous experiences may reinforce any such behaviour. Children of any ethnic or cultural group may be subjected to prejudice. Involve family members in addressing such circumstances.

◆ Encourage all children to sometimes play with and relate to children of different cultural backgrounds and equally encourage all children to accept and welcome children different from themselves into their play and relationships.

- Think about multiculturalism. Are all the resources and curriculum plans recognising, taking account of and addressing the fact that cultures in Britain are often ranked in a racial hierarchy and may not be equally valued by everyone?

- Encourage all children to be critically aware of and intellectually curious about everything around them.

- Think about the ethos of the setting. A short visit can result in a superficial impression or hunch, which may or may not be accurate. Should more thought be put into an evaluation? What would someone coming in really think about what the setting is doing? What are the messages given to a visitor by the physical environment? By analysing things, what are the components that comprise and define the ethos? Does this closer analysis confirm or refute the initial impression? What needs to be done to ensure that both the ethos and the analysis give positive messages about countering racism?

- Remember that the most important things to notice are the ways workers work with children and their attitudes, rather than the displays and physical environment. Resources cannot substitute for an inclusive, friendly and supportive ethos.

- Think about how the setting workers, children and their families might involve themselves in the local community, and among themselves, in order to take responsibility to break down barriers between people from different cultural backgrounds and begin the process of enabling society to be more at ease with itself.

Component 3

Strategies should be developed to support all children and adults in:

- learning positive attitudes and behaviour to those different from themselves
- countering any negative attitudes and behaviour to differences that they may have already learned
- promoting race equality.

Adults and children usually reflect their personal environments in their racial attitudes and behaviour. Unless their whole environment is positive towards racial differences they may hold the attitudes which are prevalent in our society, that is, racially prejudiced attitudes. They will have learned some of their attitudes and behaviour to differences from many sources outside the early years service or the setting.

All services and settings (whether they are subject to the statutory duty under the Race Relations (Amendment) Act to promote race equality or not) should take action to promote good relations between people of different racial groups. This means carefully and specifically considering what might be practical ways of doing this.

The adults in the service and settings should be committed to the racial equality scheme or policy that has been devised. They have a particular responsibility to ensure that the children with whom they work are provided with opportunities for learning positive attitudes to racial differences. They are also responsible for ensuring that any negative attitudes are countered in positive, sensitive and constructive ways. Recruitment practice should reflect these responsibilities.

This component requires people working with children to devise ways of enabling children to consider their attitudes and beliefs deriving from their experiences in the light of balanced and accurate information. It means providing children with the skills to seek out information before arriving at a conclusion; to be critically aware of the world around them; and to be able to empathise and reflect, so they have a basis on which to make up their own minds about concepts of fairness and justice. This is particularly important in settings unfamiliar with cultural, linguistic, religious and ethnic diversity and where the range of skin colour difference is limited.

There is also a need to address the way racist attitudes and behaviour (concepts of racism in general) are passed on from generation to generation in our society. Unless some action is taken to break this cycle, it is likely to continue.

It is important to be particularly sensitive about the way this work is undertaken as it is all too easy for people to misinterpret the reasons for it, or to undermine the implementation of a policy. Be clear about why it is necessary and involve families, children, governors, management and committee members at all stages as partners in the policy for racial equality so that, together, they all own it. Family members are particularly important here. Without their support and commitment the chance of success is hugely reduced.

➧ Know about and understand, as far as possible, the origins of racism. This will help to explain why work in largely white areas is as important as elsewhere. It will also explain how racism first took a hold, who benefited from it, how myths and stereotypes were built up, and the mechanisms used to pass on the attitudes and beliefs that have sustained it over the years. Ensure that this is done in a sensitive and non-threatening way.

➧ Think about how families can be involved in working for racial equality. Families are the most critical influences on children's thinking and lives. In agreeing to, and supporting, the policy for equality they will already have experienced some discussion and received information on the issues. Only by engaging them in the work to counter the learning of racist attitudes will it have a real chance of success.

➧ Talk with children about what they think and believe and about their attitudes to differences and similarities. If you don't know what they think, you won't be able to identify any need to provide them with other information or to raise issues with them or their families. Be informed and confident as to how a situation or conversation might emerge so that effective and supportive discussion can take place. Take particular care to ensure that any discussion does not blame anyone, or pick a particular child out, but that it addresses the issue, not children personally. By working with all children together every child is involved, so those whose attitudes may remain hidden may also have an opportunity to consider and reflect.

- Address learned impressions of racial hierarchies regularly by planning strategies to help children to unlearn any negative attitudes and behaviour that they may have already learnt based on language, skin colour, physical features, ethnicity, culture, religion or belief. Work with children using Persona Dolls and circle time.

- Plan a programme to introduce children to the wider world in which we live. Provide accurate information about this world. Think about, identify and counter the commonly held stereotypical images of what the world is like, especially to a child, and provide a range of accurate, positive and countervailing images. For example, images of Africa often ignore countries like Egypt and focus entirely on traditional homes rather than high-rise buildings, and those of Native Americans reinforce bows and arrows depicting violent behaviour.

- Use Persona Dolls and circle time to develop children's concepts of empathy and understanding, respect for differences between people, the ability to stand up for themselves and to support and challenge unfairness when they see or hear it.

- Provide opportunities for children to hear and consider a variety of viewpoints. In order to learn how to consider conflicting pieces of information objectively, children need the experience of understanding how to evaluate them: What questions do they need to ask? What further information should they seek? What criteria are they using to make their judgments? The ability to evaluate can be encouraged through exercises that may be completely unrelated to anti-discrimination, for instance by asking children to suggest venues for a forthcoming outing, compiling a list from their suggestions, then asking them for their views on the good and bad points of each venue (their *reasons* for wanting or not wanting to visit each place). The children then vote for their favourite venue, and of course go on the trip itself. This kind of process can be referred to at any time and used in discussing such things as racist incidents.

- Monitoring of the racist incidents (including any name-calling) may reveal issues that need to be considered. It may also be important to encourage all children to participate equally in discussions and story-telling. Circle time can be the basis for this, where each child is responsible for the well-being of the others.

- Provide children with opportunities for workers to support them in taking their own actions to counter racist attitudes, unfairness and injustice, including racist incidents and other name-calling.

- Take specific action to counter negative attitudes to asylum seekers, migrant workers, Travellers, Roma and Gypsies, unfamiliar religions, including Islamophobia, antisemitism and sectarianism.

- Develop strategies to raise issues of concern, to empower children to ask questions, to question conflicts and help them address them positively – for example, if appropriate, in discussions about any violence or disturbing events that they may have heard about or seen on television or nearer home. The experience of everyday practice will highlight issues that need to be addressed strategically. For example, if all children in the setting are white, there will be lots of work to be done to raise awareness, empathy and factual knowledge of people from other ethnic and cultural groups as well as the possibly limited perspective of their own ethnic group.

▶ Prepare children in advance and with sensitivity, so far as possible, to deal with potential acts of terrorism, fear and disasters and support families and children affected by them.

▶ Provide children with the skills to be critically aware, to empathise and reflect, so that they have a basis on which to make up their own minds about concepts of fairness and justice. Most of the points raised above contribute to the development of these skills. Respect for all children and encouraging them to think, to listen, to change their minds without feeling foolish and to learn in an atmosphere of mutual support and trust will foster the conditions where these skills can best be learned.

▶ Take specific action to bring the lives of people from the local community into the setting so that it becomes the living experience of everyone – by people visiting, visits locally or further afield. Talk about how workers, children and their families can all feel they belong to their local community and how workers in the setting can be advocates for their local community.

▶ Consider the role of the setting in helping to reduce community tensions and making the world more harmonious – building up inter-ethnic communication between families both inside and outside the setting, taking an active part in local community activities and supporting concerns about injustice.

▶ Check all that is done to ensure that the duty to promote race equality (whether the setting has this statutory duty or not) is being implemented in practice.

The mechanisms to support the implementation of the framework

Component 1

The process of developing a scheme or policy for race equality should ensure that everyone working in the service or setting, management, governors, committee and elected members, family members, children where appropriate and relevant members of the local community are:

- involved in devising, implementing and monitoring its scheme/policy for racial equality
- committed to its implementation and to monitoring its effectiveness.

The process of including everyone in drafting the scheme or policy is likely to involve people in different ways and levels of detail though all need to understand the principles of what is being done. An experienced person at a high level should be appointed to have overall responsibility for the scheme or policy, the preparation of its action plan and for its implementation. Fully and actively consulting with all the people potentially involved and with a stake in the outcomes will encourage a sense of real participation and belonging. Involving children, management, governors, committee members, family members, children and relevant members of the local community, devise the following.

- A scheme or policy for race equality, to cover all aspects of the organisation (policies, procedures and practice) of the service and setting, including employment, the delivery of the service, involvement of volunteers, admissions, assessment, translation and interpreting, the curriculum and, in the setting, a strategy for countering the learning of, or the existence of, any racially prejudiced attitudes and racist behaviour.

- A statement about the vision of the policy or scheme – What is its main objective?

- A detailed programme for implementing the scheme or policy – the action plan – including timescales, allocation of responsibilities and details of the practice in employment and services for young children and their families.

- A policy to address racial harassment, name-calling and other incidents, including implementation and monitoring procedures and family involvement – which links to the human resources procedures and racist incident reporting, where appropriate.

- An ongoing monitoring, analysis and evaluation mechanism to ensure the scheme or policy is being implemented in practice at all levels. This will involve the collection of data monitored by ethnicity.

- Procedures for rectifying any discrimination (unlawful or otherwise) or inequalities found as a result of the analysis.

- A budgeting mechanism for implementing the scheme or policy to ensure that, so far as possible, no financial constraints limit its implementation.

- A plan for any training that's necessary to implement the scheme or policy effectively.

- A mechanism for raising issues of concern at meetings of workers, with family members and members of the relevant local communities.

- An item on agendas of meetings of workers, management, governors, committee members and those with families to allow for participants to review, address and consider the scheme or policy and implementation programme on a regular basis.

- A way for ensuring that everyone working with children is able to describe, justify and communicate the setting's approach to racial equality issues with parents and family members, children, governors, management, committee members and members of the local community.

- A policy ensuring that children's records are as full as possible, including relevant information on ethnicity, religion (if any), language(s) spoken and language(s) spoken at home, details of the child's developing language capabilities and the child's full name, with the personal and family names identified and in the correct order.

- Methods of ensuring that new parents and family members are introduced to the policy with sensitivity and given opportunities for sufficient time and discussion to understand its implications for them and, where appropriate, to make comments on it.

◆ A specific part of the policy to address how work is done with children to involve them in contributing to the local, national and global communities, getting to know about them, developing a sense of belonging to them and how to take positive action to break down barriers between different ethnic and cultural communities both inside and outside the setting.

Component 2

All aspects of the local authority early years service and the settings should be free of unlawful racial discrimination, comply with any statutory duties to promote race equality and aim to counter other forms of racial discrimination that are not covered by the law.

Both the local authority early years service and the settings must comply with the amended Race Relations Act 1976 by monitoring employment and the delivery of the service, by collecting ethnic data, analysing and evaluating it, by complying with any statutory duties and identifying and considering practices and procedures that might be discriminatory but are not covered by the law, for example racist name-calling between children. Although the voluntary, private and independent sector settings do not have statutory duties in the same way as public authorities do, they are equally subject to the provisions of the Race Relations Act. As a principle, local authorities and any partnerships should require equal compliance with the law for all settings irrespective of their statutory duties.

◆ Access any relevant information on the early years service and settings from the local authority's racial equality or Children's services section. And ensure that:
  – everyone understands the basis and implications of the amended Race Relations Act 1976, including its statutory requirements, and what constitutes direct and indirect discrimination
  – everyone in the setting understands and is committed to implementing the statutory requirements of the amended Race Relations Act – to eliminate unlawful racial discrimination and to promote equality of opportunity and good relations between people of different racial groups
  – an experienced person in the setting is responsible for racial equality issues; for understanding what constitutes unlawful racial discrimination in detail; and what forms of discrimination are not unlawful but are unacceptable, for example racist name-calling between children or from a child to an adult
  – the setting charges and trains someone to have some understanding of the amended Race Relations Act and liaises with others in the service and authority who have responsibility to implement it
  – in procuring any services (training, goods, curriculum resources and so on) racial equality issues are fully addressed

    – in any decisions being made, the impact on black and other minority ethnic groups is assessed – the race equality impact assessment

    – everyone understands the less obvious forms of unlawful racial discrimination, including: institutional racism; and incidents of less favourable treatment in the curriculum of early years settings, for example as a result of racial stereotyping or provision of limited access to the full range of learning resources. Less favourable treatment in day-to-day practice can only usually be identified by careful observation and recording.

◆ Provide support and training on the reasons for conducting ethnic monitoring and how to do it in practice.

◆ Collect data, by self-identification or by family members, on the ethnic origins of:
    – the children and all those working in the service or the settings at all levels
    – people who apply for and are offered jobs, and any other selection decisions at all stages
    – people who apply for and gain promotion, access to in-service support and training and any other benefits
    – children who apply to attend the setting and who are offered places, and all stages of the admissions procedure
    – all forms of assessment and tests
    – any exclusions.

◆ Analyse this data to identify any disparities and inequalities. Compare the success rates of the various ethnic groups in employment, access to benefits and admissions. If any group is failing disproportionately to be offered a job, a place in a setting, any decision towards a job or place or something else, examine the possible reasons for this. Be watchful of any possible discrimination against particular ethnic groups of people, or sub-groups, for example look at gender within an ethnic group overall, despite the success of a particular individual(s) or particular group overall.

◆ Look for the causes of any inequalities, and amend procedures to remove any discrimination found. Continue to monitor the data to ensure that no discrimination remains.

◆ Compare the ethnic composition of the workers in the service, the settings and the children in the setting with the ethnic composition of the local relevant community. If one does not reflect the other at all levels, check what might be the reasons. For example, are people from some particular ethnic groups not applying for jobs in the service and the settings at every level and for places in the early years setting? If not, try to find out why and, wherever possible, seek to change it. Consider using the positive action sections of the Race Relations Act in training or employment or setting targets to address any discrepancies, if appropriate.

◆ Examine the admission arrangements and criteria for places in the settings, and the job descriptions and person specifications for jobs to see if any criteria, any work experience, qualifications or requirements are potentially discriminatory (directly or indirectly). For example, are any tests (formal or informal) given to applicants possibly culturally biased? Is any qualification or experience required for jobs that people from a particular ethnic group would be less likely to have than others? Are any such requirements justified? Are the ways that any waiting lists operate unfair to certain black or other minority ethnic groups?

➧ Consider how the children of new arrivals – for example, refugees, asylum seekers, Travellers, Roma and Gypsies, and migrant workers who might be living only temporarily in the area – might attend settings. Consider holding places open for Travellers where they are known, potentially, to be arriving in the area.

➧ Ensure that all vacancies for jobs and for early years settings are widely advertised and available in places where they are likely to be seen by communities that are not usually included.

➧ Examine how the admission criteria are put into practice. Is the process fully accessible to all groups?

➧ Consider whether there is any discrimination in other aspects of the service, for example in the available resources, curriculum (hidden or overt) or training.

➧ Consider whether there might be forms of discrimination that are not unlawful, for example, name-calling between children or the omission of appropriate diets and learning resources reflecting the cultures of many of the children in the settings.

➧ Ensure that all of those involved in the recruitment of workers are trained in equality principles – in devising the application form, placing the advertisement, drawing up the job description and person specification; and in short-listing, interviewing, appointing and giving feedback to applicants.

Making it all work

Equality in our lifetime.

(Title of a seminar on the Discrimination Law Review, Greater London Authority, November 2006)

There are no magic ways of getting rid of racism and many people may feel disheartened by trying to do it and not getting very far.

Only a strategic approach with a commitment and the political will to implementing racial equality throughout the early years service – from central government to every early years setting – has any chance of effecting real change. That is the challenge and the task for this millennium.

Useful addresses and contacts

1990 Trust

Suite 12 Winchester House
Cranmer Road
London
SW9 6EJ
0207 582 1990
blink1990@blink.org.uk
www.blink.org.uk

A black information link – an independent community interactive site for black communities.

Anti Racist Teacher Education Network (ARTEN)

19 Hillbury Road
London
SW17 8JT

This is a national network committed to improving the quality of initial teacher education for the benefit of staff, students and children.

Babyfather Initiative

Barnardo's
Tanners Lane
Barkingside
Ilford
Essex
IG6 1QG
0208 498 7596
neil.solo@barnardos.org.uk
www.barnardos.org.uk

This project aims to encourage responsible parenting among black men, especially those separated from their children.

Black Childcare Network

PO Box 35646
London
SE12 ORE

The Black Childcare Network works in a voluntary capacity to raise and share issues of concern to black people working with, and caring for, young children.

Black Londoners' Forum

18 Victoria Park Square
Bethnal Green
London
E2 9PB
0208 709 9781
info@blacklondon.org.uk
www.blacklondon.org.uk

The Black Londoners Forum is a proactive organisation, which seeks to advance the economic, cultural and social well-being of Black and Ethnic Minority Londoners. The Forum does this by engaging primarily with Black Londoners but also with key agencies and institutions.

Community Insight

The Pembroke Centre
Cheney Manor Industrial Estate
Swindon
SN2 2PQ
01793 431773
books@communityinsight.co.uk
www.communityinsight.co.uk

Community Insight is a specialist bookseller in early childhood education and playwork.

Early Childhood Forum (ECF)

c/o Early Childhood Unit
National Children's Bureau
8 Wakley Street
London
EC1V 7QE
0207 843 6000/6078
www.ncb.org.uk/ecf

The Early Childhood Forum is a coalition of about 50 professional associations, voluntary organisations and interest groups, which meets five times a year at the National Children's Bureau. ECF aims to bring together partners in the early childhood sector to debate issues, celebrate differences and develop consensus to champion quality experiences for all young children from birth to eight and their families. It promotes inclusion and challenges inequalities. The Forum is coordinated by the Early Childhood Unit at NCB. ECF has developed its own definition of inclusion: 'Inclusion is a process of identifying, understanding and breaking down the barriers to participation and belonging.'

Early Childhood Unit

020 7843 6064
ecu@ncb.org.uk
www.earlychildhood.org.uk

See NCB for more details.

Early Years Equality (EYE)

2nd Floor, St. John's House
St John's Square
Wolverhampton WV2 4BH
eye@earlyyearsequality.org
www.earlyyearsequality.org

EYE is a national network of people working to encourage antiracist practices in the education and care of young children. It campaigns for equality and justice, holds conferences, publishes relevant information and materials, acts as a consultant on training and making videos, offers advice and support, responds to proposed and existing legislation and publishes a newsletter. Together with nine other European countries, it has produced guidelines for trainers and teachers on an anti-bias approach in the early years.

Equality and Human Rights Commission

3 More London
Riverside Tooley Street
London
SE1 2RG
0203 117 0235
www.cehr.org.uk

The Equality and Human Rights Commission aims to enforce equality legislation on age, disability and health, gender, race, religion or belief, sexual orientation or transgender status and encourage compliance with the Human Rights Act 1998. It is a non-departmental public body whose purpose is to reduce inequality, eliminate discrimination, strengthen good relations between people and protect human rights. It has offices in London, Manchester, Cardiff and Glasgow.

Institute of Race Relations (IRR)

2–6 Leeke Street
London
WC1X 9HS
0207 837 0041 / 833 2010
info@irr.org.uk
www.irr.org.uk

The Institute of Race Relations (IRR) is an independent educational charity established to carry out research and publish and collect resources on race relations throughout the world. It concentrates on responding to the needs of Black people and making direct analyses of institutionalised racism in Britain and the rest of Europe. It is at the cutting edge of the research and analysis that informs the struggle for racial justice in Britain and internationally. It seeks to reflect the experience of those who suffer racial oppression and draws its perspectives from the most vulnerable in society.

Intermix

PO Box 29441
London
NW1 8FZ
0207 485 2869
contact@intermix.org.uk
www.intermix.org.uk

Intermix offers a view of mixed race experience, information, support and the chance to build a community around and within a mixed race experience.

Language or multi-ethnic curriculum support services

Although not established specifically for work in the early years, many local education authorities are responsible for language support services for children who are learning English as an additional language; and curriculum support services for all children about our multiracial, multifaith, multicultural, multilingual society. These are staffed by teachers, bilingual support workers and others, usually under specific funding, working both in their centres and in schools. While their brief is to concentrate specifically on working with minority ethnic children, they have tried to widen out their concerns to work with all children. Many have worked in early years provision and most have been influential in raising issues about racism wherever they were able to do so. They have, wherever possible, given limited funding, organised and run courses about racism for early years workers.

Letterbox Library

71–73 Allen Road
London
N16 8RY
0207 503 4801
info@letterboxlibrary.com
www.letterboxlibrary.com

Letterbox Library celebrates equality and diversity in the best children's books. It is a non-profit-driven cooperative which supplies quality multicultural, non-sexist and special interest titles that have been pre-selected by an independent panel of teachers, librarians and parents. The selection is unique, with many titles unavailable elsewhere. It is often used by training colleges, advisers and inspectors.

Multicultural resources centres

Some local authorities have multicultural resource centres, perhaps as part of their professional or teachers' development centres. See the phone book for LEA address.

National Association for Language Development in the Curriculum (NALDIC)

Serif House
10 Dudley St
Luton
LU2 ONT
01582 724724
enquiries@naldic.org.uk
www.naldic.org.uk

NALDIC is a professional organisation concerned with the achievement of bilingual pupils. It disseminates information and represents the views of teachers and other professions on educational issues that affect the teaching and learning of bilingual pupils

National Association of Teachers of Travellers (NATT)

Anthea Wormington
Newham Traveller Education Service
Credon Centre
Kirton Rd
Plaistow
London
E13 9BT
0208 430 6279
gharrisonwhite@cornwall.gov.uk
www.natt.org.uk

NATT provides the national platform for teachers of Travellers to share good practice and promotes this through its activities. The Association also represents and supports members at a national level by addressing issues with a number of organisations including the DCSF and other government departments.

National Centre for Language and Literacy

The University of Reading
Bulmershe Court
Earley
Reading
RG6 1HY
0118 378 6801
ncll@reading.ac.uk
www.ncll.org.uk

A unit within the University of Reading that provides advice through courses, conferences and publications on all aspects of language and literacy learning. It supports Access to Information on Multicultural Education Resources (AIMER) – a database is available to members on the website.

National Children's Bureau

8 Wakley Street
London
EC1V 7QE
0207 843 6000 / 6078
enquiries@ncb.org.uk
www.ncb.org.uk

The National Children's Bureau (NCB) promotes the voices, interests and well-being of all children and young people across every aspect of their lives. As an umbrella body for the children's sector in England and Northern Ireland, it provides essential information on policy, research and best practice for members and other partners. Within the NCB there is the Early Childhood Unit (ECU), which aims to ensure that all who work with young children and their families can access the best information and support to improve their policies and practice. ECU encourages discussion and debate about the needs of young children and develops practical projects to support practitioners.

People in Harmony

49 Ledgers Road
Slough
Berkshire SL1 2RQ
01753 552559
info@pih.org.uk
www.pih.org.uk

People in Harmony is an interracial antiracist organisation which promotes the positive experience of interracial life in Britain today and challenges the racism, prejudice and ignorance in society.

Persona Doll Training

51 Granville Road
London
N12 OJH
0208 446 7591
personadoll@ukgateway.net
www.persona-doll-training.org

Persona Doll Training has developed an innovative, non-threatening experiential programme built around life-like culturally appropriate cloth dolls. Participants learn how to confidently use the Persona Dolls with children to build on their understanding of fairness and their ability to empathise and to unlearn any misinformation and prejudices they may have absorbed from the world around them.

Racial Equality Councils

Most areas have a local council for racial equality, which provides local information on organisations and resources. See the phone book for address.

Race Equality Foundation (formerly REU)

Unit 35 Kings Exchange
Tileyard Road
London
N7 9AH
0207 619 6220
office@reunet.demon.co.uk
www.raceequalityfoundation.org.uk

This is an organisation promoting black people's right to services which are accessible, appropriate, accountable and adequate. In its work with children it also addresses issues of racial equality in early years services. It undertakes training, consultancy, research and development, project work, national conferences and workshops, publications, resource facilities and networking with black individuals and organisations. It runs the Strengthening Families, Strengthening Communities programme.

Race on the Agenda (ROTA)

Suite 101
Cremer Business Centre
37 Cremer St
Shoreditch
London
E2 8HD
0207 729 1310
rota@rota.org.uk
www.rota.org.uk

Race on the Agenda is a social policy think tank that works with London's Black, Asian and minority ethnic communities towards achieving social justice by the elimination of discrimination and promotion of human rights, diversity and equality of opportunity. ROTA achieve these aims by informing London's strategic decision-makers about the issues affecting the BAME voluntary and community sector (VCS) and the communities it serves and by making government policy more accessible to London's BAME organisations.

Refugee Council

240–250 Ferndale Road
Brixton
London
SW9 8BB
0207 346 6700
www.refugeecouncil .org.uk

The Refugee Council gives advice and works with asylum seekers and refugees. It gives direct help and support and also works with them to ensure their needs and concerns are addressed.

Save the Children

1 St John's Lane
London
EC1M 4AR
0207 012 6400
supporter.care@savethechildren.org.uk
www.savethechildren.org.uk

Save the Children works to right the fundamental wrongs that affect children.

Working Group Against Racism in Children's Resources (WGARCR)

Unit 34 Eurolink Business Centre
49 Effra Road
London
SW2 1BZ
0207 501 9992
positiveimages@wgarcr.org.uk
www.wgarcr.org.uk

This is a nationwide network of people working to remove racist images and stereotypes from children's books, toys and other learning resources because of their damaging effects on all children. It aims to identify resources that reinforce racism and adopt appropriate strategies for their removal. It encourages the production and use of non-racist resources. It campaigns on specific issues and responds to inquiries from teachers, carers, parents, librarians and others. It organises regular conferences on a range of issues, including children's racial identities. It publishes selection criteria for toys and books and trains and advises publishers, suppliers and others on their use. It marked the European Year Against Racism and Xenophobia by conducting a survey to measure the success of the struggle against racism in children's resources. As part of its work it aims to set up regional support groups.

References

Adams, S and Moyles, J (2005) *Images of Violence: Responding to children's representations of the violence they see*. Featherstone Education Ltd.

Ahmed, S (2004) *The Cultural Politics of Emotion*. Edinburgh University Press.

Akhtar, S and Stronach, I (1986) 'They call me blacky: A story of everyday racism in primary schools', *Times Educational Supplement*, 9 September.

Alderson, P (2000) *Young Children's Rights: Exploring beliefs, principles and practice*. Jessica Kingsley Publishers / Save the Children.

Alibhai, Y (1987) 'The child racists', *New Society*, 4 December.

Alibhai-Brown, Y (1999) *True Colours: Public attitudes to multiculturalism and the role of the government*. Institute for Public Policy Research.

Alibhai-Brown, Y (2000) *Who Do We Think We Are?* Penguin Books.

Alibhai-Brown, Y (2001) *Mixed Feelings: The complex lives of mixed-race Britons*. The Women's Press Ltd.

Anti Racist Teacher Education Network (ARTEN) (2002) *Framework for Anti Racist Teacher Education*.

Aspinall, P, Song, M and Hashem, F (2006*) Mixed Race in Britain: A survey of the preferences of mixed race people for terminology and classification. Interim report*. University of Kent, People in Harmony and The Inheritance Project (a joint project, a pilot study prior to the ESRC funded project for which see below). Available on People in Harmony website www.pih.org.uk / features / mixedraceinbritain_report2.pdf.

Aspinall, PJ, Song, M and Hashem, F (to be published in 2008) 'Ethnic Options of "Mixed Race" People in Britain' (an ESRC funded project), University of Kent.

Baig, R with Lane, J (2003) *Building Bridges for our Future: The way forward through times of terror and war*. Early Years Equality.

Baker, C (1997) *Foundations of Bilingual Education and Bilingualism*. Clevedon: Multilingual Matters.

Baldock, P (2004) 'Take root: good practice – multiculturalism', *Nursery World* 11 November.

Ball, M (1997) *Consulting with Parents: Guidelines for good practice*. National Early Years Network.

Barnabas, J (2006) *Accessing Early Years in London: Refugee women's experiences*. Refugee Women's Association http: / / www.refugeewomen.org

Barrett, H (2008) *Hard to Reach Families: Engagement in the voluntary and community sector*. Family and Parenting Institute.

BBC (British Broadcasting Corporation) (1996) 'Rural racism', *Farming Today*, BBC Radio, Midlands and East, 25 May.

Belafonte, H (2007) 'I chose to be civil rights warrior', *Guardian*, 14 March.

Bernard Van Leer Foundation (2007) *Early Childhood Matters: Promoting social inclusion and respect for diversity in the early years.* Bernard Van Leer Foundation.

Bhavnani, R (2001) *Rethinking Interventions in Racism.* Commission for Racial Equality with Trentham Books.

Bhavnani, R, Mirza, SM and Meetoo, V (2005) *Tackling the Roots of Racism: Lessons for success.* The Policy Press.

Bloom, L (1971) *The Social Psychology of Race Relations*, London: George Allen and Unwin.

Bourne, J (2001) 'The life and times of institutional racism', in *Race and Class*, a special report on 'The three faces of British racism' 43, 2, October–December.

Bourne, J (2007) 'In defence of multiculturalism', *Institute of Race Relations briefing paper 2.* http://www.irr.org.uk/pdf/IRR_Briefing_No.2.pdf

Bradford, B (2006) *Who are the 'Mixed' Ethnic Group?* Office for National Statistics (ONS). Download from http://www.statistics.gov.uk/articles/nojournal/Mixed_ethnic_groups_pdf.pdf

Brain, J and Martin, M (1983) *Child Care and Health for Nursery Nurses.* London: Hulton Educational.

Brent Early Years Development and Childcare Partnership (2001a) *Heart of Learning: Supporting children in the Foundation Stage.* Video and booklet.

Brent Early Years Development Childcare Partnership (2001b) *Equality Audit.*

Britkids. www.britkid.org.uk. A website on race, racism and life for Britkids.

Brooker, E (2002) *Starting School: Young children learning cultures.* Open University Press.

Brown, B (1998) *Unlearning Discrimination in the Early Years.* Trentham Books.

Brown, B (third revision 1999) *All Our Children: A guide for those who care.* BBC/Early Years Equality.

Brown, B (2001) *Combating Discrimination: Persona Dolls in action.* Trentham Books and Persona Doll Training video.

Brown, B (forthcoming 2008) *Equality in Action: A way forward with Persona Dolls.* Trentham Books.

Brown, R and Lido, C (2006) *Effects of the Media Priming Positive and Negative Asylum Seeker Stereotypes on Thoughts and Behaviour.* Economic and Social Research Council.

Bruegel, S and Weller, S (2006) *Locality, School and Social Capital.* www.esrcsocietytoday.ac.uk

Bryson, C and others (2005) *Use of Childcare Among Families from Minority Ethnic Backgrounds.* Sure Start/The National Centre for Social Research.

Cabinet Office (2003) *Ethnic Minorities in the Labour Market.*

Cantle, T (2005) 'England: A segregated country?' in Bunting, M (ed) *Islam, Race and Being British.* The Guardian/Barrow Cadbury Trust.

Cemlyn, S and Clark, M (2005) 'The social exclusion of Gypsy and Traveller children' in Preston, G (ed) *At Greatest Risk.* Child Poverty Action Group.

Cesaire, A (1997) *Notebook of a Return to my Native Land.* Bloodaxe Contemporary French Poets.

Chamba, R and others (1999) *On The Edge: Minority ethnic families caring for a severely disabled child*. Policy Press.

Chambers, C, Funge, S, Harris, G, and Williams, C (1996) *Celebrating Identity: A resource manual*. Trentham Books.

Children's Workforce Development Council (CWDC) (2006a) *Early Years Professional National Standards*.

Children's Workforce Development Council (CWDC) (2006b) *Early Years Professional Prospectus*.

Child's Eye Media. *A Child's Eye View of Festivals: Chinese New Year, Diwali, Eid-ul-Fitr, Hanukkah*. www.childseyemedia.com

Clark, A and Moss, P (2001) *Listening to Young Children: The Mosaic Approach*. National Children's Bureau.

Coard, B (1971) *How the West Indian Child is Made Educationally Subnormal in the British School System*. London: New Beacon Books.

Commission for Racial Equality (CRE) (1989 revised 1996) *From Cradle To School: A practical guide to racial equality in early childhood education and care*.

Commission for Racial Equality (1993) *Job Advertisements and the Race Relations Act: A guide to Section 5*. (This does not take account of the new definition of indirect discrimination, GOQs and the 2000 amendment – a new version is planned.)

Commission for Racial Equality (1996) *Roots of the Future: Ethnic diversity in the making of Britain*.

Commission for Racial Equality (2000) *Learning For All: Standards for racial equality in schools*.

Commission for Racial Equality (2002a) *Statutory Code of Practice on the Duty to Promote Race Equality*.

Commission for Racial Equality (2002b) *A Guide for Public Authorities*.

Commission for Racial Equality (2002c) *A Guide for Schools*.

Commission for Racial Equality (2002d) *Ethnic Monitoring: A guide for public authorities/local government*.

Commission for Racial Equality (2003a) *Race Equality and Public Procurement: A guide for pubic authorities and contractors*.

Commission for Racial Equality (2003b) *Evaluation of the Public Duty to Promote Race Equality and Good Relations*.

Commission for Racial Equality (2003c) *Briefing on Gypsies and Irish Travellers*. Safe Communities Initiative/Defeating organised racial hatred.

Commission for Racial Equality (2004a) *YouGov survey* 19.7.04.

Commission for Racial Equality (2004b) *Gypsies and Travellers: A strategy for the CRE 2004–2007*.

Commission for Racial Equality (2004c) *Public Authorities and Partnerships: A guide to the duty to promote race equality*.

Commission for Racial Equality (2005a) *40 Years of Law Against Racial Discrimination*.

Commission for Racial Equality (2005b) *Statutory Code of Practice on Racial Equality in Employment*.

Commission for Racial Equality (2005c) *Gypsies and Travellers: The facts*.

Commission for Racial Equality (2005d) *CRE Report: Gypsies and Travellers – Britain's forgotten minority.*

Commission for Racial Equality (2005e) *Good Race Relations Guide: Voluntary sector guidance.*

Commission for Racial Equality (2005 onwards) *Catalyst,* email newsletter.

Commission for Racial Equality (2006a) *Catalyst,* email newsletter, March.

Commission for Racial Equality (2006b) *Common Ground: Equality and good relations and sites for Gypsies and Irish Travellers.*

Commission for Racial Equality (2007a) *Race Relations 2006: A research study.* Ipsos MORI.

Commission for Racial Equality (2007b) *Ethnic Minorities in Great Britain.* CRE factfile.

Commission for Racial Equality (2007c) *A Lot Done, A Lot To Do: Our vision for an integrated Britain.*

Commission on Integration and Cohesion (CIC) (2007a) *Our Interim Statement.*

Commission on Integration and Cohesion (CIC) (2007b) *Our Shared Future.*

Commission for Racial Equality / Schneider Ross (2002) *Towards Racial Equality: An evaluation of the public duty to promote race equality and good relations in England and Wales.*

Communities and Local Government (2006) *Improving Opportunity, Strengthening Society: One year on – A progress report on the Government's strategy for race equality and community cohesion.*

Communities and Local Government (2007) *The Road Ahead: Final Report of the Independent Task Group on Site Provision and Enforcement for Gypsies and Travellers.*

Connolly, P (1998) *Racism, Gender Identities and Young Children: Social relations in a multi-ethnic inner-city primary school.* Routledge.

Connolly, P (undated) *Fair Play: Talking with children about prejudice and discrimination.* Barnardo's (Northern Ireland) / Save the Children.

Connolly, P, Smith, A and Kelly, B (2002) *Too Young to Notice? The cultural and political awareness of 3–6 year olds in Northern Ireland.* Community Relations Council.

Cook, E and Lane, J (2002 / 2004) 'Dealing with racial incidents', *Network News* (the newsletter of Early Years Equality), 4, 1, February 2002 and *Practical Pre-School*, 44, March 2004.

Cousins, J (1999) *Listening to Four Year Olds: How they can help us plan their education and care.* National Early Years Network / National Children's Bureau.

Craig, G, Ali, N, Ali, S, Atkins, L, Dadze-Arthur, A, Elliott, C, McNamee, S and Murtuja, B (2007) *Sure Start and Black and Minority Ethnic Populations.* Sure Start, National Evaluation. Report 020.

Creaser, B and Dau, E (1996) *The Anti-Bias Approach in Early Childhood.* Harper Educational, Australia.

Crystal, D (2000) *Language Death.* Cambridge University Press.

Darling, B and Hedge, A (1992) *Fair Interviewing.* Trentham Books.

Dawes, J (2006) *Using Empathy Dolls with Young Children: Ideas for developing inclusive practice and supporting early emotional literacy.* Leeds City Council.

Daycare Trust (2003) *Parents' Eye: Building a vision of equality and inclusion in childcare services.*

Daycare Trust (2004) *Positive Practice: Achieving equality in childcare. A guide for practitioners.*

Daycare Trust (2007) *Listening to Black and Minority Ethnic Parents about Childcare.*

Daycare Trust/National Centre for Social Research (2006) *Ensuring Equality: Black and minority ethnic families' views on childcare.* Daycare Trust.

Dell, C (2006) 'All about the global dimension in education', *Nursery World*, 2 November.

Denton-Brown, S (2006) Item describing the School for Peace methodology in the village of Neve Shalom/Wahat al Salam, Israel where Jewish and Palestinian Israeli children learn to live together. *TES*, 4 August.

Department for Children, Schools and Families (2007a) *Supporting Children Learning English as an Additional Language: Guidance for practitioners in the Early Years Foundation Stage.*

Department for Children, Schools and Families (DCSF) (2007b) 2005/2006 'Childcare and Early Years Providers Survey: Overview report'. Research Report RR009.

Department for Children, Schools and Families (2007c) *Race Equality Scheme Update.*

Department for Children, Schools and Families (2007d) *Single Equality Scheme.*

Department for Children, Schools and Families (DCSF) (2007e) *Securing Sufficient Childcare: Guidance for local authorities, Childcare Act 2006.*

Department for Children, Schools and Families (2008a) *The Inclusion of Gypsy, Roma and Traveller Children and Young People: Strategies for building confidence in voluntary self-declared ethnicity ascription.*

Department for Children, Schools and Families (DCSF) (2008b) *Everyone's Welcome: How Sure Start Children's Centres are serving their communities.*

Department for Children, Schools and Families (2008c, forthcoming) leaflet for parents whose children are learning English as an additional language.

Department for Children, Schools and Families (DCSF)/Communities and Local Government (CLG)(2007) *Guidance on the Duty to Promote Community Cohesion.*

Department for Education and Employment (DfEE) (2001*) National Standards for Under-eights Day Care and Childminding.* Standard 9, Equal Opportunities.

Department for Education and Skills (DfES) (2001) *Early Years Development and Childcare Partnership: Implementation planning guidance 2002–2003.*

Department for Education and Skills (DfES) (2003a) *Aiming High: Raising the achievement of Gypsy Traveller pupils. A guide to good practice.*

Department for Education and Skills (DfES) (2003b) *Every Child Matters.*

Department for Education and Skills (DfES) (2003c) *Aiming High: Raising the achievement of African-Caribbean pupils.*

Department for Education and Skills (DfES) (2004) *Aiming High: Understanding the educational needs of minority ethnic pupils in mainly white schools.*

Department for Education and Skills (DfES) (2005a) *Foundation Stage Profile: National results for 2004.*

Department for Education and Skills (DfES) (2005b) 'Ethnicity and Education: The evidence on minority ethnic pupils', *Research Topic Paper.*

Department for Education and Skills (DfES) (consultation 2005c) *Inclusion, Equality and Diversity: Data.*

Department for Education and Skills (DfES) (2006a) *National Occupational Standards in Children's Care, Learning and Development.*

Department for Education and Skills (DfES) (2006b) *National Occupational Standards in Playwork.*

Department for Education and Skills (DfES) (2006c) 'Childcare and Early Years Providers Survey Overview Report' cited in CWDC (2006) *Recruitment, Retention and Rewards in the Children's Workforce, Appendix 1.*

Department for Education and Skills (DfES) (2006d) *Bullying Around Racism, Religion and Culture: How to prevent it, and what to do when it happens. Advice to schools.*

Department for Education and Skills (DfES) (2006e) *The Children's Workforce Strategy: The government's response to the consultation.*

Department for Education and Skills (DfES) (2006f) *The Government's Response to the Consultation on the Early Years Foundation Stage.*

Department for Education and Skills (DfES) (2007a) *The Early Years Foundation Stage.* (This includes the *Statutory Framework for the Early Years Foundation Stage*; and *Practice Guidance for the Early Years Foundation Stage: Setting the standards for learning, development and care from birth to five.*)

Department for Education and Skills (DfES) (2007b) *School Admissions Code.*

Department for Education and Skills (DfES) (2007c) *Childcare Sufficiency Assessments: Guidance for local authorities.* Statutory Guidance.

Department for Education and Skills (DfES) (2007d) *National Standards for Leaders of Sure Start Children's Centres.*

Department for Education and Skills (DfES) (2007e) *Creating the Picture: Guidance – curriculum and standards.* Primary National Strategy.

Department for Education and Skills (DfES)/Department of Health (2006) *Sure Start Children's Centres Practice Guidance: Revised version.*

Department for Education and Skills (DfES)/Department for Work and Pensions (DWP) (2006a) *Choice for Parents, the Best Start for Children: Making it happen. An action plan for the ten-year strategy: Sure Start children's centres, extended schools and childcare.*

Department for Education and Skills (DfES)/Department for Work and Pensions (DWP) (2006b) *The Early Years Foundation Stage: A consultation on a single quality framework for services for children from birth to five.*

Department for Education and Skills (DfES)/NCB (2005/2006) A series of 4 conferences, *Participation and Belonging: Ensuring equality for every child.* National Children's Bureau/DfES.

Derbyshire, H (1994) *Not in Norfolk: Tackling the invisibility of racism.* Norwich: Norwich and Norfolk Racial Equality Council.

Derman-Sparks, L (2004) 'Early childhood anti-bias education in the USA', in van Keulen, A (ed) *Young Children Aren't Biased, Are They?! How to handle diversity in early childhood education and school.* Amsterdam: B.V.Uitgeverij SWP.

Derman-Sparks, L (2006) 'Where are we now? Anti-bias/anti-racism early childhood and primary education in the USA,' *Race Equality Teaching*, Spring.

Derman-Sparks, L and the ABC Task Force (1989) *Anti-bias Curriculum: Tools for empowering young children.* National Association for the Education of Young Children, USA.

Derman-Sparks, L and Ramsey, P (2003) 'What if all the kids are white? Anti-bias/multicultural education with white children', *International Journal of Equity and Innovation in Early Childhood,* 1, 1.

Dhalech, M (2000) 'Rural race equality work in the South West of England', *Multicultural Teaching,* 19, 2.

Dickins, M (2002) 'All About: Anti-discriminatory practice', *Nursery World,* 3 January.

Dickins, M (2005) 'Inclusion: Resources', *Practical Pre-School.* May.

Dickins, M with Denziloe, J (2003) *All Together: How to create inclusive services for disabled children and their families. A practical handbook for early years workers.* National Children's Bureau.

Dixon, B (1992) *Playing Them False: A study of children's toys, games and puzzles.* Trentham Books.

Donnellan, C (ed) (2006) *Racial Discrimination.* Independence Educational Publishers.

Doughty, S (1988) 'Racist check on toddlers', *Daily Mail,* 6 October, front page.

Draycott, P and Robins, L (2005) 'Say hello to – a multi-faith, multi-cultural resource to aid learning in the Early Years', *RE today.*

Drummond, MJ, Rouse, D and Pugh, G (1993) *Making Assessment Work.* National Children's Bureau.

Drury, R (2007) *Young Bilingual Learners at Home and School: Researching multilingual voices.* Trentham Books.

Dryden, L and Hyder, T (2003) 'All about: Supporting children new to English', *Nursery World,* 1 May.

Ealing Council (2003) 'Listening: Pupil's voices, experiences and advice', in *Preventing and Addressing Racism in Schools* (including nurseries).

Early Childhood Forum (ECF, formerly the Early Childhood Education Forum) (1998, second edition 2003) *Quality in Diversity in Early Learning: A framework for early childhood practitioners.*

Early Childhood Forum (ECF, formerly the Early Childhood Education Forum) (2006) *Strategy and Policy Agenda 2006–9.* www.ncb.org.uk/ecf

Early Childhood Forum (ECF, formerly the Early Childhood Education Forum) (2007) *Championing Young Children's Rights and Entitlements.* ECF/National Children's Bureau.

Early Childhood Forum/Sure Start/National Children's Bureau (2005) *Participation and Belonging in Early Years Settings.* A short leaflet. National Children's Bureau.

Early Years Trainers Anti Racist Network (EYTARN) (1993a), *Racism: The white agenda.*

Early Years Trainers Anti Racist Network (EYTARN) (1993b) *On the Spot: Dealing with racism.*

Early Years Trainers Anti Racist Network (EYTARN) (1995a) *Best of Both Worlds: Celebrating mixed parentage.*

Early Years Trainers Anti Racist Network (EYTARN) (1995b) *Partnership with Parents: An anti-discriminatory approach.*

Early Years Trainers Anti Racist Network (EYTARN) (2001) *A Policy for Excellence: Developing a policy for equality in early years settings.* (With an appendix on name-calling.)

Early Years Equality (EYE, formerly the Early Years Trainers Anti Racist Network) (2005) *Mother Tongue Posters: It's good to speak your mother tongue.*

Edwards, SO, Derman-Sparks, L and Ramsey, P (2006) *What If All The Kids Are White? Anti-bias multicultural education with young children and families.* Teachers College Press.

Edwards, V (1996) *The Other Languages: A guide to multilingual classrooms.* The National Centre for Language and Literacy, University of Reading.

Elfer, P (ed) (1995) *With Equal Concern: Training material to ensure day care and educational provision for young children takes positive account of the 'religious persuasion, racial origin and cultural and linguistic background of each child' (Children Act 1989).* National Children's Bureau.

Elfer, P (2005) 'Observation matters' in Abbott, L and Langston, A (ed) *Birth to Three Matters: Supporting the framework of effective practice.* Open University Press.

Elfer P, Goldschmied E, and Selleck D (2003) *Key Persons in the Nursery: Building relationships for quality provision.* David Fulton Publishers.

Elliott, J (1970) *The Eye of the Storm.* A film by Jane Elliott, various distributors see websites.

Equal Opportunities Commission (EOC) (2007) *Moving On Up: Promote people not stereotypes.*

Equiano, O (1789) *The Interesting Narrative of the Life of Olaudah Equiano or Gustavus Vassa, the African, by Himself.* Available as a Penguin Classic.

Eshun, E (2005) *Black Gold of the Sun: Searching for home in England and Africa.* Hamish Hamilton.

Essex County Council (2007) *Dealing with and Recording Racist Incidents in the Early Years and Childcare Settings.* Available from Early Years and Childcare Service 189 Main Road, Broomfield, Chelmsford, Essex CM1 7EQ. Tel. 01245 512300.

Essex EYDCP (2001) *A World of Opportunities: A working guide for equal opportunities practice.* This is being updated.

Finch, S (2000) *Towards a Non-violent Society: Checkpoints for early years.* Forum on Children and Violence, National Children's Bureau.

Fryer, P (1984) *Staying Power: The history of Black People in Britain.* Pluto Press.

Gaine, C (2005) *We're All White, Thanks: The persisting myth about 'white' schools.* Trentham Books.

Galbraith, JK (1992) *The Culture of Contentment.* Penguin.

Garforth, H and others (2006) *Growing Up Global.* (Demonstrates how global education can be a thread running through teaching and learning right from the start.) Reading International Solidarity Centre (RISC).

Gay, G (1985) 'Implications of selected models of ethnic identity development for educators', *Journal of Negro Education*, 54, 1.

General Teaching Council for England (GTCE) Achieve project. See http://www.gtce.org.uk/networks/achieve/achieveresources/

Gill, D and Lane, J (2004) a series of three articles – 'Working together for racial equality: The key principles', 'Equality in the early years: How can you ensure best practice in your setting' and 'Learning to unlearn: Counter racist attitudes with a comprehensive strategic approach across your setting', *Nursery Education*, April, May and June.

Gillborn, D and Mirza, HS (2000) *Educational Inequality: Mapping race, class and gender – a synthesis of research evidence.* Ofsted.

Gillborn, D and Warren, S (2003) *Race Equality and Education in Birmingham.* Commissioned by Birmingham City Council and Birmingham Race Action Group. (Has references to early years.) See www.birmingham.gov.uk/equalities

Gilliam, W (2005) Prekindergarteners *Left Behind: Expulsion rates in State prekindergarten systems.* Yale University Child Study Center.

Gilroy, P (2004) *After Empire: Melancholia or convivial culture?* Routledge.

Gilroy, P (2005) 'Take two: Race and faith post 7/7', a discussion between Paul Gilroy and Herman Ouseley. *Guardian,* 30 July.

Gilroy, P 'Is faith defining the race equality project?' in an email dialogue with Herman Ouseley in Bunting, M (ed) (2005) *Islam, Race and Being British.* The Guardian/Barrow Cadbury Trust.

Glasgow City Council (2008) *Different Together: Anti-racist curriculum for Glasgow – an approach for early years centres.*

Gopinath, R (2004) 'Putting equality on the agenda', *EYE News,* March, 2, 1.

Guardian (2005) 'Report reveals hierarchy of hate', 7 March.

Guishard-Pine, J (2006) 'Men in Black Families: The impact of fathering on children's development', *Race Equality Teaching,* Spring.

Gutzmore, C (1995), speaking at a seminar organised jointly by the Black Childcare Network, the Early Childhood Unit of the National Children's Bureau and the Early Years Trainers Anti Racist Network.

Hall, S (1971). *Revealed: How the UK media fuelled race prejudice.* A report of a BBC television talk. See http://www.thechronicle.demon.co.uk/tomsite/8_6_1rev.htm

Hall, S (2001) 'The Multicultural Question', *Pavis Papers in Social and Cultural Research.* No. 4. The Open University, Faculty of Social Sciences.

Hall, K, Bance, J and Denton, N (2004) *The Role of Childcare in Women's Labour Market Participation: A study of minority ethnic mothers.* Women and Equality Unit, dti.

Hardyment, C (1996) 'Toytown gone mad', *Daily Telegraph,* Weekend section, 13 April, 1.

Henderson, P and Kaur, P (1999) *Rural Racism in the UK.* Community Development Foundation.

Holden, A and Billings, A (2008) *Interfaith Interventions and Cohesive Communities: The effectiveness of interfaith activity in towns marked by enclavisation and parallel lives.* Unpublished source, submitted to the Home Office, January 2008, University of Lancaster.

HM Government (2005a) 'Children's Workforce Strategy: A strategy to build a world-class workforce for children and young people – a consultation document'.

HM Government (2005b) *Common Core of Skills and Knowledge for the Children's Workforce.*

HM Treasury, DfES, DWP, dti (2004) *Choice for Parents, the Best Start for Children: A ten year strategy for childcare.*

Home Office (2005) *Improving Opportunities, Strengthening Society: The government's strategy for racial equality and community cohesion.*

House of Commons Committee of Public Accounts (2007) *Sure Start Children's Centres,* 38th report, June.

Houston, G (2004) *Beyond the Welcome Poster: Equal life, equal chances.* Posters and photopack, Early Years Equality.

Houston, G (2007) *Mixed race **not** mixed up! A good practice guide for Early Years practitioners: Supporting children from multi racial families in Early Years settings.* Early Years Equality.

Houston, G and Gopinath, R (2003) 'Foundation Stage Profile: Implications for inclusion', *EYE News,* October.

Hyder, T (2005) *War, Conflict and Play.* Open University Press.

Hyder, T and Rutter, J (1998) *Refugee Children in the Early Years: Issues for policy-makers and providers.* Save the Children/Refugee Council.

1990 Trust Blink website www.blink.org.uk.

Ifekwunigwe, J (ed) (2004) *Mixed Race Studies: A reader.* Routledge.

Ignatieff, M (2005) quoted in Bunting, M (ed) *Islam, Race and Being British.* The Guardian in association with Barrow Cadbury Trust.

Include Me TOO and Early Years Equality *My Family My Culture.* Posters of black and minority ethnic disabled children and their families. IM2 and EYE websites.

Information Centre about Asylum and Refugees (ICAR) (2006) 'Destitution among refugees and asylum seekers' *ICAR briefing.* May.

Inspire training for ECOs. email: info@inspire.eu.com.

Institute of Race Relations. *IRR News: Independent race and refugee news network.* Free weekly email bulletin http://www.irr.org.uk/subscribe

Institute of Race Relations (1980) 'Anti-racist not multicultural education', IRR statement to the Rampton Committee on Education, *Race and Class,* XXII, 1, Summer.

Institute of Race Relations (1982) *Roots of Racism and Patterns of Racism.*

Institute of Race Relations (Undated) *HomeBeats: Struggles for Racial Justice.* A multimedia CD-ROM (A multimedia journey through time from the Caribbean, Asia and Africa to the making of modern Britain.)

Islington, London Borough of (undated, approx 2002) *Bilingualism and Multilingualism.*

Japanese mother living in the USA (1998), *Guardian,* 18 July.

Jay, E (1992) *Keep them in Birmingham: Challenging racism in southwest England.* London: Commission for Racial Equality.

Jeffcoate, R (1979) *Positive Images: Towards a multi-racial curriculum.* London: Writers and Readers Publishing Cooperative.

John, G (2005) The 'White Paper': Higher standards, better schools for all. A comment. www.gusjohnpartnership.com

Johnson, C and Willers, M (2004) *Gypsy and Traveller Law.* LAG Books.

Jones, S (1991) *The 1991 Reith Lectures,* BBC Radio 4.

Joseph Rowntree Foundation (2008) *Parenting 'Mixed' Children: Negotiating difference and belonging.*

Kahn, T and Young, N (2007) *Embracing Equality: Promoting equality and inclusion in the early years*. Pre-school Learning Alliance.

Kapasi, H (2006) 'Race equality training in early years', *Race Equality Teaching*, Spring.

Kapasi, H (2007) 'Being antiracist' in Brown, F and Taylor, C (ed) *Foundations of Playwork*. Open University Press, Buckingham.

Kapasi, H and Lane, J (2008) 'Approaching Race Equality Training in the Early Years', *Race Equality Teaching*, Summer.

Kazimirski, A, Southwood, H and Bryson, C (2006) *Childcare and Early Years Provision for Minority Ethnic Families*. Daycare Trust / National Centre for Social Research.

Kenner, C (2004) *Becoming Biliterate: Young children learning different writing systems*. Trentham Books.

Kenway, P (1994) *Working with Parents*. Save the Children in association with Reading and Language Information Centre.

Knowles, E and Ridley, W (2006) *Another Spanner in the Works: Challenging prejudice and racism in mainly white schools*. Trentham Books.

Kundnani, A (2007) *The End of Tolerance: Racism in 21st century Britain*. Pluto Press.

Kureishi, H (2005) A 1986 essay reprinted in *The Word and the Bomb*. Faber and Faber.

Kutner, B (1958) 'Patterns of mental functioning associated with prejudice in children', *Psychological monographs*, 72.

Kwhali, J (2006) 'Colour neutral: The absence of black voices in Early Years', in *Race Equality Teaching*, Spring.

Lane, J (1989) 'The playgroup / nursery' in Cole, M (ed) *Education for Equality: Some guidelines for good practice*. Routledge Education.

Lane, J (1998) 'Ethnic monitoring: Why, how and about what' in Early Years Trainers Anti Racist Network *Planning for Excellence: Implementing the DfEE guidance requirement for the equal opportunity strategy in Early Years Development Plans*. EYTARN.

Lane, J (1999a) *Opening up Access to Qualifications and Training for Candidates from Minority Ethnic Groups: Guidelines for study centres*. CACHE. (Available from Early Years Equality)

Lane, J (1999b) 'From rhetoric to reality: Zero racial tolerance', *Early Years Educator*, July, 1, 3.

Lane, J (2001a) 'Dealing with prejudice and discrimination: The issues and in practice', *Practical Pre-School*, 2, January.

Lane, J (2001b) 'What's in a name?' *Under Five Contact*, July / August.

Lane, J (2002a) 'Working together within a 'no-blame culture', *Network News* (the newsletter of EYE) July, 4, 2.

Lane, J (2002b) 'Working for equality with children under the age of three: Identifying the issues that we need to think about', CD-ROM *Birth to Three Matters*.

Lane, J (2003a) 'The road to racial equality' *Nursery Education*, December.

Lane, J (2003b) 'Sharing a policy for excellence: Using EYE's publication to work with equal opportunity coordinators in developing a policy for equality in early years settings', *EYE News*, June.

Lane, J (2004a) *Promoting Race Equality in Early Years*. Sure Start.

Lane, J (2004b) *Thinking About an Incident*. Available from jane@janelane.plus.com

Lane, J (2005a) 'I've just seen a wave as big as our house, Daddy: The importance of providing scope for children to talk about things that worry them, including disasters such as the tsunami', *Early Years Educator*, March website: http://www.earlyyearseducator.co.uk/pages/issues/march05/disaster.htm

Lane, J (2005b) 'A recipe for change: Equality, diversity and food', *Nursery World*, 14 April.

Lane, J (2005c) 'A discussion paper on some aspects of terminology in the field of racial equality and the early years'. See www.childrenuk.co.uk (back issue October 2005)

Lane, J (2005d) Understanding starts with respect: Cultural diversity', *Practical Professional Child Care*, May.

Lane, J (2005e) 'Promoting racial equality: What words should we use?', *Practical Pre-School*, July.

Lane, J (2005f) 'Rightly so: What can settings do when a parent's wishes clash with their principles?' *Nursery World*, 21 July.

Lane, J (2005g) 'Why settings must ensure they are safe havens for children', *Early Years Educator,* 7, 6, October. Special free download – www.intered.uk.com/index.php?site=eye.

Lane, J (2005h) 'Facing terror: Terrorist attacks are frightening and can have a big effect on children and adults', *Nursery Education*, November.

Lane, J (2005i) *Response to DfES consultation document on children's workforce strategy*. Available from jane@janelane.plus.com

Lane, J (2005j) 'Equality coordinators in early years settings: a sample job description and person specification for an equality coordinator'. www.childrenwebmag.com

Lane, J (2006a) 'Woolly Thinking: Political correctness and racism in children's resources', *Nursery World*, 30 March.

Lane, J (2006b) *Right From the Start* A commissioned study of antiracism, learning and the early years. Focus Institute on Rights and Social Transformation (FIRST). www.focus-first.co.uk

Lane, J (2006c) 'A distortion too far', *Race Equality Teaching*. Summer.

Lane, J (2006d) Some suggested information/resources that may be helpful in working for racial equality in the early years. See www.childrenwebmag.com/articles/child-care-articles/racial-equality-information-for-early-years-workers

Lane, J (2007a) 'Culture, ethnicity, language, faith and equal respect in early childhood: Does 'getting it' matter?' in *Education Review: New Directions Home? The challenges and opportunities of modern childhood*. 20, 1, Spring.

Lane, J (2007b) 'Preface' in Kahn, T and Young, N *Embracing Equality: Promoting equality and inclusion in the early years*. Pre-school Learning Alliance.

Lane, J (2007c) 'Seething with cynicism or Appreciating the advances', Talk given at *Where's the Trust?* – a conference organised by the Early Childhood Unit/NCB for the Voices of black workers in the early years network, London June 20.

Lane, J and Ouseley, H (2006) 'We've got to start somewhere: What role can early years services and settings play in helping society to be more at ease with itself?' *Race Equality Teaching*, Spring.

Lane, J with Owen, S (2004/2005) 'Everyone belonging: What does inclusion mean for your setting?' *Nursery Management Today*, 3, 6, January/February.

Lawrence, P (2006) 'Lost for words? Thinking about terminology', *Race Equality Teaching*, Spring.

Lawrence, P and Lane, J (2006) 'Where are the voices of black and other minority ethnic workers in the early years? Setting up a network' in *Race Equality Teaching*, Spring.

Lewis, M (2005) *Asylum: Understanding public attitudes.* Institute for Public Policy Research.

Lincoln, B (2007) a paper as part of the e-conference on Mixedness and Mixing, September. http://www.intermix.org.uk/events/Bradley%20Lincoln.asp

Lindon, J (2006) *Equality in Early Childhood: Linking theory and practice.* Hodder Arnold.

Livingstone, K (Mayor of London) (2006) BBC Radio 4 *Today* programme, 28 September.

Lloyd, N and Rafferty, A (2006) *Black and Minority Ethnic Families and Sure Start: Findings from local evaluation reports.* National Evaluation of Sure Start (NESS).

Local Government Management Board (LGMB) (1998) *Social Services Workforce Analysis 1997: Workforce survey main report.* London.

Macdonald, I and others (1989) *Murder in the Playground: The report of the Macdonald Inquiry into racism and racial violence in Manchester schools.* Longsight Press, London.

Mackenzie, L (2003/04) 'A burning issue – recent coverage of Gypsies and Travellers in context', *Connections*, Winter.

Macpherson, W (1999) *The Stephen Lawrence Inquiry: Report of an inquiry by Sir William Macpherson of Cluny.* Stationery Office.

Marlow, B and Peck, R (2005) *Problems of Early Years Education in Gypsy and Traveller Communities.* Preschool Learning Alliance.

Maxime, J (1991) *Towards a transcultural approach to working with under-sevens*, conference report for the Early Years Trainers Anti Racist Network (EYTARN) and the National Children's Bureau.

McAuliffe, A (ed) (2004) *Listening as a Way of Life.* A series of 5 leaflets. National Children's Bureau/Sure Start.

McAuliffe, A with Lane, J (2005) *Listening as a Way of Life: Listening and responding to young children's views on food.* National Children's Bureau.

Media Initiatives For Children project. The US' Partnerships of the Peace Initiatives Institute (Pii) selected the early years organisation NIPPA (Northern Ireland Pre-school Playgroups Association) as its partner for this project. www.pii-mifc.org

Miles, B (2006) 'Anti-Traveller racism', *Race Equality Teaching*, Spring.

Millennium Cohort Study (MCS) 'Children of the 21st century: Second survey', in Hansen, K and Joshi, H (ed) (2007) *A Users Guide to Initial Findings.* Centre for Longitudinal Studies, Institute of Education, London University/ESRC.

Miller, J (1997) *Never Too Young: How young children can take responsibility and make decisions.* National Early Years Network/National Children's Bureau.

Modood, T, Berthoud, R and Smith P (1997) *Ethnic Minorities in Britain: Diversity and disadvantage* (the fourth national survey of ethnic minorities). London: Policy Studies Institute.

Mori (2004/2006) A survey commissioned by the Committee on Standards in Public Life.

Multiverse www.multiverse.ac.uk

National Assessment Agency (2007) *Guidance Notes: Assessing children who are learning English as an additional language.*

NALDIC (National Association for Language Development in the Curriculum) (1998a) 'Guidelines on Bilingualism', *NALDIC Working Paper 3.*

NALDIC (National Association for Language Development in the Curriculum) (1998b) 'Guidelines on Baseline Assessment for Bilingual Children', *NALDIC Working Paper 4.* (Contact NALDIC for a copy.)

National Children's Bureau (NCB) (2006) *Parents, Early Years and Learning Resource Pack.* DfES (now DCSF).

National Children's Bureau (NCB) (2007) *Where's the Trust?* A conference organised by the Early Childhood Unit/NCB for the Voices of black workers in the early years network, London, June 20.

National Children's Bureau/Sure Start (2004) *Working with Young Children from Minority Ethnic Groups: A guide to sources of information.* NCB.

National Quality Improvement Network (NQIN) for the early years, childcare and play sectors (2007) *Quality Improvement Principles: A framework for local authorities and national organisations to improve quality outcomes for children and young people.* National Children's Bureau.

National Refugee Integration Forum (NRIF) www.nrif.org.uk – children and young persons, early years.

National Union of Teachers (NUT)(2006) *The Muslim Faith and School Uniform: Wearing the* hijab *and other Islamic dress in schools.* NUT guidelines. www.teachers.org.uk

National Union of Teachers (NUT)(2007) *Born To Be Great: A Charter on Promoting the Achievement of Black Caribbean Boys.*

Newbery, H (2006) 'Making a difference – never give up!', *Race Equality Teaching*, Spring.

Nizhar, P (1995) *No Problem? Race issues in Shropshire.* Race Equality Forum for Telford and Shropshire.

Norfolk Traveller Education Service (1997) *Where Does Education Begin?* Video. Norfolk County Council.

North Yorkshire County Council (2001) *Traveller Children: Learning at home and at school in the early years.* North Yorkshire Traveller Education.

OECD (2005–2007) *Education at a Glance.*

Office for National Statistics (ONS) (2006) *Labour Force Survey: Ethnicity revised.*

Ofsted (undated) *Nursery Education Inspection: Guidance on equality of access and opportunity.*

Ofsted (1996) *The Education of Travelling Children: A survey of educational provision for Travelling children.*

Ofsted (2001a) *Evaluating Educational Inclusion: Guidance for inspectors and schools.*

Ofsted (2001b) *Guidance to the National Standards* [Separate guidance for each of the five forms of day care].

Ofsted (2003) *Provision and Support for Traveller Pupils.*

Ofsted (2005a) *Every Child Matters: School inspection framework.*

Ofsted (2005b) *Race Equality in Education: Good practice in schools and local education authorities.*

Ofsted (2007a) *Race Equality Scheme: Draft for consultation.*

Ofsted (2007b) *Race Equality Scheme: Consultation.*

Ouseley, H (2006) said in a lecture for Black History Month organised by the South East Region of the TUC, October 23.

Ouseley, H and Lane, J (2006) 'Early Years Foundation Stage: Response to the consultation on a single quality framework for services to children from birth to five', *Every Child Matters: Change for children.* DfES/DWP (Comments submitted to EYFS consultation.)

Ouseley, H and Lane, J (2007) Some comments on the consultation. Comments submitted to the Commission for Integration and Cohesion.

Owen, C (2005) 'Looking at numbers and projections: Making sense of the census and emerging trends', in Okitikpi, T (ed) *Working with Children of Mixed Parentage.* Lyme Regis: Russell House Publishing.

Owen, C (2006) *Special analysis of Labour Force Survey.* (See Appendix 3 for details.)

Oxfordshire County Council (2003) *Traveller Children and the Early Years.* Available from Advisory Services for the Education of Travellers, The Harlow Centre, Raymund Road, Oxford OX3 0PG.

Paley, VG (1979) 'Preface' to 2000 edition of *White Teacher.* Harvard University Press.

Parekh, B (2005) 'The curry house waiter: The poppadom paradox', *Guardian, 1 August.*

PBS Parents website, 'Talking with kids about the news', 'Age-by-age insights' covers talking about war and violence with preschoolers www.pbs.org/parents/talkingwithkids/war/index.html

Penn, H (2006) 'Contesting Early Childhood: Unequal childhoods', Contesting Early Childhood Conference, Institute of Education, London.

Persona Doll Training (2001) *Persona Dolls in Action.* Video with support book. Available from 51 Granville Road, London N12 OJH.

Persona Doll Training (2004) *Celebrating Diversity: Inclusion in practice.* Video with support book. Available from 51 Granville Road, London N12 OJH.

Platt, L (2007) *Poverty and Ethnicity in the United Kingdom.* Published for the Joseph Rowntree Foundation by The Policy Press.

Plowden Report (1967) *Children and their Primary Schools.* A report of the Central Advisory Council for Education (England), 1. HMSO.

Pollack, M (1972) *Today's Three Year Olds in London.* Heinemann.

Pool, H (2005) *My Fathers' Daughter: A story of family and belonging.* Hamish Hamilton.

Portsmouth *EMAS Early Years Project* www.blss.portsmouth.sch.uk

Portsmouth City Council (undated) *Young Children Learning English as an Additional Language (EAL): Why it is important for young children to maintain and develop their home language.*

Pre-school Learning Alliance (PLA) (revised 2001) *Equal Chances: Eliminating discrimination and ensuring equality in pre-school settings.*

Pre-school Learning Alliance (PLA) (2005) *Policies for Early Years Settings.*

Qualifications and Curriculum Authority (QCA) *Respect For All: Valuing diversity and challenging racism through the curriculum.* www.qca.org.uk/301.html

QCA/DfEE (2000) *Curriculum Guidance for the Foundation Stage.*

QCA/DfES (2003) *Foundation Stage Profile: Handbook.*

Refugee Council (2005) *The Truth about Asylum: Tell it like it is.* (A pocket guide to asylum and immigration facts, a guide to sensible discussions.) Available from http://www.refugeecouncil.org.uk

Renewal.net, *Ethnic monitoring: Monitoring involvement and outcomes.* Search via http://www.renewal.net

REU (now the Race Equality Foundation) *Strengthening Families, Strengthening Communities: An inclusive parent programme.*

Reynolds, T (2005) *Caribbean Mothers: Identity and experience in the UK.* London: Tufnell Press.

Rich, D and others (2005) *First Hand Experience: What matters to children.* Rich Learning Opportunities.

Riches, R (2007) *Early Years Outreach Practice: Supporting early years practitioners working with Gypsy, Roma and Traveller families.* Save the Children.

Richardson, B (ed) (2005) *Tell it like it is: How our schools fail Black children.* Bookmarks Publications/Trentham Books.

Richardson, R and Miles, B (2003) *Equality Stories: Recognition, respect and raising achievement.* Trentham Books.

Richardson, R and Wood, A (1999) *Inclusive Schools, Inclusive Society: Race and identity on the agenda.* Race on the Agenda/Trentham Books.

Road, N (2004) 'Are equalities an issue? Finding out what young children think', in McAuliffe, A (ed) *Listening as Away of Life*. National Children's Bureau/Sure Start.

Runnymede Trust (2003) *Complementing Teachers: A practical guide to promoting race equality in schools.*

Rutland, A (2003) *How Children Grow to Control their Ethnic Prejudices in Public.* Economic and Social Research Council.

Salusbury World. www.salusburyworld.org.uk

Sandler, G (1972) unpublished letter to the Community Relations Commission.

Save the Children (2007) for a practical comprehensive support project for early years Gypsies, Roma and Travellers, contact earlyyearsqrtprojectt@savethechildren.org.uk

Save the Children/Salusbury World (2004) *Home from Home: A guidance and resource pack for the welcome and inclusion of refugee children and families in school.* Save the Children (c/o Plymbridge Distributors Ltd. Estover Road, Plymouth PL6 7PY. Tel. 01752 202301).

Save the Children/DfES (2006) *Working Towards Inclusive Practice: Gypsy/Roma and Traveller cultural awareness training and activities for early years settings.* Save the Children.

Save the Children/Refugee Council (2001) *In Safe Hands: A resource and training pack to support work with young refugee children.*

Searchlight. www.searchlightmagazine.com.

Selleck DY, on behalf of the Oxfordshire Early Years Team (2005) 'Monitoring Quality: Inclusion/equal opportunities. Data Collection and analysis report for 2004–2005', unpublished report, available from the Early Years and Family Support team. Oxon, 01865 428096.

Selleck DY, on behalf of the Oxfordshire Early Years Team (2006a) 'Being included – being "brown", being me! Beginning at the beginning', *Race Equality Teaching*, Spring.

Selleck DY, on behalf of the Oxfordshire Early Years Team (2006b) 'Key persons in the Early Years Foundation Stage', *Early Education*, 50, Autumn.

Sen, A (2006) *Identity and Violence*. Penguin.

Shap Working Party (annually) *Shap pictorial calendar of religious festivals.* Available from PO Box 38580, London SW1P 3XF. Tel. 0207 898 1494 email admin@shapworkingparty.org.uk. www.shapworkingparty.org.uk

Simpson, L (2006) *Racial Mixing, Not Segregation in the UK*. Cathie Marsh Centre for Census and Survey Research. See www.ccsr.ac.uk/research/migseg.htm

Siraj-Blatchford, I and Clarke, P (2000) *Supporting Identity, Diversity and Language in the Early Years*. Open University Press.

Sivanandan, A (2006*)* 'Britain's Shame: From multiculturalism to nativism', an interview in *IRR News*.

Stonewall (2003) 'Profiles of prejudice: The nature of prejudice in England', a poll conducted by MORI.

Sure Start (2002) *Birth to Three Matters: A framework to support children in their earliest years.* (With CD-ROM, including several items on equality issues, i.e. 'Working for equality with children under the age of three', 'A strong child, culture and community'.)

Sure Start (2004a) 'Sure Start: For everyone – promoting inclusion, embracing diversity, challenging inequality', *Inclusion Pilot Projects Summary Report*.

Sure Start (2004b) *Childcare and Early Years Workforce Survey (2002/03)*.

Sure Start (2005a) *Children's Centre Practice Guidance.*

Sure Start (2005b) *Use of Childcare among Families from Minority Ethnic Backgrounds.*

Sure Start (2008) *The Impact of Sure Start Local Programmes on Three Year Olds and Their Families*. National Evaluation of Sure Start research team.

Swann Report (1985) *Education for All: Report of the Committee of Inquiry into the education of children from ethnic minority groups*. London: HMSO.

Sylva, K and others (2007) *Promoting Equality in the Early Years: Report to the Equalities Review.* Effective Pre-school and Primary Education (EPPE) 3–11 Project, Institute of Education, London University. (A longitudinal study 2003–08. Research commissioned by the Equalities Review.)

Taylor, J (2006) *Start With a Difference: Promoting race equality in the early years – a Jewish perspective*. The Jewish Council for Racial Equality.

Teacher Training Agency (TTA) (2000) *Raising the Attainment of Minority Ethnic Pupils: Guidance and resource materials for providers of initial teacher training.*

Teacher Training Agency (TTA) (2004) *Foundation Stage Audit Materials.*

Thomas, H (2006) 'Veil hang-ups may pass', *TES Opinion*, 27 October 2006.

Tikly, L, Caballero, C, Haynes, J and Hill, J (2004) 'Understanding the educational needs of mixed heritage pupils'. University of Bristol (in association with Birmingham LEA). *DfES Research Report 549*. Full report on DfES website.

Times Educational Supplement (2006) 'Lessons on resolving conflict'. Report by Reva Klein. 7 August

Times Educational Supplement (2007a) 'Spate of racist complaints against Polish pupils'. Report by Glenn, J and Barnett, L of complaints received by the Polish Educational Society in London. 30 March.

Times Educational Supplement (2007b) 'Life on the hill gives pupils new outlook on racism'. Report by Ruth Hedges about where a largely white working class school and a largely Asian school in Leeds merged. 13 April.

Times Educational Supplement (2007c) 'Not a black and white issue: Mixed-race pupils are the fastest growing minority in Britain and want to be heard in their own right'. Report by Nick Hilborne. 3 August.

Together for Children (tfc) (2007) *Toolkit for Reaching Priority and Excluded Families.*

Travellers Times. www.travellerstimes.org.uk

Tyler, C (ed) (2005) *Traveller Education: Accounts of good practice.* Trentham Books.

Van Ausdale, D and Feagin, J (2001) *The First R: How children learn race and racism.* Rowman and Littlefield.

Vandenbroeck, M (1999) *The View of the Yeti: Bringing up children in the spirit of self-awareness and kindredship.* Bernard van Leer Foundation.

Van der Eyken, W (1984) *Day Nurseries in Action.* Department of Child Health Research Unit, University of Bristol, Bristol.

van Keulen, A (ed) (2004) *Young children aren't biased, are they?! How to handle diversity in early childhood education and school.* Amsterdam: B.V. Uitgeverij SWP.

Walker, Alice (1989) *The Temple of my Familiar.* New York: Harcourt Brace Jovanovich.

Walker, R (2006) *When We Ruled.* London: Every Generation Media.

Wanless, P, Dehal, I and Eyre, R (2006) *Getting it. Getting it right: Exclusion of Black Pupils – Priority Review.* DfES. Formally published by DfES in March 2007.

Williams, P (1997) 'Seeing a Colour-Blind Future: The paradox of race', *The 1997 Reith Lectures*, BBC Radio 4, London.

Winston, R (2005) *Child of Our Time.* BBC.

Wolverhampton Early Years Team (2003) *For all of us.* Social inclusion pilot video. Free if still available. Tel. 01902 555956

Wong, J L. (1996) 'Multicultural aspects of developing urban schools' grounds' in *The Challenge of the Urban School Site, Learning Through Landscapes.* Black Environmental Network (BEN) http://www.ben-network.org.uk//uploaded_Files/Ben_1/ben_file_1_2.pdf.

Working Group Against Racism in Children's Resources (1991) *Guidelines for the evaluation and selection of child development books.* London: WGARCR.

Working Group Against Racism in Children's Resources (WGARCR) (1995) *Guidelines for the Evaluation and Selection of Toys and Other Resources.* London: WGARCR. www.wgarcr.org.uk (Other resources are available from Letterbox Library and Community Insight.)

Zealey, C (1995) 'The importance of names' in *Coordinate Collection.* London: National Early Years Network.

Further reading

This list covers research publications on the early age that children learn their attitudes to racial/ethnic differences.

Ammons, R (1950) 'Reactions in a projective doll-play interview of white males two to six years of age to differences in skin colour and facial features', *Journal of Genetic Psychology*, 76.

Clark, K (1955) *Prejudice and Your Child*. Boston, MA: Beacon Press.

Connolly, P (1998) – see References.

Connolly, P and others (2002) – see References.

Goodman, M (1952) *Race Awareness in Young Children: A cultural anthropologist's study of how racial attitudes begin among four year olds*. New York: Collier Books.

Horowitz, E (1936) 'Development of attitudes towards Negroes', *Archives of Psychology*, 194.

Menter, I (1989) 'They're too young to notice: Young children and racism' in Barrett, G (ed) *Disaffection from School: The early years*. Falmer Press.

Milner, D (1983) *Children and Race: 10 years on*. London: Ward Lock.

Morland, J (1962) 'Racial acceptance and preference of nursery school children in a Southern city', *Merrill-Palmer Quarterly*, 8.

Pushkin, I (1967) 'A study of ethnic choice in the play of young children', unpublished PhD thesis, London.

Radke, M, Sutherland, J and Rosenberg, P (1950) 'Racial attitudes of children', *Sociometry*, 13.

Stevenson, H and Stewart, E (1958) 'A developmental study of racial awareness in young children', *Child Development*, 29.

Troyna, B and Hatcher, R (1992) *Racism in Children's Lives: A study of mainly white primary schools*. Routledge/National Children's Bureau.

Van Ausdale, D and Feagin, J (2001) – see References.

Vaughan, G (ed) (1972) *Racial Issues in New Zealand*, Auckland: Akarana Press.

Winston, R (2005) *Child of Our Time*. BBC.

Appendix 1: Some thoughts about terminology

The terminology used in this book applies to Britain. It may or may not be applicable elsewhere. Care should always be taken when using terminology in non-British contexts.

(a) Terms used to describe people

African-Caribbean: people whose heritage is African from the Caribbean.

Asian and South Asian: people from, or originating from, India, Bangladesh, Pakistan and Sri Lanka; not from countries, such as China, that are in the northern part of Asia. South Asian is the most accurate term, but the census categories use the term *Asian* and for that reason it has been included here for information.

Asylum seekers: people who are fleeing persecution in their homeland, have arrived in another country, made themselves known to the authorities and exercised the legal right to apply for asylum.

black, Black: people who are discriminated against because of their skin colour. These words are usually used as 'political' terms, to unite the people who are discriminated against. Some people use the term 'Black' to refer specifically to people of African-Caribbean or African origin. (For a more detailed discussion, see pages 8 and 76.)

ethnic minority, ethnic majority: people whose ethnic group is in a minority or majority in a country. They include people of all skin colours. As with the term *minority ethnic* it is important to acknowledge that, although they may have a common experience of racism, this group comprises a variety of different groups each with different backgrounds, experiences and needs – they are not a homogeneous group. Even within one category, members may have very different histories, backgrounds and needs. For example, the term *Black African* may include particular groups, such as asylum seekers from particular countries, with very specific needs.

minority ethnic, majority ethnic: these terms are often preferred to the two above as they make more explicit that everyone has an ethnicity, whether it is in the majority or the minority.

mixed race: mixed heritage, dual heritage, multiple heritage, mixed parentage, and mixed race are among the terms that are variously used in Britain to describe people whose parents or forebears are from different ethnic backgrounds to each other. Sometimes the term is qualified with the background, as in the census categories, for example White and African-Caribbean, White and Asian, etc. Viewed in its widest context many of us may be as yet unaware of our own personal heritages, as Ekow Eshun found when he discovered that one of his ancestors was a white slave trader (see page 115; and Eshun 2005). Although there are advocates for all these terms, none is universally accepted; and among those accepting certain terms there often remain reservations about them, there being no fully acceptable alternative. This demonstrates the complications and the very strong feelings often associated with them. While individuals are able to define their own specific heritages, agreeing an umbrella term for all heritages is problematic.

There are particular differences between advocates who prefer race to be used and those who prefer heritage.

The term *race* is sometimes refuted because of its apparent acceptance of the long-derided concept of biologically determined races, even if the term is in common usage as well as in legislation. Others prefer it, as at least it appears to denote the specific aspects of skin colour which, in the context of a racist society, are critical determinants of racial equality.

Some prefer *heritage* as it covers all ethnicities (and some people also suggest ethnicity includes nationality) and see it as, of course, including skin colour differences and notions of ancestry and descent. Others reject it as they think it appears to equate differences between ethnicities, where both are white, with differences of skin colour. Ethnic differences between white people may evoke xenoracism but differences in skin colour may evoke racism and all its historical implications.

Similarly there are differences of opinion about the term *mixed* because it is seen to imply something mixed up, a mixture rather than something exclusive in its own right. Some view 'mixedness' with particular scorn. Other problems include the concept of dual heritage when the reality may be multiple heritages. The word *parentage* is also subject to different interpretations.

There is consequently no term that pleases everyone, nor even one that may be completely acceptable to a majority of people. It is a matter of personal choice, recognising sensitivity and not causing offence – it is a no-win situation. Even where people comprise the same ethnic mixture, what may be acceptable to one person may not be appropriate to another. Also, sometimes there is a conflict between what people feel themselves to be and how others may perceive them, which may lead to particularly strong views about terminology. It is important to listen to and respect what is being said and felt. (The term 'half-caste' is offensive and should never be used. It is a negative term suggesting that a person doesn't really fit in anywhere.)

To provide information for the 2011 census and to try to ascertain the preferences of people who describe themselves in one of the above ways, a pilot survey of preferences was conducted (Aspinall and others 2006). A follow-up survey is in process (Aspinall and others 2008). The term 'mixed race' was preferred in the pilot survey – referring to 'people who are mixes of white and any minority ethnic racial/ethnic group'. Some saw it as being only mixes of black and white people.

The term 'mixed race' is used in this book as an interim compromise and for simplicity, though recognising that some readers may prefer other terms. (For further discussion, see page 191.)

'non-white': a term that is unacceptable because it assumes that white is the norm and has associated implications of somehow being not normal or even abnormal. It is demeaning, disrespectful and reinforces concepts of inequality. Although white people are the majority group in Britain, and might therefore be described in some situations as the norm, this does not detract from the consequences of racism on the use of such terminology. Although 'not white' does not have quite these implications and is therefore more positive, it nevertheless implies 'them' and 'us'. To be a *non*-anything is seldom positive, except when reversing the common assumptions such as in non-disabled and non-vegetarian. Would the lone man in a group of women ever be described as a non-woman, that is, not present in his own right? It is always better to describe exactly who is being categorised in positive terms and not in relation to someone else. (See Case study 20, page 79.)

refugees: people whose asylum application has been successful and are allowed to stay in another country having proved that that they would face persecution back home.

Travellers, Roma and Gypsies and other travelling communities: although often abbreviated to 'Travellers' to avoid the previously derogatory use of these terms, now, because of the wide range of groups included, it is less acceptable – the full inclusive phrase being preferred. However, as with the term *black*, the term 'Traveller' is used here to avoid clumsy repetition while recognising its unacceptability. It covers a wide range of cultural and ethnic groups of people who are traditionally nomadic, whether they still are or not. If they are nomadic they move around, but the majority now live in houses or on permanent sites, usually travelling seasonally. Only Irish Travellers and Romany Gypsies have been specifically determined in law to be ethnic groups and are therefore covered by race equality legislation. It is irrelevant whether they have a settled lifestyle or not. Travellers are one of the most discriminated against groups, and often experience racism.

Nomadic Travellers travel from place to place seeking work but, because most of their original work is no longer in demand, they have adapted to other trades. They include English and Welsh Gypsies (some of whom may be Romany Gypsies); fairground (Showmen) and circus people; Irish and Scottish Travellers; Bargees and New Travellers (who are generally seeking an alternative way of life, and are not Travellers by ethnic group); and, more recently, European Roma who have obtained refugee or immigrant status. Although nearly all Travellers experience discrimination it is Romany Gypsies, Roma and Irish Travellers who are subjected to the most racial abuse. Romany Gypsies and Irish Travellers are defined as racial groups under the Race Relations Act.

The term 'Traveller' has a capital 'T' ('travellers' would include tourists and commercial travellers). The term 'Gypsy' has a capital 'G' (see section 'Travellers, Roma, Gypsies and mobile communities' on page 195 for further details). Some Roma see the term 'Gypsy' as derogatory, because it has often been used in a derogatory way.

white, White: this is, again, a political term. It refers to people who are not 'black' and who are usually, but not always, of European origin, whose skin colour or tone is light. Most white people are not subject to racism but Jewish, Irish, Traveller, Roma, Gypsy and some refugee and asylum seekers and other migrant people, who are white, do experience racism but in different ways from black people (see xenoracism). (See page 8 for some further discussion and see above for discussion of the term 'non-white'.)

'working class': this term is in inverted commas to denote some of the controversies in the use of the term. Dividing people into 'class' groups (working, middle and upper, usually with subgroups of each) is problematic for several reasons – including the way class is defined or measured (the existing, and largely recognised as limited and inadequate, measures such as 'free school meals', occupation, home address, etc.); its often associated hierarchy of classes; and the powerful pride that different people often have in belonging to particular classes. This has led to some ambivalence – a reluctance to use the term against the need to monitor equality of treatment and outcomes for such groups. The particular term *working class* is sometimes, and wrongly, used in a demeaning way. There is no law against discrimination on class or socioeconomic grounds.

Those who do not fit into any of the above categories: people may simply be described as coming from their country of origin. Note that countries such as South Africa, Ghana, Kenya and Egypt all belong to the continent of Africa.

Everyone can make mistakes. What is needed is the confidence to become familiar with these words and to use them appropriately as part of a commitment to remove racism, by talking about them in an atmosphere of trust and by not being afraid to make a mistake and learn from it.

(b) Some other terms

As with the previous group of words, some of the following may change their interpretation over time.

antiracist, antiracism refer to resources, policies, practices and procedures that recognise the existence of racism in its many forms and take appropriate action to remove it. Antiracism recognises racism as being the major obstacle to racial equality.

antisemitism is usually defined as racism against Jewish people. However it applies to Arabic people who also speak the same family of Semitic languages as Jewish people (Hebrew).

assimilation requires the absorption of minority cultures into the majority culture. It is not based on equal value and respect, but on an assumption of the longer established community as a norm.

classism: all those practices and procedures that, both historically and in the present, disadvantage and discriminate against people because of their class.

colonialism is a system of exploitation of a country, controlled by a more powerful and often distant country.

cultural racism occurs when people are discriminated against because of their culture. (See definition of *culture* below.)

culture everyone has a culture as a result of their lives and experiences. It includes all those factors that have contributed to these experiences. It is not just the high days and festivals but also the minutiae of everyday life. Elements of culture may include factors such as language, social class, religious beliefs and practices, traditions, dress and food. No culture is superior or inferior to another. The way this term is used here should not be confused with its other meaning – intellectual and aesthetic activity, i.e. 'cultured'. (For further discussion, see page 80.)

diversity is used to refer to the variety of whatever is under discussion. It does not, however, automatically imply that the various parts are either equally valued or equally treated. It is very frequently used where the equality aspects are neither explicit nor implicit (see page 81 for further discussion).

disableism: all those practices and procedures that, both historically and in the present, disadvantage and discriminate against people because of their disability.

ethnically monitored data (for example, information about the ethnic composition of the local community) refers to the ethnicity of people on whatever information (data) is being collected. Data is collected in various ways, according to the reason for collecting it. There should always be a clear reason for collecting data monitored by ethnicity, including an explanation of why it is needed and what will be done with it in terms of data protection, plus a clear statement of confidentiality (that the identity of individuals surveyed will not be available). It is important, wherever possible, that the ethnicity of a person is identified by themselves (that data is self-identified) and not determined by someone else. (Note: Although 'Datum' is the singular of data, convention generally means that the word data is usually used in the singular, rather like the word agenda.)

ethnic monitoring is the process of collecting ethnically monitored data. The purpose is to analyse and evaluate it to identify any disparities, any potential or existing racial discrimination, unequal outcomes, unmet service needs, unequal access to or take-up of services and any more specific information according to the circumstances.

ethnicity refers to an individual's identification with a group sharing some or all of the same culture, lifestyle, language, religion, nationality, geographical region and history. Every person has an ethnicity. Concepts of 'ethnic food', 'ethnic dress', 'ethnic music' and 'ethnic people' are therefore nonsense. (For further discussion, see page 81.)

ethnocentrism is the process of viewing or interpreting the world from the perspective of a particular ethnic group. 'Eurocentrism' is, for example, viewing the world from a European perspective. For example, thinking about languages in general but only using European languages is ethnocentric and Eurocentric. Thinking specifically about European languages would be correct. 'Africentrism' is focusing on Africa, interpreting the world from an African perspective, often deliberately to redress previous trends.

imperialism is a system in which a country rules another country, usually having used force to obtain power over it.

integration provides for the co-existence of minority cultures with the majority culture. It is a two-way process, each being of equal value and being equally respected

multiculturalism means cultural diversity – that diversity can either be a good thing, leading to integration, or a bad thing, leading to separatism. It means cultures influencing one another, interacting and opposing racism. (For further discussion see page 142.)

multicultural education means an education for all children that values and reflects the realities of all cultures equally. Crucial to this is that racial hierarchies of the various cultures are removed – by antiracist education. (For further discussion see page 128.)

non-racist refers to resources, policies, practices and procedures that take a neutral approach to racism, neither acknowledging it, denying it nor opposing it.

race is a term in everyday use – but it is a controversial term. The word comes from historical attempts to categorise people according to their skin colour and physical characteristics. There is no scientific basis for this term and its divisions into biologically determined groups, and it is now accepted that variations within such groups are as wide, or wider, than variations between people of notionally different races. Individuals, not nations or races, are the main sources of human variation. There are some strong feelings about its usage.

To indicate the controversy associated with its usage some academic articles put the word 'race' into inverted commas.

racial assumptions are when generalisations are made that the behaviour or characteristics, whether real or imagined, of one person or a few persons from a particular racial or ethnic group are believed to be typical of all people from that racial or ethnic group.

racial discrimination is the treatment of people of a racial or ethnic group or groups less favourably than others would be treated in the same circumstances. Under the Race Relations Act 1976 racial discrimination is defined specifically, in several ways, to cover particular situations and circumstances (see Chapter 8 for details).

racial group refers to those who are of, or belong to, the same race. They have the same racial origins. There is a specific definition under the Race Relations Act 1976 (see page 240).

racial harassment refers to verbal, non-verbal or physical aggression towards people of a different racial group. If the target or wronged person believes that it was because they belong to a particular racial group then, unless proved otherwise, it is usually defined as racial harassment, whatever other people may say. In some situations children may not realise they are being racially harassed or abused, but adults who witness it will be able to identify it. It is defined under the amended Race Relations Act (see page 247).

racial hierarchy refers to a racist ranking of factors including the languages, cultures, nationalities, skin colours, physical features and ethnicities of people in an order ranging from important to less important, less worthy. This ranking results in these aspects of black people usually being ranked negatively.

racial hatred and racial violence are when strong overt negative hostility against people of a different racial group lead to verbal or physical assault against them.

racial prejudice is a negative opinion or attitude about people of various races, based on false or inadequate evidence. It is a tendency to judge people in a particular way and is often self-perpetuating because the (usually negative) judgement of people from different races prevents any interaction with them. Surveys in Britain show that white people are more likely to be racially prejudiced than others. However, racial prejudice often exists between many ethnic groups. Racial prejudice, where some groups are marked out as different, is found in most parts of the world.

racial stereotyping is categorisation (usually negative) of a whole racial group of people because of the actions or behaviour of one person, or a few people, or of an imagined belief or as the result of racial prejudice. It is also when a general stereotype is transferred to a particular person. It often becomes part of the cultural legacy. It is still stereotyping even if the stereotype is positive – for example, 'being good at sport', 'having a sense of rhythm' or 'having the gift of the gab' are all racial stereotypes when applied to groups of people.

racism refers to all those practices and procedures that, both historically and in the present, disadvantage and discriminate against people because of their skin colour, ethnicity, culture, religion, nationality or language (see Chapter 2 for more detailed discussion).

Racism in Britain is usually seen as against black people. But there is also racism against some white people – see *xenoracism* below.

institutional racism – see page 33 for a description. It has some similarities to 'indirect racial discrimination', as defined under the Race Relations Act 1976. As so many social, economic and political decisions are in the hands of white people and have been so historically, the reality is that white people rarely experience institutional racism in Britain.

sectarianism – a rigid adherence to a particular sect, party or denomination, usually a religious group, and involving hostility, conflict and often violence towards other religious groups within a context of bigotry and dogmatism.

segregation occurs where different communities live, work or are educated separately. It may arise from discriminatory practices or procedures, by choice or chance or by one community fleeing from the other. Where an area is 100 per cent from one community and is associated with persecution it is called a ghetto. So far as is known there are no ghettos in England.

structural racism is where the existing structures of the society have the effect of discriminating against particular racial or ethnic groups of people but is not a result of individual action or of an institutional nature. It occurs as a result of the way society is structured and the way power is positioned. For example in the 1950s, '60s and '70s, the industrialised areas of Britain specifically recruited South Asian and African-Caribbean workers because of rapid increases in industrial production and to help recovery after the Second World War. These were the very same areas that experienced severe decline in manufacturing in the 1980s. Despite 20 or 30 years' living in those regions, these populations were still not established in the community in terms of such things as secure employment, and so they suffered disproportionately from the effects of long-term unemployment during the 1980s.

state racism occurs when aspects of state procedures, for example, certain immigration procedures and legislation, though racially discriminatory, are not covered by the amended Race Relations Act 1976.

xenoracism is the term used to describe the discrimination that some white people experience – for example Travellers, Roma, Gypsies, Irish and Jewish people and some refugees, asylum seekers and other migrants (such as recently arrived people from eastern Europe and the Balkans) – based on their histories and nationalities. It is mostly directed at those displaced by dispossession and globalisation. Although this involves aspects of racism it is not the same as that experienced by black people.

Appendix 2: Further points for reflection on the possible reasons for not addressing racism

Possible reasons for not addressing racism include:

- denying that racism exists, being unaware, or the presence of racism just 'not occurring' to them
- not understanding and accepting, or really wanting to acknowledge, the power of the embedded nature of racism to influence everyone's lives, not really taking it seriously
- not really listening to, or positively seeking out, the voices and stories of black people and their experiences, their frustration and relative powerlessness, rather than just reactively hearing them
- being somewhat apprehensive when they see people around, obviously from cultures other than their own and sometimes speaking languages that they do not understand, and wondering if it is ever possible to see them in any way other than as strangers
- not seeing instances of prejudice as part of the whole gamut of racism but seeing them as clearly unfortunate and unacceptable but not something affecting them or their own lives personally
- genuinely assuming that racial equality was 'done' some time ago, that it is now implicit, that inequalities are largely things of the past and that everything has now moved on
- being alert to the issue but, as nothing drawing unwelcome attention to it has cropped up in everyday practice so far, continuing as before and justifying this by 'sort of keeping an eye out' for any warning signs in the future
- using terms and words without understanding or reflecting on their real meaning and, if questioned, just dismissing it as political correctness
- being reluctant to be the first person to raise issues of racial equality for fear of upsetting the boat and being isolated
- not being prepared or willing to take personal responsibility for questioning, finding out, learning and understanding why some children's life opportunities are affected by discrimination and racism
- not seeing the particular experiences, opinions and ideas of black people as part of the fabric of understanding the role of early years in society from which everyone can learn – to learn what everyone is missing from these opportunities

- feeling strongly that black people are getting a raw deal, sometimes making friends with them but nevertheless not seeing their own lives as part of the system that oppresses black people
- perceiving any excessive publicity given to non-British people, for example asylum seekers, as favouritism when the priority should be 'to look after one's own' British first, allowing this to influence their attitudes to black children and their families and not recognising how the media feeds this resentment
- not being aware of the role of the Race Relations Act generally, or taking the statutory duties of the Race Relations (Amendment) Act seriously
- being unprepared for any unexpected changes – because those with power do not consistently and positively espouse the value of living in a vibrant multicultural, multiethnic community or prepare society for the changes that accompany this and, instead, only react when there is a crisis – and consequently feeling such changes are negative, thus impacting on their work with children and their families
- not noticing the lack of black representation on nearly all important bodies
- usually thinking about racial equality as an afterthought – perhaps because it is known through legislation that something has to be done
- unwittingly perpetuating racism by not challenging the racist thinking and behaviour of any children, black or white, and being insufficiently aware or supporting children and their families who are on the receiving end of racism
- assuming that just mentioning something about equal opportunities, especially in writing, somehow deals with it, is sufficient and that there is nothing more to do and no need to spell out what it means in practice
- unwittingly perpetuating racism by not challenging the racist thinking and behaviour of white children because everyone in the setting is white
- living, socialising, and working mainly with white people, and not having issues of racial equality as part of their lives so they have never experienced real communication and friendship with any black people and so have never experienced or shared their experiences together
- denying the evidence of racism in society as having any impact on early years practice; and seeing those who challenge this view and try to address it as emotive, ideological and out of touch with the way practitioners work, and likely to deter them from even considering its implications
- thinking that if there are no black people around then there isn't really an issue, so nothing needs to be done at this stage and even, possibly, thinking they do not have a right to do anything by imposing their commitment on others
- feeling insufficiently knowledgeable – and afraid of exposing this to others
- being disappointed that effort and commitment put into training, supporting and consulting with people makes little impact on most practitioners and, hence, giving up trying
- berating oneself for not doing enough but not really knowing what to do and how to do it
- thinking all is well because there are black people in the work situation but not realising that most are on low grades and that, in reality, there is very little true mutual communication except in passing the time of day
- thinking it is someone else's responsibility, that is, the person responsible for these sorts of issues, perhaps someone responsible for 'diversity'
- wishing, perhaps unconsciously, to avoid issues that may be confrontational and upsetting and make people feel bad – pushing issues of discrimination and poverty to one side because they are uncomfortable so they are not talked about, almost as if to talk about them is improper

- despite the fact that it is known that the press trivialises and distorts issues of racial equality, nevertheless half-believing that there must be some truth in what is being written and that people who raise issues are perhaps a bit 'over the top' and have a 'chip on their shoulder'
- believing that no-one will be checking on this issue so they can afford to let it go, especially when they are pressed for time
- seeing it as someone else whose expertise and responsibility it is to raise issues of equality and do what is necessary
- not having the courage to address it
- being already frantically busy so this just cannot be on the top of their work list
- in writing initial drafts of policies, feeling overwhelmed when someone suggests equality is not being addressed, dismissing the idea as already implicit ('everyone knows what we mean'), suggesting that such comments can be incorporated later at a consultation stage
- knowing there is an issue but not giving themselves opportunities to discuss, consider and reflect on it. Dismissing specific instances of racism as just part of life's problems, not one of theirs – genuinely working hard on other important issues but not these ones
- being apparently surprised when black people tell it like it is, how it affects all aspects of their daily lives, as if this is shocking and painful news to them
- not being part of campaigns for equality, antiracist groups or groups challenging injustice so consequently being relatively unaware of these activities and concerns.

Appendix 3: Breakdown of mixed identities in UK

Percentages with a white partner

	Men	Women
Black Caribbean	38.6	26.1
Black African	15.2	10.6
Other Black	41.8	44.6
Indian	8.1	9.8
Pakistani	5.3	2.5
Bangladeshi	1.7	0.6
Other Asian	18.6	31.6
Chinese	17.7	36.5

Source: Special analysis of the Quarterly Labour Force Survey conducted by Charlie Owen of the Thomas Coram Research Unit, Institute of Education, University of London. Data are for Great Britain and include only people aged 16–59 who have a partner, married or cohabiting.

(Material from the Labour Force Survey is Crown Copyright. It has been made available by the Office for National Statistics through the UK Data Archive and has been used with permission, 2006.)

Appendix 4

Promoting race equality in early years

SureStart

Guidance

Introduction

This paper has been written for

- local authority early years officers
- area officers with responsibilities for equality, policy or training issues (in early years and children's partnerships or local authorities)
- equality coordinators in early years settings

It aims to clarify the responsibilities for ensuring the implementation of race equality in early years settings, taking account of the requirements of the Race Relations (Amendment) Act 2000.

This paper was written by Jane Lane, Policy Director, Early Years Equality (EYE) and is endorsed by the Sure Start Unit.

What are the duties?

Background to the law

The Race Relations (Amendment) Act 2000 is a result of the Macpherson report into the murder of the black teenager, Stephen Lawrence. It outlaws racial discrimination in public authority functions that were not already covered by the 1976 Race Relations Act. The 1976 Act outlawed racial discrimination and covered statutory and non-statutory early years organisations and provision in education, employment, housing and the provision of goods, facilities and services. However, the amendment extends the Act's powers to make racial discrimination unlawful for any listed public authority in any of its functions.

What the law says

The law requires all listed public authorities to comply with the **General duty** to make the promotion of race equality central to their work. Some public authorities also have **specific duties** placed on them to make arrangements to help them meet the General duty. This statutory public duty means there is no choice about complying; it applies to all public authorities whatever their minority ethnic population. A lack of resources is no excuse for non-compliance.

What is the public duty?

The General duty means that all listed public authorities must have a due regard to the need to:

- eliminate unlawful racial discrimination
- promote equality of opportunity and
- promote good relations between people of different racial groups

Effectively, this requires authorities to take account of race equality in policy making, service delivery, employment practice and other functions within existing funding.

Promoting race equality in early years

The **specific duties** are a means for public authorities to meet the general duty. These include the preparation and delivery of a Race Equality Scheme, which is essentially a three-year strategy and action plan that states how the public authority will arrange to fulfil its general duty under the Act. The Race Equality Scheme should state which functions and policies have been assessed as relevant to the performance of the general duty to promote race equality and what arrangements it has for meeting its specific duties, i.e. assessing and consulting on the likely impact of its proposed policies on the promotion of racial equality; monitoring its policies for any adverse impact on the promotion of race equality; publishing the results of such assessments and consultations; ensuring public access to information and the services which it provides; training staff in their responsibilities under the Act and reviewing progress on a rolling three-year programme.

Showing that the duty has been met – ethnic monitoring

Ethnic monitoring is necessary to demonstrate that policies for promoting equality are working in practice and measuring any adverse impact. Monitoring is the process of collecting, analysing and evaluating data on the ethnicity of people in relation to the processes of employment, admissions and the experiences and opportunities available and outcomes achieved. It is a way of identifying potential discrimination and whether policies on promoting equality of opportunity and good relations between people of different racial groups are being implemented. If monitoring reveals any discrepancies, they need to be examined and the reasons for them ascertained. Consultation with all concerned about categories to be used and data protection issues should be undertaken.

Who is responsible?

What is a 'public authority'?

A public authority is any organisation with functions of a public nature. Public authorities include private organisations that carry out public functions. Government departments, local authorities and Primary Care Trusts are examples of public authorities.

Is there a public duty when working in partnerships?

Partnerships are single bodies bringing together representatives of various organisations to pursue common aims. They include 'umbrella' organisations working for children and families, early years or children's partnerships. They are not themselves public authorities and are therefore not bound by the race equality duty. However, where a public authority is a member of a partnership, wholly or significantly, it has a duty to promote race equality in the work carried out by the partnership, both the General duty and the specific duties. It must also ensure that the other partnership members are aware of the authority's legal responsibilities.

Voluntary, private, independent and community organisations, as partnership members, are bound by the law on racial discrimination but not by the race equality duty.

A CRE publication provides further details - see the further information section at the end of this paper.

Responsibilities in early years

Early years settings (including nurseries, nursery schools, children's centres, neighbourhood nurseries, early excellence centres and out-of-school care) which are directly run or maintained by the local education authority, and day nurseries run by social services departments of local authorities, will be bound by the General and specific duties for a public authority.

Sure Start local programmes will have local authority and Primary Care Trust representatives on their partnership boards - so the local authority and Primary Care Trust, as public authorities, will have responsibility to ensure the duties are fulfilled.

Voluntary, independent and private early years and childcare settings/services do not have the same statutory duty as public authorities. However, the principles of equity and justice underpinning the law should be applied by all settings as good practice. Furthermore, where the provision is overseen, coordinated or advised by the local early years or children's partnership (which, as indicated above, has public authority membership), the local authority will have responsibility to ensure the duties are fulfilled.

Practice implications for early years settings

The following are duties for publicly run settings and good practice for private, voluntary and independent settings. These steps need to become part of everyday routine practice.

Early years and childcare settings need to

- examine all their existing policies, procedures and practices and assess whether they promote racial equality in all that they do
- devise a strategy to evaluate the impact of all they do on all children and their families in the area and whether they might advantage or disadvantage families from particular racial groups
- take advice and support from the local authority and attend training provided by it
- ensure that all members of staff understand the law is important

They need to **eliminate unlawful racial discrimination:**

- examine all their policies, practices and procedures to ensure there is no discrimination on racial grounds
- monitor and review - collect information on ethnicity, analyse it and evaluate the effectiveness of policies, procedures and practices to help establish whether discrimination occurs
- remove discrimination if identified

They must **promote equality of opportunity:**

- ensure that everyone in the setting is equally valued, treated with equal respect and concern, and that the needs of each are addressed
- ensure that each child and family has equal access and entitlement to all available opportunities for learning, experiences and resources

Promote good relations between people of different racial groups

Children reflect the attitudes and values of all around them, including racial attitudes and values. While eliminating racial discrimination and promoting equality of opportunity are important in ensuring race equality, they are insufficient in themselves to counter any prevailing racist attitudes and behaviour. In order to offset the process whereby children may learn to be racially prejudiced at an early age, specific and positive action needs to be taken on a regular basis to ensure children:

- develop positive attitudes and behaviour to all people, whether they are different from or similar to themselves
- unlearn any negative attitudes and behaviour that they may have already learnt
- value aspects of other people's lives (such as their skin colour, physical features, culture, language or religion) equally rather than seeing them as less worthy than theirs or ranking them in a racial hierarchy

It is important to recognise and accept that the need to eliminate unlawful racial discrimination and promote equality of opportunity and good relations applies equally in all areas, whether rural, suburban or urban. This is as important where the children are largely from one racial group as it is in multiracial, multicultural, multilingual settings. It is an essential part of promoting good relations between people of different racial groups and provides children with a basis for understanding race equality in their future lives.

Settings should also ensure that the needs of every child and adult are identified and addressed and that everyone shares an ethos to promote race equality in practice. Planning a strategic approach will enable short and long-term objectives to be realistic as well as effective.

Settings should prepare and maintain a written statement on promoting race equality, giving details of how it is to be implemented. They should monitor and assess how their policies affect families, staff and children from all racial groups and make changes to remove any disadvantage or discrimination. As a minimum, this means monitoring ethnic data on employment and admissions, observing and recording which

Promoting race equality in early years

children access what services and devising methods of consulting with everyone involved in the setting – staff, children and their families.

Practice implications for local authorities and their early years and children's partnerships

Local authorities and their early years and children's partnerships are in a position to identify and have an overview of the needs of all members of the local community. In response to its general and specific duties the local authority should:

- **assist settings to comply with their duties**

  including by:
  - providing training courses on the general and specific duties
  - offering information, support and advice
  - providing a central supply of supportive resources for sharing with settings
  - supporting staff to recognise and challenge discrimination knowledgeably and confidently
  - supporting any equality coordinators in settings
  - ensuring a requirement to comply with the principles of the duties within contractual and funding agreements

- ensure compliance and that monitoring is put in place

  including by ensuring that:
  - what is learnt in training is put into practice
  - Children's Information Services (CISs) comply with their duty
  - all settings and childminder networks have a racial equality policy
  - the ethnic data collected by settings is monitored and analysed effectively
  - race equality principles are central to the procurement process for any contracted-out services (for example, meals) and training
  - any non-public authority partnership members are aware of how the public duty affects them

Sources of support

Local authorities and settings are supported and encouraged to comply with their duties by central government departments and agencies.

The **Sure Start Unit** (part of the Department for Education and Skills and the Deparment of Work and Pensions) ensures - through the annual review and self assessment process - that local authorities comply with their duty to monitor the impact of all their activities on minority ethnic families and their children.

Through its inspection process, **Ofsted** ensures that settings promote equality of opportunity and anti-discriminatory practice for all children (Standard 9 for Section 122 inspections and Section 10 inspections) and that inspectors fully understand the implications of the Race Relations (Amendment) Act 2000.

The **Learning and Skills Council and Teacher Training Agency** ensure that early years teachers/workers are provided with the understanding, knowledge and skills in their initial and in-service education to comply with the public duty through their oversight of training courses.

Promoting race equality in early years

Definitions of racial discrimination

The Act sets out explanations of what discrimination covers.

Direct discrimination means treating a person in a particular racial group less well than someone in the same or similar circumstances from a different racial group. The motive for such treatment is irrelevant.

Indirect discrimination occurs when a provision, criterion or practice, applied equally to everyone, puts people from a particular racial group (based on race or ethnic or national origin) at a disadvantage because they cannot comply with it. This will be unlawful unless it can be shown that the provision, criterion or practice is a proportionate means of achieving a legitimate aim.

Indirect discrimination also occurs when a requirement or condition, applied equally to everyone, has a disproportionate adverse effect on people from a particular racial group (based on colour or nationality) because they cannot comply with it. This will be unlawful if it cannot be justified on non-racial grounds.

Customs, practices and procedures that may have been in place for a long time may have an indirectly discriminatory impact on particular racial groups, even though this was never the intention.

Segregation – segregating a person from others on racial grounds constitutes less favourable treatment.

Victimisation – the law protects a person who is victimised for bringing a complaint of racial discrimination under the Race Relations (Amendment) Act 2000 or for backing someone else's complaint.

For further details of these definitions see the CRE website: www.cre.gov.uk

(**Note:** racial group or ethnic background covers the following – colour, race, nationality including citizenship or ethnic or national origins.)

Further information

Commission for Racial Equality (CRE) (2002) 'Statutory Code of Practice on the duty to promote race equality'

Commission for Racial Equality (CRE) (2004) 'Public Authorities and Partnerships: a guide to the duty to promote race equality'

Early Years Trainers Anti Racist Network (2001) 'A Policy for Excellence: developing a policy for equality in early years settings'

Lane, J (1999) 'Action for racial equality in the early years: understanding the past, thinking about the present, planning for the future', National Early Years Network. Available from EYE and the National Children's Bureau. Recommended by the CRE

The CRE website provides information, links to more detailed advice, and downloadable publications: www.cre.gov.uk

The Sure Start website provides links to further more detailed advice, information, sources of case studies, support, and links to more detailed advice: www.surestart.gov.uk

Appendix 5: Some of the most significant government documents

The documents are given in chronological order.

Acts

Race Relations Act 1976

Race Relations (Amendment) Act 2000

Education Act 2002

Children Act 2004

Childcare Act 2006

Education and Inspections Act 2006

Equality Act 2006

Other documents

Plowden Report (1967) *Children and their Primary Schools.* A report of the Central Advisory Council for Education (England) ('The Plowden Report'), HMSO, London.

DfES/Institute of Education, University of London (1997–2003) *The Effective Provision of Pre-School and Primary Education (EPPE) Project* – A longitudinal study.

QCA/DfEE (2000) *Curriculum Guidance for the Foundation Stage.*

DfEE (2001) National Standards for Under-eights Day Care and Childminding Standard 9, Equal Opportunities.

Sure Start (2002) *Birth to Three Matters: A framework to support children in their earliest years.*

DfES (2002) *Researching Effective Pedagogy in the Early Years* (REPEY).

Study of Pedagogical Effectiveness in Early Learning (SPEEL 2002) Sure Start.

Commission for Racial Equality (2002) *Statutory Code of Practice on the Duty to Promote Race Equality.*

DfES (2003) *Every Child Matters.*

QCA/DfES (2003) *Foundation Stage Profile: Handbook.*

Ofsted (2005) *Every Child Matters: School inspection framework.*

Sure Start (2004) *Childcare and Early Years Workforce Survey.*

Sure Start (2004) *Listening as a Way of Life.* A series of 5 leaflets. National Children's Bureau (McAuliffe, A. (ed))

DfES (2004) *Every Child Matters: Next steps.*

DfES (2004) *Every Child Matters: Change for children in Schools.*

DfES (2004) *Parents: Partners in learning.*

DfES (2005) *Common Assessment Framework.*

DfES (2005) *Extended Schools: Access to opportunities and services for all.*

DfES (2005) *National Professional Qualification in Integrated Centre Leadership.*

DfES (2005) *Foundation Stage Profile: National results.*

Sure Start (2005) *Children's Centres Practice Guidance.*

DfES/Sure Start (2005) *Key Elements of Effective Practice* (KEEP).

DfES/DH (2004) *National Service Framework for Children, Young People and Maternity Services.*

HM Treasury, DfES, DWP, dti (2004) *Choice for Parents, the Best Start for Children: A ten year strategy for childcare.*

Teacher Training Agency (2004) *Foundation Stage: Audit materials.*

HM Government (2005) *Children's Workforce Strategy: A strategy to build a world-class workforce for children and young people* – a consultation document.

HM Government (2005) *Common Core of Skills and Knowledge for the Children's Workforce.*

Ofsted (2005) *Early Years Inspection Framework/School Inspection Framework.*

Children's Workforce Development Council (2006) *Early Years Professional National Standards.*

DfES/DWP (2006) *Choice for Parents, the Best Start For Children: Making it happen. An action plan for the ten year strategy: Sure Start Children's Centres, extended schools and childcare.*

DfES (2006) *Parents, Early Years and Learning Resource Pack.* National Children's Bureau.

DfES/DWP (2006) *The Early Years Foundation Stage: Consultation on a single quality framework for services for children from birth to five.*

DfES (2006) *The Government's Response to the Consultation on the Early Years Foundation Stage.*

Sure Start (2006) *National Occupational Standards in Children's Care, Learning and Development.*

DfES/DH (2006) *Sure Start Children's Centres Practice Guidance: Revised version.*

Children's Workforce Development Council (CWDC) (2006) *Early Years Professional National Standards.*

CWDC (2006) *Early Years Professional Prospectus.*

Communities and Local Government (2006) *Improving Opportunity, Strengthening Society: One year on – a progress report on the government's strategy for race equality and community cohesion.*

Commission on Integration and Cohesion (2007) *Our Shared Future.*

Department for Children, Schools and Families (DCSF) (2007) *Securing Sufficient Childcare: Guidance for local authorities, Childcare Act 2006.*

Department for Children, Schools and Families (DCSF)/Communities and Local Government (2007) Guidance *on the Duty to Promote Community Cohesion.*

DfES (2007) *The Early Years Foundation Stage.*

DfES (2007) *Creating the Picture.*

DfES (2007) *National Standards for Leaders of Sure Start Children's Centres.*

DfES (2007) *Childcare Sufficiency Assessments: Guidance for local authorities.*

Appendix 6: Comments on HM Government consultation paper on the Children's Workforce Strategy (2005)

HM Government (2005a) 'Children's Workforce Strategy: A strategy to build a world-class workforce for children and young people – a consultation document' – proposals for raising the status of the early childhood workforce within a coherent framework of qualifications and so forth.

It fails to:

- examine barriers to equal representation of black people in the workforce (i.e. racist attitudes, assumptions, stereotypes, discrimination, institutional racism)
- consider that staff from black and other minority ethnic communities are very likely to be disproportionately at lower levels than white people
- address the disproportionately few early years qualified black teachers. Therefore as the new children's centres require a teacher to be responsible for specific areas of work, there are few black people with these responsibilities and status
- mention the need for ethnic monitoring or statutory requirements of RR(A)A
- identify the critical need for training the trainers; and initial, in-service and leadership training, in order to ensure that future and existing staff are committed to equality. It cannot be assumed that teachers have a better understanding of racism than some voluntary sector trained people
- mention positive action.

Appendix 7: Recommendations in *Inclusion Pilot Projects Summary Report* (2003) Sure Start

The recommendations of 'Sure Start: For everyone – Promoting inclusion, embracing diversity, challenging inequality', *Inclusion Pilot Projects Summary Report* (Sure Start 2003)

- the DfES and LA to be monitored for inclusive language/anti-discriminatory practice
- a need for ethnic monitoring, using RR(A)A
- a need for local authority named officers to monitor data across settings
- a need for designated equality posts at local authority and setting levels
- a need for mandatory training for local authority, Ofsted and setting staff
- a re-think of all training, including leadership and training the trainers
- an enforcement of National Equal Opportunities Standard
- a need to designate Centres of Excellence on equalities
- ethnic minority achievement grant (EMA or EMAG) funding to be accessible to voluntary, independent and private (VIP) sector
- the need for new funding to implement all the above.

So far as is known, none of the above have been implemented.

Appendix 8: Government publications on racial equality with relevance to early years issues

The following are given in chronological order.

Swann Report (1985) *Education For All: Report of the Committee of Inquiry into the education of children from ethnic minority groups.* London: HMSO.

Ofsted (1996) *The Education of Travelling Children: A survey of educational provision for Travelling children.*

Macpherson, W (1999) *The Stephen Lawrence Inquiry: Report of an inquiry by Sir William Macpherson of Cluny.* Stationery Office.

TTA (2000) *Raising the Attainment of Minority Ethnic Pupils: Guidance and resource materials for providers of initial teacher training* – includes a section on early years.

Ofsted (undated) *Nursery Education Inspection: Guidance on equality of access and opportunity.*

Ofsted (2000) *Educational Inequality: Mapping race, class and gender: A synthesis of research evidence* (Gillborn and Mirza).

Ofsted (2001) *Evaluating Educational Inclusion: Guidance for inspectors and schools.*

Ofsted (2003) *Provision and support for Traveller pupils.*

DfES (2003) *Aiming High: Raising the achievement of African-Caribbean pupils – guidance.*

DfES (2003) *Aiming High: Raising the achievement of Gypsy Traveller pupils – a guide to good practice.*

DfES (2003) *Aiming High: Raising the achievement of minority ethnic pupils.*

Cabinet Office (2003) *Ethnic Minorities in the Labour Market.*

Sure Start (2003) 'Sure Start: for Everyone: Promoting inclusion, embracing diversity, challenging inequality', *Inclusion Pilot Projects Summary Report.*

DfES (2004) *Aiming High: Understanding the educational needs of minority ethnic pupils in mainly White schools.*

dti (2004) *The Role of Childcare in Women's Labour Market Participation: A study of minority ethnic mothers.* Women and Equality Unit.

dti (2004) *Diversity and Difference: Minority ethnic mothers and childcare.* Women and Equality Unit.

Sure Start (2004) *Promoting Race Equality in Early Years*. (Lane)

Sure Start (2004) *Working with Young Children from Minority Ethnic Groups: A guide to sources of information*. National Children's Bureau.

DfES Research Report 549 (2004) *Understanding the Educational Needs of Mixed Heritage Pupils*. University of Bristol (in association with Birmingham LEA) (Tikly, Caballero, Haynes and Hill).

Sure Start (2004) 'Are equalities an issue? Finding out what young children think' in *Listening as a Way of Life*. National Children's Bureau (Road in McAuliffe (ed)).

Qualifications and Curriculum Authority (QCA) *Respect For All: Valuing diversity and challenging racism through the curriculum*. www.qca.org.uk/qca_6753.aspx

DfES (2005) *Ethnicity and Education: The evidence on minority ethnic pupils* – includes a section on the Foundation Stage Profile.

DfES (consultation 2005) Inclusion, equality and diversity – data.

DfES (2005) *Ethnicity and Education: The evidence on minority ethnic pupils*.

Ofsted (undated) *Nursery Education Inspection: Guidance on equality of access and opportunity*.

Sure Start (2005) *Use of Childcare among Families from Minority Ethnic Backgrounds*. National Centre for Social Research (Bryson, Bell, Barnes and O'Shea).

Home Office (2005) *Improving Opportunities, Strengthening Society: The government's strategy for racial equality and community cohesion*.

Department for Communities and Local Government (2006) *Improving Opportunity, Strengthening Society: One year on – a progress report on the government's strategy for race equality and community cohesion*.

Sure Start (2006) *Black and Minority Ethnic Families and Sure Start: Findings from local evaluation reports*. National Evaluation of Sure Start (NESS) (Lloyd and Rafferty).

Ofsted (2005) *Race Equality in Education: Good practice in schools and local education authorities*.

DfES (2006) *Working towards Inclusive Practice: Gypsy/Roma and Traveller cultural awareness training and activities for early years settings*. Save the Children.

DfES (2007) *Getting it. Getting it right: Exclusion of Black pupils – Priority Review*. (Wanless, Dehal and Eyre).

Ofsted (2007) Race Equality Scheme: draft for consultation.

DfES/Sure Start (2007) 'Sure Start and Black and Minority Ethnic Populations', *Sure Start National Evaluation Report 020* (Craig, Adamson, Ali and others).

Department for Children Schools and Families (2007) *Race Equality Scheme Update*.

Department for Children Schools and Families (2007) *Single Equality Scheme*.

Department for Children Schools and Families (2007) *Supporting Children Learning English as an Additional Language: Guidance for practitioners in the Early Years Foundation Stage*.

Department for Children, Schools and Families (2008) *The Inclusion of Gypsy, Roma and Traveller Children and Young People: Strategies for building confidence in voluntary self-declared ethnicity ascription*.

Index